Simon Elmer

The
Road
to Fascism

For a Critique of the Global Biosecurity State

Published in Great Britain in 2022 by

Architects for Social Housing
Fairford House
Kennington Lane
London SE11 4HW
e-mail: info@architectsforsocialhousing.co.uk
website: www.architectsforsocialhousing.co.uk

ISBN 978-1-4710-6819-5 (clothbound)
ISBN 978-1-4716-0172-9 (paperbound)

Cover design by Architects for Social Housing
Printed and bound by Lulu Press, UK

For the non-compliant

Contents

I asked myself: why talk to them?

They only acquire knowledge in order to sell it.

They want to know where cheap knowledge

Can be sold on for a profit. Why

Would they want to listen

To words against buying and selling?

They want to win

And won't hear anything said against winning.

They don't want to be oppressed

They want to oppress.

They don't want progress

They want a head start.

They're obedient to anyone

Who promises them they can command.

They sacrifice themselves

So that the altar will remain standing.

I wondered, what should I say to them?

I decided that it was this.

— Bertolt Brecht, 1941

Preface

We are — we are constantly being told — living in 'unprecedented times', facing 'unprecedented circumstances' requiring 'unprecedented measures' for which there is no historical precedent and because of which — is the unstated implication — those in power cannot be held to account for the consequences of their actions. 'Unprecedented', however, is one of those words that should set alarm-bells ringing in the head of the historical materialist, implying, as it does, that we are in a moment about which history can teach us nothing, but which signals, in practice, that the speaker either doesn't know what they're talking about (the journalist and scientist) or is deliberately dissembling what they are in fact doing (the politician and capitalist). History tells us that we should always be suspicious when those in power start claiming we are in a moment about which history can tell us nothing. The call to forget the past is always made in the service of power; but there are very few things that history cannot teach us. Once upon a time, we studied history precisely in order to learn from it, rather than stumbling around without memory in the apparently unprecedented newness of the present. Whether that present is a product of ignorance or deceit, the past inevitably has a lot to tell us about supposedly 'unprecedented' moments, and so it is with the coronavirus 'crisis'.

The two years between March 2020, when the 'pandemic' was officially declared by the World Health Organization and the UK Parliament passed the Coronavirus Act 2020, and March 2022, when the date set for the expiry of the Coronavirus Act was reached and the last of the 582 coronavirus-justified Statutory Instruments made into law were revoked, have left us now, six months later, in our own reenactment of that 'phoney war' that stretched for eight months between the UK's declaration of war against Germany in September 1939 and Germany's invasion of France in May 1940. With the lifting of the thousands of regulations by which our lives were ruled for two long years there has been an understandable desire to believe that the coronavirus 'crisis' is over and we will return to something like an albeit 'new' normal. But as new crises have sprung up to take its place — war in the Ukraine, monkeypox, the so-called 'cost of living crisis' and the return of the environmental crisis — it has become increasingly difficult not to look back on 'lockdown' as only the first campaign in a war that has not been declared by any government but is no less real for that. Waged by the international technocracies of global governance that, under the cloak of the 'pandemic', have assumed increasing power over our lives since March 2020, this war is not being fought against foreign countries but against the populations of their member states. Trialled for compliance under lockdown, the weapons of this war are Digital Identity, Central Bank Digital Currency, Universal Basic Income, Social Credit, Environmental, Social and Governance criteria, Sustainable Development Goals, and all the other programmes instrumental to the United Nation's Agenda 2030. If they haven't been already, these look likely to be launched in a *Blitzkrieg* campaign, possibly this winter, with the World Health Organization advising European countries to reimpose mandatory masking and 'vaccination'. Just like the winter of 1939-1940, now is the deep breath before the storm.

My comparison with the opening of the Second World War, however, is not merely an analogy. I am not alone in thinking that the willingness of our governments to use the forces of the state against their own populations during the 'pandemic' on the justification of protecting us from ourselves signals a new level of authoritarianism — and something like the return of fascism — to the governmental, juridical and cultural forms of the formerly neoliberal democracies of the West, and one of the aims of this book is to examine the validity of this thesis. My purpose in doing so, however, is not to pursue an academic question about the meaning and historicity of the term 'fascism', but rather to interrogate how and why the general and widespread moral collapse in the West since March 2020 — another indicator of fascism — has been effected with such rapidity and ease, and to examine to what ends that moral collapse is being used. It is here, I believe, that history can tell us something about these supposedly 'unprecedented' circumstances and measures.

Something, but not everything. For while historical fascism arose in the context of the imperialism of European nation states and their struggle for power, a hundred years later that struggle has been reduced to their united and virtually unopposed 'roll-out' of the programmes, technologies and regulations of what has been hailed as the Fourth Industrial Revolution. And while our economic, security and military alliances are dividing the globe into new axes of geopolitical influence, in the West — by which I mean Europe, North America and Australasia — the war we face is not between nation states but a civil war waged against our institutions of democratic governance and the division of powers between executive, legislature and judiciary. Insofar as these institutions and this division are being dismantled and replaced by the rule of international technocracies composed of the board members of private corporations and the unelected representatives of national governments, this 'war', more accurately described, represents a *revolution* in Western capitalism from the neoliberalism under which we have lived for the past forty years. What it is revolving into, and the conclusion my thesis on fascism will seek to demonstrate, is the new totalitarianism of the Global Biosecurity State.

This book was preceded by eighteen months of research and writing between March 2020 and October 2021, during which I published more than two dozen articles about the coronavirus 'crisis' on the website of Architects for Social Housing (ASH), the architectural practice and community interest company for which I am Head of Research. These found an unexpectedly wide readership, with over 320,000 people from 190 countries visiting the articles on our website. In response to this interest, ASH published these articles in three collections, *COVID-19: Implementing the UK Biosecurity State* (published in September 2020); *Brave New World: Expanding the UK Biosecurity State through the Winter of 2020-2021* (published in March 2021), and *Virtue and Terror: Resisting the UK Biosecurity State* (published in October 2021). When, in February 2022, I started writing the current book, which I conceived as a single work rather than a collection of articles, I therefore took as given the major conclusions I had reached from the preceding two years of research. Although, by now, the same or similar conclusions have been reached by many others, these are still sharply at odds with the official narrative about the coronavirus 'crisis' that many more continue to believe in or at least to obey. So, although I have referred to some of these conclusions in the discursive footnotes to this book, I will try to summarise their main points in this preface; because it is on them that the argument for my thesis about the return of fascism and the totalitarianism of the Global Biosecurity State is founded.

In 'Giorgio Agamben and the Biopolitics of COVID-19', which I published in April 2020, I showed that the lockdown restrictions removing our rights and freedoms were not being imposed in response to a public health crisis that represented no more of a threat than seasonal influenza but in accord with mechanisms and technologies of biopower that had turned our health 'status' into the object of a global political strategy.

In 'Manufacturing Consensus: The Registering of COVID-19 Deaths in the UK', which I published in May 2020, I showed how, through changes to disease taxonomy, to the criteria for attributing a death to Coronavirus Disease 2019 (COVID-19), to the procedure for identifying the underlying cause of death on a death certificate, to the protocol for diagnosing infection with Severe acute respiratory syndrome coronavirus 2 (SARS-CoV-2), to identifying the clinical presence of COVID-19, and to the recording and reporting of deaths, the number of deaths officially attributed to COVID-19 has been grossly and deliberately exaggerated many times above the actual deaths that can be attributed to the disease with any medical accuracy.

In 'The State of Emergency as Paradigm of Government: Coronavirus Legislation, Implementation and Enforcement', published the same month, I showed that, on the basis of these deliberately falsified figures and under cover of the politically-declared 'emergency period' they were used to justify, the UK Government was implementing the first regulations, privatisations, programmes and technologies of a future UK biosecurity state which, at that stage, comprised the NHS Test and Trace programme and the Joint Biosecurity Centre (JBC).

In 'Lockdown: Collateral Damage in the War on COVID-19', which I published in June 2020, I showed that, across the world, there was no correlation between the severity of lockdown restrictions and a reduction in the deaths attributed to COVID-19; that, to the contrary, the withdrawal of medical diagnosis, care and treatment under lockdown was a major contributor to the increase in excess deaths; and that lockdown was having a disproportionately negative impact on the poorest and most economically vulnerable while financially benefiting the wealthiest and most economically powerful.

In 'The Science and Law of Refusing to Wear Masks: Texts and Arguments in Support of Civil Disobedience', also published in June, I showed that face coverings had been mandated not on their effectiveness as a barrier to viral transmission — for which they are at best ineffective and at worst dangerous to the health of the wearer — but rather to encourage social compliance with the regulations of the biosecurity state; and that 'asymptomatic transmission' as the driver of infection was a myth manufactured to terrorise the population into obedience to lockdown restrictions.

And in 'The New Normal: What is the UK Biosecurity State?', which I published in two parts in July 2020 ('Programmes and Regulations') and August 2020 ('Normalising Fear), I showed that, far from responding to an unprecedented 'crisis' in public health, the so-called 'New Normal' into which we were being encouraged to 'Build Back Better' had been prepared by the economic, political, legal and cultural apparatus of neoliberalism; but that the use of emergency powers to implement the Global Biosecurity State, and the willingness with which the populations and institutions of Western countries were complying and collaborating with this technocratic and globalist coup, had its most recent historical precedent in the rise of fascism in Europe between the two world wars and the state of emergency under which the laws for the protection of people and state were made in the Third Reich between 1933 and 1945. This, in summary, comprised the major conclusions from my first collection of articles, *COVID-19*.

What would go on to constitute my second collection, *Brave New World*, began with 'Bonfire of the Freedoms: The Unlawful Exercise of Powers conferred by the Public Health (Control of Disease) Act 1984', which I published in November 2020, and in which I showed that the coronavirus-justified regulations that were removing more and more of our civil liberties in the UK had been made unlawfully and were, therefore, in violation of our constitutional rights and freedoms.

In 'The Betrayal of the Clerks: UK Intellectuals in the Service of the Biosecurity State', also published in November, I showed that, far from challenging the abuse of power by the national governments and international corporations that were dismantling our democracy under cover of this manufactured 'crisis', our institutions of medicine, education and letters were instead providing scientific legitimacy, ideological indoctrination into and intellectual credibility to the social practices of the New Normal.

In both 'Bread and Circuses: Who's Behind the Oxford Vaccine for COVID-19' and 'Bowling for Pfizer: Who's Behind the BioNTech Vaccine for COVID-19?', published, respectively, in November and December 2020, I showed that, far from being independent public bodies operating objectively for the health and safety of the British public, the Government departments and regulatory agencies responsible for granting temporary authorisation to unlicensed and still experimental COVID-19 'vaccines' were funded and guided by the pharmaceutical companies and global financiers whose products they were authorising; and that all these companies had records of corruption, malpractice, manslaughter, cover-ups and bribery of officials from which only their vast profits and political lobbying had saved them from prosecution.

In 'Our Default State: Compulsory Vaccination for COVID-19 and Human Rights Law', published in January 2021, I showed that, in response to a Government consultation on the legal barriers to compulsory 'vaccination', jurists specialising in the ethics of neuro-intervention had advised that, based on the assumption that those refusing to be injected willingly were endangering the lives of others, injection with COVID-19 'vaccines' could be made compulsory under the Mental Health Act 1983, and that our biological state by default warrants intervention by the UK biosecurity state.

In 'Lies, Damned Lies and Statistics: Manufacturing the Crisis', published the same month, I showed that, of the roughly 80,000 deaths officially attributed to COVID-19 in 2020, at least 40,000 were caused by the withdrawal of diagnosis, care and treatment for heart disease, cancer, dementia, diabetes and the other major causes of death in the UK; that this is a conservative estimate, and doesn't include the more than 20,000 excess deaths in care homes that were swept under the COVID-19 carpet; and that, even with these exacerbated causes of death, the age-standardised mortality rate in 2020, during a supposedly civilisation-threatening pandemic, was the twelfth lowest since records began in 1942.

And in 'Cui Bono? The COVID-19 "Conspiracy"', which I published in February 2021, I showed that the 'conspiracy theories' to which any challenges to the official narrative about the coronavirus 'crisis' have been reduced, far from threatening to undermine the ideological hegemony of the Global Biosecurity State, have in practice been one of the tropes by which that hegemony has been maintained; and that what we have been undergoing since March 2020 is neither a viral 'pandemic' that threatens Western civilisation nor an international 'conspiracy' of secret cabals — nor even, as many opposed to the authoritarianism of biosecurity believed, some sort of communist coup — but a revolution in Western capitalism into a new form of totalitarianism.

In what would begin my third collection of articles, *Virtue and Terror*, 'Behind the Mask, the Conspiracy!', published in May 2021, I showed that, during this revolution in capitalism, claims about what is true and what is false are no longer being subjected to discursive measures and empirically verifiable evidence, and have instead been reduced to a question of authority and the belief in an apotheosised 'Science', which has taken the place and role of religion in Western secular societies.

In 'March for Freedom: London, 29 May, 2021', published the same month, I showed that the fact the largest demonstrations in UK history against lockdown restrictions and 'vaccine' mandates — which had brought millions of citizens out in protest — were being ignored by both the corporate media and our elected representatives in Parliament represented a collusion between Government and the fourth estate that called into question the UK's status as a democracy.

Finally, in 'The UK "Vaccination" Programme', published in three parts between September and October 2021, I showed (in Part 1: 'Adverse Events and Deaths'), that mass injection of the populations of the West with experimental 'vaccines' may one day turn out to be the most-deadly of the measures imposed as a condition of our release from lockdown; that (in Part 2. 'Virtue and Terror') the removal of the rights and freedoms of 68 million UK citizens wasn't the unfortunate consequence of the failure of such measures to halt the spread and impact of a new disease that threatens the public health of the UK, but rather the product of the success of two years of regulations and programmes in implementing the transition from neoliberalism into the constitutional dictatorship of the UK biosecurity state; and, finally (in Part 3: 'Resistance'), I showed how, through acts of non-compliance and civil disobedience, we can begin to reassert our right to question, resist and overthrow the totalitarian future awaiting us.

It is not necessary for the reader to accept every one of these conclusions in order to derive some benefit from the current work. Indeed, part of the object of this study is to sketch the larger context in which to understand how what for two years was contemptuously dismissed as 'conspiracy theories' now constitute the reality in which our immediate future is about to unfold with terrifying speed and finality. The question confronting us now is not one of doubt or belief in the reality that is all around us, but of how to oppose it before we are submerged into the new totalitarianism.

Since the revocation of coronavirus-justified regulations in the UK, much of the resistance to the various programmes and technologies of biosecurity has become bogged down in challenging the justification for the lockdowns and demonstrating the injurious and fatal effects of the 'vaccination' programme. And while there is value and importance in this work — particularly in halting the criminal injection and indoctrination of the young — it has been accompanied by a reluctance to look at what these programmes have prepared our compliance for in the next stage of the Global Biosecurity State. Although implemented on the various justifications of convenience of access and movement within the Global Biosecurity State, national security against present and future biological, cyber or military threats now all placed in the in-tray marked 'terrorist', and, of course, the great environmental catch-all of 'saving the planet' from global warming, these programmes will be implemented outside of any immediate threat such as that represented by the coronavirus 'pandemic', and can expect less compliance, perhaps, than that which met the restrictions on our human rights and freedoms under lockdown. For this reason, they are likely to be implemented quickly and all at once, with Digital Identity holding our biometric data made a condition of numerous freedoms, cash withdrawn from circulation and replaced by Digital Currency controlled and programmed by central banks, and a Social Credit system of compliance monitored by artificial intelligence and policed by facial recognition technology all a reality to which we will wake up one day with no choice but compliance or having our access to the rights of citizenship removed by default.

This is the context in which I have written this book, which is neither an academic study of the history of fascism nor a journalistic account of the past two-and-a-half years, but a work of political theory. Some of the chapters are written around the work of other writers on different aspects of fascism and totalitarianism, including the Italian semiotician and cultural critic, Umberto Eco, the Italian critical theorist, Fabio Vighi, the French sociologist and philosopher, Georges Bataille, the German literary critic, Walter Benjamin, the Austrian economist, Friedrich Hayek, the English novelist and journalist, George Orwell, the Italian philosopher, Giorgio Agamben, and the German political theorist, Hannah Arendt. And although the book has been written for a popular rather than a scholarly readership, I haven't shied away from addressing the political, legal, economic, cultural, philosophical, psychological and moral issues raised by the Global Biosecurity State. Indeed, the positive response to my articles in the three collections that preceded this study have encouraged me to think that there is a wider readership in the UK for this level of analysis than we are made to believe by our rigorously anti-intellectual culture. In this respect, I hope my book will provide a more historical and practical framework in which to understand and respond to the past two-and-a-half years than the vituperative, sectarian, authoritarian and politically naive character of what debate there is in Parliament, the mainstream media or on social media platforms.

As readers familiar with the work of Hayek will recognise, my title is taken from his enormously influential book, *The Road to Serfdom*, which was published in the UK in 1944 during the Second World War. Intent as he was on refuting the Marxist argument that fascism was the reaction of a decaying capitalism to the rising threat of socialism, Hayek argued that Italian fascism, German National Socialism and Soviet communism all had common roots in central economic planning and the resulting power of the state over the individual. He therefore opposed the UK following the model of socialism that had been laid out in the hugely popular Beveridge Report in 1942, and which the post-war Labour Government would fail to implement fully in the creation of the Welfare State. In doing so, he also laid the grounds for the neoliberal revolution in the late 1970s that conquered the West and which has brought us to this point. So although I share neither Hayek's equation of fascism with socialism nor his championing of liberalism and capitalism as defenders of the rights of the individual — both of which have been refuted by the return of fascism in the political, juridical and cultural forms of the most advanced capitalist economies over the past two-and-a-half years — Hayek's fears and warnings about the threat of the state to the freedom of the individual are even more relevant today than they were eighty years ago. If 350 million Europeans had lived under fascist governments for a decade and more when Hayek was writing, how should we describe the digital serfdom to which the Global Biosecurity State is reducing the more than 900 million people living in the former neoliberal democracies of the West today? It's under the banner of this warning, therefore, that I'm publishing *The Road to Fascism*.

— September 2022

The
Road
to Fascism

1. The Return of Fascism

'At its fullest development, fascism redrew the frontiers between private and public, sharply diminishing what had once been untouchably private. It changed the practice of citizenship from the enjoyment of constitutional rights and duties to participation in mass ceremonies of affirmation and conformity. It reconfigured relations between the individual and the collectivity, so that an individual had no rights outside community interest. It expanded the powers of the executive — party and state — in a bid for total control. Finally, it unleashed aggressive emotions hitherto known in Europe only during war or social revolution.'

— Robert Paxton, *The Anatomy of Fascism*, 2004

1. The Axe in the Bundle

For my generation, which grew up during the neoliberal revolution implemented in this country by the Governments of Margaret Thatcher, the accusation of 'fascist!' was most closely associated with the character of Rick, played by a young Rik Mayall in *The Young Ones*, a television series that was screened by the BBC between 1982 and 1984. Emblazoned with political lapel badges opposing everything and everyone, Rick was the stereotype of political impotence that was not, unfortunately, confined to student anarchists but extended to the entire British Left after the defeat of the Miners' Strike in 1985. This stereotype has continued up to today with Antifa, the anarchist movement which — before most recently advocating locking up the 'unvaccinated' and joining police in opposing anti-lockdown protesters in Germany — was known for calling far-right groups 'fascist'. This has attracted the censure and mockery of an older generation who lived through fascism in Germany, Italy and occupied Europe, and who look with frustrated tolerance at a generation raised on the relative freedom won by them in the Second World War. From this perspective, the accusation of 'fascism' was an expression of the apparent end of history for the children of Europe's middle-classes, who were too busy developing the orthodoxies of multiculturalism, political correctness and identity politics to notice the very real and unorthodox politics going on beyond the borders of Europe, most obviously in the expansion and violence of US imperialism in South America, East Asia and the Middle East. While accusations of 'racism', 'sexism', 'antisemitism' and all the other 'isms' learned by rote in the institutions of political correctness are now made publicly, with impunity, without proof, on a daily basis and with often ruinous effect for the accused, 'fascism', in contrast, has been made all but unusable, its use identifying the speaker as unworthy of attention, childish, innocent of history. And while I am horrified at how the adolescent accusations of woke ideology have found such rapid translation into ever more repressive laws further removing our human rights and civil liberties under the guise of protecting us from ourselves and others, I have, by and large, agreed with reserving the term 'fascism' for its historical manifestations.

Fascism, as I have written previously, is particular to a certain stage in the development of capitalism and a certain formation of the capitalist state, arising out of the relatively late unification of the Italian and German nations in 1871, the desire of their governments and perhaps their people to share in the colonial spoils on which the British and French empires had fed for centuries, and in response to, respectively, humiliation and defeat in the Great War, the revolutionary upheavals of 1918-19, post-war hyperinflation, the stock market crash of 1929 and the Great Depression that followed.[1] There are, undoubtedly, many more factors contributing to the coming to power of fascist and authoritarian governments in Italy (1922-43), Lithuania (1926-40), Hungary (1932-45), Germany (1933-45), Portugal (1933-74), Bulgaria (1934-35), Latvia (1934-40), Austria (1934-45), Greece (1936-44), Romania (1937-44), Czechia (1939-45), Albania (1939-43), Slovakia (1939-45), Spain (1939-75), France (1940-44), Serbia (1941-45), Croatia (1941-45) and Norway (1942-45), including the long history of antisemitism in Christian Europe, the revival of nationalism by the Great War, and the threat presented to capitalism by the Russian Revolution in 1917 and the formation of the Union of Soviet Socialist Republics in 1922. And, given the complexity and contingency of these historical forces, what justification can there be for using the word 'fascism' in anything other than a historical context? None, I would have

---

1. See the pages titled 'Historical Precedents for the Biosecurity State' in Simon Elmer, 'The New Normal: What is the UK Biosecurity State? (Part 2. Normalising Fear)' (28 August, 2020), collected in *COVID-19: Implementing the UK Biosecurity State* (Architects for Social Housing, 2021), pp. 225-230.

said, and for this reason have always avoided using this term to describe the imperialism, militarism and increasing brutality of the West's politics, laws and military aggression since 1945.

Until now. In this book, I'm going to look at what the term 'fascism' means 100 years after it first came to power in the Kingdom of Italy in 1922; what grounds there are for using it to describe the current formations of power within the Global Biosecurity State and technologies of the Fourth Industrial Revolution in 2022; and what are the benefits and dangers of using this term. My point in doing so is not to adjudicate over a question of terminology proper to an academic discussion in which I have no interest, but to alert us to the seriousness of the threat we are facing from the revolution in capitalism we have been undergoing in the former neoliberal countries of the West since March 2020, where our continued failure to counter this revolution will lead, and, finally, the necessity of doing so before — as happened in Europe in 1939 — the world is thrust into a disaster from which it cannot extract itself except at the cost of millions of lives. Indeed, as I write, this brink may already have been crossed. But even if it has, we should be in no doubt about what is driving this revolution, what its political aims are, and what means it will employ to attain them, and not be afraid to call it what it is. I believe that, not in its economic infrastructure, certainly, but in its ideological superstructure — that is to say, its emerging governmental, juridical and cultural forms — its name is 'fascism'.

I want to start by distinguishing what I mean by the return of 'fascism' from 'neo-fascism'. The latter is a term used by neoliberal governments and their media to describe far-right groups in Europe and the USA that nostalgically look back to the 1930s, even when their nations and people suffered under historical forms of fascism. Favoured as a pejorative description by anarchists, antifascists, socialists, social democrats and liberals who see no problem in thereby aligning themselves with right-wing governments, this term has functioned to turn our eyes away from what has always been the real threat of the return of fascism. This is not, in my opinion, from these violent but largely impotent political and cultural movements, but rather from the neoliberal governments themselves, which are not above using neo-fascist groups to further their own geopolitical agendas —

most recently, for example, conveniently deciding that Vladimir Putin's Russia is more 'neo-fascist' than Volodymyr Zelenskyy's until recently 'neo-Nazi' Ukraine.[2]

The word 'fascism' comes from *fascio*, the Italian word for 'bundle', and etymologically from the Latin *fasces*. Originating with the Etruscan civilisation, from which it was adopted by the Ancient Romans, the *fasces* was a bundle of rods surrounding an axe with the blade projecting that, carried by a lictor or bodyguard, symbolised the legal authority and supreme power of command *(imperium)* over the Roman military. *Imperium* was the form of authority held by a Roman citizen elected to the office of civic magistrate, including consuls, praetors, and proconsuls, and in Roman law was distinguished from and superior to the coercive power of the law *(potestas)* or individual prestige and influence *(auctoritas)*. On the magistrate's command, however, the *fasces* could also serve a more practical function, with the rods being used for corporal punishment and the axe for capital punishment. The unity of the bundle, therefore, was only achieved at the cost of the subjection of the individual to the obligations of citizenship, which were modelled on the military and were enforced with all the authority and power of the state.

Revived in the Twentieth Century, most famously by the Italian fascist movement, the *fasces* was used as a symbol of civic authority beyond and before Fascist Italy. It appeared, most inconveniently, on the reverse of the ten-cent 'Mercury' coin struck by the United States Mint between 1916 and 1945, surrounded by the words *E pluribus unum* ('Out of many, one'), which was the motto of the USA until 1956 (when it was replaced by 'In God We Trust'). This isn't surprising, given that the USA has modelled its empire on that of Rome, and in doing so has adopted not only the latter's terminology of Republic, Senate and Legislature but also its classical architecture and its military symbolism, the most obvious borrowing from which is the Imperial Eagle. Taken by the Founding Fathers from the military standards of the all-conquering Roman legions they wished to emulate, the eagle was also adopted, and for the same reasons, by the Third Reich. And unlike the Nazi *swastika* — an ancient symbol even older than the *fasces* that has become anathematised and even illegal to display in some

---

2. See, for example, from the same neoliberal newspaper two years apart, Kevin Rawlinson, 'Neo-Nazi groups recruit Britons to fight in Ukraine', *The Guardian* (2 March, 2020); and Jason Stanley, 'The antisemitism animating Putin's claim to "denazify" Ukraine', *The Guardian* (26 February, 2022).

countries — the *fasces* continued to be used as a symbol of collective power long after the Second World War. To an extent, this reflects the difference of censure imposed by the victorious Allies on, respectively, National Socialist Germany and Fascist Italy, but it also tells us something about the structure of state power. A pair of bronze *fasces* still appear, to this day, behind the House Rostrum in the US House of Representatives. Indeed, in a distant echo of Rome, the seat of my former local magistrates, Lambeth County Court, has a bas-relief of a *fasces* over the door of its Neo-classical building, which was completed in 1928. In 2017, however, as part of the Government's drive to privatise as much of the UK state as possible, the court was closed and the property sold by the freeholder — the Duchy of Cornwall, which owns most of the land in this part of London — to the aptly-named property developer Lucrum, which in Latin means 'profit', 'advantage', 'love of gain', 'avarice'.

It would be wrong, therefore, to see the authoritarian unity symbolised by the *fasces* as belonging to a historical period and politics now surpassed. Instead, fascism should be understood as a latent presence in the structure of all judicial, executive and legislative authority, and a warning of what can happen when the individual and his rights are subsumed within the politically declared needs of the collective. Fascism, in this sense of the word, is the other side of the coin that is struck when we agree — willingly, out of convention or under duress — to the formation of the state. For this reason alone, it would be not only historically incorrect but also politically naive to confine fascism to the past. On the contrary, fascism — I am not alone in believing — is making a return to our politics; or, perhaps more accurately, fascism is unveiling the axe it has kept hidden in the bundle of rods with which our backs have been beaten on the justification of the 'common good'.

2. The Rise of Global Governance

Over the past two-and-a-half years, this all-but universally embraced common good — the ultimate, irreducible, transparent and utterly illusory referent by which all biosecurity 'measures' have been justified — has been decided not only or even primarily by the elected governments of nation states, but also and with increasing authority by the various institutions and organisations of global governance that have been formed by the West mostly since the Second World War. To remind us of the membership, extent and reach of their unelected and largely unaccountable merger of corporate and government power, these include, but are not limited to:

- The Bank for International Settlements (BIS), originally founded in 1930 to oversee the payment of reparations after the Great War, with a membership of 61 central banks in 2022.
- The United Nations (UN), founded in 1945, with 193 member-states in 2022.
- The International Monetary Fund (IMF), founded in 1945, with 190 member-states in 2022.
- The World Bank, founded in 1945, with 189 member-states in 2022.
- The World Health Organization (WHO), founded in 1948, with 194 member-states in 2022.
- The North Atlantic Treaty Organization (NATO), founded in 1949 to oppose the Union of Soviet Socialist Republics, it continues today with 30 member-states in 2022.
- The Council of Europe, founded in 1949, with 46 members states in 2022.
- The European Court of Justice, founded in 1952, with 27 member-states in 2022.
- The European Economic Community, founded in 1957, and incorporated into the European Union (EU) in 1993, with 27 member-states in 2022.
- The European Commission, founded in 1958.
- The European Management Forum, founded in 1971, renamed the World Economic Forum (WEF) in 1987, with over 1,000 member-companies in 2022, and whose Board of Trustees includes the Managing Director of the IMF, the President of the European Central Bank, the Director General of the World Trade Organization, the UN Envoy for Climate Action and Finance, and the CEO of BlackRock.
- The Trilateral Commission, founded in 1973, with roughly 400 members from North America, Europe and the Asia-Pacific region in 2022.
- The Society for Worldwide Interbank Financial Telecommunication (SWIFT), founded in 1973, linking more than 11,000 financial institutions in over 200 countries in 2022.

- The European Council, founded in 1975, with 27 heads of state or government of the EU member-states in 2022, plus the President of the European Council and the President of the European Commission.
- The Group of Six (G6), founded in 1975, expanded to the G7 in 1977, to the G8 in 1997, and to the G20 in 1999, with 20 member-states in 2022, including the UK, the US and the European Union.
- The Group of Thirty (G30), founded in 1978 by the Rockefeller Foundation, with 30 members in 2022 comprised of the current and former heads of the central banks of 17 countries, including the UK and US, the Federal Reserve Bank of New York, the European Central Bank, the Bank of International Settlements, the International Monetary Fund and the World Bank.
- The Intergovernmental Panel on Climate Change (IPCC), founded in 1988, with 195 member-states in 2022.
- The World Trade Organization (WTO), founded in 1995, with 164 member-states in 2022.
- The European Central Bank (ECB), founded in 1998.
- The Global Alliance for Vaccines and Immunization, founded in 2000, renamed GAVI the Vaccine Alliance in 2014, and funded (in order of proceeds between 2016 and 2020) by the UK, the Bill & Melinda Gates Foundation, the USA, Norway, Germany, France, Canada, Italy, the Netherlands, Australia, Sweden, Japan, the European Commission and 20 other countries.

As an example of the axe blade hidden in this bundle of unelected power claiming to protect the world from, among other things, the return of historical fascism, on 3 March, 2022, as coronavirus-justified regulations were revoked across Europe and NATO declared its proxy war on Russia, the European Council adopted a decision to authorise the opening of negotiations for an international agreement on Pandemic Prevention, Preparedness and Response.[3] Under this agreement, the 194 member-states of the World Health Organization will be legally bound to implement restrictions on human rights and freedoms, such as mandatory face masks, lockdowns, compulsory vaccination and Digital Identity,

---

3. See World Health Organization, 'World Health Assembly agrees to launch process to develop historic global accord on pandemic prevention, preparedness and response' (1 December, 2021); and European Council, 'An international treaty on pandemic prevention and preparedness' (last reviewed 25 March, 2022).

on the judgement of the WHO. The basis of this agreement is Article 19 of the WHO Statutes, which states that the General Assembly of the World Health Organization can adopt agreements that, if passed by a two-thirds majority, are binding on all member states. Under these agreements, nation states, including the UK and the 193 other members of the WHO, will in principle concede their sovereignty to decide which restrictions the elected executive and legislature will impose on their populations. Crucially, once written into a legally-binding treaty, the efficacy or logic of these so-called medical 'measures' — none of which have been used before as responses to viral epidemics, and all of which have been shown over the last two-and-a-half years to be ineffective, dangerous and to endanger more people than SARS-CoV-2 — will no longer be open even to what little debate we've had in this country. Instead, the WHO will effectively become a global form of the UK's Scientific Advisory Group for Emergencies (SAGE), a politically appointed technocracy to which the governments of nation states can defer when they choose to, and which serves to depict undemocratic forms of governance as technical responses to new crises.[4] Indeed, this international technocracy is the new paradigm of governance to have emerged from under the cloak of the coronavirus 'crisis', and its globalist intentions become more apparent every day. 'No one is safe until everyone is safe', the slogan that first entered public discourse around February 2021 and was quickly adopted by the G7, the United Nations, the World Health Organization, the European Union, GAVI and an ever-increasing number of Western governments, including the UK, Germany, France, Spain, Portugal, the Netherlands, Norway, Greece, Serbia, the Ukraine and the USA, is as perfect an expression of the totalitarian aspirations of the Global Biosecurity State as *'Ein Volk, ein Reich, ein Führer'* was of the Third Reich.[5]

This is only one example of many, but it's on the evidence of such unilaterally imposed biosecurity programmes that my argument for the return of fascism is built. The 'crisis' in public health manufactured in response to SARS-CoV-2 has

---

4. On the membership and funding of SAGE, see Simon Elmer, 'The Betrayal of the Clerks: UK Intellectuals in the Service of the Biosecurity State' (12 November, 2020), collected in *Brave New World: Expanding the UK Biosecurity State through the Winter of 2020-2021* (Architects for Social Housing, 2021), pp. 25-52.

5. See Robert Hart, 'Nobody Is Safe Until Everyone Is Safe': World Leaders Call for Global Pandemic Preparedness Treaty', *Forbes* (30 March, 2021).

been the occasion and justification both to expand the power of existing organisations of global governance and to justify the implementation of new programmes, new powers of enforcement, new ideologies and new technologies that will bring to a completion the erasure of the nation state as the dominant form of governance in the West, and to replace it with the expanded powers of an international technocracy for which national governments will primarily function as the administrators and enforcers of its laws and policies. Since at least 2018 the Trilateral Commission has promoted the use of Artificial Intelligence to analyse, monitor and shape the behaviour of citizens; in October 2019, the World Bank proposed acting as a central repository of data relating to good practices of countries implementing Digital Identity, facilitating the transfer of information to interested parties and incentivising compliance with preferential loans and grants; in August 2020, the IMF recommended that data from our online browsing, search and purchase history should be used to determine the credit rating of a citizen or business; in April 2022, the Intergovernmental Panel on Climate Change declared that annual greenhouse gas emissions must be reduced by 43 per cent by 2030 and reach Net Zero emissions by 2050 through a global reduction in energy and material consumption; in March 2021, SWIFT expelled Russia from its banking system; and in September 2022, the European Commission announced that, should the electorate of Italy not vote for its preferred candidate, they had the 'tools' to cut funds to Italy, as it already has to Poland and Hungary.[6]

Undoubtedly, forty years of neoliberalism have paved the way and removed most of the political, state and ideological obstacles to this revolution in Western capitalism; but the construction and implementation of the Global Biosecurity State, the violence with which its dictates have been enforced by nation states, and the readiness with which the residual forms of democracy in civil society have accepted, accommodated and become instruments for its programmes, represents the transition to a New World Order which draws much of its politics (technocratic rule), juridical procedures (a permanent state of emergency) and ideology (biosecurity) from historical fascism. Fascism is not just a form of

---

6. See Trilateral Commission, 'Task Force Report on Artificial Intelligence' (25 March, 2018); World Bank Group, 'Practitioners Guide' (October 2019); IMF, 'Financial Intermediation and Technology: What's Old and what's New?' (7 August, 2020); Paul Collins, 'IPCC climate report 2022 summary: The key findings'; and Wilhelmine Preussen, 'Von der Leyen's warning message to Italy irks election candidates', *Politico* (19 October, 2022).

governance, a configuration of the state or a social contract, but how these are imposed on a population; and the increase in state violence against the populations of previously neoliberal democracies in the two years since March 2020 marks a watershed to a new and terrifying willingness of Western governments to use the power of the state against its own citizens.

What distinguishes the return of fascism from the fascist states of a century ago is, obviously and necessarily, the different stage of capitalism we have reached today. Fascist Italy and Nazi Germany operated within an imperialist model of capitalism which, as I have said, represented the attempt of these countries to catch up with the more established imperialisms of the UK and France, and even of the Netherlands, Belgium, Spain and Portugal. To some extent, this accounts for the crudity and violence of their implementation, using military conquest to accelerate hundreds of years of colonial expansion, economic exploitation and resource extraction. A century later, the finance capitalism of the last forty years has reached the stage where global corporations wealthier than all but the very wealthiest countries are now intent not only on dictating the economic infrastructure of our societies but also on using their monopoly to create a new politics — a politics which, in the sense that it erases the division of powers on which the *polis* is founded, is the end of the classical model of politics.

It's in this sense that the World Economic Forum, which of all the institutions of global governance formed since the Second World War has been the most open about its intentions to create an unelected international technocracy, has become emblematic of this revolution, even though its power to effect such change pales beside other, far more powerful, global organisations.[7] Much has been made about the revelations that many Cabinet members in the governments of the former neoliberal democracies of the West are former Young Global Leaders, a sort of WEF Ivy League for Europe created in 1993 by Klaus Schwab, the founder and Executive Chairman of the World Economic Forum, with members from over 90 countries in 2022; and certainly many of the most active promoters of the Global Biosecurity State appear to have passed through its doors.[8] Alumni occupying former or current ministerial positions in Western

---

7. See World Economic Forum, 'This is what a new model of governance could look like' (17 January, 2022).

8. See World Economic Forum, 'The Forum of Young Global Leaders: Who We Are'.

governments include Tony Blair, the former Prime Minister of the UK; Angela Merkel, the former Chancellor of Germany; Nicolas Sarkozky, the former President of France; Sebastian Kurz, the former Chancellor of Austria; Jean-Claude Juncker, the former Prime Minister of Luxembourg and former President of the European Commission; Justin Trudeau, the current Prime Minister of Canada; Chrystia Freeland, the Canadian Deputy Prime Minister and Minister of Finance; François-Philippe Champagne, the Canadian Minister of Innovation, Science and Industry; Emmanuel Macron, the President of France; Amélie de Montchalin, the French Minister of Public Sector Transformation and the Civil Service; Marlène Schiappa, the former French Minister Delegate in charge of citizenship; Alexander De Croo, the Prime Minister of Belgium; Ida Auken, the former Danish Minister for the Environment; Lea Wermelin, the current Danish Minister for the Environment; Karien van Gennip, the Dutch Minister of Social Affairs and Employment; Leo Varadkar, the Irish Minister for Enterprise, Trade and Employment; Niki Kerameus, the Greek Minister of Education and Religious Affairs; Jens Spahn, the former German Minister for Health; Annalena Baerbock, the German Minister for Foreign Affairs; Sanna Marin, the Prime Minister of Finland; Annika Saarikko, the Finish Deputy Prime Minister and Minister for Finance; Viktor Orbán, the Prime Minister of Hungary; and Jacinda Ardern, the Prime Minister of New Zealand. That's just the figures in publicly-elected office. In this respect, the WEF is the think-tank for the geopolitical aspirations of Western capitalism, the far more powerful equivalent of Policy Exchange in the UK, formulating, announcing and indoctrinating its populations into supporting the policies of international technocracies rather than national governments. And just as the UK Government is the administrative body of UK capital, so too the economic forces behind the WEF, the WHO, the EU and the UN are the real drivers of this revolution in capitalism. I'll look in more detail at what these forces are in chapter 4.

In its economic infrastructure, therefore, which includes the emerging technologies and markets of the Fourth Industrial Revolution, what I'm arguing is the return of fascism in the West is qualitatively different from historical fascism in Europe; but in the ends to which that revolution is being put and the effects it is having on our governance, our laws and our society, it bears comparison.[9] The

---

9. See Department for Digital, Culture, Media and Sport, 'The Fourth Industrial Revolution' (16 October, 2017). My commentary on this speech by Matt Hancock, who would be the UK's

current revolution — which, as I will go on to argue, is the West's response to the systemic crisis in capitalism unresolved by the Global Financial Crisis of 2008-2009 — is effecting our transition to a new form of fascism: one formed not around the nation states of imperialist capitalism, but around the Global Biosecurity State of an international technocracy. Indeed, what the past two-and-a-half years have shown to those who believed — or at least argued — that the European Union and its attendant Court, Commission, Parliament, Council and Central Bank represented some last defence of human rights and freedoms against the predations of global capital is that, to the contrary, it is one of the international forums in which the policies the nation state will enforce are made without any representative or direct vote from their populations. As we will soon see, that will be whether those policies are for an open-ended programme of mandatory 'vaccination' against future 'pandemics' declared by the World Health Organization, the implementation of Digital Identity combining blockchain technology, artificial intelligence and biometric scanners as a condition of access to the rights of citizenship, the move to Central Bank Digital Currency that logs every transaction we make and is programmed with restrictions and limits on expenditure linked to our health status, individual carbon footprint and social compliance, or a system of Social Credit linked to the Internet of Things modelled on that used in the People's Republic of China.[10] This is the axe in the bundle of rods that's been wielded over our heads since March 2020 on the justification of the common good. This, I believe, is where we can accurately speak of fascism having returned as the present to which the road we've so blindly followed has led us. In the following chapters, I'll be looking at the evidence for the return of fascism to the West in its respective ideological, juridical, economic, psychological, cultural, political, biopolitical, governmental and moral aspects.

Minister of Health during lockdown, can be read in the pages titled 'Disruption and Redeployment', section 5 of Simon Elmer, *'Cui Bono? The COVID-19 "conspiracy"'* (19 February, 2021), collected in *Brave New World*, pp. 151-155.

10. See, for example, Daniel Boffey, 'EU must consider mandatory Covid jabs, says Von der Leyen', *The Guardian* (1 December, 2021); Frank Hersey, 'UN explores digital identity sector to inform legal identity progress', *Biometric* (15 November, 2021); Tim Wallace, 'Bank of England tells Ministers to intervene on digital currency programming', *The Telegraph* (21 June, 2021); and Drew Donnelly, 'China Social Credit System Explained — What is it and How Does it Work?', *NH Global Partners* (22 July, 2022).

2. Eternal Fascism

'It does not surprise me that Italy is at the moment spearheading the development of a technology of governance that, in the name of public health, renders acceptable a set of life conditions which eliminate all possible political activity, pure and simple. This country is always on the verge of falling back into fascism, and there are many signs today that is something more than a risk.'

— Giorgio Agamben, interview on Swedish Public Radio, April 2020

Another variation on the use of the word 'fascism' in a contemporary context was coined by the Italian semiotician, novelist and political commentator, Umberto Eco, who grew up in Fascist Italy in the 1930s, and who in June 1995 published a text in *The New York Review of Books* titled 'Ur-Fascism'.[1] Conceding that fascism, in its historical form, had little chance of returning in a Europe drunk with celebrating the formation of the European Union, Eco was interested in why this term — rather than Falangist (Spain), or Cagoulard (France), or Quisling (Norway), or Ustaše (Croatia), or even Nazi (Germany) — became the privileged synecdoche for different authoritarian nationalist movements. Eco is insistent that this was not because Italian fascism, although the first fascist movement to come to power, contained the essence of totalitarian movements. On the contrary, unlike National Socialism or even Stalinism, Italian fascism had no coherent doctrine, combining political revolution with monarchy, military conquest with the Catholic Church, state absolutism with private business. Unlike the Third Reich or the Soviet Union, there was no unified model of fascist culture, with neoclassical architecture being built alongside modernist buildings, and avant-garde writers and artists that were denounced as degenerate by Adolf Hitler and bourgeois by Joseph Stalin tolerated and even celebrated under Benito Mussolini. That didn't mean that political dissidents in Fascist Italy weren't arrested, tortured and executed, that the freedom of the press wasn't abolished, that the trades unions weren't dismantled, that the legislature wasn't bypassed, and that laws weren't issued

---

1. Umberto Eco, 'Ur-Fascism', *The New York Review of Books* (22 June, 1995), collected in *How to Spot a Fascist*, translated by Ricard Dixon and Alastair McEwan (Harvill Secker, 2020).

direct by the executive without democratic oversight. But while there was only one form of Nazism, just as there was one form of Falangism, there are, Eco argued, many fascisms that combine some but not all its elements. Some are imperialist, some atheist, some anti-capitalist, some anti-Semitic, but none of these elements are necessary to all. From this proposition comes the point of Eco's article, which is to outline the typical features of what he calls 'Ur-fascism or Eternal Fascism', of which he describes fourteen. These fourteen features of fascism cannot be organised into a system, some contradict each other, and some characterise other forms of despotism; but it is enough, Eco says, for just one to be present in any given society for fascism to form around it.

In what follows, I'm going to quote from Eco's descriptions of these typical features of Eternal Fascism, and then give examples of their presence in the new ways of thinking and feeling, the new meanings and values, the new social practices and behaviours, the new relationships and kinds of relationships, that have formed over the past two-and-a-half years around and in response to the coronavirus 'crisis' and the Global Biosecurity State that has been constructed on the justification of combatting it.

1. Fourteen Features of Fascism

1. The first feature of Ur-Fascism is the cult of tradition. As a consequence, there can be no advancement of learning. Truth has already been spelled out once and for all, and we can only keep interpreting its obscure message.

The most prevalent demonstration of this first feature of fascism has been the mantra, repeated over and over by every government implementing the Global Biosecurity State in order to justify its removal of the human rights and civil liberties of its citzens, to 'Follow the Science!' In doing so, science — which is a set of discursive and practical procedures for testing a hypothesis about the physical and natural world and, by a repeatable practical demonstration, proving it to be either true or false — has instead been hypostatised as an eternal and unchanging Truth. Science, in other words, has been turned into its opposite, which is religion, the dictates of whose high priests — the Chief Medical Officers of nation states, the Chief Executive Officers of pharmaceutical companies, or the

Leadership Team of the World Health Organization — must be followed without question, unchallenged by the emergence of new evidence they themselves are not required to produce for debate or to justify the practices they impose. It is in this sense that the obedience of hundreds of millions of citizens in the Global Biosecurity State to its dictates has accurately been described as a cult.[2]

2.   Traditionalism implies the *rejection of modernism*. The Enlightenment, the Age of Reason, is seen as the beginning of modern depravity. In this sense, Ur-Fascism can be defined as irrationalism.

On the justification of following this monotheistic, absolute and therefore fundamentally unscientific 'Science', Western governments have imposed arbitrary 'measures' without medical foundation or logical justification. These include so-called 'social' distancing, enforced mask-wearing, plastic dividers between tables in restaurants and schools, directional arrows in shops, pavements and parks, anti-bacterial soap dispensers at the entrance to every building and venue, and all the other instruments and practices of cultic compliance. As was revealed by the publication of the advice on the mandating of masks by the World Health Organization and, in the UK, by the Scientific Advisory Group for Emergencies, the primary function of such 'measures' is to create fear in the minds of the public and thereby increase obedience and acquiescence to the restrictions to our human rights and civil liberties.[3] It is a measure of the irrationalism by which we are now ruled that overt support for such

---

2. See Giorgio Agamben, 'Medicine as Religion' (2 May, 2020), collected in *Where Are We Now? The Epidemic as Politics*. Second updated edition. Translated by Valeria Dani (Eris, 2021), pp. 49-54.

3. See World Health Organization, 'Advice on the use of masks in the context of COVID-19' (5 June, 2020). For a summary of the politicisation of masking, see Simon Elmer, 'The Science and Law of Refusing to Wear Masks: Texts and Arguments in Support of Civil Disobedience' (11 June, 2020); collected in *COVID-19*, pp. 159-187. The by-now notorious advice from the Scientific Pandemic Influenza Group on Behavioural Science (SPI-B) was that: 'A substantial number of people still do not feel sufficiently personally threatened; it could be that they are reassured by the low death rate in their demographic group. The perceived level of personal threat needs to be increased among those who are complacent, using hard-hitting emotional messaging.' See Scientific Advisory Group for Emergencies, 'Options for increasing adherence to social distancing measures' (22 March, 2020).

cultic practices has come from the World Health Organization, the European Medicines Agency, the Medicines and Healthcare products Regulatory Agency in the UK, the Robert Koch Institute in Germany, and the Centers for Disease Control and Prevention in the US, and been met with collusive silence by, among other institutions of science, the Nobel Foundation, the Lindau Institute, the Royal Society and the National Academy of Sciences.

3.   Irrationalism also depends on the cult of *action for action's sake*. Action being beautiful in itself, it must be taken before, or without, any previous reflection. Thinking is a form of emasculation. Therefore, culture is suspect insofar as it is identified with critical attitudes. Distrust of the intellectual world has always been a symptom of Ur-Fascism.

The primary example of this feature of eternal fascism has been the readiness of governments to impose so-called 'lockdowns' on their populations in response to the terrorised public's demand for immediate action, and the online censorship, public denunciation and media campaigns to slander and delegitimise anyone who dares to adopt a critical attitude to such action. The readiness with which corporate 'Fact Checkers' have been accepted as the Orwellian Thought-Police of the Global Biosecurity State, and the ease with which accusations of 'conspiracy theory' continue to be levelled at anyone who dares to think for themselves, including previously eminent scientists and still independent political thinkers, testifies to the anti-intellectualism of Eternal Fascism. Although the irony may be as lost on them as it will be to those who look to such organisations for objective guidance, no less an authority than the European Commission, the executive body whose unelected members propose new laws on its own initiative, has published a guide to identifying conspiracy theories, which they define as 'the belief that certain events or situations are secretly manipulated behind the scenes by powerful forces with negative intent'.[4]

4.   The critical spirit makes distinctions, and to distinguish is a sign of modernism. In modern culture, the scientific community praises disagreement as a way to improve knowledge. For Ur-Fascism, disagreement is treason.

---

4. See European Commission, 'Identifying conspiracy theories'.

The extension of this anti-intellectualism and demand for reactive action is the unprecedented level of censorship that has taken over public life in the former neoliberal democracies of the West. This has been imposed above all against the scientific community, whose every attempt to raise questions, ask for proofs, or propose alternative explanations and courses of action — in other words, to adhere to the principals of scientific procedure — is met with accusations that in doing so they are endangering lives and, last winter in Canada, threatening the security of the state, thereby justifying the use of emergency powers to crush dissent and punish dissenters. The other side of this coin is the equally unprecedented compliance with which previously competing and politically opposed corporate media outlets and platforms have collaborated, both with governments and with each other, to repeat a single, homogeneous and unquestioned narrative in support of the Global Biosecurity State.

5.   Disagreement is a sign of diversity. Ur-Fascism grows up and seeks consensus by exploiting and exacerbating the natural *fear of difference*. The first appeal of a fascist or prematurely fascist movement is an appeal against the intruders. Thus Ur-fascism is by definition racist.

Just as, under the official ideology of multiculturalism, forty years of neoliberalism created a global, corporate, ersatz, homogeneous monoculture that has reached into every corner of the globe — colonising indigenous cultures, destroying alternative cultures and appropriating what remained of the counter-culture — so today, behind its commitment to diversity, the Global Biosecurity State has been built on a fundamental fear of the other. The medical apartheid in Western societies instigated by 'vaccine' passports, and the system of segregation, exclusion and punishment of intruders being constructed on their imposition, is the technological implementation of this ideology.[5] Like the 'safe

---

5. There is already extensive and, since a Federal Judge forced the US Food and Drug Administration to publish the data from Pfizer's clinical trials, rapidly growing evidence that the 'vaccines' temporarily authorised for use in the UK to combat the effects and spread of COVID-19 do neither, and cannot, therefore, be considered to be vaccines, even by the constantly altered definition of what a vaccine can and should do. For this reason, when using this word in the context of the COVID-19 'vaccination' programmes, I always place it in inverted commas. See Simon Elmer, 'The UK "Vaccination" Programme: Part 1. Adverse Drug Reactions and Deaths' (15 September,

spaces' of woke orthodoxy, these have been implemented on fear of difference, fear of contradiction, fear of the body, fear of death, fear of whatever threatens to break into the online world of biosecurity.

This is a space in which everyone — or, more accurately every-body — is policed by everyone else, everyone is a potential informant, in which anyone deviating from the imposed norm is censored, punished, banished and erased from the records of everyone but the police, the security services and the information technology companies dictating the norms of that world. The Global Biosecurity State has been modelled on this online space, which, as social media platforms demonstrate every day, is built on fear, hatred and division, on the unquestionable certainties of ignorance, on communities of identification formed around victimisation, on the homogenisation of heterogeneous social elements through mandatory programmes of indoctrination, on enforced orthodoxies of compliance, on what, behind their facades of inclusivity, are quite clearly fascist principles. Perhaps more accurately, the Global Biosecurity State is the totalising homogeneity of this online space, into which the heterogeneous populations of nation states are being subsumed.

6.   Ur-Fascism derives from individual or social frustration. One of the most typical features of historical fascism was the *appeal to a frustrated middle class*, a class suffering from an economic crisis or feelings of political humiliation, and frightened by the pressure from lower social groups. In our time, when the old 'proletarians' are becoming petty bourgeois (and the lumpen proletariat are largely excluded from the political scene), the fascism of tomorrow will find its audience in this new majority.

Historically, fascist governments have drawn their strongest support from the petty bourgeoisie (shopkeepers and small businessmen) and from rural areas (tenant farmers and small landowners), the inbred conservatism of whose populations are always a crisis away from conformity with fascism. Undoubtedly, though, the strictest adherents to and loudest advocates of the restrictions and requirements of the Global Biosecurity State have been the middle classes of the

---

2021), collected in *Virtue and Terror: Resisting the UK Biosecurity State* (Architects for Social Housing, 2021), pp. 39-70.

West, who appear quite ready to 'work from home' for the rest of their lives while their consumer goods are served by delivery drivers and their business is conducted via online platforms. Indeed, as their economic buffer zone has begun to collapse under two years of lockdowns and the ensuing inflation, compliance with the biosecurity state has become the new measure by which the middle-classes differentiate themselves from the working class, who make up a disproportionate number of those resisting its imposition.[6]

As a consequence, discrimination against the sociable, the unmasked and the unvaccinated as a public display of conformity with fascism has increased enormously over the past two-and-a-half years, and precisely among the demographic that defined itself — and was never hesitant to denounce others for not following its example — on its anti-discriminatory virtues. I will address this in greater detail in chapter 7, but we've seen this most glaringly among what congregates under the name of the Left, who are more accurately described as liberals as indoctrinated into the orthodoxies, programmes and technologies of the Global Biosecurity State as they were those of multiculturalism and political correctness.

7. At the root of the Ur-Fascist psychology there is the *obsession with a plot*, possibly an international one. The followers must feel besieged. The easiest way to solve the plot is the appeal to xenophobia. But the plot must also come from the inside: Jews are usually the best target because they have the advantage of being at the same time inside and outside.

On the face of it, this might seem like a description of the 'far-right conspiracy theorists' to which the COVID-faithful reduce anyone who questions the medical efficacy or political aims of imposing the regulations and programmes of the Global Biosecurity State on the populations of their countries; but the same could be said of those who have collaborated in turning the unmasked, the undistanced, the untracked, the untested and the unvaccinated into threats worthy of the harshest punishments. Indeed, it was the COVID-faithful who for two years lived in a state of siege imposed by their own governments, while the non-compliant

---

6. On the class dimension to resistance and compliance in the UK, see Simon Elmer, 'Behind the Mask, the Conspiracy!' (17 May, 2021), collected in *Virtue and Terror*, pp. 9-22.

ignored or refused to obey those governments' attempts to deprive them of their rights and freedoms. And it is the latter who have been characterised and denounced in this country — by the Government, by Parliament, by the National Health Service, by our police forces, by the pharmaceutical companies, by the press and media, and by their fellow citizens — as the 'enemies within' who should very firmly be banished from society with all the force of the law.

To this extent, the uncompliant have taken up the burden most recently borne, in the West, by the Muslim and the terrorist. As it was against the Jew and the communist in Nazi Germany, the xenophobia of the biosecurity-compliant citizen is directed not against the foreigner without but against those who, by refusing to comply, have become the foreigner within. As numerous heads of governments imposing biosecurity states have openly declared — including Emmanuel Macron, Olaf Scholz, Mario Draghi, Karl Nehammer, Scott Morrison, Jacinda Ardern, Joe Biden and Justin Trudeau — the 'unvaccinated' will no longer be treated as part of French, German, Italian, Austrian, Australian, New Zealand, US or Canadian society.

8.   The followers must feel humiliated by the ostentatious wealth and force of their enemies. Jews are rich and help each other through a secret web of mutual assistance. However, the followers [of Ur-Fascism] must be convinced that they can overwhelm the enemies. Thus, by a continuous shifting of rhetorical focus, the enemies are at the same time too strong and too weak.

The Global Biosecurity State has at its disposal not only the wealth and credit of individual nation states, whose governments have expended several generations of debt to impose its restrictions and programmes on their populations, but also of the international corporations with whom they have forged new alliances, and in particular with information technology, pharmaceutical, security and outsourcing companies. And yet, at the same time, these governments have taken action, in collaboration with private companies, to deprive resistance to the biosecurity state of funding raised by their populations. The most instructive example was that of Canada, where truckers demonstrating against 'vaccine' mandates were described by government and media as 'right-wing extremists' who were 'plotting to kill police officers', thereby justifying the

Canadian Government's appropriation of the millions of dollars raised to support their protest on the GoFundMe crowdfunding platform.[7] Like the underground resistance led by the fabricated Goldstein in George Orwell's *Nineteen Eighty-Four*, the enemies of the biosecurity state, like the virus itself, are both everywhere and everywhere being defeated, and all biosecurity-compliant citizens are called to join the struggle against them through their total obedience to the government.

9. For Ur-Fascism there is no struggle for life but, rather, life is lived for struggle. Thus, *pacifism is trafficking with the enemy*. It is bad because *life is permanent warfare*. This, however, brings about an Armageddon complex. Since enemies have to be defeated, there must be a final battle, after which the movement will have control of the world. But such a 'final solution' implies a further era of peace, a Golden Age, which contradicts the principle of permanent war.

Our own 'final solution', which has been proposed by the World Economic Forum and adopted by every government subscribing to its programme, is to 'build back better' from the global lockdown; and our Golden Age is the variously called 'New Normal' or 'Great Reset' of the Fourth Industrial Revolution.[8] From the very start, the response to a threat to public health that has never existed and which the governments of the world manufactured into a 'crisis', has been very deliberately characterised as a 'war on COVID', the medical meaninglessness of which hasn't stopped this mantra being taken up and echoed by every institution in every country in the West. And while the high priests of COVID have warned that this war will never be won and that the virus will always be with us — with the threat of future strains and new threats justifying further lockdowns hanging over our heads for the foreseeable future — we are, already, seeing how this war on COVID, just as it seemed to have been 'won', has been expanded into more conventional forms of warfare in the Ukraine.

---

7. See Justin Ling, 'Ottawa protests: "strong ties" between some occupiers and far-right extremists, minister says', *The Guardian* (16 February, 2022).

8. See HM Government, 'Our Plan to Rebuild: The UK Government's COVID-19 Recovery Strategy' (May 2020), and Klaus Schwab and Thierry Malleret, *COVID-19: The Great Reset* (Forum Publishing, July 2020).

10. Elitism is a typical aspect of any reactionary ideology, insofar as it is fundamentally aristocratic, and aristocratic and militaristic elitism cruelly implies *contempt for the weak*. Ur-Fascism can only advocate a *popular elitism*. Every citizen belongs to the best people of the world, the members of the party are the best among the citizens, every citizen can (or ought to) become a member of the party. But there cannot be patricians without plebeians. In fact, the Leader, knowing that his power was not delegated to him democratically but was conquered by force, also knows that his force is based upon the weakness of the masses; they are so weak as to need and deserve a ruler. Since the group is hierarchically organised (according to a military model), every subordinate leader despises his own underlings, and each of them despises his inferiors. This reinforces the sense of mass elitism.

In June 2021, leaders of the G7 nations at the summit held in Cornwall were photographed freely mixing with the UK's hereditary Head of State, Queen Elizabeth II, while being waited on by masked and socially-distanced workers required by their employers to be fully 'vaccinated'.[9] At a time when the rest of the UK population were living under the third Government-imposed national lockdown and fines of £10,000 for gatherings of the equivalent size, this encapsulated the division of society into the global 'elite' to whom the rules of biosecurity do not apply and the masses to whom they do. In the UK, however, the outrage of the general public was most raised by the reports of the numerous social gatherings and parties held at 10 Downing Street throughout the 'pandemic'; and the attendance of Boris Johnson at many of these events briefly threatened his survival as Prime Minister — until the 'crisis' in the Ukraine conveniently distracted a newly terrified and hate-filled population into forgetfulness.[10] Like the 'Two Minutes Hate' in *Nineteen Eighty-Four*, both these occasions for public outrage primarily served to reaffirm the necessity and efficacy of obeying restrictions on our human rights and civil liberties that have been repeatedly proven to be unnecessary, ineffective, injurious and increasingly fatal. They thereby served not to undermine, but instead to further justify, the regulations of the UK biosecurity state.

---

9. See 'The Queen and Royal Family host G7 leaders for joint dinner at Eden Project', *ITV News* (11 June, 2021).

10. See 'Partygate: A timeline of the lockdown gatherings', *BBC* (19 May, 2022).

Long before this stage-managed spectacle, however, two years of unrelenting attacks, slander, dismissals, derision, mockery, threats, hate and disgust directed from every quarter of the state and civil society against those who refused to obey orders from this self-appointed elite has created a popular elitism of compliance. Hierarchically stratified by public and online virtue signalling, this has reduced the non-compliant, in the minds of the COVID-faithful, to a semi-criminal and diseased underclass, unworthy and undeserving of human rights or the freedoms of citizenship — into, indeed, the *Untermenschen* of the Global Biosecurity State.

11. In such a perspective, *everybody is educated to become a hero*. In every mythology, the hero is an exceptional being, but in Ur-Fascist ideology heroism is the norm. This cult of heroism is strictly linked with the cult of death.

One of the more instructive spectacles created to promote the existence of a public health 'crisis' in the UK was the state-led adulation of NHS staff as 'heroes'. This was initiated with the 'clap for the NHS' ritual that was trialled for compliance in Italy and then performed every Thursday evening in the UK by those obeying the Government's instructions to remain at home. Partly as a consequence of this spectacle, when the third UK lockdown was officially lifted in July 2021, some UK residents had actually followed the Government's instructions, implemented with the full support of the NHS, to remain in their homes since March 2020. This adulation was further propagated by the child-like drawings thanking the NHS that were mass produced for those who wished to signal their obedience. This hero-worship served the by-now firmly entrenched belief that the population of the UK should be locked down to 'save the NHS', a progressively defunded public service that, until March 2020, was meant to serve the people of Britain. But perhaps the most explicit image of this cult of heroism was the widely-circulated image of superheroes from US comics depicted bowing in reverence to NHS staff.[11] From their willingness to embrace this trite propaganda and their own online behaviour — which continues to oscillate between assuming the role of a spiritual guru and a hysterical patient — it appears

---

11. See 'Superheroes bow to NHS angels in stunning artwork on businessman's garage door', *Daily Mail* (19 May, 2020).

NHS staff are only too ready to believe their own hype. Just what the UK Government really thought of these 'heroes' became clearer when, in November 2021, the new Secretary of State for Health, Sajid Javid — the previous holder, Matt Hancock, having been forced to resign for breaking his own lockdown restrictions — announced to Parliament that NHS staff who refused to be injected with a COVID-19 'vaccine' would be sacked.[12]

In contrast to historical fascism, however, in which death was promoted as the reward for a heroic life in the service of the nation state, in the biosecurity state death has been all but outlawed, with the death of every 80-year-old testing positive for SARS-CoV-2 (which is to say, the average 'COVID-19 death' in the UK) lamented as a 'tragedy' deserving of national mourning. The exception are the vast numbers of deaths that have already occurred and are expected to occur in the future from the removal of medical diagnosis for cancer, treatment for heart disease, care for dementia and the other primary causes of death in the UK, which will far surpass anything attributed to COVID-19, about which neither the medical profession nor the media have anything to say.[13]

12. Since both permanent war and heroism are difficult games to play, the Ur-Fascist transfers his will-to-power to sexual matters. This is the origin of machismo (which implies both disdain for women and intolerance and condemnation of nonstandard sexual habits, from chastity to homosexuality). But since even sex is a difficult game to play, the Ur-Fascist hero tends to play with weapons — doing so becomes an ersatz phallic exercise.

The enforcement of the regulations and programmes of the Global Biosecurity State has occasioned a significant increase in the violence and unaccountability of the police forces of Western nations, who are now armed and armoured like their counterparts in the military and augmented by counter-terrorist paramilitary units. These have used pepper spray, tear gas, rubber bullets, water-cannons and armoured-cars reportedly mounted with sonic and heat weapons in order to assault protests against lockdowns and 'vaccine' mandates by unarmed

---

12. See Sajid Javid, 'Health Secretary statement on Vaccines as a Condition of Deployment', *Department of Health and Social Care* (9 November, 2021).

13. See Simon Elmer, 'Lies, Damned Lies and Statistics: Manufacturing the Crisis' (27 January, 2021), collected in *Brave New World*, pp. 112-136.

and unarmoured civilians, including the elderly, women and children. This should make it apparent, once and for all, that the expansion in the number and capabilities of the weapons of the police and security forces of the former neoliberal democracies of the West in the twenty years since '9/11' has not been accomplished in order to protect us from external threats to our safety from terrorists. On the contrary, it has been in anticipation of the social uprisings and protests we've seen across the world in response to the violence of the Global Biosecurity State. This, rather than Eco's rather cod-Freudianism, is the reason for the unprecedented levels of state violence we saw during the 'pandemic'. But if we take what Eco calls a 'phallic exercise' to mean the exercise of state power — which has nothing 'ersatz' about it — against the populations of nation states, then undoubtedly the two years since March 2020 saw a display of machismo at levels new in the West except, perhaps, among our strutting leaders, both male and female. Indeed, since the Cabinet of Prime Minister Theresa May underwent who knows what PR course in public relations, all our Ministers of State adopt a heroic stance when appearing in public as ludicrous as it is revealing about how they see themselves.[14]

At the same time, under the guise of protecting adolescents and young adults from a disease to which they are statistically immune, the UK biosecurity state hasn't shrunk from advising its obedient citizens to abstain from certain sexual practices, to practice a new form of 'safe sex' (not face to face), or to give up sex altogether 'for the common good', as though it were trying to recreate the Junior Anti-Sex League from Orwell's *Nineteen-Eighty-four*.[15] As for children, the vast financial and institutional resources concurrently being used to promote so-called non-binary and trans-sexual identities even among pre-pubescent infants appears to be directed toward a similar goal. Certainly, the erasure of intimacy won't stop at social distancing and masking, and will endeavour, as the biosecurity states of historical fascism did, to impose its restrictions and obligations on sexual intercourse (the extreme example being the prohibition on 'miscegenation' in the Third Reich). The monitoring and manipulation of human sexuality has always been used by authoritarian and particularly totalitarian states

---

14. See Kate Nicholson, 'Rishi Sunak Proves That The Conservative Power Stance Lives On', *Huffington Post* (13 July, 2022).

15. See Dr. Michael Brady, 'How to have sex while managing the risk of COVID-19', *The Terrence Higgins Trust* (7 August, 2020).

to control the behaviour of its citizens; and the Global Biosecurity State has technologies to do so undreamed of by historical fascism, whether that's repressing desire in obedience to the orthodoxies of biosecurity or releasing pent-up libido in anger directed against those who fail to obey. The disdain for and violence against women Eco equated with the machismo of historical fascism and which has been authorised and encouraged today by the ideology of trans-sexualism is the manifestation of such anger, and an example of how easy it is for those in control of this ideology to direct the aggression of its acolytes.

13. Ur-Fascism is based upon a *selective populism*, a qualitative populism, one might say. In a democracy, the citizens have individual rights, but the citizens in their entirety have a political impact only from a quantitative point of view — one follows the decisions of the majority. For Ur-Fascism, however, individuals as individuals have no rights, and the People is conceived as a quality, a monolithic entity expressing the Common Will. Since no large quantity of human beings can have a common will, the Leader pretends to be their interpreter. Having lost their power of delegation, citizens do not act; they are only called on to play the role of the People. Thus, the People is only a theatrical fiction. There is in our future an Internet populism in which the emotional response of a selected group of citizens can be presented and accepted as the Voice of the People.

For the first two years of its construction, the UK biosecurity state removed many of our human rights and freedoms, including the right to liberty (Article 5 of the European Convention on Human Rights), the right to private and family life (Article 8), freedom of thought and conscience (Article 9), freedom of expression (Article 10), freedom of assembly and association (Article 11), prohibition of discrimination (Article 14), and the right to education (Protocol 2). This was itself facilitated by the prior removal of Parliament from the legislative process under a politically declared emergency period that allowed Ministers to make laws by decree, with 537 coronavirus-justified Statutory Instruments made into law prior to parliamentary approval as of 3 March, 2022.[16] As a consequence, the

16. See Alex Nice, Raphael Hogarth, Joe Marshall, Catherine Haddon and Alice Lilly, 'Government emergency powers and coronavirus', *Institute for Government* (22 March, 2021); and Hansard Society, 'Coronavirus Statutory Instruments Dashboard, 2020-2022' (9 April, 2020-17 June 2022).

Government had to fabricate the appearance of the continuation of democracy in the UK. To this end, every new regulation removing our rights, freedoms and the accountability of the Government to UK citizens was accompanied by a propaganda campaign extolling the common good as justification for this removal. The most egregious of these was that, for the benefit of 'public health', citizens of the biosecurity state must give up their right to say what goes into their own bodies, even though it has been demonstrated beyond the doubt of any but the COVID-faithful that none of the COVID-19 'vaccines' do anything to stop or inhibit either infection with or transmission of the SARS-Cov-2 virus, and present considerable risks to the health and even lives of those injected with this experimental biotechnology.[17]

In the absence of any democratic oversight of this dictatorial legislative process, the Government fell back on the facade of technocratic organisations like the Scientific Advisory Group for Emergencies, which usurped Parliament as the ultimate decider of our human rights and civil liberties, and such online tools as YouGov polls. Throughout the two years of the 'pandemic', these presented responses to probes of their carefully vetoed respondents as the equivalent of referenda. These announced that such-and-such a percentage of the population was in favour of, for example, masks in schools or mandatory 'vaccinations', even though neither had been supported by scientific evidence of their effectiveness, or even of the logicality of their imposition. In this way, the erasure of our rights, freedoms and parliamentary democracy since March 2020 has been presented as a form of direct representation, in which the ultimate arbiter of political decisions has been displaced onto an unquestionable authority called 'The Science'. The

---

17. My description of the 'vaccination' programme as 'experimental' throughout this book is based on the following conditions of its implementation. 1) The clinical trials for the AstraZeneca/Oxford viral-vector 'vaccine' won't be completed until February 2023, until February 2024 for the mRNA Pfizer/BioNTech 'vaccine', and until December 2022 for the mRNA Moderna/NIH 'vaccine'. 2) The 'vaccines' have only been granted temporary authorisation by the MHRA under The Human Medicines (Coronavirus and Influenza) (Amendment) Regulations 2020, in which the newly-introduced Regulation 174a modified The Human Medicines Regulations 2012 to allow temporary authorisation of the supply of unlicensed medicines, including COVID-19 vaccines, in response to certain threats to public health. 3) Although tested on individual humans for several infectious diseases including rabies and influenza, the messenger RNA biotechnology employed in the Pfizer/BioNTech and Moderna/NIH 'vaccines' has never before been authorised for emergency use on humans as part of a mass 'vaccination' programme.

fact that the majority of the population has fallen for such an obvious deception is proof, at the least, of the political naivety of the British public, perhaps of its wish to wash its hands of responsibility for its own future, and undoubtedly of its readiness to play the fictitious role of the 'British People' in the biopolitical theatre.

14. Ur-Fascism speaks Newspeak. Newspeak was invented by Orwell, in *Nineteen Eighty-Four*, as the official language of Ingsoc, English Socialism. But elements of Ur-Fascism are common to different forms of dictatorship. All the Nazi or fascist schoolbooks made use of an impoverished vocabulary and an elementary syntax, in order to limit the instruments for complex and critical reasoning. But we must be ready to identify other kinds of Newspeak, even if they take the apparently innocent form of a popular talk show.

From the very beginning of this manufactured 'crisis', those not ready to believe its deceptions have cited George Orwell's novel, as I have, as a model for what has happened — although Aldous Huxley's *Brave New World* would perhaps have been a better reference point. But whatever its own inspiration, in the Government propaganda that appears on every surface — from the lecterns behind which Ministers and their appointed technocrats announced the latest restrictions before bothering to inform Parliament, to the bus-stop shelters, TV screens and mobile phones through which the public continues to be indoctrinated into compliance — Newspeak slogans like 'Stay Home / Protect the NHS / Save Lives', the equally asinine 'Stay Alert / Control the Virus / Save Lives', or simply 'Hands / Face / Space', serve precisely the function Eco describes here. This is to impoverish the terms in which permissible debates are held, and thereby to shut down forums for critical thinking. We continue to see this demonstrated when any scientist, doctor or political commentator tries to introduce such thinking on News programmes, chat shows, at demonstrations, or on social media platforms, which continue to censor anyone who challenges the official narrative about the viral 'pandemic' and the biosecurity 'measures' imposed to 'combat' it. My own Twitter account was permanently suspended in March 2022 for reporting the findings from the UK Health Security Agency's latest 'COVID-19 vaccine surveillance report' and summarising the data from the Pfizer trials that was only being released under a US District Court order in response to a Freedom of

Information Request.[18] Indeed, when the Online Safety Bill becomes UK law, this censorship of data, debate and criticism will only increase.

For a hundred years we have wondered how the populations of Italy and Germany could have believed the obvious lies employed by Mussolini and Hitler to turn their nations against themselves in the name of the common good they called fascism and National Socialism; over the two-and-a-half years since March 2020 we've had a demonstration and reminder of exactly how. The politically declared common good has changed its name to 'biosecurity', but the means for imposing it, and the justifications for doing so, are remarkably similar and unchanged from a century ago. Eco concludes his article with this warning:

> Ur-Fascism is still around us, sometimes in plainclothes. It would be so much easier for us if there appeared on the world scene somebody saying: 'I want to reopen Auschwitz, I want the Black Shirts to parade again in the Italian squares'. Life is not that simple. Ur-Fascism can come back under the most innocent of disguises. Our duty is to uncover it and to point our finger at any of its new instances — every day, in every part of the world.

---

18. See UK Health Security Agency, 'COVID-19 vaccine surveillance report: Week 10' (10 March 2022); and Pfizer, 'Cumulative analysis of post-authorization adverse event reports of PF-07302048 (BNT162B2) received through 28-Feb-2021. The former document reported that, in the 4 weeks to 6 March, 2022, 286 deaths attributed to COVID-19 in the UK were not 'vaccinated', compared to 2,082 who had been triple-injected with a COVID-19 'vaccine', and that 90 per cent of the deceased, 2,642 people, had had at least one injection. The latter document reported that, in the 3 months between 1 December, 2020, when the Pfizer 'vaccine' was approved for emergency use, and 28 February, 2021, there had been 42,086 reports of 158,893 adverse events, of which 1,223 were fatal, from an unknown (redacted) number of doses. These disorders included 51,335 general disorders, 25,957 disorders of the nervous system, 17,283 musculoskeletal, 14,096 gastrointestinal, 8,476 skin and tissue, 8,848 respiratory, spine and chest, 4,610 infections and infestations, 5,590 injury, poisoning and complications, and 1,403 cardiovascular. Contradicting the widespread dismissal of adverse events as 'sore arms', these disorders were categorised as follows: cardiovascular: 1,441 cases, of which 946 were serious and 136 fatal; facial paralysis: 453 cases, 280 permanent; autoimmune: 1,050 cases, 780 serious, 57 of pericarditis or myocarditis, 12 fatal; neurological: 542, 515 serious; blood clotting: 168, 161 serious, 18 fatal; stroke: 300, all serious. Of the pregnancy disorders, there were 413 cases, of which 84 were serious. Outcomes for 270 pregnancies were that 23 resulted in spontaneous abortion, 2 in premature birth with neonatal death, 2 in spontaneous abortion with intrauterine death, and 5 outcomes were pending. Of 124 mothers participating in the trial, 75 reported serious adverse events.

As Eco wrote, it only takes the presence of one of these features for fascism to form around it, and all fourteen are present in the Global Biosecurity State. Like historical fascism, they are not all present, or all equally present when they are, in all instances of the biosecurity state. What is official policy or unofficial practice in, for example, Canada, Australia and New Zealand may not be at the same time in France or Germany, or has not yet been imposed in England; but all these features of fascism — which go beyond legislation and policy into newly-formed meanings and values, new norms of social practice and behaviour, new relationships and kinds of relationships — are present across the Global Biosecurity State. This alone, we might think, justifies using this term to describe this revolution in the former neoliberal democracies of the West. Unless Eco could see twenty-seven years into the future to describe our present with such uncanny accuracy, he was accurately describing the latent presence of fascism in the West that has re-emerged today with all its historical features intact.

2. The Political Economy of Fascism

As a semiotician and cultural critic, however, rather than an historical materialist or political economist, Eco's analysis was limited to the ideological and psychological manifestations of fascism, and therefore ignored its material driving force, which is the convergence of state power with corporate interests. Pitched at a readership of wealthy, middle-class, liberal New Yorkers ideologically committed to US exceptionalism and global capitalism as the best of all possible worlds, Eco's analysis steered well clear of proposing a causal link between these manifestations of fascism and their economic foundations, and least of all to the history of US imperialism since the Second World War. Instead, he allowed his readers to conclude that any presence of fascism in the cultures and ideologies of other countries in the 1990s can only ever be an anachronistic residue of the 1930s, and which the ideologies of multiculturalism and political correctness — both of which were in their heyday in the 1990s — would eradicate, no doubt with the help of the US military.

Auschwitz, however, to use Eco's deliberately extreme example, wasn't only a death camp but was also an industrial factory of slave labour. This labour was used by Krupp, the largest company in Europe at the beginning of the Twentieth

Century and the premier weapons manufacturer for Germany in World War Two; as well as Siemens-Schuckert, at the time Germany's largest industrial conglomerate, whose output included armaments for the German military, and is today Europe's biggest industrial manufacturing company; and IG Farben, the German chemical and pharmaceutical company that produced the Zyklon B gas used to exterminate prisoners. The camp itself, moreover, was administered with the help of IBM, the US information technology company that produced the census responsible for the racial profiling of populations subjugated by the Third Reich; and Bayer, the German chemical company that tested its products on individuals, races and ethnicities categorised by National Socialist medicine as 'life unworthy of living *(Lebensunwertes Leben)*'. As is widely known but still unrecognised, all these now international corporations are still in business today, having thrived from their 12-year collaboration with the National Socialist Government and the forced labour of hundreds of thousands of prisoners they drew from the concentration camps. At a lesser degree of enforcement, the German Labour Front, created in May 1933, and then the Law Regulating National Labour, passed in January 1934, banned strikes and other forms of industrial action in the Third Reich. The Labour Charter of 1927 had already done much the same in creating the corporative economy of Fascist Italy. Fascism, in other words — if we use this term to include National Socialism — wasn't confined to the cultural and ideological features analysed by Eco, but also described a political economy that merged government and corporate power to create an immensely powerful financial, industrial, technological and military state.

The even more powerful Global Biosecurity State of today has its own equivalents to these industrial, pharmaceutical, technological and chemical companies. These include immensely wealthy global investors like the Bill Gates Foundation, which funds and has financial influence over vast numbers of health and medical institutions, including the World Health Organization and, in the UK, the Medicines and Heathcare products Regulatory Agency, which has allowed it to influence the biosecurity policies of nation states towards mask mandates, lockdowns and experimental 'vaccination' programmes; and international pharmaceutical companies like Pfizer, Moderna, Johnson & Johnson and GlaxoSmithKline, which, besides making billions from this manufactured 'crisis', are not only effectively conducting the largest clinical trial in history of their experimental mRNA technology, but also appear to be deciding how many injections the populations of nation states must take.[19] But like IBM's role in the Third Reich, the Global Biosecurity State also includes global information technology companies like Apple, Alphabet, Meta and Tesla, which are collecting the personal data and developing the technology by which it is used to monitor, classify and control individuals according to their biosecurity profile; as well as multinational corporations like Serco, G4S, Palantir and Uniserve, to whom the coronavirus 'crisis' has been the occasion and justification for increasing the UK Government's outsourcing not only of the manufacture of the 'crisis' through immensely lucrative Test & Trace and PPE contracts but also of the security functions of the UK biosecurity state, which includes so-called 'quarantine' centres.[20] Auschwitz, as Eco wrote, doesn't have to be reopened for the camp to return as the biopolitical paradigm of the state, as I will go on to discuss in chapter 8.

This, I believe, is where the real parallel with historical fascism lies: not in its more or less anachronistic cultural manifestations (the apotheosis of Science as a new religion, irrational mandates, anti-intellectualism, censorship of criticism and dissent, discrimination and segregation, xenophobia, fear of the working class, maintaining a permanent state of war, populist elitism, hero-worship, machismo, militarism, state violence, political populism and Newspeak — none of which have exactly been lacking in the neoliberal democracies of the West over

---

19. On this alliance between international finance, pharmaceutical companies and Government regulatory agencies, see Simon Elmer, 'Bread and Circuses: Who's Behind the Oxford Vaccine for COVID-19?' (25 November, 2020), collected in *Brave New World*, pp. 53-64; and 'Bowling for Pfizer: Who's Behind the BioNTech Vaccine for COVID-19?' (9 December, 2020), collected in *Brave New World*, pp. 65-75.

20. See the pages titled 'Crime and Punishment in the UK Biosecurity State' in 'The UK "Vaccination" Programme. Part 2. Virtue and Terror' (22 September, 2021); collected in *Virtue and Terror*, pp. 98-109. As of 29 March, 2022, the total value of the contracts awarded by the UK Government in response to the 'pandemic' was £46.7 billion: of which £22.7 billion was spent on Test and Trace; £14.7 billion on PPE; £3.4 billion on hospitals and medicines; £5.1 billion on other supplies/services; and £0.8 billion on experimental 'vaccines' (with the contracts with Pfizer, AstraZeneca and Moderna all published with a notional value of £1). The largest contractor was Innova Medical Group, the US startup company founded by a car salesman that sold over a billion rapid antigen tests manufactured in China to the UK Government, with 11 contracts worth £4.248 billion. See Henry Thompson, 'Latest Updates on UK Government COVID-19 Contracts and Spending', *Tussell* (29 March, 2022).

the previous two decades), but in its political economy, about which Eco says nothing. Nor, understandably — beyond his prescient reference to an 'Internet populism' — does he say anything about the vast reach of the new technologies, systems and legislations of surveillance, data collection and population control. Between 1995, when Eco was writing, and 2022, when I am, these have expanded and penetrated not only into what we previously considered to be our private lives but also into our bodies themselves, and even, with the messenger RNA 'vaccines', into human DNA itself. The resulting capabilities and rights of the Global Biosecurity State to control us under the pretext of monitoring our health 'status' already far surpasses anything dreamed of by fascist propagandists and scientists of the 1930s.

The greatest value of Eco's article, therefore, is not in identifying the presence of fascism in the contemporary cultures and ideas of his time, which remained within the neoliberal framework of multiculturalism and political correctness, but in making an argument for the continuity of fascism beyond its historical rise, coming to power and military defeat in World War Two. In doing so, he opened up the possibility — which today has become the necessity — of identifying the return of fascism not only in our ideologies, cultures and behaviours but also in our politics, laws and economics, and most importantly of all in the new lack of distinction and forms of convergence between them. Because — and this is the parallel I will go on to examine — it is precisely this convergence of interests between the legislative authority of the nation state and the monopolies of multinational companies that defined the political economy of historical fascism.

3. The Fascist State and Human Rights

'Totalitarianism is not only hell, but also the dream of paradise — the age-old dream of a world where everybody would live in harmony, united by a common will and faith, without secrets from one another. If totalitarianism did not exploit these archetypes, which are deep inside us all and rooted deep in all religions, it could never attract so many people, especially during the early phase of its existence. Once the dream of paradise starts to turn into reality, however, here and there people begin to crop up who stand in its way, and so the rulers of paradise must build a little gulag on the side of Eden. In the course of time, this gulag grows ever bigger and more perfect, while the adjoining paradise gets smaller and poorer.'

— Milan Kundera, interview in *The New York Times Book Review*, 1980

As Umberto Eco pointed out, Italian fascism was riddled with contradictions: revolutionary yet with a king serving as Head of State; advocating the absolute authority of the state while being financed by aristocratic landowners and privately-owned companies; extoling military conquest with the backing of the Roman Catholic Church (although there's nothing new in this). But perhaps its most coherent theoretical formulation was made in *The Doctrine of Fascism*, which was co-authored in 1927 by Giovanni Gentile, the official 'philosopher of fascism', and Benito Mussolini, the Leader of Italian fascism and since 1922 the Prime Minister of Italy. In this text, which was published in 1932 in the *Enciclopedia Italiana di Scienze, Lettere ed Arti,* they laid out the totalitarian reach of fascism:

> For the fascist, everything is in the state, and nothing human or spiritual can exist, much less have value, outside the state. Thus understood, fascism is totalitarian, and the fascist state — as the synthesis and unity of all values — interprets, develops, and strengthens the whole life of the people.

> The fascist state lays claim to rule even in the economic field, and by means of the corporative, social, and educational institutions it has created, makes itself

felt in every aspect of national life; and all the political, economic and spiritual forces of the nation, framed in their respective organisations, circulate within the state.[1]

There is a difference between what Mussolini meant by a fascist 'corporation' (from the Latin *corpus*: 'human body'), which brought together federations of workers and employers' syndicates under government-appointed officials in order to ban strikes and lockouts and control production within a given area or profession (agriculture, industry, commerce, transport, banking and insurance, professional men and artists), and the commercial corporations that went on to dominate and control the politics, economics and legislation of the Western World. But it is hard not to hear in this definition of fascism a description of the totalitarian reach of the Global Biosecurity State today, which has unified the populations of former neoliberal democracies into obedience to its dictates to a greater degree of success than any government or crisis has since the Second World War.

In the initial stages of its writing, I had considerable trouble pinning down what this book was attempting to argue, partly because the government authoritarianism, state violence and legal suppression of the rights and freedoms of the populations of Western nations during the politically-declared 'pandemic' was so self-evidently fascistic that to argue the point seemed almost redundant. And as I've argued, such treatment hasn't been limited to the actions of the public sector, but has been inflicted by precisely those international corporations to which so many of the functions and duties of the state have been outsourced under forty years of neoliberalism, and which greatly expanded their reach during two years of lockdown.[2] As a result, private companies are now given the responsibility and authority to make judgements about the definition and qualification of our human rights: whether that's pharmaceutical companies deciding whether injection with their products should be mandatory, information technology companies deciding when and where our movements and

---

1. Benito Mussolini and Giovanni Gentile, *The Doctrine of Fascism*, 1932; The World Future Fund, pp. 3 and 8.

2. On the outsourcing of the UK biosecurity state to privately-owned and run companies and its consequences for democratic scrutiny and accountability, see Simon Elmer, 'Lockdown: Collateral Damage in the War on COVID-19' (2 June, 2020), collected in *COVID-19*, pp. 123-158.

associations should be tracked and recorded, or social media platforms deciding the limits of our freedom of conscience and expression.

As an example of the latter, in another re-enactment of Orwell's 'Two Minutes Hate' following the invasion of the Ukraine, Meta released a statement that the ban on 'hate speech' on Facebook and Instagram would be lifted in certain European countries if it is directed against Russian soldiers and politicians and made in the context of the war; and would permit praise for the neo-Nazi Azoz regiment in the Ukrainian armed forces it had previously banned.[3] This wasn't surprising, given that the Global Biosecurity State has been built on the fabricated, manipulated and directed hate of its national populations and international consumers: first against those refusing to wear masks or remain in their homes; then against protesters against the imposition of lockdown and 'vaccine' passports; more recently against the nurses and doctors who refused to be injected with the experimental 'vaccines'; and now against anyone failing to declare their solidarity with the US-installed puppet government of the Ukraine.

However, given the widespread perception that the restrictions on our rights and freedoms justified by the coronavirus 'crisis' are now over and in the past, and the collective amnesia that appears to be the defining characteristic of the political psychology of our time, I think it would be useful to revisit recent history. Obviously, the state violence and illegality with which the regulations and programmes of global biosecurity have been enforced over the past two-and-a-half years is beyond the scope of this book, so I'm going to focus on 'vaccine' mandates in selected countries in the Western World where they have been enforced in the 7 months before coronavirus-justified regulations were largely suspended in March 2022.

1. The Biosecurity State in Practice

From 13 September 2021, in Lithuania, under the Government of Ingrida Šimonytė, injection with a COVID-19 'vaccine' was made compulsory for all citizens. Those without a 'vaccine' passport proving their compliance or a medical

---

3. See Munsif Vengattil and Elizabeth Culliford, 'Facebook allows war posts urging violence against Russian invaders', *Reuters* (11 March, 2022); and Urooba Jamal, 'Facebook is reversing its ban on posts praising Ukraine's far-right Azov Battalion, report says', *Insider* (25 February, 2022).

exemption were banned from all 'non-essential' shops, shopping centres, cafes, bars, restaurants, indoor public venues, outdoor events of over 500 people, government buildings, gyms, bookshops, libraries, trains, banks, universities, inpatient medical care, care homes, and also from any employment involving contact with other humans. Private businesses were permitted to require injection as a condition of employment, and to suspend the non-compliant without pay, thereby circumventing legal challenges for unfair dismissal. Government inspectors conducted spot checks to ensure businesses were enforcing compliance, with the compliant public encouraged to report any business that did not, with fines for non-compliance for both businesses and customers. Armed police were stationed at larger venues to bar entry and issue fines. A spokesman for the Government issued the following statement: 'I urge you to avoid associating with the unvaccinated, because associating with the deliberately unvaccinated is the same as getting into a car with a drunk driver.'[4]

In September 2021, in Melbourne, Australia, under the Government of Scott Morrison, in response to demonstrations against 18 months of periodic lockdowns and 'vaccine' mandates for construction workers, armed riot police and anti-terrorist paramilitaries in gas masks attacked protesters with rubber bullets, pepper balls, pepper spray, stinger grenades, tear gas and armoured cars mounted with unidentified weapons. Protesters who braved this armoury were additionally threatened with $5,000 fines.[5]

In October 2021, in Italy, under the Government of Mario Draghi, students, lecturers and staff occupied the University of Turin in protest against the imposition of 'vaccine' passports (the so-called 'Green Pass') as a condition of access to both education and employment. In Trieste and Genoa, in response to unionised dock workers striking against the Green Pass as a condition of work, riot police illegally entered the ports, where they fired tear-gas canisters and water cannons against strikers and their supporters, among whom were many women and children. A port official in Trieste wearing a sash in the national colours was recorded giving the fascist salute before directing police armed with a water

---

4. Quoted in Anon, 'How recent vaccine mandate laws in Lithuania and throughout Europe have upended my family's life', *The Rio Times* (1 October, 2021).

5. See Samuel Osborne, 'COVID-19: Australian riot police fire rubber bullets at anti-lockdown protesters in Melbourne', *Sky News* (22 September, 2021).

cannon to the assault. The following month, the Prime Minister banned protest in Italy.[6]

In October 2021, in Canada, under the Government of Justin Trudeau, injection with a COVID-19 'vaccine' was made mandatory for federal public servants and workers in federally-regulated industries. Proof of full 'vaccination' for healthcare workers and public servants including teachers was enforced in most provinces and territories between October and November, with 'vaccination' mandatory for anyone over 11 years of age in Ontario in order to enter 'non-essential' businesses, and to many other public venues in the rest of Canada. In November, the mandate was extended to essential workers, including Canadian truck drivers, crossing the borders with the USA.[7]

From 15 November 2021, in New Zealand, under the Government of Jacinda Ardern, injection with the first dose of a COVID-19 'vaccine' was made mandatory for all workers in healthcare, education and prison staff, with a second injection required by 1 January 2022, and a so-called 'booster' injection by 24 February. Later cut-off dates were imposed for fire and emergency and military personnel. Private businesses were permitted to enforce injection with 1 of 8 Government-authorised COVID-19 'vaccines' as a condition of employment.[8] Ardern admitted that this would impose a 'two-tier society', with those refusing to be injected facing what she called 'tougher' restrictions on their rights and freedoms.[9]

In December 2021, in Germany, under the Government of Olaf Scholz, school children were forced every day to go to the front of their class and declare their 'vaccination' status. Those who were vaccinated were applauded, while those who were not had to explain why they were not.[10] Outside, police officers were filmed roaming through city crowds, using 2-metre rulers to enforce social distancing among shoppers; while cafés in Berlin that were handing out free

---

6. See 'Covid green pass: How are people in Italy reacting to the new law for workplaces?', *The Local* (15 October, 2021).

7. See Government of Canada, 'Mandatory COVID-19 vaccination requirements for federally regulated transportation employees and travellers' (6 October, 2021).

8. See Ministry of Health NZ, 'COVID-19: Mandatory Vaccinations' (last updated 1 August 2022).

9. See Liam O'Dell, 'Jacinda Ardern admits New Zealand will become a two-tier society between vaccinated and unvaccinated', *The Independent* (24 October, 2021).

10. See Andrea Knipp-Selke and Heike Riedmann, 'Die Spaltung der Gesellschaft ist längst in den Schulen angekommen', *Die Welt* (1 December, 2021).

coffees to both the 'vaccinated' and the 'unvaccinated' were attacked in a campaign of violence orchestrated by the media.[11]

From 7 December 2021, in Melbourne, Australia, the Premier of the State of Victoria, Daniel Andrews, has absolute and non-reviewable power to keep the population under lockdown indefinitely. At 262 days in total, the residents of Melbourne had endured the longest cumulative lockdown of any city in the world; but under the Public Health and Wellbeing Amendment (Pandemic Management) Act 2021, lockdown can now be enforced even if there are no medical 'cases' of COVID-19 (i.e. positive RT-PCR tests), and can be maintained for an indefinite period. Those breaching a 'pandemic order' can be fined up to $45,250 or face two years imprisonment, with businesses fined up to $109,000. Protests have not been banned outright, but can be stopped by the Health Minister if he believes it is 'reasonably necessary' to protect public health.[12]

From 16 January 2022, in Greece, under the Government of Kyriakos Mitsotakis, injection with a COVID-19 'vaccine' was made compulsory for anyone over 60 years of age, with a fine of €100 per month of non-compliance added to citizens' tax bills. Mitsotakis, the former CEO of a private equity firm and venture capital subsidiary of the National Bank of Greece, said the fines were not a punishment but a 'price to pay for health' and an 'act of justice for the vaccinated'.[13]

On 23 January 2021, in Belgium, under the Government of Alexander de Croo, armed and armoured riot police used tear gas and water cannons in the middle of winter against citizens defending their rights of assembly and protest against 'vaccine' mandates under EU law.[14]

From 5 February 2022, in Austria, under the Government of Karl Nehammer, injection with a COVID-19 'vaccine' was made compulsory for anyone over the age of 18, with those refusing confined to their homes. The Chancellor announced

---

11. See Laurenz Gehrke, 'Germany to tighten coronavirus restrictions', *Politico* (1 December, 2021).

12. See Rule of Law Education Centre, 'Victorian Pandemic Management Bill' (2 November, 2021).

13. See Silvia Amaro, 'Greece imposes monthly fines of 100 euros on the over-60s who refuse a Covid vaccine', *CNBC* (1 December, 2021).

14. See Johnny Cotton, 'Belgian police fire water cannon, tear gas during COVID curbs protest', *Reuters* (23 January, 2021).

that anyone leaving their home and unable to produce a vaccine passport when stopped by the police would be fined from €600 rising to €3,600 per year, with imprisonment for up to one year for non-payment.[15]

On 12 February 2022, in Paris, under the Government of Emmanuel Macron, who the previous month had declared that he wanted to 'piss off' those refusing to be injected, 7,200 armed riot police and paramilitaries violently assaulted protesters against 'vaccine' mandates with truncheons, pepper spray and tear gas. At the same time, heavily armed and armoured vehicles of the Gendarmerie, a French military force, were deployed to stop 500 vehicles in the 'Freedom Convoy' from entering the capital, with participating truck-drivers threatened with a fine, driving ban and up to two years in prison.[16]

On 14 February 2022, in Canada, the Prime Minister, Justin Trudeau, invoked the Emergencies Act to grant him emergency powers and suspend Parliament. The Minister for Finance, Chrystia Freeland, declared that anyone who protested or continues to protest against 'vaccine' mandates or donates to funding them would have their bank accounts frozen.[17] Freeland, who sits on the Board of Trustees of the World Economic Forum, also announced that any company whose trucks were used in the protest would have their bank accounts frozen and their insurance suspended. On 19 February, mounted riot police and anti-terrorist paramilitaries in armoured vehicles armed with weapons firing chemical irritants and direct impact batons, stun grenades, pepper spray and tear gas, violently assaulted protesters against 'vaccine' mandates, including the 'Freedom Convoy' of truckers in the capital, Ottawa.[18]

From 14 February 2022, in the USA, under the Government of Joe Biden, who had repeatedly claimed that this is a 'pandemic of the unvaccinated', injection with a COVID-19 'vaccine' was made mandatory for healthcare workers, with a first dose by 14 February and a second by 21 March. Hospitals, nursing

---

15. See Philip Oltermann, 'Austria plans compulsory Covid vaccination for all', *The Guardian* (19 November, 2021).

16. See Katie Weston, Chris Matthews and Peter Allen, 'French Freedom Convoy crackdown: Riot police teargas terrified diners at pavement cafes in Paris', *Daily Mail* (12 February, 2022).

17. See 'Full text of Chrystia Freeland's remarks during Emergencies Act announcement', *Toronto Star* (14 February, 2022).

18. See Greg Woodfield, John R. Kennedy and Keith Griffith, 'Ottawa police arrest 100 protesters and remove 21 trucks using emergency act powers', *Daily Mail* (19 February, 2022).

homes and surgeries failing to comply were threatened with losing Government funding for its patient health insurance programmes. In the States of Washington, New Jersey, Connecticut, Illinois, Oregon and California, and in New York City, this mandate has been extended to all state government and educational workers. The previous month, the Supreme Court blocked the Biden Administration's mandate, issued under emergency powers in September 2021, that private companies with more than 100 employees can require weekly COVID-19 tests for employees who have not been fully 'vaccinated'. This mandate would have applied to 84 million US citizens. Despite this ruling, many businesses continue to make injection a condition of work for employees, of entry to their venues for consumers, and of access to their services for customers, including students.[19]

From 15 February 2022, in Italy, injection with 3 doses of a COVID-19 'vaccine' was made mandatory for everyone 50 years of age and over, with a fine of €1,500 for non-compliance. As a result of this mandate, half a million Italians over 50 have been suspended from work and left without a salary.[20] The Prime Minister, Mario Draghi, the former President of the European Central Bank and member of the G30 who was appointed by the Italian President, announced: 'The unvaccinated are not part of our society.'

On 2 March 2022, in New Zealand, under the Government of Jacinda Ardern, riot police armed with tear gas, pepper spray and truncheons attacked protesters in the 'Freedom Camp' against 'vaccine' mandates that had been camped outside Parliament House in Wellington for three weeks, resulting in the camp being set on fire.[21]

From 15 March 2022, in the UK, under the Government of Boris Johnson, injection with a course of COVID-19 'vaccines' was made mandatory for workers in care homes. This was to be extended to healthcare and social care settings from 1 April, but all mandates were subsequently revoked on 15 March, 2022.

From 16 March 2022, in Germany, under the Government of Olaf Scholz, employees of medical establishments have to provide proof of a full course of injection with COVID-19 'vaccines'. In May, in response to legal challenges from

---

19. See Jacqueline LaPointe, 'CMS Updates Healthcare Worker Vaccine Mandate Guidance', *RevCycle Intelligence* (18 January, 2022).

20. See 'What changes about life in Italy in February 2022?', *The Local* (1 February, 2022).

21. See Brett Lackey, 'New Zealand Parliament grounds set on fire as Kiwis lose it', *Daily Mail* (3 March, 2022).

members of the medical profession, this ruling was approved by the Federal Constitutional Court. In April, a Draft Bill to make 'vaccines' compulsory for those over 60 years of age was voted down in Parliament.[22]

As I said, is it really necessary to argue for the fascism of the nation states that imposed and continue to inflict such violence and violation of the human rights of their populations? But then again, isn't this all in the past — an unfortunate and perhaps overzealous response to an unprecedented situation which is now all but over, and we can now return to something like normal, even if it is the 'New Normal', 'built back better' and more prepared for future pandemics? It is in part to challenge this view, which has dissipated much of the former opposition to the Global Biosecurity State, that I am writing this book. Let's have a closer look, then, at what happened, is happening now, and is set to happen in the immediate future to the former neoliberal societies of the West from the perspective of human rights and their subordination to the 'common good' declared by our governments.

2. Erasing Human Rights

According to a briefing on 'Legal issues surrounding compulsory Covid-19 vaccination' published by the European Parliament, as of 14 March 2022, 'vaccine' mandates in Austria have been suspended, but will be re-evaluated for re-imposition in anticipation of the next wave of infections this autumn.[23] A full course of 'vaccination' — although what constitutes this arbitrary designation changes according to the declarations of the pharmaceutical companies producing the 'vaccines' — is still obligatory for specific age groups in Italy and Greece; and for specific categories of workers (in healthcare and public services, including schools) in Germany, France, Italy, Greece, Hungary and Latvia; and employers are allowed to impose them on workers as a condition of employment in Hungary and Estonia; while access to certain public spaces (including public transport, post offices, banks, work canteens, restaurants, hotels, catering

---

22. See Kate Connolly, 'German government drops plan for Covid vaccine mandate', *The Guardian* (8 April, 2022).

23. See Maria Diaz Crego, Costica Dumbrava, David de Groot, Silvia Kotanidis, and Maria-Margarita Mentzelopoulou, 'Legal issues surrounding compulsory Covid-19 vaccination', *European Parliamentary Research Service* (14 March, 2022).

establishments, sports facilities, receptions, congresses, spas, amusement parks, gaming centres, discos and cultural centres) was only permitted for those designated as 'vaccinated' in Germany, France, Italy and Latvia; and, except for Lithuania, Slovenia and Sweden, all member states in the European Union still required travellers from other member states to present a 'vaccine' passport, although by August 2022 all EU countries except Spain, the Netherlands, Slovakia and Latvia had removed this requirement.

In many of these countries — including Germany, France, Italy, Greece and Hungary — legal challenges to the 'vaccine' mandates have been made by workers on the grounds that their human rights under the European Convention on Human Rights (and specifically Article 8, recognising the right to private and family life and protecting, therefore, the physical integrity of a person) are being interfered with; and in each case the constitutional court dismissed their claims on two bases. First, that since the mandates are a condition of their continued employment in a particular industry and therefore not compulsory — 'mandatory' meaning, in legal terms, the agreement between employee and employer to meet a requirement of their employment — workers are free to leave that industry and seek employment elsewhere. And second, that the injection with a COVID-19 'vaccine' of a given demographic (whether defined by age or the entire national population) is in the interest of public health, and therefore comes under European Convention on Human Rights conditions for interfering with qualified rights (Articles 8, 9, 10 and 11) in order to protect public safety. Several things can be said about these court rulings.

First, that ruling that a worker who may have trained and worked for years in a given industry, the prime example being in healthcare, is free to find new employment is a clear violation of the first requirement of medical treatment under UK, EU and international law, which is that it must be voluntary and not influenced by pressure from the medical profession or anyone else.[24] For example, under Article 6 of the Universal Declaration on Bioethics and Human Rights, which was adopted by the United Nations Educational, Scientific and Cultural Organization (UNESCO) in 2005:

---

24. For a discussion of the laws, codes, rights and best practices which mandatory 'vaccination' violates, see Simon Elmer' 'The UK "Vaccination" Programme. Part 2: Virtue and Terror' (22 September, 2021), collected in *Virtue and Terror*, pp. 71-109.

Any preventive (*sic*), diagnostic and therapeutic medical intervention is only to be carried out with the prior, free and informed consent of the person concerned. The consent should, where appropriate, be express and may be withdrawn by the person concerned at any time and for any reason without disadvantage or prejudice.[25]

This rules out masks, PCR tests and vaccines being mandated, or those refusing to comply being fined, arrested or having their freedoms removed. More specifically to the COVID-19 'vaccines', under the Council of Europe's Resolution 2361, which was adopted by Parliamentary Assembly on 21 January, 2021, member states of the EU must:

7.3.1. ensure that citizens are informed that the vaccination is not mandatory and that no one is under political, social or other pressure to be vaccinated if they do not wish to do so;

7.3.2. ensure that no one is discriminated against for not having been vaccinated, due to possible health risks or not wanting to be vaccinated.[26]

This resolution has been completely ignored by the constitutional courts of these European nation states. Threatening a worker with being banned from practicing their profession or trade is clearly a failure to uphold this Resolution, as well as a failure of the courts of the relevant countries to uphold the rights of the individual under EU law. Indeed, this failure has characterised all legal rulings in the Global Biosecurity State, and the UK is no exception to this rule.

Second, human rights were written into the Universal Declaration of Human Rights (1948) and the European Convention on Human Rights (1950) after the Second World War not only to give capitalism a veneer of morality in its Cold War with the more obvious morality of socialism, but precisely in order to protect the individual from the state — and specifically the return of the fascist state. They should not be abandoned, therefore, when the state — fascist or not — rules that they must be limited by what the government decides is the common good,

---

25. See UNESCO, 'Universal Declaration on Bioethics and Human Rights' (19 October, 2005).

26. See European Council, 'Covid-19 vaccines: ethical, legal and practical considerations', Council of Europe Resolution 2361 (27 January, 2021).

whether that's public health or state security. It is against the arbitrariness of those decisions, on which the fascist state was historically constructed, that human rights and their legal arbitration are meant to protect the individual. And although the rights of the individual must necessarily be balanced against those of the collective, that balance has been written, first, into the original formulation of those rights in the text of the European Convention on Human Rights, and, second, into guidance on that balance in case law made by the European Court of Human Rights in the course of enacting its functions.

That these rights and freedoms should now be cast aside at the bidding of governments of member states on the unexamined and widely contested ground that 'vaccines' of unproven efficacy, proven dangers, documented injuries including deaths, rushed clinical trials, dubious content, experimental biotechnology, censored trial data and unknown long-term consequences — and which have been mandated in order to protect us from a virus which is almost exclusively a threat to the elderly and those already suffering life-threatening illnesses — are more important to the public good than our human rights, demonstrates just how weak both national and international courts are in protecting us from the Global Biosecurity State. Indeed, far from offering a means of holding the national governments implementing the Global Biosecurity State to account, the courts have become the means for enforcing its erasure of our rights and freedoms.

Under Article 11 of the European Social Charter, contracting parties are obliged 'to take appropriate measures designed *inter alia:* (3) to prevent as far as possible epidemic, endemic and other diseases'.[27] This has been interpreted by the European Committee on Social Rights as requiring member states 'to ensure high immunisation levels'. Yet the question of whether high immunisation rates can be attained through mandatory vaccination has never been addressed by the European Committee on Social Rights; nor, more importantly, has the question of whether mandatory masking, social distancing, contact tracing, lockdown restrictions, 'vaccine' passports and all the other politically enforced 'measures' did or do anything to prevent the spread of a respiratory virus in circulation since the end of 2019.

---

27. See Council of Europe, 'European Social Charter', collected texts (7th edition) (updated: 1 January, 2015), p. 14.

And third, this subordination of the individual and his freedoms to a 'common good' declared by the government of the nation state is one of the political foundations of historical fascism. In *The Doctrine of Fascism* it states:

We were the first to state, in the face of liberal individualism, that the individual exists only in so far as he is within the state and subjected to the requirements of the state, and that, as civilisation assumes aspects which grow increasingly complicated, individual freedom becomes more and more restricted.

The concept of freedom is not absolute because nothing is ever absolute in life. Freedom is not a right, it is a duty. It is not a gift, it is a conquest; it is not equality, it is a privilege. The concept of freedom changes with the passing of time. There is a freedom in times of peace which is not the freedom of times of war. There is a freedom in times of prosperity which is not a freedom to be allowed in times of poverty.[28]

The structure of every state requires the individual to subordinate his abstract freedom to the common good in accordance with the law. It is this, at least in principle, that guarantees the protection of the individual by the state. But just as important to this social contract is the protection of the individual *from* the state. Arguing — as the Secretary of State for Justice has in order to justify the UK Government's impending reform of the Human Rights Act 1998 — that our individual rights must be balanced by 'personal responsibility' and the 'wider public interest' is political sophistry.[29] It is not the role of Governments to dictate the responsibilities of its citizens. That way lies fascism. The balance between the rights of the individual and the state is precisely what human rights were written to protect. Human rights are described in the 1776 United States Declaration of Independence, the 1789 Declaration of the Rights of Man and of the Citizen and the 1948 Universal Declaration of Human Rights as 'inalienable' precisely because they are not subject to the revisions of individual governments claiming they must be subordinated to what they decide is the common good. That is why they are

---

28. Benito Mussolini and Giovanni Gentile, *The Doctrine of Fascism*, p. 11.

29. See Ministry of Justice, 'Human Rights Act Reform: A Modern Bill of Rights' (post-consultation paper for the consultation opened 14 December, 2021, closed 19 April, 2022).

called human rights and not obligations of citizenship; and the erasure of the former by the Global Biosecurity State since March 2020 — and, most worryingly of all, the obedience of its national populations to their erasure — has laid the ground for the return of fascism today.

Over the past two-and-a-half years, in which our governments have repeatedly told us that 'we are at war' — for example, by the French President, Emmanuel Macron, in March 2020, when announcing the national lockdown of France — previously thinking citizens of neoliberal states have willingly, and even happily, subordinated their individual rights and freedoms to the 'requirements' of the Global Biosecurity State, and handed over the responsibility and judgement to decide what those requirements are to national governments, multinational corporations and international technocracies.[30] In an astonishingly short period of time, vast numbers of people who previously held a healthy suspicion of governments, pharmaceutical companies, information technology companies and the corporate media have made the decision to believe everything and anything they say with a conviction that can only be described as 'blind faith'.

This is not, however, a form of hypnosis or psychosis that some have claimed, but rather the effect and product of the return of fascism in our governance, our corporations, our media and our society, and of the impact and success of two years of unrelenting propaganda that continues to this day.[31] Certainly, the susceptibility of the public to this propaganda has assumed hypnotic dimensions, with otherwise rational adults leaving their parents to die alone and without medical treatment in care facilities when ordered to do so, injecting their children with experimental biotechnology for a disease to which they are statistically immune, and doing the same to themselves for the sake of a summer holiday abroad. However, attempts to explain the mass support for the Global Biosecurity State in terms of individual or mass psychology risks depoliticising the Global Biosecurity State. In accepting this explanation, the last two-and-a-half years of cowardice, compliance and collaboration is transformed into a temporary aberration in our neoliberal democracies excused and perhaps necessitated by a global threat to public health, rather than being identified for

30. See Rym Momtaz, 'Emmanuel Macron on coronavirus: "We're at War"', *Politico* (16 March, 2020).

31. See Andrew Orlowski, '"Mass formation psychosis" gets a warning from Google', *The Post* (5 January, 2022).

what it is, which is a revolution in Western capitalism necessitating the imposition of a fascist superstructure capable of policing, controlling and suppressing the anticipated social and political resistance.

In 'The Decline of the Nation State and the End of the Rights of Man', chapter 9 of *The Origins of Totalitarianism* (1951), Hannah Arendt, the German political theorist and escapee from the Third Reich, reminded us that history has repeatedly demonstrated that, without a nation, citizenship and a state to defend them, human rights are worth little or nothing.[32] Indeed, the Law on the Revocation of Naturalisations and the Deprivation of German Citizenship of July 1933 revoked the citizenship of naturalised German Jews and those the NSDAP Government deemed to be 'undesirables'. This was followed in September 1935 by the Reich Citizenship Law, under which those designated as Jews were stripped of their German citizenship and instead made 'subjects of the state'. This was defined as 'a person who enjoys the protection of the German Reich and in consequence has specific obligations towards it.' Finally, in November 1941, the Eleventh Decree on the Reich Citizenship Law stripped Jews of their remaining rights as subjects of the state, stipulating that any Jew living outside Germany was no longer a citizen. The first act of fascist states, therefore — whether that's the Third Reich stripping Jews and communists of German citizenship, the State of Israel stripping Palestinians and Bedouin of Israeli citizenship, the European Union declaring refugees from wars and political violence in Africa and the Middle East to be illegal immigrants, or the nation states of global biosecurity imposing 'vaccine' passports as a condition of citizenship and their leaders, as we have seen, describing the non-compliant as no longer part of society — is to render their victims stateless. I'll come back to this systemic failure of human rights when they are most needed in chapter 8, where I'll look at the techniques by which the biosecurity state, as the permanent spatialisation of the state of emergency, reduces its citizens to their biological existence; but for now it's enough to recognise that the Global Biosecurity State, in the first two-and-a-half years of its construction, has been built on ground erased of human rights.

Finally, the fact that 'vaccine' mandates, the laws for their enforcement and the punishments for non-compliance have recently been suspended in some

---

32. See Hannah Arendt, 'The Decline of the Nation State and the End of the Rights of Man', *The Origins of Totalitarianism*, 2nd revised edition (Penguin Modern Classics, 2017), pp. 349-396.

nation states, far from being the cause for celebration they have been even among those opposing the regulations and programmes of the biosecurity state, doesn't mean that the governments of the former neoliberal democracies of the West will not be prepared to use the full force and violence of the state to push through this revolution in global capitalism. And we shouldn't forget that the ineffective and dangerous mass 'vaccination' programme continues unabated, having been extended since April in the UK to children between the age of 5 and 11; and the data and reports on its negative effects, which are escalating in severity and incidence, continue to be suppressed, censored and denied investigation.[33] In August, the German Cabinet agreed on a package of restrictions to come into force in October, including mandatory mask-wearing on public transport, hospitals and care homes, supermarkets, shops and other public indoor spaces.[34] Finally, in the course of writing this book, the threat of lockdown has once again been suspended over our heads, the axe blade placed gently on our necks. Indeed, the ongoing lockdown of cities in China, following the Government's medically nonsensical 'zero-COVID' strategy, are even more severe and even more brutally imposed than the one that set off copycat lockdowns across the West in 2020, to the astonishment and delight of Western governments that believed their populations would never tolerate such authoritarianism. No, there is nothing to be celebrated in this pause for breath before the war to come between the populations of the world and the Global Biosecurity State being constructed around, between and within us — in the service of which, to echo *The Doctrine of Fascism*, all the political, economic and spiritual forces of the nation state will be placed.

---

33. For an attempt to correct this censorship, see Simon Elmer, 'The UK "Vaccination" Programme: Part 1. Adverse Drug Reactions and Deaths' (15 September, 2021), collected in *Virtue and Terror*, pp. 39-70. For analysis of the clinical trials whose data is being released by Pfizer under a court order, see Paul Thacker, 'Covid-19: Researcher blows the whistle on data integrity issues in Pfizer's vaccine trial', *British Medical Journal* (2 November, 2021); and HART: Health Advisory & Recovery Team, 'First finding from Pfizer trials' (16 June, 2022).

34. See 'COVID: German cabinet signs off on rules for autumn and winter', *DW* (24 August, 2022).

3. Towards an International Technocracy

The war in the Ukraine undoubtedly played a catalytic role in the unexpected pause in the two years of unrelenting dismantling of our rights, freedoms and democracies. As I suggested in my preface, this hiatus is comparable to the so-called 'phoney war' between the declaration of war in Europe in September 1939 and the start of hostilities in April 1940. Perhaps it would be hard for the West to put on its customary mask as staunch upholder of democracy and brave defender of human rights if its populations were living under lockdown restrictions, their citizenship dependent on obedience to mandates in violation of national and EU law; and our governments and corporate media have been as ready to wheel out these tired old stereotypes as we have been to accept them, as if the memory of the previous two years had been erased with a single wave of the now ubiquitous Ukrainian flag. Or perhaps not. It's far more likely, as I will discuss in the next chapter, that the West's imposition of economic sanctions on Russia has served to extend the time of reckoning for the repayment of the vast sums of electronic money that were injected into the collapsing global financial system in the months immediately before the coronavirus was declared a 'pandemic' by the World Health Organization. This has allowed our governments to pile even more debt on the future to pay for the expenditures of the present, while at the same time presenting an easy-to-understand explanation and convenient villain to blame for the spiralling inflation now branded 'the cost of living crisis'.[35]

In addition, some commentators attributed the temporary relaxation of restrictions to the approach of general elections in, most notably, France (April), Australia (May), Austria (September) and the USA (November). However, the re-election of Jacinda Ardern as the Prime Minister of New Zealand with a landslide victory in October 2020 suggests the majority of the populations that have lived through the revolution of the past two-and-a-half years still believe that it was 'for their own good', and that the present incumbents will be re-elected to continue the construction of the Global Biosecurity State. But even if they are not, the consensus from all political parties in the legislatures of these former neoliberal democracies equally suggests that little or nothing would change under new

---

35. See Fabio Vighi, 'From COVID-19 to Putin-22: Who needs friends with enemies like these?', *The Philosophical Salon* (14 March, 2022).

governments. Indeed, were the Labour Party to form a government in the UK, it is likely that we would be living under some of the strictest restrictions to our freedoms of any of these nation states.

What the past two-and-a-half years have shown — and that perhaps more incontrovertibly than any of the other periodic crises between which we live in the West — is that, behind the facade of democracy these national governments are there to represent, there is the rule of an international technocracy of which the United Nations and the European Union are the models inherited from the past, and the World Health Organization and the World Economic Forum are those of the present. Just as the institutions of the UK state — the Crown, the legislature, the judiciary, the civil service, the security services, the military, the police forces, the financial sector, the media — will retain their grip on power no matter which political party is elected to the Government of the UK, so the international organisations administering the Global Biosecurity State will continue to implement the revolution in Western capitalism to the new form of technocratic governance irrespective of the national governments that will execute its mandates on their populations. As an example of what's in store for us, two days after his re-election as the President of France on 24 April this year, Emmanuel Macron, in compliance with the decision of the European Commission in June 2021 to create a European Digital Identity framework, announced the Digital Identity Guarantee Service for the French electorate; 58 per cent of which didn't vote for him.[36]

In the UK, which has emerged as one of the nation states with the least severe biosecurity regulations, an example of how the biosecurity state will continue to be implemented outside the immediate context of the coronavirus 'crisis' — and instead be based on a model of authoritarian rule with whose compliance that crisis has demonstrated the population's almost total obedience — recently passed and imminent legislation in the UK includes the following Acts and Bills of Parliament. This is the fascist state in formation, for which the previous two years has prepared our acquiescence and collaboration, and shows why none of us should be celebrating the suspension of coronavirus-justified restrictions.

---

36. See Frank Hersey, 'France announces user-controlled mobile digital identity app for use with national ID', *Biometric* (28 April, 2022).

- The Telecommunications Infrastructure (Leasehold Property) Act 2021 amends The Communications Act 2003 to allow telecom network operators to gain access to multiple-dwelling buildings, most obviously blocks of council flats owned by local authorities, to erect communication transmitters or receivers. This accommodates the installation of the new 5G (fifth-generation) technology on which the Fourth Industrial Revolution, and especially the Internet of Things and Internet of Bodies, will rely for the quantum leap in computing capacity required for the expanded surveillance, data collection and interconnection capacities of the UK biosecurity state.

- The Financial Services Act 2021 amends The Anti-Terrorism, Crime and Security Act 2001 and The Proceeds of Crime Act 2002 with regard to the forfeiture of money, so that they apply to money held in accounts maintained with electric money and payment institutions. This allows funds to be automatically removed from a person's account in the event of, for example, non-payment of fines for non-compliance with 'vaccine' mandates or, as was enforced in Canada, support for or participation in protests against such mandates.

- The Health and Care Act 2022, as part of the NHS Long Term Plan, furthered the privatisation and outsourcing of the National Health Service, grants the Secretary of State authority over the NHS, and makes 42 integrated care systems statutory bodies with power over NHS commissioning and spending in England.

- The Police, Crime, Sentencing and Courts Act 2022 empowers the police to impose conditions on demonstrations, including where they are held, and that they do not cause 'unease', 'annoyance' or 'disruption', all of which are now a criminal offence punishable by up to 10 years in prison, effectively banning protest in the UK in contravention of the European Convention on Human Rights (Article 11, Freedom of Assembly and Association). It also permits the police to have access to our private education and health records, criminalises trespass on privately-owned land, and increases the maximum sentence for damaging a memorial from 3 months to 10 years.

- The Judicial Review and Courts Act 2022 empowers the law courts to suspend and limit challenges by UK citizens to the legality of, and redress for, the decisions and actions of the UK Government and other public bodies, making the UK biosecurity state even less accountable to public scrutiny and legal accountability than it was under the two-year emergency period declared in March 2020.

- The Nationality and Borders Act 2022 empowers the Home Secretary to revoke, without prior notification, the British citizenship of anyone who is not born in the UK, who is of dual nationality, who is judged to be a threat to national security, or whose behaviour is deemed to be 'unacceptable'. As the previous Home Secretary, Sajid Javid, did in 2019 with Shamina Begum, a British citizen who at the age of 15 went to join Islamic State, this will leave such persons stateless, and therefore effectively without human rights. Echoing Mussolini in *The Doctrine of Fascism*, the former Home Secretary, Priti Patel, this year described UK citizenship as a 'privilege' and not a human right.[37]

- The Elections Act 2022, despite the tiny incidence of voter fraud in the UK, makes proof of voter ID a requirement for voting, and will most likely be used to impose Digital Identity already introduced under the guise of the NHS Covid Pass.

- The Public Order Bill will extend the powers of police to criminalise protest through extending stop and search powers to allow police to search for and seize objects that may be used in the commission of a protest-related offence; as well as through the introduction of Serious Disruption Prevention Orders (SDPO) that prohibit an individual from being in a particular place, being with particular people, having particular articles in their possession and using the internet to facilitate or encourage persons to commit a protest-related offence. The court may also require a person subject to an SDPO to wear an electronic tag. Breach of an SDPO will be a criminal offence carrying a maximum penalty of six months' imprisonment, an unlimited fine, or both.

- The Online Safety Bill will hand authority for policing the internet to information technology companies, who will be obligated and empowered to censor and block access to online content deemed 'lawful but harmful'. This includes, for example, information about the adverse reactions, including injury and death, to experimental biotechnology administered as vaccines,

---

37. See Haroon Siddique, 'New bill quietly gives powers to remove British citizenship without notice', *The Guardian* (17 November, 2021).

which in the judgement of the state may inhibit the compliance of both adults and children with a given 'vaccination' programme, thereby, with regard to this legislation, exposing them to the effects of a virus and therefore causing harm. Under the cover of protecting us from harmful content, therefore, this legislation will formalise the blanket censorship of anything and anyone challenging or questioning the medical and rational basis to the Government's 'vaccination' programme, which has been demonstrated to have little or no medical benefit, considerable negative impact on the health and lives of millions of Britons, and with unknown consequences in the future. In anticipation of such practices, this September the multinational financial technology company, PayPal, removed its online payment services from groups they deemed to be uncompliant with the UK biosecurity state, including the Free Speech Union, an organisation that has campaigned to defend freedom of conscience and expression against coronavirus-justified censorship; *The Daily Sceptic*, a news website that has given a platform to those censored by the corporate-owned media for challenging the Government narrative about the 'pandemic'; UsForThem, a group of parents that campaigned to keep schools open during lockdown; Law or Fiction, a group of lawyers that sought to advise the public and hold the Government to account on the legality of the coronavirus-justified regulations it was making into law; and Left Lockdown Sceptics, a left-wing group that has challenged the collaboration of the UK Left with the biosecurity state.

- The Human Rights Act Reform by a Modern Bill of Rights will make existing rights subordinate to 'public protection' and 'national security', effectively erasing them as a legal recourse for UK citizens. By making the worst Parliament in British history the ultimate source of laws having an impact on the UK population, the UK will effectively sever its obligations under European and international human rights laws and agreements. These include the Nuremberg Code (1947), the Universal Declaration of Human Rights (1948), the European Convention on Human Rights (1950), the International Covenant on Civil and Political Rights (1966), the United Nations Convention on the Rights of the Child (1991), the Convention for the Protection of Human Rights and Human Dignity of the Human Being with Regard to the Application of Biology and Medicine (1997), and the Universal

Declaration on Bioethics and Human Rights (2005), all of which have signally failed to protect or even defend our human rights in response to the increasing authoritarianism of Western governments over the past two-and-a-half years. Once again, then, this legislation will formalise the actions of the UK Government, Parliament and Courts during the coronavirus 'crisis'.

This severance of the nation state from international laws and agreements and the suspension of human rights under a permanent state of emergency were defining characteristics of the governments of historical fascist states. At the same time, however, the UK Government is ready to sign up to the World Health Organization's resolution on Pandemic Prevention, Preparedness and Response, for which more than 70 member-states, including the European Union and the UK, are advocating a strong and legally binding international treaty. It appears that, when it serves to expand and increase the power of the Global Biosecurity State over the national population, the UK Government that was elected to an 80-seat majority on the back of the Brexit referendum is nonetheless more than willing to cede UK sovereignty to global and technocratic forms of governance intent on reducing us to a neo-feudal form of capitalism. In practice, however, rather than relieving nation states of their sovereignty, this treaty will allow national governments to justify and excuse the consequences of future decisions on lockdowns, masking, 'vaccine' mandates and all the other regulations, programmes and technologies of biosecurity as the technical decisions of an international health technocracy, and in doing so to depoliticise and therefore remove from contestation their governance of the Global Biosecurity State.

Based on this technocratic model of global governance, Digital Identity, Central Bank Digital Currency (CBDC), Universal Basic Income (UBI), Environmental, Social and Governance (ESG) criteria, Sustainable Development Goals (SDG), Social Credit, the Internet of Things (IoT) and Internet of Bodies (IoB), Smart Cities, Facial Recognition, and other programmes of the Great Reset are being introduced into the UK without the electorate — like that of every other nation state in the West — having a say or vote or even a debate in Parliament.[38]

---

38. For the imminent 'rollout' of these programmes that will fundamentally change our social contract with the UK biosecurity state, see, respectively, Department for Digital, Culture, Media and Sport, 'UK digital identity and attributes trust framework' (14 June, 2022); Bank of England, 'Central Bank Digital Currency: An update on the Bank of England's work — speech by Tom Mutton' (17

Instead, like the fifth generation of cellular networks introduced into the UK in 2019 with nothing more than a guide to best practice belatedly issued by the Government in 2022, these programmes will be unilaterally imposed by committees of technocrats drawn from the private sector as though they are mere upgrades in the technological capabilities of the infrastructure of the state, rather than the means to bring about a qualitative shift in the power of the state over the population.[39] The Fourth Industrial Revolution driving the Great Reset is not only a revolution in our technology but also in the forms of governance under which we live, from the elected parliamentary democracies of nation states to an unaccountable international corporate technocracy.[40] Beyond the mass of legislation about to undo three-quarters of a century of human rights and freedoms in Europe, these are the weapons of fascism in the Twenty-first Century; and what defences against them remained to us after forty years of neoliberalism have been dismantled over the past two-and-half years in the name of that 'common good' we now call the Global Biosecurity State.

June, 2021); Frank Hudson and Aaron Kulakiewiscz, 'Potential Merits of a universal basic income', *House of Commons Public Library* (13 June, 2022); Sarah Ward, 'Mandatory ESG reporting is here, and Finance needs to get ready', *KPMG* (20 May, 2022); Cabinet Office, 'Implementing the Sustainable Development Goals' (15 July, 2022); Government Digital Service, 'How to score attributes' (2 August 2021); UK Government Chief Scientific Advisor, 'The Internet of Things: Making the most of the Second Digital Revolution' (December 2014); Lydia Harriss and Philippa Kearney, 'Smart Cities', *Research Briefing, UK Parliament* (22 September, 2021); and British Security Agency, 'Automated Facial Recognition: ethical and legal use', *Home Office* (25 October, 2021).

39. See Department for Digital, Culture, Media and Sport, 'Code of practice for wireless network development in England' (7 March, 2022).

40. See Klaus Schwab, *The Fourth Industrial Revolution*, with an introduction by Marc R. Benioff (Portfolio Penguin, 2017); and *Shaping the Future of the Fourth Industrial Revolution: A Guide to Building a Better World*, with a foreword by Satya Nadella (Portfolio Penguin, 2018).

4. Fascism and the Decay of Capitalism

'From the moment the "normal" police and military resources of the capitalist dictatorship, together with their parliamentary facades, are no longer sufficient to hold society in a state of equilibrium, the turn of the fascist regime arrives. Through the agency of fascism, capitalism sets in motion the masses of the crazed petty bourgeoisie and the groups of declassed and demoralised lumpen proletariat — all the countless human beings whom finance capital itself has brought to desperation and frenzy.'

— Leon Trotsky, *What Next? Vital Questions for the German Proletariat*, 1932

Perhaps the most famous definition of fascism — it is the one to which I have returned over the past two-and-a-half years when attempting to comprehend what has been happening behind the facade of this manufactured 'crisis' — is that attributed to Vladimir Ilyich Lenin: 'Fascism is capitalism in decay'. What Lenin more accurately said, in *Imperialism, the Highest Stage of Capitalism* (1917), is that the rentier state — which is to say, a state that derives a substantial proportion of its national revenues from properties and securities, and whose economic foundation is monopoly capitalism — is capitalism in decay.[1] In 1935, in his article on 'The Question of Fascism and Capitalist Decay', Rajani Dutt, a member of the Executive Committee of the Communist Party of Great Britain, extrapolated from this observation to argue that fascism was an advanced stage of this process of decay, representing a regression in the development of the forces of production in the period of the general crisis of capitalism during the 1930s.[2] The actual source of this often-quoted statement, therefore, is not Lenin but Dutt. That said, historical fascism undoubtedly arose from the imperialist ambitions of European nations and the mass unemployment caused by the financial crisis after the Great War that was further exacerbated by the stock market crash of 1929 and the Great Depression that lasted, in most future fascist

---

1. See Vladimir Ilyich Lenin, 'Parasitism and the Decay of Capitalism', *Imperialism, the Highest Stage of Capitalism*, Selected Works, vol. 1 (Moscow: Progress Publishers, 1963), pp. 667-766.

2. See R. Palme Dutt, 'The Question of Fascism and Capitalist Decay', *The Communist International*, Vol. XII, No. 14 (July 20, 1935).

states, well into the 1930s. However, I don't intend to revisit here the accuracy of the predictions of capitalism's inevitable demise following yet another of the crises that occur today, a century later, with ever greater regularity, but from which it always emerges with its grip over the world even stronger. My interest, for the purposes of this chapter, is in the contention that, when the internal contradictions of capital accumulation reach such a stage that the existing social contract can no longer hold them together, society enters a period of revolution in which that contract is rewritten; and that fascism is the authoritarian form of that contract, which encompasses the entirety of the political, juridical and cultural superstructure. As I have argued previously, it is this crisis in capitalism, and not a manufactured crisis in public health, that has occasioned the rising authoritarianism of formerly neoliberal states over the past two-and-a-half years, and which I am arguing signals the return of fascism as the social contract of the Global Biosecurity State currently in formation.[3] This understanding of the term expands the limited definition of fascism as a never-repeatable historical moment between the two world wars not only to a threat inherent to the structure of the democratic state (the axe within the collective bundle of rods), but as endemic to capitalism — which is, of course, still with us, exerts greater hegemony over our world than ever, but is undergoing, nonetheless, one of the greatest crises in its recent history.

1. The Economics of Lockdown

Political economists, who are more aware than most of the devastating impact lockdown has had not only on the economies of the locked-down countries but also on the rest of the world — in which an estimated half a billion people have been pushed into poverty or worse poverty during the 'pandemic' — have belatedly started to question their government's professed reasons for imposing them.[4] And rather than a medically-unprecedented response to a supposedly civilisation-threatening pandemic that has turned out to have the infection fatality rate of seasonal influenza, the answers they have come up with instead relate the

---

3. See Simon Elmer, *'Cui bono?* The COVID-19 "conspiracy"' (19 February, 2021), collected in *Brave New World*, pp. 137-176.

4. See Manas Mishra, 'Health costs pushed or worsened poverty for over 500 million', *Reuters* (13 December, 2021).

decision to impose lockdowns to the financial crisis that threatened the global economy in September 2019, 6 months before the lockdown of people and businesses in the wealthiest nations in the world.[5]

I am not an economist, which is an almost unpardonable lack of knowledge in an historical materialist; and I have been helped enormously in my attempt to understand the political economy of the biosecurity state by the work of Fabio Vighi, Professor of Critical Theory and Italian at the University of Cardiff, and co-author with Heiko Feldner of *Critical Theory and the Crisis of Contemporary Capitalism* (2015). Vighi, whom I first heard speak at a meeting of Left Lockdown Sceptics in November 2021, has written a series of articles on the economic causes of the coronavirus 'crisis' that can be read on *The Philosophical Salon*, an online forum published by the *Los Angeles Review of Books*, and I have drawn on his analyses for much of what I write in this section.[6]

As Vighi laid out in August 2021 in his article 'A Self-fulfilling Prophecy: Systemic Collapse and Pandemic Simulation', in June 2019 the Bank of International Settlements (BIS), the central bank of all central banks, published its Annual Economic Report.[7] This began with the extraordinary statement that 'It was perhaps too good to be true' — the 'it' being the recovery from the 2007-2009 Global Financial Crisis (GFC). Describing current financial markets as 'jittery', the report identified four forces at play in the economic downturn: 1) the

---

5. The Infection fatality rate (IFR) for SARS-CoV-2 varies considerably by country and over time, but the biggest variant is age. According to the COVID-19 Forecasting Team funded by the Bill & Melinda Gates Foundation, from 15 April 2020 to 1 January 2021 the IFR at the age of 7 was 0.0023%, through to 0.0573% at 30 years of age, 1.0035% at 60 years of age, and 20.3292% at 90 years of age. See Reed J. D. Sorensen, et al, 'Variation in the COVID-19 infection-fatality ratio by age, time, and geography during the pre-vaccine era: a systematic analysis', *The Lancet* (24 February, 2022). Even these figures, however, are based on the exaggerated estimates of what the report calls 'total COVID-19 mortality'. An estimate not funded by vaccine investors of the IFR in 29 countries (24 high-income) among those under 70, which constitutes 95 per cent of the global population, has the median IFR at 0.0003% at age 0-19, 0.003% at 20-29, 0.011% at 30-39, 0.035% at 40-49, 0.129% at 50-59, and 0.501% at 60-69. See John P. A. Ioannidis, et al., 'Age-stratified infection fatality rate of COVID-19 in the non-elderly informed from pre-vaccination national seroprevalence studies', *medRxiv* (13 October, 2022).

6. See 'Speakers confirmed for "The left case against vaccine passports"', *Left Lockdown Sceptics* (9 November 2021).

7. See Fabio Vighi, 'A Self-fulfilling Prophecy: Systemic Collapse and Pandemic Simulation', *The Philosophical Salon* (16 August, 2021).

failure of labour to recover the bargaining power it has lost over the previous decades; 2) the role of finance on economies, including on real estate prices, credit developments and financial markets; 3) the lagging of trade behind productivity and consequent stagnation in growth in productivity in the most advanced capitalist economies; and 4) the social and political backlash against what it calls the 'open international economic order', which the BIS predicted will continue to cast a 'long if unpredictable shadow' over the world economy, and whose long-term challenges, it advises, should not be taken lightly:

> From a historical perspective, it is not unusual to see such surges of sentiment in the wake of major economic shockwaves: the Great Depression marked the end of the previous globalisation era. It is too early to tell how this surge will evolve; but it will clearly be a force to contend with in the years to come.[8]

What the BIS is describing here are not only the classic symptoms of a crisis produced by the internal contradictions of capitalist accumulation — according to which, as the wages of workers are deflated so too is the purchasing power of consumers, threating the profits of capitalists and resulting in an inflated credit bubble — but also the threat of the social revolution they cause in the body politic, and which it, as the bank of highest appeal on monetary policy, is more than aware presents a threat to the global financial system.[9] It's worth bearing this warning in mind when considering the violence of the restrictions imposed by the Global Biosecurity State nine months later, and how the coronavirus 'crisis' has been used to entrench its emergency powers on a permanent basis.

Of even greater concern to the BIS than the social and political rejection of globalisation, however, is the competitive threat to banks presented by the rise in power of information technology companies, whose market capitalisation far exceeds that of banks. By this measure, Apple, Microsoft, Alphabet (Google, etc.), Amazon and Meta (Facebook, Instagram and WhatsApp) make up five of the eight richest companies in the world in 2022.[10] Leveraging the vast customer bases they

---

8. Bank of International Settlements, *Annual Economic Report* (June 2019) p. ix.

9. See David Harvey, *Seventeen Contradictions and the End of Capitalism* (Profile Books, 2014).

10. See Archana Kabra, '20 Richest Companies in the World by Market Cap 2022', *The Teal Mango* (25 June 2022).

have secured through social media, e-commerce and search engines, and drawing on the vast amounts of data they have collected and the power of networks, so-called 'Big Tech' has made inroads into financial services that threaten the hegemony of central banks over the financial sector. Indeed, the entire last chapter of the report is devoted to formulating a regulatory compass for Big Techs in finance. This leads the BIS to make the following policy considerations:

> The analysis of the regulatory response to Big Techs' inroads in finance offers rich material to examine more closely and concretely some of the challenges involved. The objective is to ensure that one can reap the potentially large benefits that such technological innovations can bring about while managing the potential risks. This requires tackling delicate issues that range from financial stability to competition and data privacy. At the core of this triangle is the treatment of data, which the digital revolution has brought to the fore. Ensuring a level playing field that promotes competition under an adequate regulatory umbrella is key. Whatever the precise answer, it will require more than ever the close cooperation of different authorities, both nationally and internationally.[11]

Again, it's hard not to hear in this statement a carefully euphemised insistence that the emerging technologies and markets of the Fourth Industrial Revolution must be used to police, control and, when necessary, suppress the social and political unrest the BIS anticipates in response to the coming crisis. It also expresses the fear that Big Tech will use these technologies to monopolise financial markets. The following month, accordingly, in July 2019, the BIS called for 'unconventional policy' to 'insulate the real economy' from further deterioration in financial conditions, specifically advocating that, by offering direct credit to the economy, central banks could 'replace commercial banks in providing loans'.[12] In August 2019 — when the crisis predicted by the BIS was almost upon us, the global debt-to-GDP ratio had risen to an all-time high of 322 per cent, total debt had reached close to \$253 trillion, Germany, Italy and Japan were on the verge of

---

11. Bank of International Settlements, *Annual Economic Report*, p. xiv.

12. See Fiorella De Fiore and Oreste Tristani, '(Un)conventional Policy and the Effective Lower Bound', *BIS Working Papers*, No. 804 (August 2019).

a recession, and the economies of the UK and China were contracting — BlackRock, the largest investment fund in the world with $6.5 trillion in assets under management at the time (rising to $10 trillion in 2021), published a white paper titled 'Dealing with the next downturn'.[13] This instructed the Federal Reserve System, the twelve central banks of the USA, to inject liquidity directly into the financial system to prevent a dramatic downturn in the economy predicted to be even worse than that of the Global Financial Crisis of 2007-2009. BlackRock argued that, since monetary policy (central bank interest rates on loans and the amount of money in circulation) was exhausted and fiscal policy (government taxation and spending) would not be sufficient to reverse such a downturn, what was needed was an 'unprecedented response'. It therefore recommended 'going direct', which meant 'finding ways to get central bank money directly into the hands of public and private-sector spenders' while avoiding hyperinflation. Significantly, as an example of the dangers of the latter, BlackRock cited the Weimar Republic in the early 1920s, at precisely the time when fascism took root in both Germany and Italy. Later that month, central bankers from the G7 nations (the UK, France, Germany, Italy, Japan, Canada and the USA) met to discuss BlackRock's proposals.[14]

In response to the subprime mortgage crisis of 2007 and the Global Financial Crisis it triggered, in 2010 the US Congress had limited the amount to which the US Government would insure depositors to $250,000.[15] This meant that large institutional investors like pension funds, mutual funds, hedge funds and sovereign wealth funds had nowhere to park the millions of dollars they held between investments that was at once secure, provided them with some interest and allowed the quick withdrawal of funds like a traditional deposit account. It

---

13. See the Institute of International Finance, 'IIF Quarterly Global Debt Monitor 2019' (5 August, 2019); Phillip Inman, 'Is a global recession coming? Here are seven warning signs', *The Guardian* (25 August, 2019); and Elga Bartsch, Jean Boivin, Stanley Fischer and Philipp Hildebrand, 'Dealing with the next downturn: From unconventional monetary policy to unprecedented policy coordination', *BlackRock Investment Institute* (August 2019).

14. See Brendan Greeley, 'Central Bankers rethink everything at Jackson Hole', *Financial Times* (25 August, 2019).

15. See Federal Deposit Insurance Corporation, 'Basic FDIC Insurance Coverage Permanently Increased to $250,000 Per Depositor' (21 July, 2019).

was in response to this need that the private repo market evolved.[16] 'Repo', which is shorthand for repurchase agreement, is a contract whereby investment funds lend money against collateral assets, typically treasury debt or the mortgage-backed securities that had financed the US housing bubble. Under the terms of the contract, banks undertake to buy back the assets at a higher price, typically the next day or within two weeks. As secured short-term loans, repos are the main source of funding for traders, replacing the security of deposit insurance with the security of highly liquid collateral.

However, although the repo market evolved to satisfy the needs of large institutional investors, it also allowed banks to circumvent the capital requirements imposed by regulations on the banking system after the Global Financial Crisis.[17] As a result, by 2008 the repo market provided half the credit in the US, and by 2020 had a turnover of $1 trillion per day.[18] The danger was, a lack of liquidity in repo markets can have a knock-on effect on all major financial sectors. This happens when banks borrow from their depositors to make long-term loans or investments, and the depositors and borrowers want the money at the same time, forcing the banks to borrow from somewhere else. If they can't find lenders on short notice, or if the price of borrowing suddenly becomes prohibitive, the result is a liquidity crisis.

This is exactly what happened in September 2019, by which time the borrower side of the repo market had been taken over by aggressive and high-risk hedge funds, which were using them for several loans at once.[19] As a result, many large institutional lenders pulled out of the market, causing a sudden spike in repo borrowing rates from 2.43 per cent to 10.5 per cent in a matter of hours.[20] However, rather than letting the banks fail and forcing a bail-in of creditors' funds,

---

16. See Gary B. Gorton, 'Questions and Answers about the Financial Crisis', *National Bureau of Economic Research*, Working Paper 15787 (February 2010).

17. See Enrico Perotti, 'The Roots of Shadow Banking', *Centre for Economic Policy Research*, Policy Insight No. 69 (December 2013).

18. See Christopher Rugaber, 'Federal Reserve to lend additional $1 trillion a day to large banks', *PBS* (20 March, 2020).

19. See Tyler Durden, '"The Fed Was Suddenly Facing Multiple LTCMs": BIS Offers A Stunning Explanation Of What Really Happened On Repocalypse Day', *ZeroHedge* (9 December, 2019).

20. See Emily Barrett and Jesse Hamilton, 'Why the US Repo Market Blew Up and How to Fix It', *Bloomberg UK* (6 January, 2020).

the Federal Reserve System, following the advice of BlackRock, initiated an emergency monetary programme, injecting hundreds of billions of dollars every week into Wall Street in order to ward off substantial hikes in interest rates.[21] Over the next six months, the US Federal Reserve injected more than $9 trillion into the banking system, equivalent to more than 40 per cent of the Gross Domestic Product of the USA.[22] By March 2020, the Federal Reserve was making $1 trillion per day available in overnight loans, effectively providing backup funds for the entire repo market, including the hedge funds. But more was needed. On 15 March, under the media cover and hysteria provided by the coronavirus 'crisis', the Federal Reserve dropped interest rates to 0.25 per cent, eliminated the reserve requirement, relaxed the capital requirement, and offered discount loans of up 90 days to its preferred banks (JP Morgan, Goldman Sachs, Barclays, BNP Paribas, Nomura, Deutsche Bank, Bank of America, Citibank, etc.), which were renewed on a daily basis and continuously rolled over.[23] By July 2020, the cumulative value of these loans was $11.23 trillion. Allegedly made available to meet demands for credit from households and businesses under the lockdown that was imposed state by state between 19 March in California and 7 April in South Carolina, in practice no obligations were attached to make this effectively interest-free money available to the public through, for example, loans to small businesses, reducing credit-card rates for households or suspending payment plans on mortgages.[24] In response, demand for repo loans fell; but it took until September 2020, a year later, for interest rates to fall to 1.75 per cent.[25]

In the meantime, in September 2019, the month interest rates on the repo market spiked, the US President, Donald Trump, had established a National Influenza Task Force, a 5-year plan to accelerate vaccine development and

---

21. See Ellen Brown, 'Another Bank Bailout Under Cover of a Virus', *The Web of Debt Blog* (18 May, 2020).

22. See Malcolm Scott, Paul Jackson and Jin Wu, 'A $9 Trillion Binge Turns Central Banks into the Market's Biggest Whales', *Bloomberg UK* (7 July, 2021).

23. See Board of Governors of the Federal Reserve System, 'Federal Reserve Actions to Support the Flow of Credit to Households and Businesses' (15 March, 2020).

24. See Federal Reserve, 'The Primary & Secondary Lending Programs'.

25. See Wolf Richter, 'Fed Cut Back on Helicopter Money for Wall Street and the Wealthy', *Wolf Street* (23 April, 2020).

promote vaccine technologies to counteract a pandemic.[26] The following month, on 18 October 2019, 'Event 201', organised by the Bill & Melinda Gates Foundation, the Johns Hopkins Centre for Health and the World Health Organization, simulated an outbreak of a novel zoonotic coronavirus that, modelled on SARS, was more transmissible in the community setting by people with mild symptoms.[27] In December 2019, the World Health Organization held a Global Vaccine Safety Summit for vaccine safety stakeholders from around the world.[28] These included current and former members of the Global Advisory Committee on Vaccine Safety (GACVS), immunisation programme managers, national regulatory authorities, pharmacovigilance staff from all WHO member states, as well as representatives from UN agencies, academic institutions, umbrella organisations of pharmaceutical companies, technical partners, industry representatives and funding agencies. Then on 17 January, 2020, when total deaths worldwide attributed to COVID-19 officially numbered just 6, the WHO adopted the protocols for detecting and identifying SARS-CoV-2 set out in the Corman-Drosten paper, 'Diagnostic detection of 2019-nCoV by real-time RT-PCR', which among its numerous flaws recommended 45 cycles of thermal amplification of samples, far higher than the number at which infectious virus can be reliably detected.[29] At a stroke, this set the template for how to turn a virus with the infection fatality rate of seasonal influenza into a global pandemic.[30] Finally, in

---

26. See Administration of Donald Trump, 'Executive Order 13887 — Modernizing Influenza Vaccines in the United States To Promote National Security and Public Health' (19 September, 2019).

27. See Center for Health Security, 'The Event 201 Scenario: A Global Pandemic Exercise' (18 October, 2019).

28. See World Health Organization, 'Global Vaccine Safety Summit' (2-3 December, 2019).

29. See Victor M. Corman, et al., 'Diagnostic detection of 2019-nCoV by real-time RT-PCR', Eurosurveillance (22 January, 2020).

30. Following the WHO's lead, on 16 March 2020, the 'Guidance and standard operating procedure: COVID-19 virus testing in NHS laboratories', issued by the National Health Service, recommended a thermal cycle amplification threshold (Ct) of 45 for reverse-transcription-polymerase chain reaction (RT-PCR) tests for SARS-CoV-2, with anything below 40 to be regarded as a 'confirmed' positive. However, on 22 May, in 'Predicting infectious Severe Acute Respiratory Disease Syndrome Coronavirus 2 from Diagnostic Samples', the Infectious Disease Society of America (IDSA) reported that infectious virus was only detected with PCR tests with less than 24 cycles of amplification. On 4 August, in 'Viral cultures for COVID-19 infectivity assessment. Systematic review', the Centre for Evidence-based Medicine at Oxford University reported that,

March 2020, with the global apparatus in place, the World Health Organization partnered with the World Economic Forum to launch the 'COVID-19 Action Platform', a coalition of the world's most powerful companies that, within two months, numbered over 1,100.[31] On the same day — 11 March, 2020 — the WHO, ignoring its own previous definitions and criteria, declared SARS-CoV-2 to be a 'pandemic', and lockdowns were imposed across the neoliberal democracies of Western capitalism.[32]

That's where most of us came in, and in my case began trying to understand the lack of correlation between the impact and even existence of this 'pandemic' and the authoritarian restrictions by which our rights and freedoms were being taken from us. What most of didn't know was that the Great Reset of the world economy supposedly justified and even necessitated by the 'pandemic' was initiated 6 months before it was officially declared, and not in response to a virus. What the 6 months of emergency and unprecedented monetary measures prior to the lockdown of Western economies reveals is that, had the enormous mass of liquidity pumped into the financial sector by central banks reached transactions in the real economy, it would have triggered the hyperinflation BlackRock had warned the Federal Reserve had to be avoided. This refutes the received wisdom about the purpose and necessity of lockdown restrictions. As Vighi writes:

---

with RT-PCR tests at more than 30 cycles of thermal amplification, the virus detected was dead and therefore non-infectious. On 28 September, in 'Correlation Between 3790 Quantitative Polymerase Chain Reaction-Positive Samples and Positive Cell Cultures, Including 1941 Severe Acute Respiratory Syndrome Coronavirus 2 Isolates', the IDSA reported that, at a Ct of 25, up to 70 per cent of positives results are real positives; but that at a Ct of 30 this drops to 20 per cent; and at a Ct of 35, just 3 per cent of positive tests are real positives. Despite these findings, in October 2020, in 'Understanding cycle threshold (Ct) in SARS-CoV-2 RT-PCR: A guide for health protection teams', Public Health England advised administering RT-PCR tests at a Ct of 40, while admitting that such tests were 'not able to distinguish whether infectious virus is present'. The most extensive analysis of the numerous flaws in these protocols is that published by the International Consortium of Scientists in Life Sciences. See Pieter Borger, et al.,'Corman-Drosten Review Report. External peer review of the RT-PCR test to detect SARS-CoV-2 reveals 10 major scientific flaws at the molecular and methodological level: consequences for false positive results' (27 November, 2020).

31. See World Economic Forum, 'World Economic Forum launches COVID-19 Action Platform to fight coronavirus' (11 March, 2020).

32. See World Health Organization, 'WHO Director-General's opening remarks at the media briefing on COVID-19 — 11 March 2020' (11 March 2020).

The mainstream narrative should therefore be reversed: the stock market did not collapse in March 2020 because lockdowns had to be imposed; rather, lockdowns had to be imposed because financial markets were collapsing.[33]

Contrary to the narrative we continue to be told by our governments to this day, lockdown wasn't imposed to protect the population from a deadly and highly contagious new pathogen, but because the real economy had to be shut down — with most business transactions and consumer spending suspended under emergency powers — in order to insulate it from the vast sums being pumped into the collapsing financial sector. As of April 2022, the total assets of the US Federal Reserve ($8.9 trillion), the European Central Bank ($9.6 trillion), the Bank of Japan ($6.2 trillion) and the People's Bank of China ($6.3 trillion) had risen to $31 trillion, an extraordinary and unprecedented increase from $19 trillion in September 2019, with a corresponding increase in liabilities (currency in circulation, reserves in commercial banks, central bank securities and equity capital) and therefore in risks to the real and financial sectors of the economy.[34] And although this has fallen to 28.7 trillion in August 2022, across the globe over $41 trillion in assets, nearly half the world's GDP, are now held by central banks.[35]

But that's not all. At the same time that trillions of electronic dollars were being pumped into the global financial system, hundreds of millions of workers across the Western World were forcibly placed on furlough for months and even years on end by national governments, which effectively mortgaged in advance the future labour and production of their populations. In doing so, governments made sure that the populations of the nation states they now had the power to 'lock down' were pushed further into debt for generations to come to the financial institutions that had just been bailed out by the central banks with their money. Just as the fiscal austerity imposed by central banks after the Global Financial Crisis of 2007-2009 had punished workers for the speculations of the financial

---

33. See Fabio Vighi, 'A Self-fulfilling Prophecy: Systemic Collapse and Pandemic Simulation', *The Philosophical Salon* (16 August, 2021).

34. See Dr. Edward Yardeni and Mali Quintana, 'Central Banks: Monthly Balance Sheet' (April 2022).

35. See Alexandra Dimitropoulou, 'Economy Rankings: Largest countries by GDP, 2022', *CEO World Magazine* (31 March, 2022); and Sovereign Wealth Fund Institute, 'Top 100 Largest Central Bank Rankings by Total Assets'.

sector by reducing government spending on the economically spurious justification of 'balancing the budget', so lockdown made certain that the bailout of the banks would be paid by the workers and small businessmen whose jobs and businesses had been lost, bankrupted or placed into debt by the governments enforcing lockdown on the even more spurious justification of protecting them from a threat to public health that never existed. And just as there was no bailout for those who were unemployed, impoverished, ruined or killed by cuts to government spending, so too there is to be no bailout today for those whose jobs, savings, businesses and lives have been ruined by lockdown restrictions. Like austerity, therefore, lockdown is economic class war waged by the financial and political ruling class against the working class, and in which — as is their economic and ideological function under capitalism — the middle-classes have sided with their bosses in administering and morally justifying the restrictions of the biosecurity state.

But what, we might ask, is wrong with this? The second collapse of the global financial system in fifteen years has been averted at the cost of two years of authoritarianism, the bankruptcy of millions of small businesses, the loss of tens of millions of jobs and the impoverishment of hundreds of millions of people. But isn't that a price worth paying to avoid the collapse of capitalism and the far greater economic damage and suffering that would have caused to the world? Isn't that the 'bigger picture', as the apologists for lockdown say?

The answer to this must be a very definite 'no', not only because of the already catastrophic social, economic and political consequences of lockdown, which are very far from over, but also because the downturn in a global economy increasingly hostage to money printing and the artificial inflation of financial assets hasn't been averted but only postponed, with debt-leveraged speculation on financial assets its only escape-route left from the structural contradictions of capitalism in the Twenty-first Century. In its drive to generate surplus value, the global economy must both exploit the workforce and, increasingly, expel it from the productive process. This has resulted from the unprecedented acceleration in digitalisation under the Fourth Industrial Revolution and the accompanying change in the relations of production that revolution is producing. Ironically, these are likely to have the hardest impact on white-collar workers, whose willingness to 'work from home' has demonstrated their redundancy to their former employers. And as the report by the Bank of International Settlements indicated, as the purchasing power of a growing part of the global population has fallen, debt and immiseration have increased. This in turn has reduced surplus value, forcing capital to seek returns in the debt-leveraged financial sector (stocks, bonds, futures and derivatives) rather than investing in the real economy.

As Vighi has argued, lockdown was both a protective measure, averting the collapse of the global financial system, and an offensive programme, implementing the revolution to a social system that, in November 2021, he described as authoritarian, but which I would describe now as totalitarian. It is lockdown, therefore, that has prepared the way for the return of fascism as the political, juridical and cultural superstructure of what Vighi calls 'emergency capitalism'.[36] This appears to differentiate itself from Naomi Klein's definition, in *The Shock Doctrine*, of 'disaster capitalism', in not merely enabling private companies to profit from large-scale crises (war, poverty, famine, natural disasters, pandemics, economic collapse, military coups and political revolutions), but in manufacturing those crises to its own ends.[37] This is something Klein, in the face of all the evidence to the contrary, has dismissed as a 'conspiracy theory'.[38] But if COVID-19, according to the mainstream narrative of our governments and media, is the biggest crisis of our time, to what ends is it being put by a financial system that has just been flooded with trillions of dollars?

2. The Great Reset

In his 2013 article, 'Capitalism as Religion', the Italian philosopher, Giorgio Agamben, warned us that 'a society whose religion is credit, which believes only in credit, is condemned to live on credit'.[39] This is the society we live in now. When the US President, Richard Nixon, responded to rising inflation in the US in August

36. See Fabio Vighi, 'Slavoj Žižek, Emergency Capitalism, and the Capitulation of the Left', *The Philosophical Salon*, 24 May, 2021.

37. See Naomi Klein, *The Shock Doctrine: The Rise of Disaster Capitalism*, Knopf Canada, 2007.

38. See Naomi Klein, 'The Great Reset Conspiracy Smoothie', *The Intercept* (8 December, 2020).

39. See Giorgio Agamben, 'Capitalism as Religion', translated by Adam Kotsko in *Creation and Anarchy: The Work of Art and the Religion of Capitalism* (Stanford University Press, 2019), pp. 66-78.

1971 by suspending the convertibility of the dollar into gold, it marked the end of a system that bound monetary value not only to the gold standard but to its last remaining referent in the real world. This effectively marked the beginning of the neoliberal revolution into finance capitalism, within which money is a self-referential system of representation founded on credit. It is in this sense that Agamben (whose article is a commentary on a 1921 text by Walter Benjamin) argued that capitalism is a religion founded on belief — the Latin term for which, *credere*, is the infinitive form of the past participle, *creditum*. And after August 1971, he argued, 'money is a form of credit which is grounded on itself alone and which corresponds to nothing other than itself'.

By detaching it from any referent in the real world, however, money was separated not just from the gold standard but also, and primarily, from labour, which for most of us — which is to say, the working class that sells its labour for a salary — is the only referent there is. It was from this threshold that labour began to lose its bargaining power, with real wages in advanced capitalist economies, after being adjusted for inflation, having about the same purchasing power in the USA and, in the UK, less than they did in the 1970s.[40] Remember that this ongoing failure of labour to recover its bargaining power was identified by the Bank of International Settlements as one of the four main forces leading to the economic downturn it predicted in June 2019. And when money, and especially our money, has no referent, then the value of our labour and savings can change as quickly as that of homes during the subprime mortgage crisis of 2007-2010. Such devaluation can also happen when, as the BIS also reported, economies can no longer generate the profits to pay off their debts, and central banks create vast sums of electronic money to bail out financial institutions unable to pay the interest on their loans.

The lockdown of the Western World in the two years prior to March 2022 — the exact time set for the expiry of the Coronavirus Act when it was made into UK law in March 2020 — completed several huge strides in the Great Reset. None of these have anything to do with averting a crisis in public health, which lockdown restrictions, instead, served to exacerbate and extend. Rather, as Vighi argues,

---

40. See Drew DeSilver, 'For most U.S. workers, real wages have barely budged for decades', *Pew Research Centre* (7 August, 2018); and Ciaren Taylor, Andrew Jowett and Michael Hardie, 'An examination of Falling Real Wages', *Office for National Statistics* (January 2014).

the lockdown of the real economies of the wealthiest countries in the world achieved the following objectives:[41]

- Provided cover for central banks to print sufficient electronic money to bail out the collapsing global financial system;
- Bankrupted vast numbers of small- and medium-sized businesses, thereby accelerating the monopolisation of markets and resources by international corporations;
- Further depressed labour wages and the standard of living in the West, both of which are set to fall further as inflation continues to rise;
- Enabled the growth and normalisation of e-commerce and the explosion in the value of the global information technology and pharmaceutical companies that have dominated our government's 'responses' to the coronavirus 'crisis'.

As a result of which, over the course of the politically declared 'pandemic', the world's billionaires added $5 trillion to their fortunes, with Big Tech CEOs Larry Page ($113.6 billion) and Sergey Brin ($109.4 billion), both of Google, Jeff Bezos of Amazon ($165.1 billion), Larry Ellison of Oracle ($104.7 billion), Steve Ballmer ($92.7 billion) and Bill Gates ($129.5 billion) of Microsoft, and Mark Zuckerberg of Facebook ($71.1 billion), now making up seven of the ten wealthiest men in the USA, whose billionaires have increased their wealth by 57 per cent under the lockdown, rising from $2.95 trillion in March 2020 to $4.62 trillion in March 2022, with the total number of US billionaires increasing from 614 to 704.[42] Such vast increases in personal fortunes, however, looks set to pale beside the monopoly of the world's natural resources, markets and capital being implemented by the Great Rest.

To echo Trotsky: what next? What Vighi calls the 'controlled demolition' of the real economy is already being effected through the collapse of supply chains from Russia on the justification of economic sanctions and the interruption of

---

41. See Fabio Vighi, 'A Self-fulfilling Prophecy: Systemic Collapse and Pandemic Simulation', *The Philosophical Salon* (16 August, 2021).

42. See Americans for Tax Fairness, 'After 2 years of COVID, U.S. billionaires are $1.7 trillion, or 57%, richer' (11 March, 2022).

trade routes with China on the justification of zero-COVID lockdowns.[43] When the real economy was reopened in March 2022, businesses started trading again, consumers started buying, commercial banks resumed lending, the vast sums borrowed by commercial banks began to flow into markets, and the value of the savings and assets of the mass of working people fell accordingly. As of July 2022, inflation in the US had risen to 8.5 per cent, and in the UK to a 40-year high of 10.1 per cent, with the Bank of England predicting it will reach 13 per cent in the last quarter of 2022.[44] This will in turn justify the implementation of the World Economic Forum's long-heralded global digital infrastructure based on programmable Central Bank Digital Currency, mandatory Digital Identity and Universal Basic Income for the millions of workers made redundant by the new technologies, markets and programmes of the Fourth Industrial Revolution.[45]

War, proxy or not, has always allowed governments to load debt onto the future in order to fund whatever spending it deems necessary to the present state of emergency. In this sense alone, the governments of the West have indeed been waging a 'war on COVID', the cost of which will be laid on their civilian populations for generations, while at the same time justifying further cuts to public spending, reductions in the standard of living and spiralling inflation. Indeed, the current crisis in food and energy prices, which we were warned about in September 2021 after inflation rose from 2.040% to 3.197% the previous month, is conveniently being blamed on Russia's invasion of the Ukraine in February 2022 — as if the previous two years have been wiped from the memories of the amnesiac consumers of the corporate media.[46] And having been trialled over those two years with unexpected and astonishing degrees of compliance, lockdown — justified in the future by a new virus or strain of coronavirus, insufficient reduction in carbon emissions, a crisis in energy or food supplies, rising sea levels, wild fires

---

43. See Fabio Vighi, 'Red Pill or Blue Pill? Variants, Inflation and the Controlled Demolition of the Economy', *The Philosophical Salon*, 3 January, 2022.

44. See Bank of England, *Monetary Policy Report* (August 2022).

45. The Confederation of British Industry has estimated that, by 2030, 9 in 10 UK workers will need 'reskilling', of which 26 million workers will need 'upskilling' and 5 million will need 'retraining' for new jobs. See Edward Richardson, 'Learning for Life: Funding a world-class adult education system', *CBI* (October 2020).

46. See 'Energy crisis: Why gas prices have soared and left UK facing prospect of food shortages', *Sky News* (22 September, 2021); and United Kingdom inflation rate', *RI* (17 August, 2022).

or a myriad of other excuses yet to be invented — will be the new monetary and fiscal mechanism of global capitalism.

There can be few more convincing images of the decay of capitalism than supermarket shelves standing empty of food in the wealthiest countries in the world while millions of tons of grain rot in Ukrainian warehouses; a fifth of the world's container ships sitting in traffic jams outside congested ports, nearly a third of them in China; or UK citizens facing a choice between eating and heating their homes this winter while energy companies post record profits.[47] Spiralling inflation, war in Europe's bread basket, economic embargo against the world's largest exporter of oil and petroleum products, and interruption of trade routes with the world's largest exporter of goods, have created a perfect storm for capitalism. We are at the end of a 50-year cycle of debt from which no amount of zero-interest loans will protect us, and the last time this happened was in 1932.[48] These are the economic conditions for the return of fascism to the governance, laws and culture of the West.

As the World Economic Foundation has been open about declaring, the Great Reset will be implemented on the devaluation of our labour, savings and property, followed by multinational corporations stepping in to buy everything that can be owned or controlled. United Nations programmes will be key to this, allowing global investors to direct the flow of global capital through its Sustainable Development Goals, which increase the economic advantage of already wealthy Western economies and companies able to meet such goals over poorer countries.[49] Administered in compliance with Environmental, Social and Governance criteria which, despite the UN-branding, are set by financial asset managers like BlackRock, these enable multinationals to further their monopoly over global markets.[50] Behind their 'Green' credentials, both these programmes are instruments of what the WEF calls 'stakeholder capitalism', according to which national governments will no longer be the final arbiters of state-imposed

---

47. See Jasper Jolly and Mark Sweney, 'Big oil's quarterly profits hit £50bn as UK braces for even higher energy bills', *The Guardian* (2 August, 2022).

48. See Ray Dalio, *Principles for Dealing with the Changing World Order*, 2021.

49. See Jason Hickel, 'The World's Sustainable Development Goals aren't Sustainable', *Foreign Policy* (30 September, 2020).

50. See Gibson Dunn Lawyers, 'BlackRock, Vanguard, State Street Update Corporate Governance and ESG Policies and Priorities for 2022' (25 January, 2022).

policies, and multinational corporations, through their economic management of the global economy, form a multi-stakeholder form of global governance. It is an indicator of who will benefit from these programmes that the man to profit most from the lockdown of the real economy, Elon Musk, who invests in clean energy, green transportation, artificial intelligence and neurotechnology, increased his already vast fortune by a barely credible 850 per cent in just two years to $240 billion. At its most basic, the Great Reset is the creation of a global government whose leaders are not elected by the people of any nation state, but are self-selected according to the wealth and influence of the international companies and national economies they head on the basis that, since it was these that caused the environmental 'crisis' they have done so much to promote, only they can save the planet — and us with it — as long as we do exactly what they tell us.

The by-now infamous World Economic Forum statement that 'you'll own nothing and be happy' — perhaps the most prophetic of the Newspeak slogans to come out of the Global Biosecurity State — is both a promise of Eden and a threat of expulsion to those who don't embrace its conditions — which, as with every earthly paradise ever invented, entail total submission to someone else's absolute authority over every aspect of our lives. Ahead of the WEF's Annual Meeting in 2016, Ida Auken, the Danish MP, former Minister for the Environment, WEF Young Global Leader, Member of the Global Future Council on the Future of Cities and Urbanisation, and since 2017 a Member of the WEF's Europe Policy Group, interrupted her utopian vision of the future — 'Welcome to 2030: I own nothing, have no privacy and life has never been better' — to voice her concerns about the underclass produced by the Fourth Industrial Revolution.

> My biggest concern is all the people who do not live in our city. Those we lost on the way. Those who decided that it became too much, all this technology. Those who felt obsolete and useless when robots and AI took over big parts of our jobs. Those who got upset with the political system and turned against it. They live different kind of lives outside of the city. Some have formed little self-supplying communities. Others just stayed in the empty and abandoned houses in small 19th-century villages.[51]

51, Ida Auken, 'Welcome to 2030: I own nothing, have no privacy and life has never been better', *Forbes* (10 November, 2016).

The slums and refugee camps in which more than 2 billion people were predicted to live by 2030 long before anyone had heard of the Great Reset or Agenda 2030 appear to be the intended destination of the *Untermenschen* of the WEF's Brave New World, and I see no reason not to take them at their word when its spokespersons repeat the threat with such regularity, openness and consistency. This is not a conspiracy; this is the openly declared policy of global governance by an international technocracy. In the follow-up article he published in October 2021, 'The Central Bankers' Long Covid: An Incurable Condition', Fabio Vighi drew the parallels between this programme of immiseration and expropriation being implemented on the back of the financial crisis and the merger of government, state and private companies under historical fascism that I looked at in chapter 3:

> A cornerstone of historical fascism was industry controlled by government while remaining privately owned. It is quite astonishing that, despite the overwhelming evidence of systematic revolving doors between public and private sector, most public intellectuals have not yet realised that this is where we are heading.[52]

One public intellectual, however, who doesn't have to look outside his own nation state for a model of the slums and camps of the future, has more than realised where we are heading. As one of the ideologues of the Great Reset and a regular speaker at the World Economic Forum, Yuval Noah Harari, the Israeli transhumanist, Professor in the Department of History at the Hebrew University of Jerusalem and personal advisor to Klaus Schwab, and an author who counts Barak Obama, Bill Gates and Mark Zuckerberg among his fans and readers, hasn't been scared to lay out the aims of the Fourth Industrial Revolution with all the frankness and ruthlessness of a latter-day Joseph Goebbels:

> In the industrial revolution of the Nineteenth Century, what humanity learned to produce was stuff like textiles and shoes and weapons and vehicles, and this was enough for [the] very few countries that underwent the revolution fast enough to subjugate everybody else. What we are talking about now is like a second

---

52. Fabio Vighi, 'The Central Bankers' Long Covid: An Incurable Condition', *The Philosophical Salon* (18 October, 2021).

industrial revolution, but the product this time will not be textiles or machines or vehicles or even weapons; the product this time will be humans themselves. We are basically learning to produce bodies and minds. Bodies and minds are going to be the two main products of the next wave. And if there is a gap between those that know how to produce bodies and minds and those who do not, then this [gap will be] far greater than anything we have seen before in history.

This time, if you're not part of the revolution fast enough, then you'll probably become extinct. Once you know how to produce bodies and minds, cheap labour in Africa or South Asia or wherever counts for nothing. I think that the biggest question in the economics and politics of the coming decades will be what to do with all these useless people. I don't think we have an economic model for that. My best guess — which is just a guess — is that food will not be a problem. With that kind of technology, you will be able to produce food for everybody. The problem is more boredom — what to do with them, and how will they find some sense of meaning in life when they are basically meaningless, worthless.[53]

Harari made these comments in 2017, when he was writing his third best-seller, *21 Lessons for the 21st Century* (2018), which was praised by Bill Gates in *The New York Times*. Since then, just as Umberto Eco warned, the corporations and organisations whose interests Harari represents on the global lecture circuit have come up with another and better 'final solution' to the problem of 'useless people' in the Twenty-first Century. 'Useless mouths (*Unnütze Esser*)' was the National Socialist term for Jews who were unable to work, people with serious medical problems or disabilities, and other *Untermenschen* whose lives were deemed as 'meaningless, worthless' to the Third Reich. We shouldn't be surprised, then, that Harari — who as these comments suggest is a fascist in everything but name — has become one of the most celebrated propagandists for the Great Reset, or that the apartheid State of Israel, as I will go on to discuss in chapter 8, is the model for the Global Biosecurity State of our rapidly approaching future.

---

53. The recording of Yuval Harari's comments has been removed from YouTube, but has been downloaded and may be viewed in the online version of this chapter. See Simon Elmer, 'Fascism and the Decay of Capitalism (The Road to Fascism: For a Critique of the Global Biosecurity State)', *Architects for Social Housing* (24 April, 2022).

5. The Psychological Structure of Fascism

'The tradition of the oppressed teaches us that the "state of emergency" in which we live is not the exception but the rule. We must attain to a conception of history that is in keeping with this insight. Then we shall clearly realise that it is our task to bring about a real state of emergency, and this will improve our position in the struggle against fascism. One reason why fascism has a chance is that, in the name of progress, its opponents treat it as a historical norm. The current amazement that the things we are experiencing are "still" possible in the Twentieth Century is not philosophical. This amazement is not the beginning of knowledge — unless it is the knowledge that the view of history that gives rise to it is untenable.'

— Walter Benjamin, *Theses on the Philosophy of History*, 1940

My argument in this series of articles for the return of fascism in the political, juridical and cultural superstructure of the nation states of Western capitalism raises a question that I want to address in this chapter. How is it possible for a global economic infrastructure formed over a hundred years of increasingly rapid developments in technology and finance, including two industrial revolutions, to produce a fascist superstructure — one that should, in the classic Marxist formula, reflect, accommodate and reproduce the new relations of production it requires for capitalism to defend and enforce its hegemony over the world? How is it possible, in other words, for an emergent economic infrastructure, that is contingent upon technology and markets yet to be developed a hundred years ago, to effect a historical regression back to the political, juridical and cultural forms of historical fascism — forms that are residual, as Umberto Eco argued, in even the most advanced capitalist societies, but which are widely perceived to have been surpassed by the irreversible clock of history?[1] Indeed, is there any

---

1. The Welsh socialist, Raymond Williams, divided the ideological superstructure into the dominant, the residual and the emergent. What Williams meant by the dominant ideology is pretty self-explanatory, designating those political forms, legal structures and social practices produced by the ruling class, instrumental to their hegemony, and particular to the definite stage of development of the productive forces of a given society. However, since capitalism is always in a process of transformation, it is also always in the process of discarding redundant forms of

justification for using this term to describe the return of these latent but now, undoubtedly, resurgent forms of governance, jurisprudence and social practice if it doesn't illuminate the emergent economic infrastructure to which they appear to be the response, and which is the driving force of this revolution?

My first — and obviously inadequate — response to this question is that I am trying to understand precisely how this regression back to the fascist state, authoritarian government and a totalitarian society has been so easily implemented by multinational corporations, so readily accepted by the populations of Western capitalism, so enthusiastically adopted by the civil institutions of previously liberal societies. Hopefully, why the Global Biosecurity State should favour a return to fascism is by now obvious, given the openly stated aspirations to govern the West by an international technocracy of financial institutions, pharmaceutical companies and information technology companies and the organisations of global governance they form. Yet ideologies are not chosen by a financial elite. They are produced by the economic relations of production of a given society at a given stage of their development; and the question of how it has been possible to revive, implement and enforce the political, juridical and cultural forms of fascism with such ease is the one I am trying to answer in this book.

1. Producing the Heterogeneous

In this chapter, I want to look at an article that was published in two parts between 1933 and 1934, the years in which Hitler went from being appointed Chancellor of the Weimar Republic to making himself Leader of the Third Reich, eliminated his political opponents in both the Reichstag and his Cabinet, and made National Socialism the official ideology of German society at every level of the state, from

---

capitalist ideology. Some, however, continue to have a function, and these residual forms designate those structures which, although formed at an earlier stage of its development, still play a role in its current stage. But just as capitalism is always discarding the redundant forms of its ideology, so too it is always developing emergent forms, and it is in them that we can best see the future to which the present has given birth and is even now struggling into dominance. See Raymond Williams, 'Dominant, Residual and Emergent', *Marxism and Literature* (Oxford University Press, 1977), pp. 121-127; and my application of this division to the UK biosecurity state in the pages titled 'The Emerging Ideology', part 6 of Simon Elmer, *'Cui Bono?'*, collected in *Brave New World*, pp. 155-159.

schools, universities, trades unions, the press, culture industry and civil service to the police force, judiciary, military and medical institutions — a process they called 'coordination (*Gleichschaltung*)'. In this article, 'The Psychological Structure of Fascism', which was published in the Marxist but anti-Stalinist journal *La Critique sociale*, the French sociologist and philosopher, Georges Bataille, tried to understand and explain this sudden and overwhelming success of fascism, and in particular its appeal to the working class in Italy and Germany, both of which had strong and well-organised communist parties politically and militantly opposed to fascism.[2] To explain this unexpected historical development, Bataille formulated what he called a 'theory of heterology', which challenges much of the thinking in this country about how political movements win and hold power, and how the Left continues to view the relation between the classes. Bataille's article is written in abstract and even philosophical terms, but they are worth trying to elucidate, I think, as they can tell us a lot about the particular form in which fascism has returned to the West today, and why that return cannot be understood within the outdated political polarities of Left and Right.

The foundation of homogeneous society, Bataille argues, is production, which works to exclude all forms of non-productive or useless activity and, by the same token, all non-productive and useless people. To establish this homogeneity between the various activities that constitute a given society, a common denominator has been created. This, of course, is money, which is the calculable equivalence between the different products of social activity. As such, money is not only the measure of all activity but reduces humans to the mere function of that activity; and according to its measure, each worker in a society is worth what he or she produces. However, in capitalist economies, only the owners of capital and the means of production — that is to say, the capitalists that profit from its products — compose homogeneous society, together with the middle classes that variously benefit from that profit; while the producers of those products — the workers whose labour creates the wealth on which homogeneous society is built but who do not profit from its products — are, properly speaking, heterogeneous to society. They remain, that is to say, outside the cycle of

---

2. See Georges Bataille, 'The Psychological Structure of Fascism', in *Visions of Excess: Selected Writings, 1927-29*, edited, translated and with an introduction by Allan Stoekl, Theory and History of Literature, Vol. 14 (University of Minnesota Press, 1984), pp. 137-160.

capitalism proper, and indeed must remain there so that homogeneous society can continue to expropriate their labour. From this heterogeneity comes the revulsion, contempt, dismissiveness, hate and violence with which the working class is treated by homogeneous society, and above all by the middle classes, for whom workers are not only of another class but of another nature, unsubjugated and therefore in constant need of surveillance, regimentation and oppression in case their heterogeneity should infect homogeneous society.

It is in order to protect the homogeneous functioning of the productive forces of a given society from heterogeneous elements that the modern state exists. In a democratic order, the practical application of homogeneous society's reduction of heterogeneous elements are the various forms of parliament, upon entering which those elements more or less quickly become a part of homogeneous society. We have seen this demonstrated repeatedly by the ease and success with which nominally 'socialist' political parties, including the UK Labour Party, have become assimilated into the capitalist order, to which they now present not the least threat of subversion.

Periodically, however, the contradictions of capitalism in industrial and now post-industrial societies throw up heterogeneous elements that threaten to subvert the homogeneous functioning of production. Today we call these 'crises', but formerly they took the form of uprisings and even revolutions, as they still do in less advanced capitalist societies. When this happens, as we witnessed during the two years of the politically-declared 'pandemic', the state makes recourse not to parliament and the rule of law but rather to imperious and sovereign forms of authority that are not subject to parliaments and courts. These include the power of a hereditary or elected head of state (Crown, *Duce*, *Führer* or *Président*) to overrule the legislature and even the constitution; the Church, which always aligns itself with the authority of the state in times of crisis; the police and armed forces, whose impunity from the laws they claim to enforce is the clearest demonstration of imperious power; and, as we saw universally employed by governments during the coronavirus 'crisis', emergency powers.

All these forms of authority, however, are themselves heterogeneous to the homogeneous social order, whose existing relations of production, administrative framework and juridical forms they exist to maintain and uphold. As an example and expression of this hierarchy, on the architrave of the pediment of the west entrance to the US Supreme Court Building in Washington, DC — which was completed in 1935, a year after Bataille's article was published — are carved the words: 'Equal Justice Under Law'; but among the figures that sit in judgement *above* these words are symbolic depictions of Liberty flanked by Order and Authority, the latter of which is represented by a Roman lictor bearing a *fasces* from which the axe blade is visibly protruding. To understand the homogeneous functioning of any given society, therefore, including a fascist society, Bataille argued that we have to understand its heterogeneous elements, how they defend and enforce its economic, legal and political continuity, and how these heterogeneous elements are themselves produced by homogeneous society.

Bataille is a good etymologist. To speak of what is, by definition, always seeking to escape containment within a discursive apprehension of the world, he uses the term 'heterogeneous', from the Greek *heteros* (the other of two), and *genos* (kind). His own project, however, isn't to constitute a heterogenealogy (a family of others), but a heterology (from the Greek *logos*). Although, at the concrete level, the heterogeneous is the other of the homogeneous 'in kind', its abstract logos within a discourse has no elementary structure of kinship, and cannot be assembled according to a scientific taxonomy. Its forms, therefore, can only ever be spoken of in their diffuse relation to the self of which they are the other. As Umberto Eco would go on to argue in his article on 'Ur-fascism', whether, historically, it was the communist, the Jew or those designated by the Third Reich as 'useless mouths', or, more recently, the terrorist, the Muslim or those designated by the Global Biosecurity State as 'unvaccinated', fascism produces the other — and indeed, must produce the other — in opposition to which its own unity is formed. The heterogeneous, in other words, is both the axe around which the homogeneous bundle of rods is bound to form the authority of the fascist state, and at the same time the enemy against which that axe is wielded.

For Bataille, therefore, the unity of fascism lies in its new and particular production of the heterogeneous, which it must constantly seek to dispel from its homogeneity while at the same time reproducing it. And just as, under historical instances of fascism, the identity of the heterogenous elements did not matter — being contingent instead on the individual fascist state: with Mussolini's Italy, for example, tolerating and even embracing fascist Jews for well over a decade

85

before its alliance with Hitler's Germany — so today the high priests of the Global Biosecurity State do not discriminate between those they anathematise, swinging its propaganda machine in a few months from 'conspiracy theorists' endangering lives to 'unvaccinated' medical professionals to 'barbaric' Russian invaders. Today, the Russian national living in the West who has had his assets frozen, his trade stopped and his music and culture banned, who is forced to condemn his country and denounce his government in order to appear in public life or practice his profession, has been ostracized by our so-called 'liberal' populations with all the fervour and compliance they showed to the 'unvaccinated'. What is important — what is necessary to the unity of the Global Biosecurity State — is neither the identity nor the culpability of the ostracised and criminalised, but rather the production of the heterogeneous social elements in opposition to which homogeneous society can unify. And to protect itself from these heterogeneous elements, as we have seen, no expenditure can be too great, no decree or action too violent.

At the same time, therefore, in correlation with this impoverished, abject other, the fascist state must also create an imperious, sovereign force capable of protecting homogeneous society from these heterogeneous elements, whose threat, as Eco argued, is always exaggerated in order to justify the violence of fascist rule. Under historical fascism, this heterogeneous power was concentrated in the figure of the charismatic Leader, whether that was Mussolini, Hitler or Franco — all of whom, in common with most of the rest of Europe, thought democracy was doomed, and that the choice was between communism and fascism. Today, however, with the West citing the defence of democracy as the justification for three-quarters of a century of imperialist wars, military invasion and political intervention in sovereign states in South America, Africa, the Middle East and Asia, not even the President of the United States (now given the vaguely Roman-sounding title of 'Potus') has the absolute authority of the *Duce, Führer or Caudillo*. Indeed, for some time now the vaunted position of 'the most powerful man in the world' has been occupied by Hollywood actors, Christian fundamentalists, game-show hosts and half-senile puppets who mouth the words (and declarations of war) written by the military-industrial technocracy for which he presents the barely standing facade of democracy.

Instead, as I have argued, the sovereignty of the fascist Leader has been reinvested in the global forms of technocratic governance that have assumed such power over our governments, nation states and their populations, and which has increased enormously since March 2020. And much like citizens under historical fascism, we are now reduced to the position of children in relation to their father, slaves to their master, criminals to the police, soldiers to their general, subjects to their sovereign, rather than as civilians to their elected political representatives in Parliament and Government. Thus, the Global Biosecurity State functions as a strictly one-way street between this new international technocracy and the nation states that administer and enforce its dictates. So, although the role of the Leader has been supplanted in the new form of fascism that has re-emerged from this crisis in twenty-first-century capitalism, the imperious sovereignty of fascist rule most certainly has not.

What Bataille, in this article, called the 'psychological structure' of fascism is the pull of attraction and repulsion between these two poles of the heterogeneous: on the one hand (the right), an almost child-like reverence for and obedience to the imperious, elevated forms of authority that exist above democratic accountability and the law, and which guarantee the unity and functioning of homogeneous society; and, on the other hand (the left), a visceral revulsion for and rejection of the impoverished, the diseased, the pathologised, the ostracised and the criminalised, which threaten to subvert homogeneous society. Both these poles, which together compose the heterogeneous elements of society, lie outside the labour force, means of production and legislative and legal administration that constitute homogeneous society.

2. From Religion to War

In proposing this theory of heterology, Bataille argued that the unity of fascism does not lie in its economic infrastructure — the forces and relations of production and property ownership, which varied considerably, moreover, in the European countries where fascism had formed a government — but in this 'psychological structure'; and for Bataille, that structure is determined by its distinct unification of religious and military forces. On the face of it, there was nothing new in this. For over a century now, the US Empire has invaded, bombed and stripped resources from sovereign states to the patriotic cries of 'God bless America', just as before it the British Empire colonised a fifth of the globe to the chants of *'Dieu et mon droit'*. But by identifying the psychological structure of fascism in this unification of religion and the military, Bataille implicitly departed from the crude model of Marxism espoused by the Third International, according to which the ideological structure of a given society — its political, juridical and cultural (including religious) forms — are mere reflections of its economic infrastructure.

If this crude application of the Marxist theory of ideology had any explanatory purchase on fascism, why did Germany — during the Weimar Republic between 1919 and 1933 the most advanced industrial, scientific, philosophical and perhaps political nation in Europe — produce an ideology as culturally, intellectually and politically regressive as National Socialism? What had the most advanced capitalist nation in Europe to do with torch-lit parades, a parliament bullied by political paramilitaries in the Reichstag, and laws founded on pseudo-scientific notions of race drawn from nineteenth-century discourses of hereditary degeneracy, eugenics and mystical anthropology? How could the nation that in the early Twentieth Century alone had produced Albert Einstein in physics, Hannah Arendt in philosophy, Rosa Luxemburg in politics, Theodor Adorno in Sociology, Walter Benjamin in cultural criticism, Bertolt Brecht in theatre, Marlene Dietrich in acting, Fritz Lang in cinema, Arnold Schoenberg in music, Walter Gropius in architecture, Alfred Döblin in literature, Kurt Schwitters in poetry and Max Ernst in art, also produce Adolf Hitler, Hermann Goering, Heinrich Himmler, Josef Mengele, Carl Schmitt, Wolfram Sievers, Joseph Goebbels, Albert Speer, Arno Breker, Adolf Ziegler and Leni Riefenstahl? How could Martin Heidegger, in other words, be the most influential philosopher of the Twentieth Century and, at the same time, a signed-up member and ideological exponent of the National Socialist German Workers Party?[3]

This is a question we should be asking again — it is one I am trying to address in this book — in the wake of the last two-and-a-half years of intellectual cowardice, political credulity and cultural regression: in which science has been apotheosised by politics as a religion; in which medical reactions to disease not employed in Europe for hundreds of years have been imposed on the populations

---

3. On Heidegger's collusion with the Third Reich, see Richard J. Evans, *The Coming of the Third Reich* (Allen Lane, 2003), pp. 419-422.

of previously neoliberal democracies; in which the most educated people in the world — the Western middle classes — have believed in the efficacy of cloth masks, plastic screens and standing two metres from their fellow acolytes to stop the spread of a respiratory virus one-thousandth the width of a human hair; in which sanctimonious liberals have avidly participated in informing on and calling for the social segregation of anyone who did not obey regulations and restrictions that not only have no basis in science, medicine or logic, but which have torn up the social contract of the West that was founded on the rule of law, democratic oversight of government, the separation of executive, legislature and judiciary, and the universality, indivisibility and inalienability of human rights?

I will continue to recall the lies, deceptions and orthodoxies of faith under which we were forced to live for the two years since March 2020 and which continue today; but the point I'm arguing here is that, as with the rise of fascism in Europe in the period between the two world wars, the manufactured 'crisis' in public health that has been used to justify the imposition of the Global Biosecurity State has been a profoundly religious moment. The watchword employed by the ideologues of both the coronavirus 'crisis' and, before it, the environmental 'crisis', to 'Follow the Science!' is — to anyone who understands the evidential procedures of scientific method — a fundamentally unscientific statement.[4] It is, however, a deeply religious one. Taking my point of departure from Giorgio Agamben's commentary on the cultic practices of the biosecurity state, I have written previously about the religious foundation to the COVID faith.[5] I won't repeat my analyses here, therefore, except to say that, in opposition to science, religion apotheosises its dogma as an unquestionable Truth (with a capital 'T'), for which it provides no proofs or arguments. And in contrast to science — which under forty years of neoliberalism has increasingly come to resemble it — religion demands absolute belief from its acolytes, anathematises deviations from its orthodoxies as heresy, and responds to questions and challenges with censorship

---

4. See, for example, James Butler, 'Follow the Science', *London Review of Books* (16 April, 2020).

5. See, in particular, Simon Elmer, 'The Religion of Medicine', section 6 of 'The New Normal: What is the Biosecurity State? (Part 1: Programmes and Regulations)' (31 July, 2020), collected in *COVID-19*, pp. 209-215; and 'Biosecurity as Cultic Practice', section 7 of '*Cui Bono?* The COVID-19 "Conspiracy"' (19 February, 2021), collected in *Brave New World*, pp. 159-164.

and punishment, to administer which it draws on all the powers of the secular state.

This religious, regressive, irrational, and fundamentally unscientific approach to knowledge, the debates that produce it and the proofs it requires, describes, exactly, the actions of the Global Biosecurity State over the past two-and-a-half years. That it has done so around a discourse of disease — which has never quite escaped its religious explanation as divine punishment for moral failings (something we should have learned from the reaction to the AIDS epidemic) — has made this manufactured 'crisis' particularly amenable to the revival of the religious dogma and cultic practices of the biosecurity state at this historical moment. Indeed, if we understand so-called 'health measures' — face masking, physical distancing, prohibited public spaces, proscribed actions, restricted consumptions, banned social interactions, ritual ablutions, ingested salvations — as the interdictions and practices of a new religion, they begin to make far more sense. But the construction of the biosecurity state in response to a 'pandemic' has also, I would argue, prepared the ideological ground for the return of fascism as the political, juridical and cultural superstructure produced by the current revolution in global capitalism.

In the recent transition from a Western World under lockdown to a Western World under the threat of war with Russia and its allies, we are seeing the political movement from the 'war on COVID' trumpeted by the ideologues of the Global Biosecurity State to the war on those who represent a barrier to the hegemony of its international technocracy. As I discussed in the previous chapter, the Great Reset depends on the immiseration of the real economy to achieve the financial monopoly of an international technocracy whose geopolitical axes are in the course of being decided. Whether it's an external war waged against enemy states outside its military alliances (the North Atlantic Treaty Organization or a new Moscow-Beijing axis) or an internal war waged against manufactured enemies within (the foreigner, the terrorist or the virus), war has always been a structural necessity of fascism — at once justifying the government's removal of the human rights of citizens and the suspension of the democratic process under a state of emergency, and in doing so manifesting the sovereign and imperious character of its authority over homogeneous society.

One possible explanation of why biosecurity restrictions have temporarily been lifted in the West is that we are undergoing the transition from the religious phase of the Global Biosecurity State, which reordered homogeneous society according to new cultic practices and dogma, to its military phase; but both have existed side by side from the start, with the power of the nation state that for two years was turned against its own people returning to its former function. The difference between the past forty years of neoliberalism and the return of fascism today is that, while the former directed the violence of the capitalist state externally in military invasions and wars — with El Salvador, Grenada, the Persian Gulf, Panama, Iraq, Kuwait, Afghanistan, Yemen, Libya and Syria being only the most well-known — in the latter those forces are being directed internally, by riot police, counter-terrorism paramilitaries and homeland security services, against the populations that vote for, fund and turn a blind eye to its violence. In the two years since March 2020, the forces that for decades have been employed externally in wars of aggression against sovereign nations have been turned by the governments of the Global Biosecurity State against those who sat by and voted for them to turn the rest of the world into their killing fields. Now those fields are being expanded by NATO.

Like most on the political Left in the interwar period, Bataille understood fascism as the response of capitalism to the growing threat of an international working-class movement. And the ability of fascism to unite religious and military authority in the politically new figure of the Leader derived from the fact that, in opposition to communism, which sought to exacerbate the class war, fascism was characterised by the 'uniting of classes'. This power of unification, Bataille argued, was derived from the military aspect of fascism, which erased the class differences of its recruits beneath a uniform that homogenised both appearance and actions. Of course, beneath that homogeneity lay a hierarchical military structure even more stratified than that of social class, and whose head was the fascist Leader. But today, the response to COVID-19 has similarly erased the political differences of party, newspaper and electorate beneath the military flag of the 'war on COVID'. Conservative and Labourite, *Telegraph* and *Guardian* reader, entrepreneur and environmentalist — all have united in their advocacy of restrictions, their calls for greater punishments, their demands to suspend our human rights and freedoms. Indeed, maintaining social distancing, obeying directional arrows on the floors of shops and in the street, and participating in collective rituals like clapping for the NHS or the Ukraine, transpose into civilian life such military forms as standing to attention, marching in formation and military parades, with the individual identity of the biosecurity recruit erased beneath the uniformity of both mask and behaviour. What is erased by fascism, in other words, is not the distinctions of class and rank but rather the political identity and agency of the recruit.

3. Assimilation into the Homogeneous

Fascist unity, however, is not only the unification of military and religious authority in the figure of the Leader and the symbolic uniting of different social classes in the erasure of the political identity of the individual. 'It is also', writes Bataille, 'the successful uniting of heterogeneous elements with homogeneous elements, of sovereignty, properly speaking, with the state.'[6] Under fascism, the democratic principle of the sovereignty of Parliament and Nation — like the previously inalienable human rights of its citizens — are all subordinated to the state. As I've already quoted Mussolini writing in The Doctrine of Fascism: 'Everything is in the state, and nothing human or spiritual can exist, much less have value, outside the state.'[7] By successfully eradicating all forms of heterogeneous subversion, the historical fascist state aligned itself with the interests of the capitalists, which is to say, with homogeneous society. However, as a result of this recourse to fascist heterogeneity, which threatened the homogeneity of production based on ideological notions of competition and free enterprise, 'the very structure of capitalism', Bataille writes, 'finds itself profoundly altered'. Without Italian landowners and German industrialists being compelled to align themselves, respectively, with fascism and National Socialism, these political movements would never have formed governments. In a revision to the classic Marxist model of ideology, therefore, the fascist state is in a reciprocal relationship with the economic infrastructure that ultimately determines its formation.[8] However, that the unity of fascism is in its psychological structure rather than in the economic

6. Georges Bataille, Visions of Excess, p. 155.

7. Benito Mussolini and Giovanni Gentile, The Doctrine of Fascism, p. 3.

8. See Karl Marx, 'Preface to A Critique of Political Economy', collected in Selected Writings, edited by David McLellan (Oxford University Press, 1977), pp. 388-392.

conditions that serve as its base doesn't mean that the stage of development of the global economy and the crisis it faced didn't provide the different fascist states with a common economic determination; and the same is true today. Indeed, after a century of globalisation it is even more true.

From the immense resources and productive forces squandered on the two world wars in the Twentieth Century to the vast accumulation of wealth by the most powerful commercial corporations in the world today and, most recently, the $33 billion in 'military aid' the US is sending to its Ukrainian puppet government to wage its proxy war on Russia, the production of the imperious, sovereign pole of heterogeneous authority is not only opposed to its impoverished, abject pole, but also produces it.[9] The poverty of the global working class is not an unfortunate consequence of the failure of capitalism to feed, clothe, house, educate and care for the health of the population of the globe, but instead the product of its success in keeping the labour force that produces its wealth from sharing in its profits. The unproductive expenditure of material and labour, whether in lockdown or the permanent state of war in which the USA has existed since World War Two is, first of all, the consumption of those resources to ends that are kept from the producers of the wealth it consumes. It's not by chance that the USA, the wealthiest nation in history, has a defence budget of $773 billion this year — more than the next 9 countries combined, and over 10 per cent of all federal expenditure — but doesn't have free health care.[10] To maintain the relations of production of homogeneous society, the labour time in which the working class can be fed, housed and educated must be squandered in producing the sovereign and imperious forms of heterogeneous authority before which they are then commanded to kneel in obedience and, eventually, convinced to revere as their protectors. We shouldn't forget that it is the financial sector the governments of the West have bailed out with $10 trillion of electronic money to which the working class is now in debt for generations to come. In this respect as in so many others, the coronavirus 'crisis' is a demonstration of how homogeneous society produces the poles of the heterogeneous, both the imperious and the impoverished. And

---

9. See Christina Wilkie and Thomas Franck, 'Biden asks congress for $33 billion to support Ukraine through September', *CNBC* (28 April, 2022).

10. See Secretary of Defense Lloyd J. Austin III, 'The Department of Defense Releases the President's Fiscal Year 2023 Defense Budget' (28 March, 2022); and Peter G. Peterson Foundation, 'US Defense Spending Compared to Other Countries' (11 May, 2022).

yet, it is the corporate leaders of this international technocracy that have emerged from the 'pandemic' they declared as the sovereign and imperious authority before which the newly impoverished and abject must now bow in obedience and fear if not yet in universal reverence.

From these principles, Bataille concludes his article with a discussion of the different possibilities of the working class being joined by elements of homogeneous society (the middle classes and even individual capitalists) dissociated from it by the crises arising from the contradictions in capitalism. It is only as such, he argues, that heterogeneity can form a potentially subversive force of change in society. Bataille sees these possibilities being determined by the existing and historical political structures of a given society, and above all by its imperious and sovereign forms of heterogeneous authority. Italy, for example, after the Great War, had a weak monarchy that made it susceptible to fascism; and in Germany the revolution had overthrown the Kaiser and replaced him with the legislatively impotent Weimar Republic that increased nostalgia for the authoritarianism of the Second Reich. In both countries, therefore, which only attained national unity, respectively, 51 and 62 years before forming a fascist government, and which had emerged from the Great War humiliated and defeated, an imperious heterogeneous authority was lacking, making both nations susceptible to the militarism of fascist sovereignty. For the multinational successor states created, restored or expanded by the Treaty of Versailles from the dissolved Austro-Hungarian and Russian empires (Austria, Hungary, Czechoslovakia, Yugoslavia, Poland and Romania) the lack of a recognised heterogeneous authority, whether Emperor or Czar, was even greater. While in Spain, both the military dictatorship and the monarchy had been deposed, making way for the doomed Spanish Republic.

The UK, in contrast, had as its Head of State a hereditary monarch who is still wheeled out today at the first sound of grumblings from the unfailingly patriotic and royalist British working class; and France had the French Revolution, to which protesters against lockdown still appeal when they sing *La Marseillaise* and wave the *Tricoleur*, demonstrating their apparently unshakeable equation of *liberté, égalité, fraternité* with the continuity of the French Republic. It would appear, therefore — and the unopposed accession of Charles III to the throne of the United Kingdom in the month I publish this book has reaffirmed this function

— that in a constitutional monarchy of long-standing the sovereign is so closely connected with homogeneous society that its authority has become naturalised as an unchangeable part of its structure; while in a democratic republic like France or the USA, the sovereign appears as that which has already been overthrown in the glorious moment of its founding. The imperious elements of the heterogeneous, therefore, are both immobilised and immobilising, while only its impoverished elements can bring about change. Not for nothing are the memorial statues of George Washington and Abraham Lincoln both depicted with their hands resting on the *fasces*.

To form itself into a force for change, however, the heterogeneous elements of society must include not only that part of the working class that has become conscious of its subversive and even revolutionary potential but also those elements of the middle classes dissociated from homogeneous society by its disintegration. However, during such crises the dissociated elements of homogeneous society are not necessarily attracted to its subversive elements. On the contrary, and as we saw during the coronavirus 'crisis', in the demonstrations, marches and protests against the UK biosecurity state the middle-classes, and particularly those on the political Left, were conspicuous by their almost total absence. Instead, the imperative force of attraction exerted by heterogeneous forms of authority — which reached a peak during the recent Lying-in-State of Queen Elizabeth II — mobilised homogeneous society in the direction of the restoration of the temporarily broken contact between the masses of the obedient working and middle classes and sovereign authority, which they were and are only too willing to obey. Just as, in historical fascist states, the *Duce* and the *Führer* exerted not just a military authority but also a religious power of attraction over the masses, so the subjects of the UK biosecurity state, in Orwell's words, have learned to love Big Brother.

These considerations, strictly speaking, lie outside the scope of this chapter, though I will return to them at the end of this book; but Bataille's conclusions on his own time, which proved to be accurate, do not offer much hope for us today:

> In principle, it seems that revolutionary movements that develop in a democracy are hopeless, at least so long as the memory of earlier struggles against a royal authority has been attenuated and no longer necessarily sets heterogeneous

reactions in opposition to imperious forms. In fact, it is evident that the situation of the major democratic powers, where the fate of the Revolution is being played out, does not warrant the slightest confidence: it is only the very nearly indifferent attitude of the proletariat that has permitted these countries to avoid fascist formations.[11]

Bataille was quick to add that the rapidly-changing world of concrete reality cannot be constrained by such theoretical constructions, and he held out hope that fascism, which he said threw the very existence of a workers' movement into question, nevertheless demonstrated what energies such a movement could mobilise when awakened to the awareness of its affective forces. Just as it's from the ranks of the working class that an imperious sovereignty draws its means of affective action to fight its wars and enforce its laws, so it's against this class that the entire apparatus of the state directs its powers of oppression in Parliament, law court and the media, turning the 'heroes' in our police forces and military into football 'hooligans' with the stroke of a pen, the click of a camera. Nearly ninety years later, however, Bataille's description of the indifference of the proletariat to its subversive — let alone revolutionary — potential paints a more accurate picture of the working class of the West than his hopes of a heterogeneous force that would turn the weapons of fascism against itself.

I want to end these considerations on the psychological structure of fascism and why it has returned today with a passage from a contemporaneous text that addresses precisely this subordination of the working class by fascism — in Bataille's terms, the appropriation of the subversive potential of the heterogeneous elements of capitalism to homogeneous bourgeois society. In 1936, in his now famous article on 'The Work of Art in the Age of Mechanical Reproduction', Walter Benjamin, the German critic from whose writings my epigraph to this chapter is drawn, and who would himself die trying to escape from fascism four years later, wrote:

Fascism attempts to organise the newly proletarianised masses while leaving intact the property relations which the masses strive to abolish. Fascism sees its salvation in granting these masses not their rights, but instead a chance to

---

11. Georges Bataille, *Visions of Excess*, p. 159.

express themselves. The masses have the right to change property relations; fascism seeks to give them expression while keeping these relations unchanged. The logical result of fascism is the aestheticising of political life.[12]

Nearly ninety years have passed since Benjamin's prophetic words, and in the formerly neoliberal democracies of the West the masses have long since given up asserting their right to change property relations let alone bringing that change about. Instead they are content — or, more accurately, they demand now above all other things — their right to express themselves with the toys with which they have been distracted from their historical role and, finally it seems, enslaved by the spectacles of fascism. Of all the new buzzwords and phrases to emerge from the propaganda machine of the Global Biosecurity State with which the nation states of Western capitalism have spoken in one voice, perhaps the most quoted is the declaration of the World Economic Forum, to which I have already referred, that after the Great Reset, when we have embraced the Fourth Industrial Revolution and fascism is the New Normal, 'we will own nothing and be happy'.

This was, perhaps, Benjamin's greatest insight into our still distant present. Clarifying what he meant by the aestheticising of political life, Benjamin wrote: 'In great ceremonial processions, giant rallies and mass sporting events, and in war, all of which are now fed into the camera, the masses come face to face with themselves.' Benjamin was thinking of the Nuremberg rallies and the use Hitler's Minister for Propaganda, Joseph Goebbels, made of the new technologies of mass communication in 1930s Germany, especially cinema and the radio. Today, however, this spectacle has been reduced to the size of a smart-phone screen, by which the masses are confronted, at every moment of every day, with their own face; and ever-proliferating social media platforms grant us the unlimited scope to express ourselves while doing absolutely nothing to change the property relations overseen and enforced by this technology. On the contrary, the will to self-expression is not only the ideological basis of the identity politics by which the potentially subversive heterogeneous elements in our societies are assimilated into an homogeneous order but also, as the Bank of International Settlements

---

12. Walter Benjamin, 'The Work of Art in the Age of Mechanical Reproduction', collected in *Illuminations*, edited and with an introduction by Hannah Arendt, translated by Harry Zohn (Fontana Press, 1973), pp. 234.

warned, the source of the already enormous financial power and growing political power of the handful of information technology companies that administer the Global Biosecurity State.

This doesn't mean, however, that the political spectacle has lost its uses to fascism, at least not for the moment. The first two years of lockdown were accompanied, for the citizens of the UK biosecurity state, by the European Football Cup, the Wimbledon tennis championships, the British and Irish Lions rugby tour to South Africa, the delayed Summer Olympics in Japan, the Winter Olympics in China and, in the empty stadiums of the English Football Premier League, the ritual of 'taking the knee'. Originally an act of non-compliance in protest against the systemic racism in US society enacted during the national anthem that is played before games of American football, this gesture, which in international matches is now performed after the anthems, is another example of how the heterogeneous and potentially subversive elements in a society are co-opted into and assimilated by the homogeneous order. Indeed, insofar as this gesture, like that of wearing a face mask, has become a mandatory ritual with which few sportsmen dare not comply, the left-hand pole of the heterogeneous has been transformed into the right-hand pole, and a gesture originally aligned with the impoverished and abject (the Black working-class) is now employed to uphold the homogeneous system of their oppression.

More recently, we've had the ritual of clapping in support of the Ukraine — a spectacle that repeats the clapping for the NHS during the first lockdown of the UK — and the corresponding ban on everything Russian, from commodities to culture. Under the political consensus created by such spectacles, Chelsea Football Club, which since 2003 has been owned by the Russian oligarch and gangster, Roman Abramovich, has now been forcibly sold to another billionaire currently approved by the UK state. In response to protests against this decision, Thomas Teuchel, the German manager of the club, told the UK media: 'There is no second opinion about the situation [in Ukraine]'.[13] Televised to the nation on *Match of the Day*, a programme not normally known for commenting on military conflict around the world (it has made no equivalent condemnation of the far longer and more destructive wars in Yemen or Gaza), this is the very doctrine of

---

13. See 'Chelsea boss Thomas Tuchel says fans should not have sung Abramovich's name during minute's applause', *ITV News* (7 March, 2022).

fascism, in which every citizen must adopt the political positions and repeat the political statements of their Government, and any deviation from that orthodoxy is censored and punished on the grounds, as Eco wrote, that all disagreement is a threat to the security of the state and therefore a form of treason.

The fact that the espousal of this view, which has been unanimously repeated by the now homogeneous UK media, is in contravention of our legal rights to freedom of thought (Article 9 of the European Convention on Human Rights) and freedom of expression (Article 10), is further proof that the politically-declared state of emergency under which we lived for two years in the UK has not been lifted with the formal suspension of coronavirus-justified regulations and restrictions this March. On the contrary, those nominally temporary measures are no longer the enforced exception and are now the obeyed rule in the 'New Normal' under whose flag the homogeneity of the fascist state has been imposed. That they are now unquestioningly accepted by the UK public outside of any legal framework indicates how far we have descended into unthinking obedience and willing servitude over the past two-and-a-half years, and shows that — without us realising it — we are now a fascist society in everything but name, and ready to form a properly fascist state under the new forms of sovereign authority that rule over the Global Biosecurity State.

In the previous chapter, I made some predictions about the consequences of the current crisis in capitalism and the resort to heterogeneous forms of authority by our international technocracies to avert the collapse of the global financial system, which included the lockdown of the real economy in the West for two years. If fascism has returned to our politics, laws and cultures, like historical fascism it is in anticipation of the expected social and political reactions to the global plummet in living standards, not only among the already impoverished heterogeneous elements of society, but also in elements of homogeneous society. Capitalism has progressively developed the means first to crush and then to seduce the working class of the West into compliance, but it needs the middle classes to administer the apparatus of the state, although far less than previously as more of their functions are taken over by the next generation of technology and the monopoly of the economy by multinational corporations increases. This is precisely the type of crisis in capitalism that Bataille identified as having the potential to unite the heterogeneous elements of society into a force for social and political change. As I discussed in chapter 4, the Bank of International Settlements warned that such a challenge to the 'international global order' should not be underestimated, and will be 'a force to contend with for years to come'.

From this point of view, the hugely increased government authoritarianism and state-authorised violence in Western societies during the politically-declared 'pandemic' was a test-case of the even greater violence and authoritarianism to come, and which the totalitarianism of the Global Biosecurity State is designed to control and suppress in advance. Although the economic infrastructure of the Global Biosecurity State, therefore, is necessarily different from the economic conditions that gave rise to fascism in Europe in the 1920s, not only has it also risen from a crisis in Western capitalism that is the latest in what can justifiably and accurately be described as its long decay, but many of the superstructural forms of historical fascism have returned in the nation states of the West. As I've argued, the sovereign, imperious elements of Western societies are no longer invested in the fascist Leader, but have instead been assumed by the global forms of technocratic governance by which we are now ruled. Like historical fascism, the authority of this technocracy is both religious and military; but this time they are united not in the authoritarian nationalism of the nation state but in the totalitarianism of the Global Biosecurity State. Indeed, biosecurity, which has supplanted parliamentary sovereignty as the ultimate source of law and the supreme power in the former Western democracies, is the unification of religious and military power; and it's under its absolute authority — the authority of fascism — that we are now living.

6. The Aesthetics of Totalitarianism

'There is, of course, no reason why the new totalitarianisms should resemble the old. A really efficient totalitarian state would be one in which the all-powerful executive of political bosses and their army of managers control a population of slaves who do not have to be coerced, because they love their servitude. To make them love it is the task assigned, in present-day totalitarian states, to ministries of propaganda, newspaper editors and school-teachers. But their methods are still crude and unscientific. The love of servitude cannot be established except as the result of a deep, personal revolution in human minds and bodies.'

— Aldous Huxley, Foreword to *Brave New World*, 1946

1. The Culture of Kitsch

In the Western World there is a common misperception, for which the 'Holocaust' industry is largely responsible, that the aesthetics of fascism is one of hyper-masculinity — the figures of Mussolini and Hitler gesticulating like marionettes, the serried ranks of soldiers lined up in the Piazza Venezia in Rome or goose-stepping across the rally grounds at Nuremberg, the regimented austerity of Guiseppi Terragni's neo-classical buildings and the bulging muscles of Josef Thorak's statues of the ideal man. And undoubtedly this is partly true. But we view these spectacles through the lens of a history that has turned Hitler into Charlie Chaplin's *The Great Dictator*, the Nuremberg Rallies into George Lucas's *Star Wars*, and Arno Breker's Aryan *Ubermenschen* into Sylvester Stallone's *Rambo*. By turns comic ridicule, monstrous caricature or phallic absurdity, it's as if we were looking back on the shambling Boris Johnson, villainous Klaus Schwab or preening Donald Trump in 50 years' time. What we have missed — more accurately, what has been made transparent by the appropriation of fascist politics to the spectacle of post-war capitalism — is the heightened emotion and unity that was created around these spectacles. What we respond to today as sinister or comic or sentimental was experienced at the time — and there are ample testimonies to these effects — as willing submission to a Leader, the joyous unity of a people, the aesthetic ideal to which a national art should aspire.[1]

As the symbolism of the *fasces* makes clear, this is the aesthetics of fascism, perhaps best expressed in the National Socialist motto of '*Kraft durch Freude* (Strength through Joy)'. Behind the fascist salute, the SS uniform and the neo-classical memorial there was the ideal state, the dream of a unified people, the commemoration of fallen heroes, like the Honour Temples built in Munich in 1935 to house the sarcophagi of the sixteen members of the then nascent National Socialist German Workers Party who were killed in the failed Beer Hall Putsch of 1923. While the National Socialist Government that was formed in 1933 embraced the industrial and technological advances of modernity to construct the totalitarian state of the Third Reich, National Socialist art, which had its roots in nineteenth-century German Romanticism, was a violently anti-modernist and conservative aesthetic. At once sentimental and maudlin, it was better represented by paintings such as Adolf Wissel's *Kalenberg Peasant Family* (1939), which was purchased by Adolf Hitler for his personal collection, than the Aryan musclemen that stood outside his chancellery.

This aesthetics, however, was not limited to fascism but characterises all totalitarian states, then and now. A corrective to the West's Hollywood-constructed perception of what lay behind the Iron Curtain was provided in the 1980s by the translation and sudden popularity of the books of the Czech writer, Milan Kundera. Set in and around Prague, his novels provided an insight into daily life in a totalitarian society; and while they contained the tropes familiar to readers of John le Carré and other spy novels that Western ideologues were happy to promote, they also painted a picture of totalitarianism that at once looked back to historical fascism and forward to our present. His breakthrough novel, *The Book of Laughter and Forgetting*, first published in 1979 from Kundera's enforced exile in France and translated into English in 1980, contained a scene set on 28 June 1950, two years after the Communists had come to power in what was then Czechoslovakia. The day before, Milada Horáková, a National Assembly representative of the Socialist Party, had been executed together with the Czech surrealist and historical materialist, Záviš Kalandra, for the crime of plotting to

---

1. See Milton Mayer, *They Thought They Were Free: The Germans, 1933-45*, with a new afterword by Richard J. Evans (University of Chicago Press, 2017).

overthrow the state. André Breton, the French poet and leader of Surrealism, had written an open letter condemning the accusations against his old friend, and Kundera was appalled to see the former surrealist poet, Paul Éluard, dancing in the street at some state-sanctioned celebration.[2] Although estranged from Éluard, who had joined the French Communist Party in 1942 and after the war emerged as the celebrated poet of Stalinism, Breton had asked him to intercede in and condemn the judgement against Kalandra. 'But Éluard', wrote Kundera, 'was too busy dancing in the gigantic ring encircling Paris, Moscow, Warsaw, Prague, Sofia and Athens, encircling all the socialist countries and all the Communist parties of the world.'

In an interview with the US novelist, Philip Roth, published in *The New York Times Review of Books* in November 1980, Kundera revealed that this scene of Éluard dancing in Prague had actually taken place; but he might have been thinking too — the passage has always raised in my mind — of the famous photograph of the Barmaley Fountain taken by Emmanuil Evzerikhin in 1942 during the siege of Stalingrad. This shows the statues of six children — they wear the neckties of Soviet Young Pioneers — holding hands and dancing in a circle around a crocodile, set against the burning wreck of the city. For most cultures the ring is a symbol of unity and happiness, but for Kundera the structure of a ring embodies the condition on which all totalitarianisms are formed. Unlike a row of dancers, which is open to entry from new members joining at either end, the ring is a closed formation, and once you leave it there is no return. The integrity and purity of its form, therefore, is only achieved on the condition of the exclusion of those outside its circle. As every wallflower sitting on the edge of a dance-floor knows, you're either in the ring of dancers or you're on the outside. And for the strength of the unity and the bond of its joy to be sustained, the dancers must justify and explain — at least to themselves — the exclusion of those on the outside. The ring of dancers, therefore, is the expression of totalitarian society, in which everyone must demonstrate their belonging, their belief, their unity, at every moment and joyfully. As Kundera told Roth:

---

2. See André Breton, 'Open Letter to Paul Eluard', in *Free Rein*, translated by Michel Parmentier and Jacqueline d'Ambrose (University of Nebraska Press, 1995), pp. 229-231.

Totalitarianism deprives people of memory and thus retools them into a nation of children. All totalitarianisms do this. And perhaps our entire technical age does this, with its cult of the future, its cult of youth and childhood, its indifference to the past and mistrust of thought.[3]

This is the aesthetics of kitsch as defined by the US art critic, Clement Greenberg, in his 1939 article, 'Avant-Garde and Kitsch'. Greenberg's concern was to distinguish the art of the avant-garde — in painting Pablo Picasso, in poetry T. S. Eliot, in literature James Joyce — he wanted to promote from the mass-produced culture of industrial societies, which he called 'kitsch', and which he equated with 'vicarious experience and faked sensations'.[4] Examples of kitsch, Greenberg said, are the illustrations for covers of *The Saturday Evening Post* by the American illustrator, Norman Rockwell — whose heir in the US culture industry of today is Steven Spielberg — and, in the Soviet Union, the art of socialist realism, which had been made the official culture under Stalin since 1934. Although Greenberg didn't cite him individually, therefore, kitsch includes the public works of the Soviet sculptor, Romuald Iodko, who designed the Barmaley fountain in Stalingrad that survived the assaults of the *Wehrmacht*.

Kitsch, therefore, was not particular to fascism, but rather a product of the expanded role of culture in the modern state. When that state was totalitarian, however — and in this respect Greenberg, like Friedrich Hayek, didn't distinguish between Stalinism, Nazism and fascism — the always tenuous distinction between culture and propaganda dissolved. Like most apologists for US imperialism, however, Greenberg remained blind to the political function of US culture, which after the Second World War went on to dominate the world we live in now. But if we expand his reference to totalitarianism to encompass the most totalitarian culture ever created — the mass culture of US consumerism since the Great War, which colonised the Western World during the Cold War and has achieved almost total global dominance since the dissolution of the Soviet Union in 1991 — his description of its political function is as true today as it was then.

---

3. See Philip Roth, 'The Most Original Book of the Season', *The New York Times Review of Books*, 30 November, 1980; reprinted as an appendix to Milan Kundera, *The Book of Laughter and Forgetting*, translated by Michael Henry Heim (Penguin Books, 1983), pp. 229-237.

4. See Clement Greenberg, 'Avant-Garde and Kitsch', in *Art and Culture: Critical Essays*, Beacon Press, 1961, pp. 3-21.

'The encouragement of kitsch', Greenberg wrote, 'is merely another of the inexpensive ways in which totalitarian regimes seek to ingratiate themselves with their subjects'.[5]

All of which brings us down to the present, in which kitsch defines what passes for art and culture in a UK suddenly devoid of both, and nowhere more so than in the construction of the ideological superstructure of the biosecurity state over the past two-and-a-half years. As an example of which, *The National Covid Memorial Wall* on London's South Bank is state-sanctioned kitsch. Produced by street-art activists Led by Donkeys, it has been described by *The Guardian* newspaper — perhaps the most unstinting national advocate of biosecurity programmes, lockdown restrictions and 'vaccine' mandates and denouncer of protesters as 'right-wing conspiracy theorists' — as 'a memorial to the UK's largest peacetime mass trauma event in more than a century'.[6] Owned by St. Thomas' Hospital and under the jurisdiction of Lambeth Council, in April 2021 the wall served as the backdrop to a photograph of the suitably masked and concerned-looking London Mayor, Sadiq Khan, as part of his successful campaign to be re-elected. Begun a month earlier, in March 2021, the wall's 150,000 pink hearts, painted uniformly under directions displayed on permanent plaques, are meant to represent the officially enshrined number of deaths then attributed to COVID-19.

We now know — and many of us have suspected since this lie was first told — that the actual number of deaths caused by COVID-19 in the UK is many times lower than this deliberately inflated figure. On 16 December, 2021, the Office for National Statistics grudgingly revealed that, between March 2020 and September 2021, deaths attributed to COVID-19 in England and Wales in which the deceased had no pre-existing health conditions numbered 17,371, of which 13,597 (78 per cent) were 65 years of age or older; while in Scotland, between March 2020 and

---

5. Clement Greenberg, *Art and Culture*, p. 19.

6. See Dorian Lynskey, 'Wall of love: The incredible story behind the national Covid memorial', *The Guardian* (18 July, 2021). Examples of this newspaper's promotion of the regulations and programmes of the UK biosecurity state include George Monbiot, 'It's shocking to see so many leftwingers lured to the far right by conspiracy theories' (22 September, 2021); Nicola Davis, Ashley Kirk and Pamela Duncan, 'Covid lockdown shows signs of working in England, expert says' (19 November, 2020); Nicola Davis, 'Do Covid vaccine mandates work?' (3 December, 2021); and Andrew Gregory, 'Covid passports could increase vaccine uptake, study suggests' (13 December, 2021).

November 2021, there had been just 884 such deaths, 585 of which (66 per cent) were 70 or over.[7] Then a month later, the Office for National Statistics further revealed that, between 1 February 2020 and 31 December 2021, just 6,183 deaths in England and Wales had COVID-19 listed as the only cause on the death certificate.[8] 4,596 of these deaths (75 per cent of the total) were of people 70 years of age or older, and 3,388 (55 per cent) were 80 or older, roughly the average life expectancy in the UK. Just 1,587 people under 70 died with COVID-19 as the only cause of death. 3 of them were under 20.

Admittedly, COVID-19 can be responsible for precipitating the death of someone who is already suffering from cancer or heart disease or dementia or some other fatal health condition — over all of which, however, under changes to the certification of deaths in the UK, COVID-19 must always takes precedence in identifying the 'underlying cause'; so the latter figure of just over 6,000 deaths is not the definitive count over this period. But it and the former figure of around 18,000 deaths in two years point toward the actual impact of COVID-19 on overall mortality in the UK, which is nowhere near the 150,000 hearts on *The National Covid Memorial Wall*. These figures also show that, even among those with no pre-existing health conditions or other listed cause of death, COVID-19 is still overwhelmingly a danger to the elderly, and has never constituted a threat to the health of the general public.

It's also necessary, if we are to understand the ideological role of such memorials, to put these figures into context of mortality rates in the UK, something the UK Government, media and NHS never did in their eagerness to terrorise the population into compliance with lockdown restrictions. In the five years before the coronavirus 'crisis' reached the UK, between 26,000 and 30,000 deaths in England and Wales had their underlying cause identified as influenza or

---

7. See Office for National Statistics, 'Deaths from COVID-19 with no other underlying causes' (16 December, 2021), FOI Ref: FOI/2021/3240; and National Records of Scotland, 'Deaths involving COVID-19 by pre-existing conditions, by age group, March 2020 to November 2021'. Even these reductions from the official totals aren't sufficient, however, as under WHO classifications U07.2, U09.9 and U10.9, a death can be attributed to COVID-19 if it is merely the 'suspected' cause, occurred from any cause after infection, or is from a multisystem inflammatory cause 'associated' with COVID-19.

8. See Office for National Statistics, 'COVID-19 deaths and autopsies Feb 2020 to Dec 2021' (17 January, 2022), FOI Ref: FOI/2021/3368.

pneumonia every year.[9] In 2019, the year before the 'pandemic' was declared, there were 1,752 deaths reported on UK roads, which is similar to the level seen every year since 2012.[10] That's more than the number of people under 70 who died of COVID-19 alone in two years. Each year in the UK, around 6,000 people die following an accident at home, and falls are the largest cause of accidental death among over-65s.[11] That's more than the 4,994 people over 65 who died from COVID-19 alone in two years. Also in 2019, there were 5,691 registered deaths by suicide in England and Wales, which is nearly as many as died from COVID-19 alone in 2020 and 2021 combined.[12] In comparison, in 2018, the most recent year for which the ONS has published the figures, 40,214 people died from heart disease in the UK, 26,579 from dementia, 18,587 from lung cancer, and 14,708 from influenza and pneumonia.[13]

As I wrote in the preface, I've published several articles about how the coronavirus 'crisis' has been manufactured through changes to disease taxonomy, changes to the medical criteria and procedures for attributing the cause of death, data manipulation and a lack of context in publishing it, and above all of the effects of lockdown itself on the health and lives of the nation.[14] Even the corporate media, earlier this year, belatedly admitted that the official figures are far too high; although, as the Government threatened us with lockdown again, there was a backlash of new wildly increased estimates.[15]

---

9. See Office for National Statistics, 'Deaths from influenza and pneumonia 2015-2020' (30 November, 2020).

10. See Department of Transport, 'Reported road casualties Great Britain, annual report: 2019' (30 September, 2020).

11. See Becky Hickman, 'The biggest cause of accidental injuries at home are falls — how can we prevent them?', *RSA* (12 October , 2021).

12. See 'Suicides in England and Wales: 2019 Registrations', Office for National Statistics (1 September, 2020).

13. See Office for National Statistics, 'Leading causes of death, UK: 2001 to 2018' (27 March, 2020).

14. See Simon Elmer, 'Manufacturing Consensus', collected in *COVID-19*, pp. 66-93; 'Lockdown', collected in *COVID-19*, pp. 123-158; and 'Lies, Damned Lies and Statistics', collected in *Brave New World*, pp. 112-136.

15. See Sarah Knapton, 'High Covid death rates skewed by people who died from other causes, admits Sajid Javid', *The Telegraph* (19 January, 2022); and Naomi Grimley, Jack Cornish and Nassos Stylianou, 'Covid: World's true pandemic death toll nearly 15 million, says WHO', *BBC* (5 May, 2022).

The truth is, we'll never know how many people died of COVID-19 in the UK, because the bodies have been cremated and autopsies were not conducted under changes to the law made by The Coronavirus Act 2020.[16] But the Government's claim of nearly 150,000 deaths 'with' COVID-19 in two years — raised to an even more improbable 200,000 by August 2022 — is clearly a product of criteria designed to terrorise the population into compliance with the construction of the Global Biosecurity State around, between and within us over the past two-and-a-half years. It's a principle of quantum physics that the observed is a product of the conditions of observation, and this manufactured 'crisis' has been a demonstration of the truism that what we call 'facts' are a product of the discursive procedures designed to produce them. However, although we'll never know the truth, we can still identify a lie when we see one, and the coronavirus 'crisis' is a lie — one of the biggest in modern history, if not the biggest: a unique product of our global political economy and the power of digital technology to manufacture a virtual reality more convincing than the evidence of our own experience. In this respect, as in the immense economic and human cost of the lockdowns it justified and which are very far from being over, it belongs in the long line of crimes against humanity and the lies invented to conceal them by totalitarian regimes, from the gulag of the Soviet Union to the US-led invasion of Iraq.

By any measure, for the World Health Organization to designate a virus with an infection fatality rate similar to seasonal influenza and to which most of the population was statistically immune as a 'pandemic' was as politically motivated as the decision of our Government to declare an 'emergency period' that justified it removing our constitutional rights and freedoms for two years; but to commemorate this period in a 500-metre long wall of pink hearts is kitsch. We might ask where the equivalent wall is for the far more numerous deaths of people at the same age from the major killers in the UK, which are mourned by their family and friends but pass without a public memorial year after year? Where is the

---

16. Under Section 19 of the Coronavirus Act 2020, which was made into law on 25 March 2020, a doctor who had not seen the deceased was empowered to certify the cause of death as COVID-19 without the body being referred to a coroner for a confirmatory medical certificate before cremation of the remains. See Simon Elmer, 'The State of Emergency as Paradigm of Government: Coronavirus Legislation, Implementation and Enforcement' (12 May, 2020), collected in COVID-19, pp. 94-122.

commemoration of the tens of thousands who will die from the cancer and heart disease undiagnosed and untreated during the reduction of healthcare under lockdown? Where is the memorial to the tens of thousands of elderly citizens suffering from dementia who were left to die in care homes under 'Do Not Resuscitate' orders while the state banned them from treatment in our emptied hospitals?[17] Since COVID-19, according to all the evidence, was not a pandemic and hasn't been experienced as such by the British people outside the propaganda with which we continue to be indoctrinated, from where do these pink hearts come? The answer is: from the enshrinement of kitsch as the official culture of the biosecurity state.

2. The Ideology of Woke

What Greenberg called 'kitsch', a loanword from the German language, is today called 'woke', which comes from African-American vernacular English. Like kitsch, behind the sentimentality and diversity of woke culture there lies the force of the authoritarian state. As Greenberg wrote in 1939 (this is the full passage from which I quoted earlier):

> Where today a political regime establishes an official cultural policy, it is for the sake of demagogy. If kitsch is the official tendency of culture in Germany, Italy and Russia, it is not because their respective governments are controlled by philistines, but because kitsch is the culture of the masses in these countries, as it is elsewhere. The encouragement of kitsch is merely another of the inexpensive ways in which totalitarian regimes seek to ingratiate themselves with their subjects [18]

The same can be said of the relation between culture and politics today. It would be politically naive to believe that the Conservative Government of Boris Johnson or of his successor, Liz Truss, cares about the proclaimed values of woke; yet it is on the hegemony of this ideology that the erasure of our democracy,

---

17. See Dave West, 'NHS hospitals have four times more empty beds than normal', *HSJ* (13 April, 2020); and Angeline Albert, 'CQC uncovers "serious concerns" of human rights breaches linked to blanket do not resuscitate orders', *Care Home* (18 March, 2021).

18. Clement Greenberg, *Art and Culture*, p. 19.

our rights, our freedoms and our politics is being justified by the UK biosecurity state.

To take just one example, in anticipation of the Police, Crime, Sentencing and Courts Act, which was made into UK law on 28 April, National Rail and London Underground now display notices by the British Transport Police informing passengers that 'touching someone inappropriately', 'making unsolicited remarks' and 'staring at someone in a sexual way' now constitutes 'sexual harassment', and encourages the victims of such touching, speaking and staring — or, crucially, those who claim to have witnessed such acts — to report the incident to the British Transport Police. It remains to be seen whether this will lead to an epidemic of denunciations from a righteous public empowered to enact vengeance against the non-compliant. But just as, in the two years since March 2020, the rights and freedoms of the entire population were removed on the justification of protecting us from a virus that constituted a threat almost exclusively to the elderly and already seriously ill, so now, on the justification of reducing the harassment of women in public, more and more of our behaviour, our speech and our actions are being subjected, under primary legislation, to surveillance, monitoring, control and punishment. To state the obvious, the intrusive staring, physical abuse and verbal harassment we need protecting from is that of the UK biosecurity state, whose powers of digital surveillance, media manipulation, facial recognition technology, private data storage, and police assault, arrest and punishment have increased beyond measure or justification over the past two-and-a-half years. Indeed, some of the transport posters are illustrated with staring eyes, representing both the eyes of the public on which the state has placed its prohibition, and the eyes of the state monitoring us for non-compliance. As he has been for some time now, Big Brother is watching us.

The National Covid Memorial Wall is only one example of kitsch being used to entrench the new ways of thinking and feeling, the new meanings and values, the new social practices and behaviours of the Global Biosecurity State in UK society. As I've mentioned, the 'clap for the NHS' was one of the first state rituals to encourage public collaboration by 'outing' non-compliance through a sort of aural panopticon — and a realisation, significantly, of the Black Lives Matter slogan that 'silence is violence'. But other cultural forms include the manipulative and shaming NHS posters of 'Covid-19 patients' daring us not to comply with, obey or believe the Government's justifications for lockdown restrictions with variations on the phrase: 'Look her in the eyes and tell her you never bend the rules'. Another was the bullying and assault of citizens in the public realm by police officers acting far beyond any legislative basis, and which, documented and reported across both social and corporate media, served to dissuade similar lack of compliance from the general public. Perhaps most ubiquitous were the infantilising 'Thank you/We Love You' NHS rainbow posters imitating the drawing of a child that became almost obligatory in the window of every pub, shop or home under lockdown — and which, as Kundera said, sought to turn us into a nation of children.

As examples of the UK biosecurity state trying — with generally overwhelming success — to ingratiate itself with its citizens, these all rely on what we today take as given and therefore do not see, which is the introduction of aesthetics into politics. As I discussed in the previous chapter, as early as 1935 the German cultural critic, Walter Benjamin, identified the aestheticising of politics that has become so ubiquitous in the former neoliberal democracies of the West as a product of fascism. But over the past two-and-a-half years it has become not only all pervasive and unrelenting, but now has at its service all the forces of the state and the private sector. This includes the almost weekly spectacle of protests by the mostly urban, white, middle-class acolytes of woke ideology that represent the ideal citizen of the Global Biosecurity State — masked at all times, tracked by their own smart phones, tested regularly and at their own expense, injected as many times as they're told to, compliant with whatever regulations the Government imposes. Obedient.

More recently, as I discussed in the previous chapter, we've had the ritual of 'taking the knee' as a protest against 'any form of discrimination', and which has been extended from sportsmen to woke politicians. This includes, in the UK, the leader of the Labour Party, Keir Starmer, who had himself photographed performing this gesture in June 2020, when the Conservative Government, under the third Amendment to the Health Protection (Coronavirus, Restrictions) (England) (Amendment) (No. 3) Regulations 2020, had banned protest in the UK.[19] Proscribed forms of discrimination presumably excludes that authorised by

---

19. See Andy Gregory, 'Black Lives Matter: Keir Starmer takes knee in solidarity with "all those opposing anti-black racism"', *The Independent* (9 June, 2020).

Western governments' 'vaccine' mandates, or committed by the governments or companies or sovereign investment funds that own the English Premier League's clubs, whether that's the United Arab Emirates, Saudi Arabia, Egypt, Russia, China, Thailand, the USA or, indeed, the UK itself. As an example of sport being used to wash the dirty reputations of investors, 'taking the knee', which originally signalled a quarterback ending play and running the clock down, has turned the disruptive gesture of the American footballer, Colin Kaepernick — a quarterback who has been blacklisted from playing professional football in the US for his protest — into another example of the obligatory virtue signalling by which woke ideology exerts its cultural influence and, increasingly, its legislative authority over us.

The universal compliance of every media, sporting, cultural and artistic institution in the West with the vilification of everything Russian, and the virtue signalling of compliance through the display of Ukrainian flags, is a demonstration and continuation of the unprecedented political consensus created by the Global Biosecurity State over the past two-and-a-half years. Quite apart from the political naivety of participating in such public displays, none of these cultural spectacles would look out of place in a fascist state. None of them do look out of place according to the fascist aesthetics of the UK biosecurity state. If we weren't certain already, the farcical willingness with which the UK population has responded to the Government's suggestion to either take up arms against Russia or open their homes to Ukrainian refugees shows just how susceptible the population is to state propaganda.[20] Indeed, we are reaching such a state of compliance — a genuinely fascist state of citizenship — that there is almost nothing that, as a nation, we won't believe, obey or do.

In the course of writing this book I watched the recording of a discussion titled 'What is . . . Fascism?' that was held in October 2017 at the Battle of Ideas, a forum at which I have spoken on a couple of occasions, but which is liberal in its political orientation, its primary aim being to defend and practice freedom of speech.[21] On the panel were three academics: Kevin Passmore, Professor of

---

20. See James Randerson, 'UK's Liz Truss: I support Brits who take up arms against Putin', *Politico* (27 February, 2022); and Michael Gove, '"Homes for Ukraine" scheme launches' (14 March, 2022).

21. See Jacob Furedi, Jane Caplan, Roger Griffin, Kevin Passmore and Bruno Waterfield, 'What is . . . Fascism?', *Battle of Ideas*, 29 October 2017.

History at Cardiff University; Roger Griffin, Professor of Modern History at Oxford Brookes University; and Jane Caplan, Professor Emeritus of Modern European History at Oxford University and Visiting Professor at Birkbeck, University College London; plus a journalist, Bruno Waterfield, the Brussels Correspondent for *The Times* newspaper. The academics — as is their wont — took refuge in problematising the term 'fascism' as a description of a single and unified ideology, political movement or government; but all the panel unreservedly confined the accusation of fascism to the usual suspects — Russia and far-right groups in Europe and the USA — without once addressing whether fascism is a term that can be applied to the neoliberal democracies of the West.[22] The most the Chair, Jacob Furedi, a journalist for *The Daily Mail*, would concede is that the Brexit referendum signalled a return of nationalism to the political agenda of the UK. But it never occurred to any of the panel that the Government that had Julian Assange under lock and key for five years in the Ecuadorian Embassy, that imprisons refugees from war and political oppression in immigration camps, and that the previous year had passed the Investigatory Powers Act 2016 into law, could for a moment be described as 'fascist'.[23]

---

22. This blinkered definition of fascism is characteristic of the taxonomic concerns of academic studies. See, for example, the pages titled 'Other Times, Other Places' in Robert O. Paxton, *The Anatomy of Fascism* (Penguin Books, 2005), pp. 172-205.

23. Nicknamed the 'Snoopers' Charter', the Investigatory Powers Act 2016 requires internet service providers and mobile phone companies to keep records of everyone's browsing histories for 12 months, including on social media, e-mails, voice calls and mobile phone messaging services, and gives the police, security services and a range of Government Departments access to the data, as well as new powers to hack into computers and phones to collect communication data in bulk. Authorities able to access the internet connections records of UK citizens include the Metropolitan Police Service, the City of London Police, the British Transport Police, the police forces of Scotland and Northern Ireland, of the Ministry of Defence, of the Royal Navy, Military and Air Force, the Security Service, the Secret Intelligence Service, GCHQ, the Home Office, the Ministries of Defence and Justice, the National Crime Agency, the Department of Health, and 26 other authorities. The Act was described by Edward Snowden — the former US National Security Agency contractor turned whistle-blower who in 2013 revealed that GCHQ had been routinely collecting, processing and storing vast quantities of global digital communications, including e-mail messages, posts and private messages on social networks, internet histories, and phone calls — as the 'most intrusive and least accountable surveillance regime in the West'. See Simon Elmer, 'Legislation for the UK Surveillance State', section 3 of 'The New Normal (Part 1. Programmes and Regulations)', *COVID-19*, pp. 198-202.

The audience, however, wasn't satisfied with the panel's sophistry, and demanded a definition of fascism, in response to which Professor Griffin offered this example of the political naivety of middle-class liberalism:

> I can understand the nostalgia for a homogeneous thought. On the other hand, I celebrate and love the fact that I'm living in such an atomised and pluralistic society that I can sit here and spout off and be denigrated, and it really doesn't matter, because it's the absolute plurality of the sort of society that I'm living in, which I love, and allows me intellectual freedom, and means that I can deliver lectures at Oxford Brookes without fear of the Gestapo coming in. And I would say that there is a very real threat to the understanding that what makes this possible historically is a celebration of difference and a celebration of tolerance . . . which means that we do not resort to violence and slogans in order to reduce the complexity of the world and the infinite chaos of our inner selves to some sort of marching simulacrum of a human being.

This tub-thumping declaration of the virtues of Western liberalism, which would be risible in *The Guardian* but is unforgivable in a Professor of Modern History, was met with applause and self-congratulatory calls of 'hear-hear!', as though they were debating in the House of Commons. It had apparently never occurred to Professor Griffin that the reason he is allowed to mouth such platitudes without interference from MI5, GCHQ or the Metropolitan Police Service is because nothing he says presents a threat to the UK state, and that, if anything he said ever did so, he would find his 'pluralist', 'tolerant', 'intellectually free' society as subjected to corporate censorship, state violence and visits from the police as those who have opposed the implementation of the Global Biosecurity State over the past two-and-a-half years.

Finally, Bruno Waterfield concluded the proceedings with a bullish call to maintain trust in people, apparently because that is what maintains the democratic order, and a warning against what he called 'ideologies of mistrust':

> Politics increasingly today is not seen as the rationality of autonomous individuals pursuing conscious interests, but based much more on the idea that humans are motivated by deeper, irrational identification with certain political or racial

groupings, for example. If the true motives of people are beyond the power of reason, then liberal democracy is a lie, a joke, less than a veneer. . . . You need to maintain that optimistic sense, which is a historical reality, that human beings are constructive, that they are not irrational creatures who are driven by passions and dark irrational impulses.

It's difficult to imagine on what historical evidence this statement could be made with any veracity in 2017. Five years later, in 2022, it's hard to hear it as anything other than an example of the bad faith with which middle-class liberals live their increasingly illusory relation to finance capitalism.[24] Asserting as much, however, already says too little and too much: too little, in that it psychologises a class attitude that is also a product of a political ideology that has been long in the formation and which the coronavirus 'crisis' has allowed to assume its official status; and too much, because it risks dismissing what must be understood if we are to understand and change how highly-educated, politically-interested professionals who see themselves as opposed to fascism have become the facilitators and apologists for its return. I agree with Waterfield that liberal democracy is a lie and less than a veneer, although hardly a joke; but in the face of his reaffirmation of Enlightenment rationalism against the baneful influence of identity politics, the coronavirus 'crisis', to the contrary, has shown that the citizens of neoliberal democracies are, incontrovertibly, driven by the dark, irrational impulses he describes — though not, as we have seen, beyond the power of reason to direct their fears and hatreds to political ends.

This is why woke, which likes to present itself as a counter culture speaking for the marginalised and oppressed, is now the official ideology of the Global Biosecurity State, justifying mass surveillance of the population, censorship of dissent, and the expansion of state control over biological life. When trans-activists, for example, declare that any male who declares himself to be female should be treated in every aspect as a female, and that anyone who questions this orthodoxy endangers the lives of transsexuals and should therefore be censored and even arrested, they contribute to and share in the culture of enforced orthodoxies by which the Global Biosecurity State has declared that

---

24. See Simon Elmer, 'Whatever Happened to the Middle Class? Bad Faith and the Culture Industry', *Architects for Social Housing* (10 May, 2019).

anyone questioning the COVID-19 'vaccine' programme is endangering the lives of those who may think twice before being injected, and should therefore be censored and even arrested. In both these examples, whether its trolls on Twitter or the UK Government, those making the declaration have decided unilaterally on the desired outcome (separation of sexual difference from biology and mass compliance with the 'vaccination' programme), and are ready to use the force of the state to enforce compliance, even if that means destroying the reputations and livelihoods of individuals or fining and arresting them.

The possible consequences of such censorship include, in the example of unexamined trans-orthodoxies being enforced through government legislation, public policy and company practice, the biological and emotional development of children being chemically suppressed through so-called 'puberty blockers'; irreversible mutilations performed as medical procedures on the judgement of adolescents and in some cases as a form of self-harming; the dangers of sexually-active males having access to female-only areas and forms of social practice; misogyny and violence against women disguised and excused as trans-rights; the erasure of female identity as a form of charade; and, more generally, the normalisation of a transhumanist agenda at the heart of the technologies and programmes of the Great Reset. In the example of 'vaccine' mandates the consequences include the adverse drug reactions, including irreparable damages to the immune system, heart inflammation and deaths, following injection with experimental bio-technology; the normalisation of discrimination against, and interference with the human rights of, the non-compliant, including being banned from employment and medical care; and, on the justification of enforcing such mandates, the implementation of Digital Identity, Facial Recognition, Social Credit, and all the other programmes of the Global Biosecurity State. And yet, in both these examples, which are also models of how woke ideology will serve to implement biosecurity programmes in the future, none of these consequences have ever been publicly examined or debated, and those calling loudest for and enforcing censorship of that absent debate have never been required to argue or provide evidence for their claims, which have instead been unilaterally adopted as part of the new ideology of biosecurity.

It's for this reason alone that trans-rights — which, even after the huge institutional support and financial backing this movement has received, still apply to only a fraction of a percentage of the population — have become so central to the Global Biosecurity State. Under the colonisation of the West's media, cultural and education institutions by woke, the subjective experience of race, of colour, of ethnicity, most recently of sexual difference and above all of the reviled and unrelentingly attacked working class, is being erased beneath the totalising homogeneity of positive discrimination, enforced diversity and unconscious-bias training, representational quotas and all the other programmes of social homogenisation. Just as the neoliberal ideology of multiculturalism created a global monoculture, so the government and corporate funding and institutional and educational hegemony of woke ideology has subsumed contrary social and political opinions and practices within the homogeneity created by monopolised cultural markets. Indeed, no other movement since fascism has been as adept as woke at creating a nexus for cultural, legal and political change to shore up a failing capitalism, or has more rapidly attained ideological hegemony in the West. And like fascism before it, woke's first task has been to destroy the Left as a viable opposition.

A far cruder use of woke ideology was demonstrated to the world when Justin Trudeau, the Prime Minister of Canada and global champion of neoliberal diversity and inclusivity who in June 2020 had 'taken the knee' at a Black Lives Matter protest in Ottawa, variously described protesters in the same city against his 'vaccine' mandates in January 2022 as 'right-wing', 'violent', 'hate-filled', 'disgusting', 'extremists', 'vandals', 'thieves', 'abusive', 'intimidatory', 'anti-vaxx', 'anti-science', 'racist', 'anti-black', 'anti-Semitic', 'Islamophobic', 'homophobic', 'transphobic', 'misogynistic' an 'insult to truth', and a 'fringe minority' with 'unacceptable views' who should 'not be tolerated'.[25] As confirmation of which, he sent in armed and armoured mounted police and counter-terrorist paramilitaries supported by armoured cars to assault, arrest and imprison them.[26]

---

25. See Leyland Cecco, 'Justin Trudeau takes a knee but is silent on reforms to policing', *The Guardian*, 6 June, 2020. Trudeau made his accusations against the protesters on numerous media platforms, including his Twitter account; but for a summary of the Canadian Government's campaign of slander, see Kurt Mahlburg, 'In Canada it's truck versus tweets and the trucks are winning', *Mercatornet* (11 February, 2021).

26. For documentation of the military-grade weapons and violence employed by the Canadian Government against the Canadian people, see Greg Woodfield, John R. Kennedy and Keith Griffith, 'Trudeau's trucker crackdown begins', *The Daily Mail* (18 February 2021).

Later, he declared to the Canadian Parliament that any MP who stood with the truckers was 'standing with the *swastika*'.[27] Trudeau then evoked emergency powers to freeze the bank accounts of anyone who supported the protest.

What Trudeau didn't address was the legality of the mandates against which the protesters were demonstrating, their rights to bodily autonomy under Canadian and international law, the efficacy and dangers of the still experimental 'vaccines', or the economic consequences for the non-compliant of being discriminated against according to their 'vaccination' status. Instead, the Canadian citizens who had elected him to office were first insulted, then assaulted and finally arrested and in some cases imprisoned for standing up for their human rights. This is woke ideology in power, and why it has been adopted by the Global Biosecurity State to justify the current revolution into a new totalitarianism administered by nation states and governed by an international technocracy.

Finally, beyond the economic sanctions placed on Russia by the West — which mirror the trade embargo the US Empire has inflicted on Cuba for the past 60 years and are just as political in their motivations and ineffectual in their impact — we are now expected to applaud the disgraceful spectacles of Russian and Belarusian tennis players being banned from competing in the Wimbledon tennis championships; of a Russian conductor being fired from his honorary presidency of the Edinburgh Festival; of a programme of Tchaikovsky's music being pulled from a concert by the Cardiff Philharmonic Orchestra; of the cancellation of the residency of the Bolshoi Ballet by the Royal Opera House; of the cancellation of the license to broadcast in the UK of RT News and the blocking of all Russian news channels by Sky, Freesat, Freeview, YouTube, Netflix, Facebook and Google; of the removal of Russian-brewed beers and vodkas from English pubs and bars; and of a Russian oligarch ordered by the Premier League to sell the football club he has owned since 2003, not because of the history of violence and corruption by which he made his billions from the expropriation of the Russian people, but because of his nationality.[28]

---

27. See Catherine Levesque, '"Stand with Swastikas": Emergencies Act debate turns ugly as opposition grows', *National Post* (16 February, 2021).

28. See Wimbledon, 'Statement Regarding Russian and Belarusian Individuals at The Championships 2022' (20 April, 2022); Iona Young, 'Edinburgh Festival cuts ties with Russian conductor Valery Gergiev over Putin support', *Edinburgh Live* (28 February, 2022); Matthew Weaver, 'Cardiff Philharmonic removes Tchaikovsky performance over Ukraine conflict', *The*

This is not only the liberal hypocrisy, virtue signaling, cancel culture and identity politics of woke ideology operating on the world stage, but demonstrates that the historical forces that gave rise to the scapegoating of foreigners and the show trials in National Socialist Germany and the Soviet Union in the 1930s — or, closer in time, to the USA in the 1950s — has reared its ugly head once again in the West. All these are, quite evidently, the actions of a fascist state — or, more accurately, of a satellite fascist state obeying the dictates of the US Empire, much as Austria did those of the Third Reich. Indeed, the geopolitical manoeuvring of the US in the Ukraine, and particularly in the Russian-speaking regions of Luhansk, Donetsk and Crimea, repeats that of Germany in Czechoslovakia in the years leading up to the Second World War.

In April 1938, Hitler had loudly proclaimed that Czechs were slaughtering Sudeten Germans living in the border-lands of Czechoslovakia and threatened to intervene. That September, the Munich Agreement with Britain and France conceded the annexation of the Sudetenland to the Third Reich. Emboldened by this dissolution of the multi-ethnic Czechoslovakia, which has only been created in 1918 after the dissolution of the Austro-Hungarian Empire, in October 1938 both Hungary and Poland annexed parts of Slovakia, and Carpatho-Ukraine, at its far eastern end, proclaimed itself an independent republic. During the occupation, when Czechoslovakia became the Protectorate of Bohemia and Moravia, the Nazi authorities banned Russian ballet. It's not recorded whether they also banned Russian vodka.

Admittedly, in an era in which the UK population can barely recall the lies on which the invasion of Iraq was justified less than two decades ago, one can't expect anyone to recall the history of fascism. Yet following a decade of woke ideology and our habituation to the increased degree and incidence of censorship over the past two-and-a-half years, the populations of the West's former liberal democracies, rather than condemning these actions for what they are, are collaborating in their implementation with all the unthinking obedience and righteous hate they brought to the creation of the Global Biosecurity State.

Guardian (9 March, 2022); Ellie Lorizzo, 'Royal Opera House cancels Bolshoi Ballet London tour', *The Independent* (25 February, 2022); Max Golbert, 'Russian News Channel RT Has UK License Revoked By Regulator Ofcom', *Deadline* (18 March, 2022); Martin Robinson, 'How "Pariah Russia" is steadily being cancelled by the West', *Daily Mail* (2 March, 2022); 'Roman Abramovich has been ordered by Chelsea's soccer league to sell', *NPR* (12 March, 2022).

Meanwhile, neither the totalitarian Kingdom of Saudi Arabia nor the apartheid and fascist State of Israel, despite committing some of the greatest crimes against humanity and violations of human rights of any states since the Second World War, attract none of the condemnation or concerted sanctions Western governments are inflicting on Russia. Indeed, the governments and companies in both the UK and the US continue to arm, train, trade with and give their political support to Saudi Arabia in its violent oppression and brutal execution of its own people and its genocidal war on the people of Yemen, as they do Israel in its 75-year illegal occupation of Palestine, whose people it continues to oppress, starve, imprison, torture and kill with impunity. The ideologues of woke 'standing with Ukraine' while ordering everyone else onto their knees have nothing to say about this silence or the hypocrisy of their collusion with their own governments in the geopolitical manoeuvrings of the West. In this respect, woke ideology functions as more than simply a comfort blanket for liberal inertia and bad faith, and becomes the means by which the violence of the Global Biosecurity State is justified.

Indeed, what the current revolution in the West from neoliberalism into biosecurity is demonstrating is that, far from being opposed to fascism — as it has depicted itself in the culture wars of the past twenty years — woke, with its cult of youth, its saccharine sentimentality, its suppression of memory, its embrace of mob rule, its kitsch aesthetics, its regression to cultural conservatism, its adherence to identity politics, its hatred of the working class, its politicisation of race, its allegiance to the market as the only framework for change, its advocacy of surveillance technology, its collaboration with the police, its extolling of reform over revolution, its suppression of intellectual, cultural and political debate, its normalisation of censorship as the default response to disagreement, its culture of no-platforming those who do not share its principles, its ban on books and authors that do not adhere to its ideology, its organised campaigns to socially ostracise and professionally ruin the uncompliant, the violence with which it demands allegiance to its orthodoxies, the adolescent puritanism of its sexual politics, its creation of ideological hegemony through indoctrination programmes such as 'diversity training', its hierarchy of obedience established by public demonstrations of virtue, its almost universal adoption by our media, police forces, education, sporting and cultural institutions, its enforcement by repressive legislation removing our rights and freedoms on the justification of protecting us from the heterogeneous elements of society, and above all the ease with which it has been employed by national governments, private corporations and the international technocracies they form to increase and expand their political, economic and cultural power — in short, by its facilitation of capitalism's construction of the totalitarianism of the Global Biosecurity State — woke is not liberal, and it certainly isn't socialist: woke is fascist.

7. Fascism, Neoliberalism and the Left

'English Fascism, when it arrives, is likely to be of a sedate and subtle kind (presumably, at any rate at first, it won't be called Fascism). It is quite easy to imagine a middle-class crushed down to the worst depths of poverty and still remaining bitterly anti-working class in sentiment; this being, of course, a ready-made Fascist Party. There is no chance of saving England from Fascism unless we can bring an effective Socialist party into existence. It will have to be a party with genuinely revolutionary intentions, and it will have to be numerically strong enough to act. If we do not get it, then Fascism is coming; probably a slimy Anglicised form of Fascism, with cultured policemen instead of Nazi gorillas and the lion and the unicorn instead of the swastika.'

— George Orwell, *The Road to Wigan Pier*, 1937

In March 1944, when he was a war correspondent in Paris, George Orwell, who had just completed the manuscript for *Animal Farm*, his allegory of the Russian Revolution, published a short article in the *Tribune*, a left-wing British newspaper to which he contributed a column between 1943 and 1947. This instalment was published under the title 'What is Fascism?' Beginning, much as I have in this book, with the observation that the accusation of 'fascist' or 'fascism' has been levelled at everyone from conservatives, nationalists and Catholics to socialists, communists and Trotskyists, Orwell argued that, in addition to being a term of abuse meaning 'something cruel, unscrupulous, arrogant, obscurantist, anti-liberal and anti-working class', 'fascism is also a political and economic system. Why, then', he asks, 'cannot we have a clear and generally accepted definition of it?' Orwell goes on to say that the answer to this question would be too long for his short column, and instead offers this slightly enigmatic statement:

> Basically, it is because it is impossible to define Fascism satisfactorily without making admissions which neither the Fascists themselves, nor the Conservatives, nor Socialists of any colour, are willing to make.[1]

---

1. George Orwell, 'What is Fascism?', collected in *Orwell and Politics*, edited by Peter Davison, with and introduction by Timothy Garton Ash (Penguin Books, 2001), p. 324.

Orwell, unusually, was clearly making concessions to the politics of his newspaper, while at the same time — as was very much his custom — making plain his many criticisms of socialism, which he had just explored more fully and at greater length in his novel. But he was also indicating something else, and that is the overlaps and collusions between fascism, socialism and the political forces of capitalism, including conservativism and, after the war, neoliberalism.

Seventy-eight years later, little has changed, and what has, has changed for the worse. It is not only the sanctimony and puritanism of the Left that the acolytes and foot-soldiers of woke have inherited, but also its political naivety. This has never been more apparent, or been demonstrated to more disastrous effect, than over the past two-and-a-half years, during which the Left, not only in the UK but across the former neoliberal democracies of the West, has been the loudest advocate of the Global Biosecurity State. In this it has repeated the historical failure of the Left to stop the rise and coming to power of fascism in Europe in the 1920s and 1930s. Worse, what was then a failure that bore all the hallmarks of Leftist politics — above all the incessant infighting between anarchists, socialists and communists in the face of fascist unity with capitalists and conservatives — has today become open collusion. Indeed, the willing collaboration of the Left with the violent implementation of the programmes and regulations of global biosecurity by a merger of state and corporate power has forced those of us who call ourselves socialist or communist or even anarchist to address the historical relation between fascism and the Left. In this chapter, I'm going to look at this relation, how it was reconfigured by Western capitalism after the Second World War to formulate the ideological hegemony of neoliberalism, and ask what it can tell us about the function of the Left in the new political paradigm of the West today.

1. Socialism and Fascism

We shouldn't forget that, before they came to power, both Italian fascism and German National Socialism flirted, if only in name, with socialist ideas, particularly about the organisation of the economy. This was done largely in order to appeal to Italian and German workers facing immense economic hardship and exploitation by capitalist landowners and industrialists after the Great War; to gain access to the organisational power of trades unions over the mass of industrial workers; and in a largely failed attempt to draw workers away from the strong communist parties in these two countries. And although, once these fascist movements formed their respective governments, this flirtation rapidly turned to violent anti-socialist policies in fascist states not only in Italy and Germany but across Europe, many workers continued to think of fascism as a form of socialism right up to the point when their trades unions were disbanded, their social and political organisations outlawed, and their party leaders arrested, imprisoned, tortured and murdered.

Here I take just one example from Richard Evans' *The Coming of the Third Reich*, the first volume in his trilogy, in which he follows how the National Socialist German Workers Party (NSDAP) came to power in Germany in March 1933, whereupon it set about destroying all political opposition, not only in the Reichstag but also in the strong Labour movement.[2] To this end, the 'socialist' dimension of National Socialist ideology, which resided in little more than its name, was cynically used by the NSDAP Government to subordinate unions and workers to its rule. Issued by the Reich Government of National Salvation — the coalition of the NSDAP with the conservative and nationalist German National People's Party (DNVP) required to form a majority government but whose members were appointed directly by President Hindenburg — the Law to Remedy the Distress of People and State, which granted Reich Chancellor Adolf Hitler dictatorial powers, was subsequently voted for by every party in the Reichstag except the Social Democrats and the Communist Party — the latter of which had been banned the month before. With Parliament effectively bypassed, Hitler then turned his attention to the trades unions. In April, the Government concluded an agreement with the Liberal and Christian unions to make May Day — traditionally the occasion for the demonstration of the Labour movement's numbers — into a public holiday. In return, the trades unions agreed that it would now be rebranded as the 'Day of National Labour', symbolising the union of nationalism and socialism.

---

2. The following account of the destruction of the German Left by the NSDAP Government is drawn from the pages titled 'Democracy Destroyed' in Richard J. Evans, *The Coming of the Third Reich*, pp. 350-374.

On the day itself, however, the offices of trades unions were decorated in black, white and red, the former national colours of Imperial Germany, and some workers marched under the sign of the *swastika*. Many of these had been threatened with dismissal by their unions for non-compliance; but forced or willing, this union of nationalism and socialism was short-lived. The very next day, on 2 May, 1933, SA and SS stormtroopers occupied the offices of every Social Democrat trade union, took over their newspapers, periodicals, banks and assets, and arrested leading union officials. These were taken into what the NSDAP Government called 'protective custody' — it was claimed for their own safety from the 'righteous wrath' of the German people — in Germany's new concentration camps. In response, the Christian trade unions, like their Church before them, placed themselves unreservedly under the new Government. In July 1933, the Social Democrats joined the Communists — whose combined votes (221 seats in the Reichstag) had exceeded that of the Nazis (196 seats) in the last free elections held in November 1932 — on the list of political parties banned by the Government.

For communists, however, it didn't take until a government was formed in Italy, Germany or Spain to know that fascism was both politically and economically opposed to socialism; but the blame for their success could not all be laid on the ability of capitalists to maintain their grip on the economies of these countries through the hyperinflation of the 1920s and the economic depression of the 1930s. In 1923, the exchange rate in Germany would plummet to an all-time low of 4.2 trillion marks to 1 US dollar. That June, Clara Zetkin, a representative of the German Communist Party in the Reichstag between 1920 and 1933, speaking at the Third Plenum of the Executive Committee of the Communist International, defined fascism not as the revenge of the European bourgeoisie against the militant uprising of the proletariat, but as what she called 'punishment because the proletariat has not carried and driven forward the revolution that began in Russia'.[3] For Zetkin, fascism was a result of reformist socialism, which she argued had caused both workers and revolutionary intellectuals to lose faith in communism and its capacity to change the world, and instead to place their faith in fascism and the ability of the fascist state to remake society.

---

3. See Clara Zetkin, 'The Struggle Against Fascism', in *Fighting Fascism: How to Struggle and How to Win*, edited by Mike Taber and John Riddell (Haymarket Books, 2017).

In the terms I discussed in chapter 5 on the psychological structure of fascism, the forces of attraction exercised by the new imperious elements of Italian, German and Spanish society — specifically, the sovereignty of the fascist Leader, the military model of social and political order fascism imposed, and the religious appeal of fascist dogma and ritual practices — were able to persuade those immiserated by the crisis in capitalism between the two world wars to align themselves with reconstituting homogeneous society, rather than joining its subversive heterogeneous elements to overthrow the capitalist infrastructure that was the cause of their immiseration. Fascism — and this is why it had the support of capitalists — got the rebellious workers and peasants back into the factories and fields.

Ninety years later, the same lie is being peddled, with those opposed to the totalitarianism of the biosecurity state from a libertarian position denouncing it as a form of communism, while themselves being denounced in turn by the propagandists of the Global Biosecurity State, and particularly those on the Left, as 'far-right extremists' for questioning the imposition of its totalitarian programmes. Much of the responsibility for such political naivety comes from forty years of neoliberalism, according to which the expansion of the powers of the state is always a product of the Left, while the Right is equally naively associated with its dismantling.[4] As a result, the Left needed little encouragement to believe that social distancing, the belated declaration of a state of emergency, mandatory masking, lockdown restrictions on freedom of movement and assembly, state-funded furlough, contact tracing, free testing, the collaboration between public and private sectors in the race to find a COVID-19 'vaccine', and even the imposition of 'vaccine' passports, were all forced on reluctant libertarian governments in the pockets of a ruling class only concerned about their profits by the righteous anger of the people — for whom the corporate media were, all of a sudden, speaking. But if there was some justification for the confusion of European workers in the 1930s when confronted by the alliance of fascism and capitalism, there is none today. On such lies have successive neoliberal governments since the 1980s deprived the welfare state of investment and privatised its industries and services; and the coronavirus 'crisis' has been no

---

4. See the pages titled 'The Authoritarian State' in Simon Elmer, *'Cui Bono?'*, collected in *Brave New World*, pp, 164-158.

different, with the UK Government overseeing a massive escalation in the outsourcing of the duties and jurisdiction of the state to the private sector under the cover of lockdown.[5] But one would have hoped that the last two-and-a-half years, which has overseen the greatest transfer of wealth from the poor to the rich in modern history, would have convinced workers in Europe and the West about the economic forces driving the implementation of the Global Biosecurity State, and they're neither socialist nor communist.[6]

It's from this historical perspective that I want to challenge the neoliberal claim that, historically, fascism was a product of socialism, and the corresponding claim, which derives from it, that the authoritarianism of the Global Biosecurity State under construction today represents a communist coup engineered by, or at least modelled on, the People's Republic of China. The second claim is easier to refute. As this book goes to print, China has the strictest and most brutally imposed lockdown of any country in the world, confining 33 cities and 65 million people to restrictions and obligations; and the Social Credit system into which we are being led in the West by the implementation of Digital Identity, Facial Recognition, Central Bank Digital Currency and the Internet of Bodies is undoubtedly based on the Chinese model.[7] Yet the claim that the Global Biosecurity State is a form of communism, despite being widely repeated by libertarians and conservatives alike, does little to illuminate the circumstances of our present. On the contrary, as the corporate and central bank CEOs sitting on the boards of the unelected organisations of global governance that have assumed such authority over our lives in the past two-and-a-half years should

5. In the 12 months to September 2021, 40 'Strategic Suppliers' — private sector companies whose relationship with the Government is centrally coordinated through the Cabinet Office — earned £19 billion from the UK public sector, increasing their revenue by 24 per cent, and representing 11 per cent of overall public expenditure. 20 companies accounted for 75 per cent of that expenditure, and 3 of the companies increased their growth by 100 per cent. The largest suppliers by contract value were Capita (£1.3b), G4S (£1.1b), Microsoft (£1.03b), Capgemini (£600m) and Balfour Beatty (£550m). See James Piggott, '2022 Analysis of UK Government Strategic Suppliers', *Tussell* (19 May, 2022).

6. In the first 12 months of the 'pandemic', the total wealth of the world's billionaires worldwide rose by $5 trillion to $13 trillion, and their numbers increased from 700 to a record total of more than 2,700. See Ruchir Sharma, 'The billionaire boom: how the super-rich soaked up Covid cash', *Financial Times* (13 May, 2021).

7. See Verna Yu, 'China puts 65m people into semi-lockdown ahead of party summit', *The Guardian* (5 September, 2022).

clearly demonstrate, these forces are capitalist through and through.[8] And their intention, far from overseeing a revolution into the triumph of international communism, is to create a Global Biosecurity State ruled by an unelected technocracy composed of state and corporate representatives: a properly totalitarian world the like of which we have never seen before.

But if the second claim is relatively easily dismissed as politically and economically unsupported, the first claim still needs answering, not only as a question of historical record but in order to show why and how fascism has returned to our politics, laws and cultures today in response to the threat to the international economic order. Unlike in the 1930s, however, that threat does not come from international communism but, as it also did in the 1930s, from the crisis in global capitalism which, as I discussed in chapter 4, started in September 2019, and which threatens the entire financial system. Indeed, it is because of the almost total lack of a political movement with the ability or indeed desire to propose a socialist alternative to the periodic and worsening crises of finance capitalism that fascism has returned today with such rapidity, ease and lack of organised opposition. If fascism, as Zetkin argued in 1923, was the failure of socialism to 'carry forward the revolution' and realise the 'genuinely revolutionary intentions' that Orwell, in 1944, identified as the only thing that could avert the return of fascism, what role has the Left played in its covert and disguised return today, when revolution has long been abandoned as a model of change, and self-identifying socialists are reduced to policing the boundaries of identity politics? To answer this question, we have to return to how socialism, despite the history of their violent opposition to each other, first came to be identified with fascism.

2. The Rise of Neoliberalism

As soon as fascism began to win power in Europe in the 1920s, the capitalists who immediately recognised that it could be used to crush the threat of communism began to deny loudly that fascism had anything to do with capitalism while simultaneously cutting deals with its Leaders in parliament and board room.

---

8. See Action Aid Global, et al, 'Open letter – Corporate capture of global governance: The World Economic Forum–UN partnership agreement is a dangerous threat to UN System', *International Network for Economic, Social and Cultural Rights* (20 June, 2021).

Unfortunately for the workers, when the communists were off the streets and the socialists banned from parliament, there was no-one left to oppose the fascists, and the capitalists had enabled a more authoritarian and, in Germany, totalitarian society than even they had bargained for. When the Second World War had been won, therefore, and fascism appeared defeated, the ideologues of capitalism had to win the moral high ground for its defeat. This was difficult, as before three-quarters of a century of Hollywood movies indoctrinated everyone into believing otherwise, everybody knew that it was the USSR, not the USA, that had defeated Nazism. So instead they came up with a plan to discredit socialism. This wasn't too hard, as even the victory of the Red Army hadn't wiped away the memory of Stalin's purges or his short-lived alliance with Hitler. And whether the other side was called fascism or communism, the Cold War soon drew a dividing line between the Western Bloc and the Eastern Bloc in Europe. But neither had the unemployment and suffering global capitalism had caused between the two World Wars been entirely forgotten; and not only in the UK but in France, Italy and across Western Europe, socialism was making a return. Something had to be done, and the solution, extraordinary as it seemed at the time, was to equate socialism with fascism.

One of the strongest exponents of this argument was Friedrich Hayek, the Austrian economist who in 1931 had moved to England, where he taught at the London School of Economics and wrote *The Road to Serfdom*.[9] Published in 1944 in both the UK and the USA, this book went on to become something of a *Das Kapital* for the ideologues of what came to be called 'neoliberalism'. In broad terms, this means the privatisation of state-owned industry and services; fiscal austerity in the form of decreased government employment and spending on public services; deregulation of financial and labour markets and the curbing of union power; and globalisation of trade through decreased tariffs on imports and a global division of labour. Acolytes of Hayek included Milton Friedman, the most influential economist of the second half of the Twentieth Century and one of the earliest theorists of neoliberalism; Augusto Pinochet, the President of Chile between 1973 and 1990, under whose brutal military dictatorship the neoliberal

---

9. See Friedrich Hayek, *The Road to Serfdom: Texts and Documents*; The Collected Works of F. A. Hayek, Vol II. The Definitive edition; edited by Bruce Caldwell (University of Chicago Press, 2007).

project was first implemented by students of Friedman (the so-called 'Chicago Boys'); José Martínez de Hoz, the Minister of Economy in the first years of the Argentine military junta between 1976 and 1981, when the first neoliberal reforms of the economy of Argentina were implemented; Margaret Thatcher, the Prime Minister of the UK between 1979 and 1990 who dismantled Britain's industrial infrastructure and turned London into the financial capital of the world; Ronald Reagan, the President of the USA between 1981 and 1989 who oversaw the rise and global domination of the finance industry over commodity production; and Alan Greenspan, the chair of the US Federal Reserve between 1987 and 2006 whose monetary policies were responsible for the dot-com stock-market bubble of the late 1990s and the subprime mortgage crisis of 2007-2010.[10] So although it would be adapted when applied to the advanced capitalist economies of Western nation states, neoliberalism was first implemented within the framework of military dictatorships installed by political coups engineered by the USA and financed by international corporations that expected to profit from its policies against democratically elected governments. In many aspects, therefore, the rise and colonisation of global markets by neoliberalism in the 1970s and 1980s repeated the rise and coming to power of fascism in the 1920s and 1930s; and to make the justification for its eventual hegemony required a lot of historical revisionism. That's where Hayek was so useful to the ideologues of neoliberalism.

A political manifesto rather than a work of economic theory, *The Road to Serfdom* provided Western governments with the historical and economic arguments to align the Union of Soviet Socialist Republics, their former military ally in World War Two, with German National Socialism — which the former had done more to defeat than all the Western nations put together — and in doing so to wipe clean the historical record of the West's collusion with fascism right up to the moment when it threatened its monopoly over the political economy of Europe and its global markets. One of the difficult questions the West's historical collusion with fascism raised, and which Hayek's book served to silence, is whether fascist governments were so violently opposed to socialism because fascism, politically, was the reaction of capitalism to the threat socialism posed to its hegemony. A

---

10. See Orlando Ortelier, 'The "Chicago Boys" in Chile: Economic Freedom's Awful Toll', *The Nation* (10 October, 2016); and Grace Livingstone, 'Margaret Thatcher's Secret Dealings with the Argentine Military Junta that Invaded the Falklands', *Declassified UK* (29 January, 2020).

more pertinent question for the purposes of this chapter, however, is why — if fascism, to the contrary, was opposed to capitalism — capitalist states had failed to oppose those fascist states militarily until September 1939, and capitalists within those states had financially supported fascist movements and governments long before that. This question applies not only to the two decades leading up to the Second World War, when the UK, France and the USA remained resolutely neutral in the face of fascist political coups and military invasions, but also afterwards, financially supporting fascist dictatorships in Spain and Portugal for three more decades. This contrasts with the willingness of the US to spend an estimated $9 trillion on a Cold War with international communism that spilled over into military invasion across the globe, most violently in Korea and Vietnam, which it was happy to reduce to near ruins.

Like the West's long history of engineered coups and military invasions against socialist governments and support for military dictatorship in Central and South America, Africa, the Middle East and Southeast Asia, this embrace of Portugal and Spain speaks of an alliance of capitalism with fascism against socialism, rather than a hidden identity between the latter. While still under Franco, who only overthrew the Republican Government in 1939 with the military aid of Mussolini and Hitler, and ruled an authoritarian one-party dictatorship until 1975, Spain was welcomed by the US, the UK and other Western allies into the United Nations in 1955. While Portugal, also an authoritarian one-party dictatorship from 1933 until 1974, had been a founder member of the North Atlantic Treaty Organization in 1949, just four years after the supposed defeat of fascism, was voted into the UN at the same time as Spain, and both countries joined the Organisation for Economic Co-operation and Development in 1961. The logical and historical answer, therefore, to the question of why capitalism supported fascism is that — far from being a form of socialism, as the acolytes of Hayek claim — fascism, as I am arguing in this book, was and still is at the heart of the political economy of capitalism — what I have been calling the axe blade it wields in times of crisis, when the political, juridical and ideological *fasces* bound together by its authority threatens to unravel.

Ignoring this history of the structural bond between capitalism and fascism, which continues to this day, Hayek's argument in *The Road to Serfdom* is that, since all centralised planning and organisation of the economy by the state requires a totalitarian system of administrative coercion to impose it, socialism is a stage on the road to fascism. Communism and fascism, according to this economic analysis, are different sides of the same coin, variants of totalitarianism, and only capitalism can guarantee the freedom of the individual. Besides the ongoing evidence of capitalism's long and unparalleled history of oppression and exploitation not only of individuals and nations but of entire races and classes, the fundamental flaw in Hayek's argument is that the 'free market' to which ideologues of capitalism point as the alternative to the centralised planning of the economy and the social and political tyranny to which it supposedly leads is an almost entirely fictional construct of neoliberalism. If a free market ever existed, it was in small market towns in Northern Europe during the merchant capitalism of the Seventeenth Century, and it didn't last for long. But for Hayek, writing in 1944, to describe the monopoly capitalism of the imperialist nations of his own time after a century of globalisation as a 'free market' is historically unsupportable, to put it politely.

Still less does such freedom apply to the finance capitalism of today. Perhaps the most powerful organisations of global governance in the Twenty-first Century are the financial institutions that set monetary policy — that is, interest rates and the supply of money in circulation — which, as we are seeing in the current rise in inflation in the UK, determine the fiscal policy — taxation and spending — of national governments. To call this a 'free market' structurally incapable of producing a totalitarian political system has little descriptive purchase on the neoliberalism of the past forty years, which, to the contrary, has created international corporations with monopolies not just over commodity markets but also over governments and financial institutions. It has none at all on the response of central banks, national governments and international corporations to the global financial crisis of 2019-2020 that resulted in the lockdown of the global economy and the ongoing construction of the Global Biosecurity State which, by any measure, is totalitarian in conception, intention and function.

Indeed, many of Hayek's warnings, in *The Road to Serfdom*, about the effects of the totalitarianism to which centralised economic planning supposedly leads uncannily describe the reality of the Global Biosecurity State today. For example, in his foreword to the 1956 US paperback edition Hayek writes that centralised planning has an 'increasing tendency to rely on administrative coercion and discrimination . . . and to resort to direct state controls or to the creation of monopolistic institutions where judicious use of financial inducements might evoke spontaneous efforts'; and that 'the most important change which extensive government control produces is a psychological change, an alteration in the character of the people'.[11] All of these — government coercion, legislated discrimination, state control, corporate monopoly, financial inducements and the psychological manipulation of peoples to supposedly spontaneous actions — will be familiar to anyone who has lived under some version of the biosecurity state for the past two-and-a-half years.

This doesn't mean, however, that the international technocracy intent on reducing us to the serfdom of Digital Identity, Facial Recognition, Central Bank Digital Currency, Universal Basic Income, the Internet of Bodies and Social Credit is either communist or socialist. Rather, just as happened a century ago, a decaying capitalism undergoing its latest global financial crisis has once again produced a fascist superstructure to give reality to its illusions. If the roughly $10 trillion printed by the central banks of the US and EU since September 2019 has no value outside the financial system of credit in which it circulates — and which it has been magicked into existence to uphold — at least the jackboot of the cop forcing us to obey the governments relying on those illusions for its authority can be real. Only this time, the technological capabilities and financial advances of a hundred years are producing a totalitarianism far more total than anything manufactured by historical fascism. Whether it's pharmaceutical products carrying a microchip registering when they are and are not ingested to ensure 'compliance', a quantum dot dye delivered with a vaccine that stores information about the injected person's vaccine history, a microprocessor storing encrypted payment data implanted under the skin of a person's hand to allow contactless payments, a smart-phone app that tracks an individual's carbon footprint to monitor and control their consumption, or a microchip implanted in their brain to augment reality, the Global Biosecurity State is the dream of fascism awakened to the reality of the present.[12]

---

11. Friedrich Hayek, *The Road to Serfdom*, pp. 44 and 48.

12. The microchipped tablet was announced by Albert Bourla, the CEO of Pfizer, at the World Economic Forum in January 2018; the quantum dot dye vaccine by researchers funded by the Bill and Melinda Gates Foundation at the Massachusetts Institute of Technology in December 2019; the skin implants by Walletmore, a Polish-British startup company, in April 2022; the carbon app

But if fascism, historically, was the response of capitalism to the growing threat of a working-class movement during the protracted financial crisis between the two world wars, why has it returned today, when such a movement doesn't exist in the UK, or indeed anywhere in the former neoliberal democracies of the West? As I discussed in chapter 4, what the international corporate technocracy calls 'stakeholder capitalism' is fairly open about its intensions to reduce the salaries of the workers in the Western World to something like the level to which various forms of capitalism have raised that of the workers in the rest of the world over the past 40 years — and specifically in the newly industrialised economies of Brazil, India and China. And taking a leaf out of the Israel Defense Forces' guide to international relations, the Global Biosecurity State has got its retaliation in first by effectively removing the political, juridical and cultural structures within which such a threat to its totalitarian rule might form. I refer, once again, to the warning issued by the Bank of International Settlements in June 2019, that such a threat to the 'international economic order' was already forming after the Global Financial Crisis of 2007-2009, and that its influence on the future 'will clearly be a force to contend with in the years to come'.

But isn't there a difference between what Hayek meant by the centralised planning of the economy by the governments of nation states and the economic interventions in the economy by the world's central banks, as well as by immensely powerful financial institutions like BlackRock, Vanguard and State Street Global Advisor? Between them, these three international corporate asset managers control $22 trillion in assets, and on average hold more than 20 per cent of shares in the 500 largest companies on the US stock exchange.[13] This gives them something comparable to state authority over the corporations accounting for the bulk of economic activity in the world and the Environmental, Social and Governance policies and criteria by which they operate and with which they must

---

by J. Michael Evans, the Alibaba Group President, at the World Economic Forum's annual meeting in May 2022; and the brain implant by Kathleen Philips, the Vice-President of Research and Design for imec the nanoelectronics and digital technology company, on the website of the World Economic Forum in August 2022.

13. See Olúfẹ́mi O. Táíwò, 'How BlackRock, Vanguard, and UBS Are Screwing the World', New Republic (7 March, 2022).

comply.[14] Indeed, in 2020, after the US Federal Reserve enlisted BlackRock to prop up the entire corporate bond market, the Director of the Division of Investment Management at the US Securities and Exchange Commission called the multinational investment management corporation the 'fourth branch of government'.[15] This is a long way from Hayek's description of a 'free market' as the defender and foundation of a free society; so let's have a look at his argument in more detail, and see if it can tell us anything about those overlaps and collusions between capitalism, fascism and socialism to which Orwell alluded in the same year *The Road to Serfdom* was published.

3. The Road to Serfdom

Hayek's argument for equating socialism with fascism and, conversely, capitalism with freedom rests on an account of Western civilisation that would not look out of place today on the website of the World Economic Forum, and which, like the idea of a 'free market', is a product of the ideology of capitalism, and in particular the neoliberal account of history he did so much to popularise.[16] This begins, inevitably, with the European Renaissance and proceeds, by leaps and bounds, through the emergence of market capitalism in the Seventeenth and Eighteenth Centuries to the great expansion of Western civilisation into the New World. In this history, the British Empire, unsurprisingly, takes pride of place, graciously exporting the concepts of 'freedom' and 'individualism' to its colonies before handing over the baton of 'democracy' to the USA in the Twentieth Century. What this four-hundred years of history demonstrated, according to Hayek, is that economic freedom is the foundation and guarantor of political freedom. Presumably he meant the political freedom of those who profited from this economic freedom, because he fails to mention the 300 years of the slave trade on which globalisation was founded beyond what Hayek calls 'the discovery of

---

14. See Gibson Dunn Lawyers, 'BlackRock, Vanguard, State Street Update Corporate Governance and ESG Policies and Priorities for 2022' (25 January, 2022).

15. See Annie Massa and Caleb Melby, 'In Fink We Trust: BlackRock is Now "Fourth Branch of Government"', *Bloomberg* (21 May, 2020).

16. See, for example, World Economic Forum, 'A brief history of globalization' (17 January, 2019).

some very dark spots in society'.[17] Equally, European colonialism and the economic subjugation of entire continents by globalisation are dismissed as necessary evils to the gradual increase of wealth that economic freedom brought about, at least for those with access to it. And the semi-slavery to which the industrial revolution reduced generations of workers apparently led, by the beginning of the Twentieth Century, to the working man — at least in the Western World — having acquired what Hayek describes as 'a degree of material comfort, security and personal independence which a hundred years before had seemed scarcely possible'.[18]

Although Orwell had read and reviewed *The Road to Serfdom*, Hayek, on the evidence of this statement, had not read *The Road to Wigan Pier*, which had been published only a few years earlier in 1937, and whose arguments for socialism Hayek was intent on dismissing.[19] Despite being one of England's most respected economists throughout the 1930s, Hayek also appears to have forgotten the Great Depression which put 3.5 million British workers out of work, pushed unemployment to 70 per cent in some regions, and from which the UK only fully emerged when the Government moved to a centrally-planned war economy in 1939. In his eagerness to depict the totalitarianism to which the socialist road will supposedly lead anyone who steps onto it, Hayek had not stopped to look around him at where the capitalist road had taken the workers of the West in the past decade, and indeed those of the capitalist world over the past four hundred years. This isn't surprising, because for Hayek, as for all the ideologues of neoliberalism, the subject of history is the universal man of the Renaissance, the rational man of the Enlightenment, and above all the economic man of Modernity whose buying and selling constitutes the invisible hand of Adam Smith's market — an abstraction, in other words, without class, without race, without nation, and therefore without any referent in the material world of unequal and exploitative economic relations.

According to Hayek, however, this triumphant history of the rise and apotheosis of Western civilisation came to an abrupt end with the unification of

---

17. Friedrich Hayek, *The Road to Serfdom*, p. 70.

18. Friedrich Hayek, *Ibid.*

19. Orwell's brief review of Hayek's book, originally published in the *Manchester Evening News* in January 1946, is included in '"The Intellectual Revolt": Pessimists', collected in *Orwell and Politics*, pp. 418-419.

Germany in 1871, at which point German ideas, he says, replaced English ones in the intellectual leadership of the West. And those ideas, which Hayek traces back to the usual suspects of Marx and Hegel, were socialist. Even though, in the 73 years between unification and the publication of Hayek's book, Germany spent 47 of them under the Second Reich and 11 under the Third Reich, with only the 15 years of the Weimar Republic separating them, he nonetheless asserts that the catastrophe of the Second World War into which Hitler had drawn Western civilisation was entirely attributable to the intellectual and political influence of German socialists. Even accounting for the liberal intellectual's self-regard for the power of ideas over the more material forces of history, what Hayek fails to mention in his potted history — what he doesn't account for in his demonisation of socialism — is the Great War of 1914-1918. Even more than the slave trade, colonialism and the industrial revolution — all of which have been dismissed by the ideologues of capitalism as the unfortunate but necessary evils of 'progress' — the Great War genuinely did cause the West to question its motives and trajectory. Genocide could be tolerated when it was inflicted on other races, other countries and other classes; but when the horrors of imperialism were visited on the palaces, governments and banks of Europe, even the leaders of Western civilisation had to pause for breath before returning to the monopoly capitalism that had driven the most powerful nations in the world to self-slaughter.

They had to wait a while, as the period between the two World Wars exposed every lie about capitalism and freedom, with the hyperinflation of the early 1920s impoverishing not just Germany and Italy but also Austria, Hungary, Poland and the Soviet Union; the stock market crash of 1929 laying bare the dangers of globalisation; and the Great Depression of the 1930s inflicting unemployment, homelessness and destitution on millions of workers who had never purchased a share in a company. Rather than the pernicious influence of German ideas, it was this protracted financial crisis in capitalism, which Hayek again fails to mention, that created the collective will to consider an alternative economic model by which to run the world, with some form of socialism being the forerunner. And it was this that so threatened the ideologues of capitalism who emerged from the second world war in two decades having to confront the challenge of international communism.

And what they came up with in its defence, it could be said, was Hayek and his fairytale account not only of the history of capitalism and the benefits of Western civilisation, but also of the economic, political and ideological causes of its decline. His account, however, isn't merely factually inaccurate and, even at the time, outdated in its idealist model of history, it is intellectually fraudulent; and it is on its foundation of lies that the neoliberal defence of the unparalleled and ongoing violence of capitalism has been erected. To understand this, I want to turn briefly to Hayek's economic arguments against socialism, which did so much to avert the West's eyes from the history of capitalism's culpability for slavery, colonialism, unending wars, political oppression, economic exploitation, social inequality, unemployment, poverty, homelessness and famine, all of which continue today.

Hayek began by arguing that socialism is what he calls a 'species' of collectivism, by which he means all planned economies.[20] It's an odd metaphor, which turns the economy into a biological process with one outcome, this being the poisoned fruit of albeit good intentions. This allows Hayek to argue that, although the goals of socialism may be shared by liberals — among whom he includes himself — his argument against socialism turns on the means it advocates to achieve them. These, he claims, have been used by both fascist and communist states to privilege an elite, whether that's defined racially or politically. However, contrary to what Hayek asserts, the centralised command economy of the Soviet Union, the corporatism and later directed economy of Fascist Italy and the mixed war economy of Nazi Germany were very far from being the same. In asserting their equivalence, moreover, Hayek turns socialism — which can embrace the economic policies of the Nordic model employed in Scandinavian countries since the 1930s (social corporatism, collective contract bargaining, mass unionisation of workers and state ownership of industries and services), the post-war UK welfare state, and even European social democracy — into a fixed, monolithic and mechanical system that produces, sooner or later, one product, rather than seeing it as a set of principles or values in whose achievement a planned economy is the primary but not the only means. In this Hayek displays the mechanistic view of history shared by most economists, including many socialist economists, but which is no less reductive for that.

---

20. Friedrich Hayek, *The Road to Serfdom*, p. 84.

Not only that, but having asserted that, because of its use of economic planning as a means to achieve its ends, all socialism must lead to totalitarianism, Hayek then undermines this mechanistic model by arguing that not all planning is bad. According to him, there is a good type of planning, which he calls 'planning for competition' rather than against it.[21] This new distinction rests on Hayek's unexamined anthropological assumption that the best way to co-ordinate the actions of individual humans is through competition and profit, to which capitalist ideology has reduced all human motivations. However, while Hayek goes some way to explaining why a society planned for competition creates higher profits and greater wealth for capitalists, he doesn't explain why it should produce a freer society than one planned for equality. Instead, by relying on beneficent governments and the rule of law to protect society from the corporate monopolies that the unequal acquisition of wealth has produced far more surely than planned economies have produced totalitarian governments, Hayek replaces the ideal government on which a socialist society, according to him, depends to avoid despotism with an equally ideal capitalist society. He even offers the unfortunate prediction that 'a state which allows such enormous aggregations of power to grow up cannot afford to let this power rest entirely in private control'.[22]

The two years since March 2020, in which the rule of law has been jettisoned by neoliberal governments imposing the regulations and programmes of the Global Biosecurity State, have provided a more accurate demonstration of the relationship between the wealth of corporations, the powers of the state and the freedom of populations. Indeed, when Hayek defines freedom as the freedom to 'buy and sell', it's clear that his primary concern is with the freedom of the capitalist, who constitutes a tiny percentage of the population even in the West today, and which history has shown care nothing about the freedom of workers — except that they should have as little of it as possible. But when Hayek offers the opinion that every worker should be free to enter into any trade on equal terms, that the law should recognise the worker's freedom of contract with his or her employer, and that such a contract should compensate the worker for damage to his or her health from the conditions of their work, it becomes clear that the halls of academe from which Hayek viewed the world had cushioned him from the

---

21. Friedrich Hayek, *The Road to Serfdom*, p. 90.
22. Friedrich Hayek, *The Road to Serfdom*, p. 205.

realities of class, labour and the relations of production within which the workers of capitalist economies are employed and unemployed. To call these relations 'free' turns his economics into an apologia for centuries of exploitation, poverty and suffering, which continue across the world today under the hegemony of neoliberalism and the global division of labour on which Western consumerism — not freedom — is founded.

To be fair, Hayek does at least admit that capitalism has a 'propensity' for creating monopolies instead of competition, and that when it does, he writes, 'the machinery of monopoly becomes identical with the machinery of the state'.[23] But he attributes this not to the power of larger companies to undercut smaller competitors and in doing so to take over their market share, but rather to government policies influenced by what he calls 'collusive agreement', which sounds like a polite term for corruption. However, rather than seeing such corruption as the inevitable result of the influence immensely wealthy global corporations wield over national governments, he blames this, once again and quite ludicrously, on the influence of socialist thinking on industry in Germany from the 1870s, which Hayek argues were the first companies to attain monopolies.

Presumably, from his offices at the London School of Economics, Hayek chose to forget the East India Company that rose to control half the world's trade by the mid-Eighteenth Century and practically ran the British Empire in India for a hundred years; or, closer to his own time, US monopolies like the Carnegie Steel Company or Rockefeller's Standard Oil Company, to which even Hayek would have trouble attributing socialist motivations. As for those German socialists of Hayek's fevered imagination, the monopolies that funded and built the Third Reich were not state-owned but bore the names of Germany's most powerful capitalists: Thyssen, Krupp and Siemens-Schuckert, to name just three of the two dozen industrialists who, in November 1932, petitioned the German President to appoint Hitler as Chancellor and, the following year, financed the successful election campaign of the German National Socialist Workers Party with over 2 million Reichsmark. The same could be said today about the CEO's of Amazon, Alphabet, Apple, Meta and Microsoft, five of the biggest companies by market value in the world, which not only exert a joint monopoly over the technology information

---

23. Friedrich Hayek, *The Road to Serfdom*, p. 207.

industry but use that monopoly to police the Global Biosecurity State and finance its organisations of global governance.

This time, Hayek's historical amnesia reads less like the rationalisations of the academic economist wrapped in the comforts of the upper-middle class into which he was born, and more like intellectual fraudulence. Rather than address the centuries of evidence that capitalism produces not competition but corporate monopolies which in our own time are threatening to surpass the influence and control of any centrally planned economy, and not only over international markets but also over national governments, Hayek instead falls back on the image of the small-business entrepreneur as the 'engineer' of freedom and capitalism's sacred cow of the free market. But this begs the question: if the global economy is engineered by the buying and selling of commodities and services by billions of private individuals, why has the financial industry risen to dominate the global economy as it does today?

For the purposes of this chapter, however, my interest in Hayek is less in the lack of historical and economic justifications for his equation of socialism with fascism than in how his arguments were used to create the ideological hegemony of neoliberalism in the West, which continues to champion capitalism as the defender of freedom. It is this double blindness, about both the political reality of the finance capitalism under which we have been living since the 1980s and the chimera of socialism it supposedly protects us from, that has contributed to our failure to understand the nature of the revolution in capitalism marked by the construction of the Global Biosecurity State. This failure is not only in the easily refuted description of this superstructure as 'communist', but also in the widely-held perception that, insofar as it is erasing what freedoms remained to us, the Global Biosecurity State represents a deviation from the principles of capitalism. Against all the evidence to the contrary, the vast majority of the populations who have lived in neoliberal economies for the past forty years, at least in the nation states of the West, continue to believe that capitalism is founded on a free market, on private enterprise, on competition, on consumer demand, and on other illusory self-representations of capitalist ideology, rather than, as is clearly the case, on the monopolisation of markets by global corporations, on the division and exploitation of labour by globalisation, on an economy planned and manipulated by the monetary policies of international financial organisations, and on the bailouts of banks by the nation state whenever the internal contradictions of capitalism result in the ever more frequent crises of a financial system built on credit. Contrary to what the followers of Hayek have argued for the past fifty years and more, this, and not socialism, is the road to serfdom; this, as the present is demonstrating for those with the eyes to see it, is the road to fascism.

Even Hayek, however, had an inkling of this. In the final chapter of his book, 'The Prospects of International Order', in which he warns of the dangers of conferring economic powers on international technocracies, Hayek writes:

> Any international economic authority, not subject to a superior political power, even if strictly confined to a particular field, could easily exercise the most tyrannical and irresponsible power imaginable. . . . And as there is scarcely anything which could not be justified by 'technical necessities' which no outsider could effectively question — or even by humanitarian arguments about the needs of some specially ill-favoured group which could not be helped in any other way — there is little possibility of controlling that power. The kind of organisation of the resources of the world under more or less autonomous bodies, which now so often finds favour in the most surprising quarters, a system of comprehensive monopolies recognised by all the national governments but subject to none, would inevitably become the worst of all conceivable rackets.
>
> It is curious to observe how those who pose as the most hard-boiled realists . . . believe that, once hitherto undreamed-of power is given to an international government, which has just been represented as not even capable of enforcing a simple Rule of Law, this greater power will be used in so unselfish and so obviously just a manner as to command general consent. If anything is evident, it should be that, while nations might abide by formal rules on which they have agreed, they will never submit to the direction which international economic planning involves — that while they may agree on the rules of the game, they will never agree on the order of preference in which the rank of their own needs and the rate at which they are allowed to advance is fixed by majority vote. Even if, at first, the peoples should, under some illusion about the meaning of such proposals, agree to transfer such powers to an international authority, they would soon find out that what they have delegated is not merely a technical task but the most comprehensive power over their very lives.

What is evidently at the back of the minds of the not altogether unpracticable 'realists' who advocate these schemes is that, while the great powers will be unwilling to submit to any superior authority, they will be able to use those 'international' authorities to impose their will on the smaller nations within the area in which they exercise hegemony. There is so much 'realism' in this that by thus camouflaging the planning authorities as 'international' it might be easier to achieve the condition under which international planning is alone practicable, namely, that it is in effect done by one single predominant power. This disguise would, however, not alter the fact that for all the smaller states it would mean a much more complete subjection to an external power, to which no real resistance would any longer be possible, than would be involved in the renunciation of a clearly defined part of political sovereignty.[24]

Is there a more prescient description of how the illusion of averting humanitarian disasters is being used today by the 'international' technocracies of the West, under the predominant power of the US, to impose a system of economic monopolies that include Sustainable Development Goals, Environmental, Social and Governance criteria, Central Bank Digital Currency, Universal Basic Income, Pandemic Prevention, Preparedness and Response, and other programmes of the Great Reset?

The failure to understand the reality of our present has already had disastrous consequences for what was left of our freedoms, most obviously in the belief held by the majority of the populations of the neoliberal democracies of the West that what we underwent between March 2020 and March 2022 was a perhaps overzealous and undoubtedly destructive but nonetheless justified response to a viral pandemic that threatened Western civilisation. Just as importantly, perhaps, the failure to see the Global Biosecurity State as the next stage in the development of Western capitalism has done much to paralyse the forces that might have opposed its almost uninterrupted conquest of the West in little more than two years. The simplest answer to the widely-asked question of why coronavirus-justified restrictions and regulations have so suddenly been dropped is that they are no longer needed. As demonstrated by the ready adoption of the World Health Organization's Pandemic Preparedness Treaty by every Western government

---

24. Friedrich Hayek, *The Road to Serfdom*, pp. 229-230.

without a referendum, parliamentary vote, public debate or even mention in the media, the facade of democracy the Global Biosecurity State struggled to maintain over the two years of lockdown, 'vaccine' mandates and other erasures of our human rights and freedoms is now all-but redundant outside the media platforms of information technology companies. The propaganda, of course, will continue and even increase, in order to keep the Left chattering on social media; but the political, legal and cultural superstructure of the nation state is no longer capable of holding the new international technocracy to account, and is knuckling down to its new role as administrator and enforcer of its dictates.

4. The Function of the Left

The question, then, to which I return after my long digression through neoliberalism's attempts to consign socialism to Reagan's 'ash heap of history', is why the Left of today, if it isn't proto-fascist as Hayek claimed, has collaborated so willingly with the Global Biosecurity State, which is capitalist in its economic infrastructure, fascist in its political, legal and cultural superstructure, and totalitarian in its implementation of a New World Order?[25] I've already addressed aspects of the answer in 'Political Perspectives', the opening section of the third part of my report on the UK 'vaccination' programme, a version of which was published by *Left Lockdown Sceptics* in October 2021.[26] I won't repeat all my arguments here, but I will draw on this text to make the following attempt at an answer to this question, which has so confused those on the Left who are opposed to this new form of totalitarianism.

If, by the Left, we mean in the UK the Labour Party and those trades unions, political organisations and pressure groups that advocate voting for it every time there's an election, then the UK Left has little or nothing socialist in its principles, politics or practices. For those of us who read its policies and oppose its actions in town hall and local authority, Labour is irrefutably and even openly a party whose political philosophy is founded in the principles of neoliberalism. This is,

---

25. Reagan's phrase, which he used to describe Marxism, is from the speech he gave to the UK House of Commons in June 1982.

26. See Simon Elmer, 'The UK "Vaccination" Programme. Part 3: Resistance' (1 October, 2021), collected in *Virtue and Terror*, pp. 111-140; and 'Open Letter to Left Lockdown Sceptics', *Left Lockdown Sceptics*, 17 October, 2021.

perhaps, most demonstrably evident in its collusion in the marketisation of human needs such as housing and the financialisation of those markets by global capital.[27] Moreover, anyone who has knocked around the Left also knows that, whatever its so-called 'left-wing' elements and organisations argue between elections, when it comes to supporting or opposing the policies and practices of Labour in government at municipal or local authority level, they all toe the party line, keep silent and vote Labour.

It has come as no surprise to me, therefore, that the UK Left, including not only Labourites but the wide diaspora of people who call themselves 'Leftists' and even 'socialists', have become fervent ideologues of the biosecurity state. But it's not, as Hayek and his acolytes argue, because of the inherent authoritarianism of socialism that leads it to impose a totalitarian social model at the first opportunity. There is — it can't be repeated too often — little or nothing socialist — in the Labour Party nothing, in its affiliates and fellow travellers little — about the policies or practices of the UK Left. Even those small groups and independent organisations that are openly critical of Labour have adopted the UK Left's almost universal support for biosecurity restrictions, remain indifferent to the immiseration and suffering of the UK working class they are causing, and steadfastly refused to join the millions of UK workers protesting against their imposition, having instead uncritically accepted and adopted the Government's and corporate media's dismissal of those workers as 'far-right conspiracy theorists'.[28]

I said earlier that the political naivety of the Left disposed it to welcome the regulations and programmes of the biosecurity state as the triumph of the common good over government incompetence and 'right-wing' greed; but that was two-and-a-half years ago, and naivety has become bad-faith and denial in the face of the vast apparatus of global biosecurity that's been constructed around, between and within us. That doesn't mean, however, that the Left now regrets its collaboration, which of course continues today; or hasn't obstinately confined its protests to the erasure of our rights and freedoms being enacted by

---

27. On the neoliberalisation of housing policy in the UK, see Simon Elmer, 'Supply and Demand in Centre Point Residences', *Architects for Social Housing* (6 November, 2018); and 'The Labour Party Manifesto on Housing', *Architects for Social Housing* (21 November, 2019).

28. See, for example, James Meek, 'Red Pill, Blue Pill', *The London Review of Books* (22 October, 2020).

the wave of new legislation introduced on the back of 582 coronavirus-justified Statutory Instruments, without admitting any relationship between them. The betrayals and duplicities of the Left are legion, but many socialists are still asking how it came to this.

What all the Left shares — and the origin of its otherwise inexplicable collusion with the implementation of the UK biosecurity state — is the former's decades-long infiltration by the neoliberal ideologies of multiculturalism, political correctness, identity politics and, most recently, the orthodoxies of woke, about which I wrote in chapter 6. In some organisations, the infiltration is marginal and exists, under the umbrella of 'intersectionality', in an uneasy and usually unexamined co-existence with the slogans — if not the practices — of socialism. In others, such as the Labour Party and its affiliates, what socialist principles they may once have had have been entirely replaced by the values and orthodoxies of these relatively new ideologies, which have manifested themselves in such youthful, energetic and well-funded movements as Momentum, Black Lives Matter, Extinction Rebellion, and now the masked-up advocates of the Global Biosecurity State. These are all pro-capitalist movements, hostile to the working class, and directly if not openly opposed to socialism; and it's by their principles that the Left has operated for some time in the UK as in all the former neoliberal democracies of the West. It can't be long before we see a similar movement, funded by the same or even more powerful capitalists and corporations, formed to support the next stage in the UK biosecurity state — particularly for the adoption of a Universal Basic Income for those impoverished by lockdown, spiralling inflation, rising energy prices and the mass automation of services by the Fourth Industrial Revolution. And like its predecessors, this movement of the COVID-faithful will claim a position on the UK Left by criticising the Conservative Government's response to this or the next 'crisis', and in doing so will help create an even greater consensus among UK youth and the liberal middle-classes for increased online surveillance, stricter laws, harsher sentences, more intrusive technologies of public control and greater police powers to enforce them. As we saw most publicly in the counter demonstrations organised across Canada during the blockade against 'vaccine' mandates in February 2022, the Left didn't hesitate to align itself with the Government of Justin Trudeau and the riot police he deployed, denounced truckers as 'white supremacists' and every other insult in the woke handbook, while waving placards telling working men and women facing unemployment and destitution at the hands of the biosecurity state to 'check their privilege'.

This largely middle-class, neoliberal Left, which today constitutes a homogeneous force of compliance across the biosecurity states of the West, did not suddenly become devotees of the restrictions and programmes imposed on the justification of a threat to public health that never existed. On the contrary, the Left is the Church in which the COVID-faithful have been raised, its guiding religion and cultic practices formed by the same radically conservative beliefs. To state again what should be obvious to all: no-platforming, cancel culture, misogyny disguised as trans-rights, policing of speech and opinion, and all the other symptoms of this totalitarian ideology did not emerge from a politics of emancipation, class struggle or wealth distribution. They emerged from, and are advocates for, authoritarian practices of censorship, suppression of debate and punishment of non-compliance that are culturally inseparable from the technologies of surveillance and control developed by finance capitalism to police and protect its borders. These, of course, are not the borders between the nation states that finance capitalism straddles like a colossus and across which the Global Biosecurity State now controls our movements to a degree hitherto unimaginable to the children of multiculturalism, but rather the borders between the international corporations and offshore jurisdictions through which global capital flows and scrutiny by, or accountability to, what remains of the public sector in those nation states.

Far from the Left being, as some have claimed, under some form of collective hypnosis or programming — presumably from the propaganda of the Right — it is from the Left that we hear the most Puritan demands for displays of public virtue, for the harshest punishments to be imposed on unbelievers in the new faith of biosecurity. There is a direct line of ideological influence between the Black Lives Matter slogan that 'silence is violence', the 'rebels' groomed by Extinction Rebellion to offer themselves for arrest, and the ideologues of 'zero-COVID' denying human rights to those who refuse to comply with the dictates of the Global Biosecurity State. Just as, for the past century and more, trades unions under Labour's duplicitous leadership have repeatedly sacrificed UK workers to the interests of UK capital, so the Left has handed over UK youth to the UK biosecurity state. To claim that this corporate, technocratic, authoritarian, repressive, violent and totalitarian ideology has anything in common with the emancipatory aims of socialism shows just how little the ideologues of the Left know or care about socialist politics, socialist principles or socialist practices, except insofar as it exists to suppress any organisation that attempts to enact them.

Indeed, with such willing compliance from the Left, is there any need anymore for the ideologues of capitalism to extol its supposedly unique ability to defend our freedoms? The declarations of a New World Order made at the concurrent meetings of the World Economic Forum and the World Health Organization this May strongly suggest not. As an ideological principle, 'freedom', which was largely an invention of Western propagandists after the Second World War both to differentiate Western imperialism from fascism and in order to give consumer capitalism a veneer of morality against the more obvious moral claims of socialism, is well and truly off the political agenda today. Fascism — although, as Orwell predicted, imposed under another name ('biosecurity', 'net zero', 'stakeholder capitalism', etc.), no longer under the authority of a sovereign Leader but sedate and subtle, and in this country appearing in a slimy Anglicised form — is the new common good to which all of us are being compelled to sacrifice our human rights, our privacy, our bodily autonomy, our freedoms. And the truth the Left continues to refuse to face up to is that none of this could have been achieved with such speed and ease without its collaboration.

But is that all? Can so momentous a historical failure, which may one day equal that of the failure of the Left to defeat the rise of fascism a century ago, be attributed entirely to the ideological erasure of socialism not only from the parliamentary parties and political organisations of the Left but also from the ideology of its membership and fellow travellers? If the psychological structure of fascism, as I discussed in chapter 5, is the pull between an almost childlike obedience to the imperious forms of authority that operate above the law, and a visceral hatred of the impoverished, the diseased, the ostracised and the criminalised, what can we say about the psychological structure of the Left in the West in 2022? Is the Left now, in effect, fascist? And if it is, was Hayek right, after all, about socialism being a stepping stone to fascism?

The answer to both these questions must be 'no': not only because the past forty years of neoliberalism in the West, far from overseeing the increased organisation of the economy by socialist or even social-democratic governments, have instead witnessed the outsourcing of public services to the private sector and deferral of economic policy to international financial institutions; but also because the division of the political spectrum on which Hayek's argument rested into Left and Right — with social democrats and socialists, respectively, one and two steps to the Left, and liberals and conservatives one and two steps to the right — no longer has any descriptive purchase on the political paradigm of the Global Biosecurity State.

As I argued in chapter 6, the authoritarian orthodoxies of woke ideology have been employed by self-styled 'liberal democracies' under some of the most authoritarian and anti-working-class governments in recent history — including those of Boris Johnson in the UK, Emmanuel Macron in France, Mario Draghi in Italy, Karl Nehammer in Austria and Viktor Orbán in Hungary — in order to subordinate the Left to the Global Biosecurity State. 'Subordinate' is perhaps the wrong word, because, at the same time, notionally left-wing governments — including those of Pedro Sánchez in Spain, António Costa in Portugal and Magdalena Andersson in Sweden — as well as Left political parties in opposition, have been just as ready to embrace the Global Biosecurity State on the woke principles of safety, censorship and a paternal state. And, of course, liberal and conservative governments — including those of Olaf Scholz in Germany, Mateusz Morawiecki in Poland, Alexander de Croo in Belgium, Mark Rutte in the Netherlands, Sanna Marin in Finland and Kyriakos Mitsotakis in Greece — have long since made woke orthodoxies the foundation of their political platforms, and rapidly deployed them in their opportunist response to the coronavirus 'crisis'. This unity of response by the notionally politically differentiated governments of European nation states, together with their willing subordination to the new technocracies of global governance, has demonstrated — hopefully once and for all — that Left and Right no longer exist as positions within the new biopolitical paradigm of the West.

One could argue that they haven't for some time. Tony Blair, the former Prime Minister of the UK and one of the West's most influential ideologues of neoliberalism, whose New Labour party did so much to close the Overton

Window, replaced Left and Right with what he called 'Open and Closed', with the former in favour of neoliberalism, multiculturalism and globalisation, and the latter with protectionism, cultural conservatism and anti-immigration. In this new political spectrum, in which so-called 'openness' more accurately describes the ideology of the Left, the socialist values of political emancipation, economic equality and wealth redistribution have been removed altogether, with the middle-classes enjoined to openness and the working class dismissed as closed. Of course, with the revolution of Western capitalism into the Global Biosecurity State, 'open and closed' have taken on very different meanings, with the 'open' advocates of neoliberalism now demanding lockdown, the imposition of 'vaccine' passports as a condition of travel and mandatory medical intervention as a condition of employment, and the 'closed' workers defending their rights and freedoms. Indeed, insofar as the residual polarity between Left and Right has served to divide opposition to the biosecurity state, with compliance depoliticised as obedience to medical 'measures' issued by supposedly non-political technocratic advisory boards (whether SAGE or the WHO), the collaboration of Left and Right has facilitated the imposition of the biopolitical paradigm of the state. Just as *The Road to Serfdom* allowed neoliberals to reduce politics to economics — most famously expressed in Thatcher's slogan that 'There Is No Alternative' (TINA) — the sanctimoniously repeated mantra of the COVID-faithful that the coronavirus crisis is 'above politics' is the dream of a post-political totalitarian world in which, whatever party is elected to administer its dictates, the state and its powers remain at the disposal of the same international organisations of global governance.

The Left, therefore, is not fascist, but neither is it socialist in any recognisable sense of the term. As the last two-and-a-half years have demonstrated more clearly than any other recent event in the history of the West, the Left is a residual but still functioning political form of the power of the nation state to assimilate, through the spectacles of parliamentary democracy and street protest, the potentially subversive heterogeneous elements of society into the homogeneous political order, in order to protect the productive forces of the economy from the crises of finance capitalism. The coronavirus 'crisis', and the collaboration of the Left in constructing the Global Biosecurity State, is the demonstration of this function.

8. The Camp as Biopolitical Paradigm of the State

'The fear of concentration. camps and the resulting insight into the nature of total domination might serve to invalidate all obsolete political differentiations from Right to Left and to introduce beside and above them the politically most important yardstick for judging events in our time, namely: whether they serve totalitarian domination or not.'

— Hannah Arendt, *The Origins of Totalitarianism*, 1951

What are the biopolitical forms of the new paradigm of governance that has emerged in the West from the manufactured coronavirus 'crisis' of 2020-2022?

1.   The state of emergency as the permanent form of biopower;
2.   The camp as the biopolitical paradigm of the state;
3.   Digital Identity storing biometric data linked to the Internet of Things.

We might call these, respectively, the political, spatial and juridical forms of the Global Biosecurity State in formation, which combined are superseding the formerly dominant model of politics based on the now residual and soon to be redundant separation of powers between executive, legislature and judiciary. What need is there for a legislature when the executive can make any regulation into law under a politically-declared state of emergency? What need for a judiciary when the rule of law has been superseded by a totalitarian system of surveillance, control and punishment administered by artificial intelligence? What need for an executive when the powers and authority of the state have been placed in the service of global technocracies? Indeed, as an emergent paradigm of governance, the Global Biosecurity State represents the end of the classical model of politics in the West.

The first two of these biopolitical forms of governance are repetitions of historical forms of fascism, though with far greater powers of enforcement. The third, however, is the dream of fascism, and its imposition, therefore, perhaps warrants a new term. Describing new formations of power, however, only serves a purpose if it enables a clearer understanding of and — hopefully along with that understanding — opposition to those forms. If the description of the Global Biosecurity State as the return of 'fascism' alerts the populations of the nation states enforcing it to the reality of what we are facing, then we should use this term. If, on the other hand, it allows the ideologues and propagandists of biosecurity to dismiss our warnings, as they did so successfully over the first two years of its construction with the accusation of 'conspiracy theory', then it serves the implementation of these forms. What, then, are the arguments and evidence for using the term 'fascism' to describe this new paradigm of governance? In this chapter, I'm going to focus on the use and expansion of the camp as the paradigm of the biosecurity state.

1. The Chinese Model

In the previous chapter I argued that, despite claims by libertarians opposed to the imposition of the Global Biosecurity State, the revolution in Western capitalism we are undergoing does not represent a communist coup engineered by the People's Republic of China. That does not mean, however, that China has not provided a model for the programmes of the biosecurity state. As is widely known by now, Professor Neil Ferguson of Imperial College London — whose fraudulent and exaggerated predictions of the death-toll from SARS-CoV-2 were used to justify the imposition of lockdown in the UK and the USA — in an interview in *The Times* published in December 2020 revealed that the Scientific Advisory Group for Emergencies, half of whose members were drawn from Government departments, didn't believe that the citizens of neoliberal democracies in the West would accept the removal of their rights and freedoms tolerated by Chinese citizens, and were amazed and delighted in equal measure when the imposition of lockdown restrictions in Italy suggested they would.[1] 'It's a Communist one-party state, we said. We couldn't get away with it in Europe, we thought. And then

---

1. See Neil Ferguson, et al., 'Report 9. Impact of non-pharmaceutical interventions (NPIs) to reduce COVID-19 mortality and healthcare demand', *Imperial College London* (16 March, 2020). This predicted 550,000 deaths in the UK if we did nothing, 250,000 if we isolated the vulnerable and quarantined the infected, and 20,000 if the Government that commissioned his estimates locked down the country.

Italy did it. And we realised we could.'[2] For Ferguson and his fellow technocrats in SAGE, therefore, the model for the regulations and programmes of the biosecurity state was undoubtedly China, which for some time now has subjected its citizens to a totalitarian system of digital surveillance, monitoring, control and punishment based not only on their adherence to laws but also on their compliance with the requirements of good citizenship.[3]

It's also true that the Chinese system of so-called Social Credit is one toward which we are being led through the programmes and technologies of the biosecurity state, including Digital Identity and Universal Basic Income, and which Central Bank Digital Currency will take to the next level of control. First announced in June 2014 and with implementation beginning in 2020, the year following the outbreak of SARS-CoV-2 in Wuhan, Social Credit is not yet a unified, nation-wide system, but the Chinese Government plans to make it mandatory for everyone.[4] Under this system, the trustworthiness of not just citizens but also of companies and government bodies are currently monitored and assessed by financial, criminal, governmental and online-credit data bases, but may in the future also include video surveillance, real-time data transfers, tax payments, bank loan repayments and employment disputes. According to the *South China Morning Post*, Social Credit rankings are decided by the National Development and Reform Commission, the People's Bank of China and the Chinese court system.[5] Nobody outside the Government knows how the scores are arrived at, but behaviour that

---

2. See Tom Whipple, 'Professor Neil Ferguson: People don't agree with lockdown and try to undermine the scientists', *The Times* (25 December, 2020).

3. In the first months of the 'pandemic', Nicholas Wright, a medical doctor and neuroscientist who works on emerging technologies and global strategy at University College London, the New America think-tank and the Georgetown University Medical Center, in an article also published in *Belt & Road News*, an organ of China's global strategy for infrastructure and investment in nearly 70 countries and international organisations, argued that one of the significant 'legacies' of the coronavirus 'crisis' would be the spread of digital surveillance enabled by artificial intelligence, and insisted that Western liberal democracies must overcome their historical attachment to human rights in order to keep pace with China. See Nicholas Wright, 'Coronavirus and the Future of Surveillance', *Foreign Affairs* (6 April, 2020).

4. See China Copyright and Media, 'Planning Outline for the Construction of a Social Credit System (2014-2020)' (14 June, 2014); and Jessica Reilly, Muyao Lyu and Megan Robertson, 'China's Social Credit System: Speculation vs. Reality', *The Diplomat* (30 March, 2021).

5. See Amanda Lee, 'What is China's social credit system and why is it controversial?', *South China Morning Post* (9 August, 2020).

incurs a negative score includes failing to repay a loan, bad driving, smoking in non-smoking zones, walking a dog without a leash, buying too many video games, wasting money on frivolous purchases, spending too much time on social media, and posting online what the Government deems to be 'fake news'.[6] A positive rating could result in an offer of priority health care, deposit-free renting of public housing, discounts on energy bills, and better interest rates at banks; while a negative rating could see individuals banned from flights, trains and even access to education and credit, with their expenditures limited in size and content and their internet speeds slowed down. For companies, a negative rating can mean sanctions and punishments including court orders and fines, as well as restrictions on government-approved land-use rights, public procurement and investment permits, subsidies and tax rebates. In a manner already familiar in the social-media-addicted West, citizens and companies deemed untrustworthy are publicly named and shamed.

Indeed, it is to the Chinese model of Social Credit that the former UK Secretary of State for Justice, Dominic Raab, has been preparing British citizens through the proposed reforms to the Human Rights Act, which will supplant the universality of human rights with the constantly changing obligations of citizenship within the UK biosecurity state. When these reforms become UK law — and given the professional incompetence and intellectual cowardice of the worst Parliament in British history there is no reason to believe they won't — rights described in 1948 in the Universal Declaration of Human Rights as 'indivisible, inalienable and universal' will become contingent on the citizen's compliance with the changing requirements of what international technocracies decide are the obligations of citizenship at any given moment in a permanent state of emergency. And just as China's Social Credit system also applies to companies, this has already been replicated by the UN's Sustainable Development Goals programme, which allocates capital, investment and other preferential treatment to governments and corporations according to their compliance with its Environmental, Social and Governance criteria.[7]

---

6. See Katie Canales, 'China's "social credit" system ranks citizens and punishes them with throttled internet speeds and flight bans if the Communist Party deems them untrustworthy', *Business Insider* (24 December, 2021).

7. See Thomas Brock, 'Environmental, Social, and Governance (ESG) Criteria', *Investopedia* (28 May, 2022).

History has demonstrated that neither the governments of nation states nor international courts of laws and treaties defend or uphold the human rights of stateless individuals or people; but the imposition of the Global Biosecurity State nevertheless represents a historic watershed in the conception of human rights, and therefore, I would argue, in the West's definition of what it is to be human. Indeed, when governments can decide, as they did across the Western World in 2021 and 2022, that our natural biological state is, by default, a threat to our fellow citizens, and it is therefore the state's right and duty to correct it with biotechnology injected not only into adults but also into children almost from the moment they are born, then we have clearly moved from a humanist conception of man that has been under assault for over a century into a post-human world in which the human organism is being reduced to little more than a host for the emerging biotechnologies of the Fourth Industrial Revolution.[8]

In Shanghai, the largest city in the People's Republic of China, 26 million people were kept in the most severe lockdown from April 2022 under the Government's 'zero-COVID strategy'.[9] Effectively placed under house arrest, residents were either prohibited from leaving their homes or allowed to do so at designated times to buy essential goods like food. Workers in white hazmat suits forcibly entered residents' homes to spray them with disinfectant. Businesses were closed, and millions of poorer residents who cannot afford, or do not have access to, online food services faced hunger. The worst affected were the hundreds of millions of low-income migrant labourers in China. The Chinese Government uses mass surveillance of mobile phone, rail and flight data to track down citizens who have travelled to affected regions. Individuals suspected of being infected are tracked through their credit-card transactions and CCTV footage. Neighbourhood monitors log the movements and temperatures of individuals. Facial recognition algorithms identify commuters who aren't wearing a mask or who aren't wearing one properly. Health and other databases have been integrated so that hospitals, clinics and chemists can access the travel information of their patients. Self-quarantine is enforced through location-tracking smartphone apps in compulsory wristbands. Government-issued identity cards

---

8. See Simon Elmer, 'Our Default State: Compulsory Vaccination for COVID-19 and Human Rights Law' (8 January, 2021); collected in *Brave New World*, pp. 95-111.

9. See Ed White, Andy Lin, Dan Clark, Sam Joiner and Caroline Nevitt, 'How China's lockdown policies are crippling the country's economy', *Financial Times* (1 June, 2022).

are required in order to buy SIM cards for mobile phones or tickets on state-run rail companies and airlines. Robot dogs roam streets and apartment blocks, barking orders at residents to maintain social distancing, wash their hands, test their temperature, and other biosecurity restrictions and obligations. Where the dogs can't reach, police-operated drones perform the same task. Anyone caught breaking quarantine is caught by hazmat-suited officials using man catchers and prosecuted under the new laws on pandemic management. Protesters are severely beaten by riot police. All residents in quarantined cities and blocks are required to take regular PCR-tests, with those refusing having their 'Health Code' status downgraded from green to yellow, indicating that they need isolating or medical treatment and restricting their movements. The Health Code, which is run by algorithms according to rules formulated by the Chinese Government and requires a smart phone, is linked to traffic data, operator data and financial institution payment data, and can track a person's movements within fourteen days. Those who test positive are sent to quarantine camps. Some of these are converted factories, warehouses, schools and conference centres, others are residential blocks that have been forcibly emptied of residents. The biggest are purpose-built camps that can hold up to 5,000 inmates. In the two months since late March, there were less than 140 deaths in Shanghai attributed to COVID, less than the 186 deaths caused by lockdown restrictions, including through lack of medical care and suicides.

It's difficult to keep track of how many people are affected by the 'zero-COVID' policy at any one moment in a country as large as China; but on 1 June, 2022, it was estimated that 130 million people in at least 16 cities in China were under full or partial lockdown. Since the virus was first reported in Wuhan in December 2019, two-and-a-half years before, there have been 5,226 deaths officially attributed to COVID-19 in a nation of 1.4 billion people, or 1 in every 268,000 of the population. China's zero-COVID strategy is not expected to change before autumn 2022, when Xi Jinping, since 2012 the General Secretary of the Chinese Communist Party and Chairman of the Central Military Commission, and since 2013 President of the People's Republic of China, will attempt to use the 20th National Congress of the Chinese Communist Party to cement his third term as leader, following the abolition of presidential term limits in 2018. As I wrote earlier, in September 2022, 33 cities and 65 million people are under some form of lockdown restrictions. As a demonstration of how the Chinese model of the biosecurity state works, in June this year bank depositors were stopped from attending a planned protest in Zhengzhou against the freezing of their accounts for the past two months by the simple expedient of identifying the intended protesters and turning their Health Code red, prohibiting them from travelling and confining those who tried to 'quarantine'.[10] If the libertarians are right, and China is the model for the Global Biosecurity State, then this post-human world is our immediate future, openly described and promoted by the World Economic Forum under the guise of Smart Cities, Facial Recognition, Digital ID and the Internet of Bodies, and in the course of being implemented by the nation states of the West imposing this new paradigm of governance on their populations without recourse to any recognisable democratic process.[11]

There is another model, however, and another way to answer the question of whether we should describe this new paradigm of governance as fascism. This is to look at the use of this paradigm not in the state-capitalism of China today but in neoliberal states long before the coronavirus 'crisis' was manufactured. This, I think, will give us a more accurate understanding of how the political, juridical and cultural forms of the Global Biosecurity State will be enforced on the populations of the West, who although far more servile and obedient than even the technocrats in SAGE and WHO could have believed, have had their political values formed around the concept of 'freedom' for too long to give it up all at once. There is one state, in particular, where elements of this biopolitical paradigm have already been implemented, trialled and approved by the neoliberal states of Western capitalism for three-quarters of a century, and which is therefore coexistent with the organisations of global governance created by the West after the Second World War to promote this concept as the alternative to international socialism. I refer, of course, to the apartheid State of Israel, which today more closely resembles the nation states of historical fascism than any other country, and above all in its use of the camp as the biopolitical paradigm of the state.

---

10. See Tess Wong and BBC Chinese, 'Henan: Chinese Covid app restricts residents after banking protests', *BBC* (14 June, 2022).

11. See World Economic Forum, 'G20 Global Smart Cities Alliance' (February 2022). On the imminent 'roll-out' of these programmes in the UK, see note 38 on pages 58-59 (Chapter 3, 'The Fascist State and Human Rights').

2. The Apartheid State of Israel

The exemplary application of this paradigm is the Gaza Strip, to which Palestinians escaping the *Naqba* fled in 1948, and whose borders were fixed by the armistice between Israel and Egypt in February 1949. Initially administered under the military authority of Egypt, Gaza was subsequently occupied by Israel in 1967 during the Six-Day War. In 1993, its administration was taken over by the State of Palestine, which also exercised partial authority over areas in the West Bank; but Israel retained control over its borders, airspace and territorial waters. In 2005, Israel withdrew its settlement camps and soldiers from the Gaza Strip. The following year, Hamas, the Islamic fundamentalist political party, won the Palestinian legislative elections and expelled Fatah, the social democratic party, thereby creating two separate governments in the Occupied Palestinian Territories. In response, Israel imposed a blockade on the Gaza Strip that continues to this day.

Although Israel now describes Gaza as a *de facto* independent state, it maintains direct external control over the strip and indirect control over life within it. In addition to Gaza's air and maritime space, Israel also controls six of Gaza's seven border crossings, only one of which is currently open, and it reserves and exercises the right for its military to enter Gaza at will. Israel maintains a buffer zone within the already limited territory of Gaza, which in 2010 it expanded to 300 meters, and on which newly-built Palestinian homes are regularly bulldozed and farmers who try to cultivate the land are gunned down by Israeli Defence Forces. Gaza is dependent on Israel for water, electricity, telecommunications and other utilities, and the population is not free to leave or enter, or to import or export goods freely. As a result of this blockade, Gaza today, with a population of over 2 million people on 365 square kilometres of land in which 17 percent is off limits to Palestinians, is the third most densely populated political authority in the world, and 70 per cent of its inhabitants are living below the poverty line.

In December 2021, Israel announced the completion of the enhanced militarised barrier by which its blockade of Gaza is maintained.[12] Stretching 65 kilometres (40 miles) around the Gaza Strip and out into the Mediterranean Sea,

---

12. See Anna Ahronheim, 'Israel completes upgraded barrier with the Gaza Strip', *The Jerusalem Post* (7 December, 2021).

the double-walled barrier cost US$1.1 billion to construct, extends 6 meters above ground and an undeclared number of metres below ground to block tunnels, and is armed with antennas, cameras, radars and a sea barrier. Watchtowers every 2 kilometres are equipped with remote-controlled machine guns, and motion sensors are inserted into the fence between and the ground beyond. As a result of the buffer zone beyond, 35 per cent of arable land and 85 per cent of fishing waters along the Gaza coast are off-limits to Palestinians. Under new rules of engagement for Israeli soldiers, any Palestinian in this zone is shot. After 15 years of maintained blockade, 52 per cent of Gaza's population is unemployed, 80 per cent is dependent on international assistance, 97 per cent of the drinking water is contaminated, 39 per cent of pregnant women and 50 per cent of children are anaemic, and 17.5 per cent of children suffer from chronic malnutrition, which is increasing. Israel only allows food imports that are vital for the survival of the civilian population.

In May 2021, the Israel Defense Forces, which includes 160 fighter jets, bombed Gaza with high-explosive weapons dropped on heavily populated areas for 11 days. The result was 259 Palestinians killed, including 66 children and 41 women, and 2,211 injured. In addition, 6 hospitals and 11 medical clinics were destroyed, 53 schools, a bookshop that held an estimated 100,000 books, as well as 1,042 homes and commercial units in 258 buildings, including 4 residential tower blocks. The Israeli Government claimed these towers were being used by Hamas for military purposes. However, Human Rights Watch has challenged the truth of this claim, declaring that the air strikes 'violated the laws of war and may amount to war crimes'.[13] The UN Office for the Coordination of Humanitarian Affairs estimated that 72,000 Palestinians have been displaced as a result of these strikes.[14] During the Israeli offensive, social media posts by Palestinian activists documenting the effects of the bombing on Facebook, Instagram and Twitter were censored or removed and their accounts suspended. Meta subsequently issued a statement that there had been a 'technical glitch' at the time. At the end of the month, Israeli police arrested 348 Palestinians. In August 2021, in mass protests along the Gaza barrier, 40 Palestinians were injured, including a 12-year-old boy

---

13. See Human Rights Watch, 'Gaza: Apparent War Crimes During May Fighting' (27 July, 2021).

14. See Tovah Lazaroff, 'UN: There is no 'safe place' in Gaza, 72,000 people displaced', *The Jerusalem Post* (19 May, 2021).

who was shot in the head by Israeli soldiers. Omar Hasan Abu al-Nil later died from his wounds. The protests continued into September, when more Palestinians were killed by the Israel Defense Forces. During the last days of the air strikes on Gaza, the foreign ministers of Germany, the Czech Republic and Slovakia visited Israel to expressed their countries' support for Israel.

In a speech made in the House of Commons during the air strikes, the UK Minister for the Middle East, James Cleverly, declared that Israel had a 'legitimate right to self-defence'.[15] In response to questions about the UK's arms deals to Israel, Cleverly added: 'The UK has a robust arms export licensing regime and all export licences are assessed in accordance with it'. In fact, since May 2015, the UK has licensed £400 million of arms sales to Israel: £183 million on military technology; £104 million on aircraft, helicopters and drones; £20 million on grenades, bombs and missiles; £4.6 million on armoured vehicles and tanks; £1.9 million on ammunition, and £1 million on small arms.[16] And far from having a robust licensing regime, the UK has issued 43 open licences, which allow for unlimited exports.[17] On top of this direct arming of the Israel Defense Forces, BAE Systems, the UK arms manufacturer and largest 'defence' contractor in Europe, produces 15 per cent of the value of every US F-35 fighter, the same model that was used in the bombing of Gaza in May 2021.[18] At a cost of $78 million each, Israel has ordered 50 of these stealth fighters for its 'defence'. In December 2020, Israel and the UK announced a joint military agreement whose contents are classified, but which is thought to cover air, land, maritime, space, and cyber and electromagnetic warfare.[19] The British Armed Forces already deploys Israeli-manufactured drones over theatres of war. Then in November 2021, Liz Truss, the UK's Secretary of State for Foreign, Commonwealth and Development Affairs, signed a 10-year trade and defence deal with Israel, promising a closer alliance

---

15. See Jon Stone, 'UK Government backs Israel's bombardment of Gaza', *The Independent* (20 May, 2021).

16. See 'Israel: Frequently asked questions', *Campaign Against Arms Trade* (13 May, 2021).

17. See Department for International Trade, 'Open general export licence (exports in support of joint strike fighter: F-35 Lightning II)' (6 January, 2014).

18. See BAE Systems, 'BAE Systems brings its military aircraft expertise to the development, manufacture, integration and sustainment of the F-35'; and Judah Ari Gross, 'IDF says it launched major offensive on dozens of rocket launch tubes in Gaza', *The Times of Israel* (11 May, 2021).

19. See 'UK and Israel sign military agreement', *5 Pillars UK* (7 December, 2020).

on cybersecurity and technology.[20] Israeli spyware has already been used against journalists, lawyers and human rights defenders in the UK.[21] As of September 2022, Lis Truss is the Prime Minister of the UK, and James Cleverly it's Foreign Secretary.

In February 2022, Amnesty International made a submission to the UN Human Rights Committee based on its 2022 report titled *Israel's Apartheid against Palestinians: Cruel System of Domination and Crimes against Humanity*. Among its many condemnations of the extensively documented human rights abuses by the State of Israel, this report stated:

> All governments and regional actors, particularly those that enjoy close diplomatic relations with Israel such as the USA, the European Union and its member states and the UK, but also those states that are in the process of strengthening their ties — such as some Arab and African states — must not support the system of apartheid or render aid or assistance to maintaining such a regime, and cooperate to bring an end to this unlawful situation. As a first step, they must recognize that Israel is committing the crime of apartheid and other international crimes, and use all political and diplomatic tools to ensure Israeli authorities implement the recommendations outlined in this report and review any cooperation and activities with Israel to ensure that these do not contribute to maintaining the system of apartheid. Amnesty International is also reiterating its long-standing call on states to immediately suspend the direct and indirect supply, sale or transfer of all weapons, munitions and other military and security equipment, including the provision of training and other military and security assistance.[22]

This detailed and rigorously documented 280-page report on the human rights abuses committed by the State of Israel against the Palestinian people under its power was immediately condemned by Zionist organisations around the

---

20. See Dan Sabbagh, 'Britain and Israel to sign trade and defence deal', *The Guardian* (28 November, 2021).

21. See Joe Tidy, 'Pegasus: Spyware sold to governments "targets activists"', *BBC* (19 July, 2021).

22. See Amnesty International, *Israel's Apartheid against Palestinians: Cruel System of Domination and Crimes against Humanity*, 2022, pp. 34-35.

world as an 'anti-Semitic' attack on the State of Israel.[23] An example of how identity politics is used to defend the crimes of Western imperialism, this condemnation and dismissal of the report was echoed by government ministers in the US, UK, Germany, France, Austria, the Czech Republic and Australia.[24] Then, at the end of February, Russia invaded the Ukraine, and the following month the UK's Foreign Secretary addressed the UN Human Rights Council in Geneva:

> The UK stands united in condemning Russia's reprehensible behaviour. There are no shades of grey to this conflict. It is about right and wrong. The UK is proud to be at the forefront of support for Ukraine economically, politically and defensively. We were the first European nation to send defensive weapons to the country, and we are leading the way in humanitarian support.[25]

The UK has yet to make a statement condemning the human rights abuses and war crimes committed against the Palestinian people in Israel and the Occupied Territories, who for 74 years have lived under an apartheid regime largely financed by the USA and armed by successive UK governments. Instead, as of 15 August 2022, the UK has sent £2.3 billion of military support to the Ukraine.[26]

It is a tragedy of Biblical dimensions that the Jews of Israel now more closely resemble the perpetrators of the *Shoah* than any other nation state, right down to creating their own *Untermenschen* in the Palestinian people, and Gaza is their Auschwitz. At the end of *The Origins of Totalitarianism*, where she reflects at length on the use of concentration camps in both the Third Reich and the Soviet Union, Hannah Arendt observes that, although these camps initially held first political prisoners and then professional criminals, the latter of which were used by the SS to enforce the camp's regime, the third and by far largest category of

23. See, for example, Institute for the Study of Global Antisemitism and Policy, 'ISGAP Fellows Reject Antisemitic Tropes in Amnesty Report' (23 April, 2022).

24. See Lazar Berman, '"We do not agree": UK rejects Amnesty report accusing Israel of apartheid', *The Times of Israel* (4 February, 2022).

25. Liz Truss, 'United Nations Human Rights Council, 1 March 2022: Foreign Secretary's statement', *Foreign, Commonwealth and Development Office* (1 March, 2022).

26. See Claire Mills and John Curtis, 'Military assistance to Ukraine since the Russian invasion', *House of Commons Library* (15 August, 2022).

inmates were imprisoned on purely arbitrary criteria, outside of any legal system, accusation of criminality or definition of guilt; and that it was this that constituted the function of the camp within the totalitarian systems of Nazism and Stalinism. This, she wrote, went far beyond those imprisoned in the camps:

> The aim of an arbitrary system is to destroy the civil rights of the whole population, who ultimately become just as outlawed in their own country as the stateless and homeless. The destruction of a man's rights, the killing of the juridical person in him, is a prerequisite for dominating him entirely.[27]

As the 74 years since the *Naqba* have demonstrated, this is the aim of the State of Israel, which cannot be contained within the racist ideology of Zionism or even by accusations of apartheid, but which constitutes a properly totalitarian system within which the Palestinian people are deprived of their juridical status as citizens. In her 2013 book, *Catastrophe and Redemption: The Political Thought of Giorgio Agamben*, Jessica Whyte draws the comparison between this destruction of the civil rights of an entire population and what the Italian philosopher of biopolitics calls the 'bare life' to which we are reduced by the power of the biosecurity state.

This term was first coined by Agamben in his book *Homo Sacer: Sovereign Power and Bare Life* (1995), in which he applied the concept of 'biopower' first formulated by the French philosopher and historian of ideas, Michel Foucault, to the concentration camps of the Third Reich.[28] This is not the former power of the sovereign over his subjects, which was ultimately manifested through his divine right to order their death; nor even, in the democratic model of government that succeeded it, the sovereignty of Parliament to make the laws determining what constitutes a crime and how it should be punished. Distinct from both, 'biopower' describes the institutions and technologies disposed of by the modern state — including the family, the army, the police, educational, medical and administrative institutions — not to threaten citizens with death but instead to manage, monitor, regulate, discipline and control their *lives* by making their biological existence the

---

27. Hannah Arendt, *The Origins of Totalitarianism*, p. 591.

28. The seminal exposition of 'biopower' is in Michel Foucault, 'Right of Death and Power over Life', part five of *The Will to Knowledge*, volume 1 of *The History of Sexuality*, translated by Robert Hurley (Penguin Books, 1998), 133-159.

object of a political strategy.[29] In a state of emergency, as we experienced in the West between March 2020 and March 2022, these techniques of power reduce us to our bare life, which the state then takes into its care outside of any legal framework of human rights or civil liberties. Applying this concept of bare life to the status and treatment of Palestinians in Gaza by the occupying forces of Israel, Whyte writes:

> There is a terrible and specific continuity between the absolute novelty of Auschwitz and Israel's decision to allow into Gaza only those goods that are 'vital for the survival of the civilian population'. That Israel determines the threshold of this survival by using a mathematical equation that calculates the minimum level of calories necessary to 'sustain Gaza's population of 1.5 million at a level just above the UN definition of hunger', should not blind us to the fact that what is at stake here is the attempt to reduce life to survival.[30]

By reducing the lives of Palestinians to their bare existence, the Gaza strip has been described as a concentration camp, and in function it is; but it would be more accurate to say that the entire State of Israel and the Occupied Palestinian Territories is a concentration camp: one in which more than half the population has few if any remaining rights of citizenship and lives in abject poverty under martial law, and in which the other half is trained and armed by the state and financially supported by the wealthiest nation on earth; in which certain areas are ringed by impassable walls, barbed wire and military watchtowers and its inhabitants are imprisoned, tortured and killed with impunity, while others enjoy all the luxuries of their expropriation of the inmates' wealth, which began with their land; and in which, finally, the Jews are no longer the captives and have now become the guards, but are still living, despite that, in a concentration camp.

Asserting as much, however, is now forbidden. According to definitions proposed by the International Holocaust Remembrance Alliance, 'drawing comparisons of contemporary Israeli policy to that of the Nazis' is now an example

---

29. See Simon Elmer, 'Giorgio Agamben and the Biopolitics of COVID-19' (25 April, 2020), collected in *COVID-19*, pp. 53-65.

30. Jessica Whyte, *Catastrophe and Redemption: The Political Thought of Giorgio Agamben*, State University of New York Press, 2013, p. 95.

of anti-Semitism.[31] This definition, which censors and lays the ground for criminalising any criticism of the apartheid and totalitarian State of Israel, has been adopted by 34 countries, including the UK, France, Spain, Belgium, the Netherlands, Sweden, Germany, Poland, the Czech Republic, Slovakia, Austria, Hungary, Luxembourg, Italy, Greece, Romania, Bulgaria, Estonia, Lithuania, Albania, Slovenia, Serbia, the USA, Canada and Australia, as well as the United Nations, the European Union, the Council of Europe, the Organization of American States and Israel itself — in other words, by the Global Biosecurity State of the West — but not by the Palestinian National Authority.[32] We shouldn't be surprised that one of the sources of this censorship is Friedrich Hayek's casual and contemptible assertion in *The Road to Serfdom*, whose importance to the neoliberal revolution I discussed in my previous chapter, that 'anti-Semitism and anti-capitalism spring from the same root' — this being, of course, socialism.[33]

That the neoliberal governments of the West have accommodated the imprisonment of the Palestinian people in this camp for nearly three-quarters of a century is a tragedy; but that it has done so on the justification of some form of compensation for the extermination of millions of Jews in the camps of the Third Reich is nothing short of a farce. As the reaction of the West to the report by Amnesty International demonstrated, any criticism of Israel and its treatment of the Palestinians is immediately and uncritically represented as a 'stain on the memory of the victims of the Holocaust' (etc.).[34] Beyond the forced removal of the

---

31. See International Holocaust Remembrance Alliance, 'What is antisemitism? Non-legally binding working definition of antisemitism'.

32. See International Holocaust Remembrance Alliance, 'Information on endorsement and adoption of the IHRA working definition of antisemitism'.

33. Friedrich Hayek, *The Road to Serfdom*, p. 161.

34. A translation of the Greek *holocaustoma*, meaning a 'burnt offering', 'Holocaust' was used by the Fathers of the Christian Church to translate the complex sacrificial doctrine of the Bible; but it was also used by them as a polemical weapon against the Jews, to condemn blood sacrifice. During the pogroms of the Middle Ages, the term was increasingly used to describe massacres of Jews in Europe. The semantic history of the word 'Holocaust', therefore, is essentially Christian, and its continued use in the Twentieth and Twenty-first Century to describe the systematic killing of millions of Jews and other 'subjects of the state' under the Third Reich attempts to dehistoricise, sanctify and ultimately obscure the causes and mechanisms of what was a historically, politically and legally contingent series of events. For this reason, I only use this word in quotation marks, and refer to the events it describes with the Hebrew word *Shoah*. See Giorgio Agamben, *Remnants of*

rights of an entire people, this tells us something, I think, about how the camp functions not only in the State of Israel but in the Global Biosecurity State that's been constructed over the past two-and-a-half-years on the justification of combatting a supposedly civilisation-threatening virus.

Attributing the observation to Hegel, Marx famously wrote that every great event in history occurs twice: 'the first time as tragedy, the second as farce'.[35] But in our rapidly-approaching post-historical present, tragedy and farce occur simultaneously. To take only the most obscene examples, the theft of two years of our children's lives and the abandonment of our elderly to death alone in care homes and hospitals is a tragedy; the complete lack of medical justification for doing so is a farce. The credulity with which the most educated, wealthiest and technologically advanced generation in history has consented to the erasure of its human rights is a farce; while the consequences for all of us of doing so is a tragedy whose full extent we are just beginning to perceive. The assassination of the respected Al Jazeera journalist, Shireen Abu Akleh, by Israel Defense Forces this May is a tragedy; the condemnation by the European Union and United States of America of the violent attack on her funeral by armed Israeli police is, given their unconditional support for this apartheid regime, an obscene farce.[36]

The simultaneity of tragedy and farce are the post-historical mode of our present, in which the end of history the Global Biosecurity State promises to bring about does not mean that the erasure of our humanity and freedoms will lessen, that the civil wars of the state against populations will stop, that the arming and violence of our police forces won't escalate, that wealth and power won't be increased and concentrated in fewer and fewer hands, that the middle classes of the West can't be further cretinised by technology designed to make their work-from-home lives easier, that the poor cannot be forced further into poverty, and the legally dispossessed and politically voiceless cannot be silenced once and for all, as they are in Israel and the occupied Palestinian territories. A camp in which inmates and guards coexist is a vision, and perhaps a model more applicable than that of China's quarantine camps, of the Global Biosecurity State of our future, in

---

Auschwitz: The Witness and the Archive. Translated by Daniel Heller-Roazen (Zone Books, 2002), pp. 28-31.

35. Karl Marx, 'The Eighteenth Brumaire of Louis Bonaparte', in *Selected Writings*, p. 300.

36. See 'Al Jazeera to refer journalist Shireen Abu Akleh's killing to ICC', *Al Jazeera* (26 May, 2022).

which the biopolitical legislation of the Third Reich meets the quantum leap in technology of the Fourth Industrial Revolution. And if, 77 years after the *Shoah* and 74 years after the *Naqba* — both of which mean 'the catastrophe' — we still haven't learned their historical lessons, work will not set us free.

3. The Space of the Camp

The logical and inevitable outcome of our continued compliance with medically meaningless and illegally imposed restrictions on our human rights, like social distancing, face masking, 'asymptomatic' testing, 'vaccine' passports as a condition of citizenship, 'quarantining' healthy people and mandatory medical intervention with experimental biotechnology, is the camp. But what is a camp? In 'The Camp as Biopolitical Paradigm of the Modern', part three of *Homo Sacer*, Agamben writes:

> The camp is the space that is opened when the state of exception becomes the rule. In the camp, the state of exception, which was essentially a temporary suspension of the rule of law on the basis of a factual state of danger, is now given a permanent spatial arrangement, which as such nevertheless remains outside the normal order.[37]

The 'state of exception' is the term Agamben uses to encompass the various legal bases, including the declaration of a state of emergency, for suspending the rights and freedoms of citizens.[38] This applies to both a period of time — such as the twelve years between February 1933 and May 1945 during which the Third Reich was ruled by emergency powers conferred by the twice renewed Decree for the Protection of People and State, or the politically declared 'emergency period' under which the UK was governed between March 2020 and March 2022 — and a spatial arrangement defining and delimiting the application of this

---

37. Giorgio Agamben, *Homo Sacer: Sovereign Power and Bare Life*, translated by Daniel Heller-Roazen (Stanford University Press, 1998), pp. 168-169.

38. See Giorgio Agamben, *State of Exception*, translated by Kevin Attell (University of Chicago Press, 2005); and Simon Elmer, 'Historical Precedents for Emergency Powers', section 1 of 'The New Normal (Part 1. Programmes and Regulations)', collected in *COVID-19*, pp. 188-223.

period.[39] Because of this, Agamben argues, we find ourselves in the presence of a camp every time such a space is created in law — paradoxically by designating a place outside the law, a properly heterogeneous space therefore — irrespective of who is held there, on what justifications, the design and layout of its structure, what crimes are committed within its limits, or how the camp is designated.

As an example and warning of the ambiguity and deception in the designation and purpose of camps, the complex of huts to the west of the earliest architectural plans for Auschwitz-Birkenau, dated October 1941, was designated as a 'Quarantine camp *(Quarantänelager)'*.[40] When the camp opened in March 1942, the block of huts to the north were used to hold male prisoners of various nationalities; that August, those to the south were turned into a women's camp; and by July 1943, both blocks held over 10,000 women prisoners.[41] The entire complex, which was never completed, was designed to hold 100,000 inmates, all of whom, upon entering the camp, would be reduced to their bare life. As Agamben writes:

> The camp is produced at the point at which the political system of the modern nation-state . . . enters into a lasting crisis, and the state decides to assume directly the care of the nation's biological life as one of its proper tasks.[42]

As we have seen, this describes the 'care' taken by the State of Israel over the lives of the 2 million Palestinians imprisoned in the Gaza camp, and by the Chinese Government over the 65 million citizens currently quarantined under its 'zero-COVID' strategy.

The birth of the camp, which notoriously dates back to the concentration camps of the British Empire during the Second Boer War of 1899-1902, when they were used to target an entire nation and depopulate whole regions, but which found its most extreme application under the Third German Reich, signalled the political space of modernity. 'Today,' Agamben writes, 'it is not the city but rather

---

39. See Simon Elmer, 'The State of Emergency as Paradigm of Government', collected in *COVID-19*, pp. 94-122.

40. See 'Architecture of Murder: The Auschwitz-Birkenau Blueprints', Yad Vashem.

41. See Auschwitz-Birkenau: Former German Nazi Concentration and Extermination Camp, 'The Organizational Structure'.

42. Giorgio Agamben, *Homo Sacer*, pp. 174-175.

the camp that is the fundamental biopolitical paradigm of the West'.[43] As such, the camp regulates not only the laws but also the norms of human behaviour. Anticipating the Global Biosecurity State of today, Agamben, who was writing in 1995, argued that every attempt to rethink the political space of the West must begin with the awareness that the classical distinction between the private life of the citizen living at home and their public life in the city no longer exists.

> There is no return from the camps to classical politics. In the camps, city and house became indistinguishable, and the possibility of differentiating between our biological body and our political body — between what is incommunicable and mute and what is communicable and sayable — was taken from us forever. And we are not only, in Foucault's words, animals whose life as living beings is at issue in their politics, but also — inversely — citizens whose very politics is at issue in their natural body.[44]

Is there a clearer description of the assault on the human that has been undertaken across the world since March 2020 under the guise of protecting us from a virus, by national governments and global technocracies that have used this manufactured 'crisis' to take our biological existence into their care, even against our will, and in doing so tried to reduce our citizenship to bare life? Let's look at an example of the camps that have sprung up in what was formerly thought of as one of the most liberal of the neoliberal democracies of the West, ostensibly in response to the coronavirus.

Manigurr-ma Village, a residential mining camp in Howard Springs in the Northern Territory of Australia, was master-planned and designed by the US-headquartered multinational engineering firm AECOM. In 2014, the camp received the State commendation award for Urban Design in the Northern Territory Architecture Awards. In March 2020, however, following the WHO's declaration of the 'pandemic', the Northern Territory government renamed the camp the Centre for National Resilience, and began using it to 'quarantine' Australians repatriated from overseas, regardless of their state of health.[45] Under a politically-

---

43. Giorgio Agamben, *Homo Sacer*, p. 101.

44. Giorgio Agamben, *Homo Sacer*, p. 188.

45. See 'Public and Environmental Health Act 2011. COVID-19 Directions (No. 55) 2020 – Directions for Quarantine Facilities', Northern Territory of Australia (12 November, 2020).

declared state of emergency, all Australians on Commonwealth-facilitated flights into the Northern Territory were required to undertake 14 days of mandatory supervised quarantine at a cost of $2,500 AUD for an unvaccinated individual and $5,000 for a family or couple.[46] Before being permitted to leave the camp at the end of 2 weeks, inmates had to produce a negative RT-PCR test with a cycle threshold (Ct) of 40-45. Refusal to do so incurred a further 7 days incarceration at an additional cost of $1,750 AUD for an individual and $3,500 for a family.

According to instructions to camp inmates laid out by the Chief Medical Officer, a person in 'quarantine' must obey the following restrictions and directions:

- Stay in the person's allocated room, including on any veranda space allocated to the room, unless permitted by an authorised officer;
- When not in their room, or on their veranda, residents must take all reasonable measures to stay at least 1.5 metres away from any other person in the quarantine facility, except for the person's spouse, *de facto* partner, child or parent;
- Wear a face mask when outside their room unless an authorised officer permits the person to remove the face mask;
- Comply with any directions given by an authorised officer to avoid congregating in a quarantine zone;
- Must not leave the quarantine zone in which the person's allocated room is located unless the person is escorted by an authorised officer, except in an emergency.
- Failure to comply with these instructions, or with any other instructions from a camp officer, is a criminal offence punishable by fines ranging from $5,000 AUD for an infringement notice up to a maximum of $62,800.[47]

In November 2021, three teenagers escaped from the camp, and following a state-wide manhunt were arrested by the Northern Territory Police. None tested positive for SARS-CoV-2. At the time, a total of 58 people in the Northern Territory had tested positive with a RT-PCR test out of a state population of 250,730, and

---

46. See Howard Maclean and Karen Elphick, 'COVID-19 Legislative response — Human Biosecurity Emergency Declaration Explainer', Parliament of Australia (19 March, 2020).

47. See 'Public and Environmental Health Act 2011. COVID-19 Directions (No. 52) 2021 – Directions for Quarantine Facilities, Northern Territory of Australia (31 August, 2021).

not a single death had been attributed to COVID-19. As of February 2022, 5 deaths had been attributed to COVID-19 in the Northern Territory after a period of nearly 2 years. 6 people have tried to escape the camp. All have been apprehended. Of the 2,639 deaths attributed to COVID-19 in Australia between March 2020 and 31 January, 2022, 92 per cent had underlying health conditions, with an average of three conditions per deceased.[48] Chronic cardiac conditions were the primary underlying health condition of those whose deaths were attributed to COVID-19. During the same period, roughly 100,000 Australians died from cancer, 32,000 from heart disease, 30,000 from Alzheimer's disease and dementia, and 10,000 from diabetes. Of the 273,901 deaths in Australia over this period, COVID-19 was identified as the 38th highest cause of death, representing less than 1 per cent of all fatalities nationwide. The average age of death was 83 for men and 86 for women. In the nearly two years since SARS-CoV-2 reached Australia, only 83 people out of a national population of over 26 million had COVID-19 identified as the sole cause of their death, without other underlying causes.

In July 2021, the Australian Government announced the contract to build a Centre for National Resilience in Melbourne, Victoria, and the camp opened in February 2022.[49] Another, being built in Brisbane, Queensland, was set to open this June; and a fourth in Perth, Western Australia, is still under construction. All three camps currently have a planned capacity of 1,000 inmates each. Those who point to the comforts of the isolation cells in which inmates are kept compared to the converted shipping containers in China and mock the idea that these 'quarantine facilities' should be called camps, or who point out that, appalling as they are, the conditions of life in the Gaza Strip are not as terrible as they were in Auschwitz — as if this refuted any comparison between them — miss the point made by Agamben. Whatever their ostensible use, designation, location or design, the camp is the permanent spatialisation of the state of emergency, and those interred in them are deprived of their status as citizens and reduced, instead, to their bare life, over which the biosecurity state has complete control. What is done with that life is a matter of degree, not of kind. Indeed, it is the

---

48. See Natalie Brown, '"Scare campaign": Underlying health issues involved in 92 per cent of Aussie Covid deaths', *News* (16 February, 2022).

49. See Department of Finance, 'Centres for National Resilience', Australian Government, 2021.

normalisation of the camp as a form of residence, fitted with the surveillance technologies of the Fourth Industrial Revolution presented as entertainment systems, that points most clearly towards their future use. In distinguishing the mechanisms of biopower from the punitive measures threatened by the law, Foucault wrote:

> Another consequence of this development of bio-power was the growing importance assumed ·by the action of the norm, at the expense of the juridical system of the law. The law always refers to the sword. But a power whose task is to take charge of life needs continuous regulatory and corrective mechanisms. Such a power has to qualify, measure, appraise and hierarchise. I do not mean to say that the law fades into the background or that the institutions of justice tend to disappear, but rather that the judicial institution is increasingly incorporated into a continuum of apparatuses (medical, administrative, and so on) whose functions are for the most part regulatory. A normalising society is the historical outcome of a technology of power centred on life.[50]

If apologists for the use of the camp as a 'temporary measure' don't think this paradigm of governance won't expand under the technocratic governance of the Global Biosecurity State and its increasingly violent and unaccountable enforcement by the police, security services and military, they have forgotten — or more likely have never known — everything history has to teach us about our immediate future.

The use of camps today in order to deprive people of their juridical status as citizens is not confined, of course, to 'quarantine' centres in Australia and China or to the Gaza Strip in the State of Israel. On the contrary, the economic, geopolitical, security and military axis of the West to which the UK belongs is in many ways founded on the camp. I will only briefly refer here to the USA, in which 22.8 million people — 6.9 per cent of the national population — do not have citizenship, and which, in addition to the more than 200 immigrant detention centres within its national borders, has an unknown number of camps across the

---

50. Michel Foucault, *The History of Sexuality*, p. 144.

world in the more than 80 countries in which the US has over 750 military bases.[51] It is from these that the Guantánamo Bay detention camp draws its prisoners, just as Auschwitz drew its prisoners from the archipelago of concentration camps across the Third Reich and occupied territories of Europe. The ongoing criminality of the actions of five successive US Governments in Guantánamo Bay, or indeed in every other country in which the US has a military presence, is outside the parameters of this book; but the forms of torture used against the inmates of Guantánamo Bay, who have been kept imprisoned for years and even decades without charge or trial or access to legal representation under either US criminal or international law, include the following:

- Solitary isolation for between 1 and 12 weeks;
- Sensory deprivation for between 12 and 48 hours;
- Sensory bombardment by sound and light for 3 to 48 hours;
- Standing handcuffed in stress positions for 12 to 48 hours;
- Physical beatings for 1 to 4 hours;
- Water boarding for between 30 minutes and 6 hours;
- Repeated suffocation with a plastic bag for between 30 minutes and 4 hours;
- Threatened by dogs for 3 to 30 minutes.[52]

All these tortures are prohibited under the third Geneva Convention of 1949 on the treatment of prisoners of war, by the International Covenant on Civil and Political Rights of 1966, and by the Convention Against Torture and other Cruel, Inhuman or Degrading Treatment or Punishment of 1984 — none of which have jurisdiction in the state of exception to which the Guantánamo Bay detention centre, as Agamben wrote, gives a permanent spatial arrangement. Reduced to the status of bare life, even those who try to escape these tortures by killing

---

51. See Altaf Saadi, Maria-Elena De Trinidad Young, Caitlin Patler, Jeremias Leonel Estrada and Homer Venters, 'Understanding US Immigration Detention', *National Library of Medicine* (22 June, 2020); 'Detention by numbers', *Freedom for Immigrants*; and Mohammed Hussein and Mohammed Haddad, 'Infographic: US military presence around the world', *Al Jazeera* (10 September, 2021).

52. See Didier Faustino and Kostas Grigoriadis, 'The Logic of Guantánamo', *The Funambulist* (19 December, 2016); and Bridge Initiative Team, 'Factsheet: Torture at Guantánamo Bay Detention Centre', Georgetown University (19 July, 2020).

themselves through hunger strikes are force-fed by their guards. In response to challenges to the ethics of this practice, US Navy Captain Robert Duran responded: 'We do it to preserve life'.[53] This is the ultimate goal of biopower: to so deprive human beings of their rights that no act committed against them can any longer be regarded as a crime. What it produces is a biological entity; but this bare life is an abstraction from social and political life, that unity of the corporeal and the spiritual we call a human being. And as Agamben has consistently argued for the past quarter of a century, it is the governance of this abstraction that is the goal of the technologies of biopower, of which the camp is the juridico-political paradigm. Guantánamo Bay, which like the Gaza Strip is separated from the rest of Cuba by a militarised border fence, is the most extreme form of the camp in the West that we know of today — though Saudi Arabia, to which the UK is the second-largest arms dealer after the USA, has even worse camps in which to imprison, torture and kill the migrant workers it no longer needs.[54] But there is a legal and spatial continuity between Guantánamo Bay and the comfortably appointed Centres for National Resilience in Australia, a shared spatial arrangement of the state of exception that the difference in degree between the tortures in the former and the removal of freedoms in the latter does not erase; and both point toward the new biopolitical paradigm of governance in the West.

For Agamben, therefore, the real — which is to say, historical — function of human rights lie elsewhere than in their repeated failure to protect the stateless and homeless. On the contrary, Agamben argues that the Declaration of the Rights of Man and of the Citizen approved by the National Constituent Assembly of France in 1789 served to inscribe bare life, for the first time, in the juridico-political order of the nation state. With the declaration (Article 3) that: 'The principle of all sovereignty resides essentially in the nation', the former subject of the divinely authorised sovereign of the *ancien régime* was transformed into the citizen of the sovereign nation state, from which the authority of any individual or government body 'emanates'. From the start, however, there was an ambiguity about whether these were human rights (*droits de l'homme*) or rights of citizenship (*droits du citoyen*). If our 'birth' is identified with our 'nation' — both of which have

---

53. Tom Leonard, 'Inside Guantanamo Bay: Horrifying pictures show the restraint chairs, feeding tubes and operating theatre used on inmates in terror prison', *Daily Mail* (27 June, 2013).

54. See Human Rights Watch, 'Saudi Arabia: Migrants Held in Inhuman, Degrading Conditions' (15 December, 2020).

their etymological origin in the Latin *natio* — our rights, as Arendt pointed out, have repeatedly been shown to be contingent upon our status as citizens of a sovereign state. This ambiguity was most fully exposed by the National Socialist credo of '*Blut und Boden* (Blood and Soil)', which made bare life into the foundation of the Third Reich, from which those not conforming to this sanctified unity of birth, nation and sovereign *(Ein Volk, ein Reich, ein Führer)* were either expelled or erased, having first been stripped of citizenship by The Reich Citizenship Law of September 1935.

However paradoxically, therefore, human rights, far from protecting citizens with their expression of eternal and supposedly meta-juridical values, are the foundation of modern biopolitics. Beginning with the 3 million Europeans made stateless in the wake of the Great War, which increased to 40 million after the Second World War, this separation between the rights of man and the rights of the citizen is today most widely enacted in the camps in which an unknown number of the nearly 90 million refugees worldwide are currently detained.[55] Indeed, under the new paradigm of biosecurity, the concept of citizenship is being transformed into something resembling the bare life of the refugee. This is the context in which the new Nationality and Borders Act 2022, which came into effect this April, has empowered the Home Secretary to remove, without prior notification, the British citizenship of anyone not born in the UK, or who is of dual nationality, or who is judged to be a threat to national security, or whose behaviour is deemed to be 'unacceptable' — as an example of which the Government has suggested 'the glorification of terrorism'.[56] Given that, in November 2021, the UK Government designated Hamas a terrorist organisation, this might now include condemning air strikes on the Gaza Strip — a right of conscience and expression no longer merely condemned as anti-Semitic but now justification for being rendered stateless and homeless.[57]

Although Agamben, in *Homo Sacer*, compares bare life to the vegetative state in which medical science has for some decades now been able to keep a human being alive for many years, a more appropriate comparison in the

---

55. See United Nations High Commissioner for Refugees, 'Figures at a Glance' (16 June, 2022).

56. See Home Office, 'Nationality and Borders Bill: Deprivation of citizenship factsheet' (March 2022).

57. See Home Office, 'Islamist terrorist group Hamas banned in the UK' (26 November, 2021).

biosecurity state is with the residents of care homes under coronavirus-justified restrictions, which for many of them continue to this day. Isolated in their rooms for months on end, subjected to unrelenting terrorism on television, deprived of access to normal medical care from GPs too terrified to visit, refused visits from their family and, even when permitted them, prohibited from physical contact, prohibited from leaving what had become and for many remains their prison, residents were transformed into a form of bare life, in which most of their human rights had been removed on the justification of keeping them alive, whatever the cost. As Captain Duran said: 'We do it to preserve life'. The fact that huge numbers of them died, most probably of the dementia from which 70 per cent of residents of care homes suffer, and which was then falsely attributed to COVID-19 under the deliberately inaccurate testing protocol, demonstrated the lack of medical justification for such measures, which to a lesser degree have been imposed on the rest of the population with a similar degree of disastrous consequence.[58]

Since the 1980s, when privately-funded care homes under successive Thatcher Governments tripled in number in a decade, their purpose has been to extend the lifespan of the human organism whatever the cost to the quality of life of the person it houses, or indeed to those paying for its extension.[59] The increase in the lifespan of populations in the West, which in the UK has risen 25 years over the past century and 10 years since 1970, is now one of the most lucrative markets into which the medical care and pharmaceutical industries have expanded, effectively draining the elderly of whatever savings and assets they may have previously passed on to their spouse or children over a protracted biological existence whose cynical financial exploitation and violation of the dignity of human life the coronavirus 'crisis' has exposed for what it is.[60] Indeed, most of us can expect to end our lives in a legal state of bare life, deprived of our rights and at the mercy of the private companies to which the state has handed the responsibility and duty of prolonging our biological existence for as long as is medically possible. Not only our lives, therefore, but even our deaths will be lived under the biopolitical paradigm of the camp.

---

58. See Alzheimer's Society, 'Facts for the media about dementia' (19 July, 2022).

59. See Sarah Munson, 'A history of care homes', Care home (7 August, 2020).

60. See Aaron O'Neill, 'Life expectancy (from birth) in the United Kingdom from 1765 to 2020', Statista (21 June, 2022).

More recently, however, in his commentaries on the 'pandemic', Agamben has come up with a figure of bare life that expands the legal state of exception in which the imprisoned, the comatose and the care-home resident exist to the entire population of the Global Biosecurity State:

What is the figure of bare life as it has been integrated into the management of the pandemic? It is not the sick, who are nonetheless isolated and treated in a manner unprecedented in the history of medicine. It is, on the contrary, the infected, or, as the paradoxical formula would have it, the asymptomatic case (a category to which we all potentially — and perhaps without even knowing it — belong). What is at stake is not health, but rather a life that is neither in health nor in sickness but that, by virtue of being potentially pathogenic, can be deprived of its freedoms and subjected to all kinds of prohibitions and controls. All men are, in this sense, potentially asymptomatic cases. The sole identity of this life that fluctuates between sickness and health consists in being the recipient of tests and vaccines that, as a sort of baptism for a new religion, define the inverted figure of what was once called 'citizenship'. Baptism is in this instance no longer permanent but necessarily temporary and renewable, because the neo-citizen (who will from now on always have to exhibit a certificate) no longer has inalienable and indivisible rights, but only obligations that must be endlessly revisited and updated.[61]

In order to bring about this redefinition of citizenship in Western democracies as the potentially asymptomatic patient of a biopolitics, the camp must become the permanent spatialisation of a state of exception whose limits, both temporal and physical, is the Global Biosecurity State.

Agamben concluded his thoughts on the camp with this warning — which has gone unheeded, it appears, by anyone except the architects of the 'crisis' on which the Global Biosecurity State has been constructed, and certainly by the intelligentsia of the West — philosophers, scientists and jurists — whose servile and willing complicity with its construction has surpassed, if anything, that of

---

61. Giorgio Agamben, 'Bare Life and the Vaccine' *Quodlibet* (16 April, 2021); collected in *Where Are We Now?*, p. 98.

European intellectuals of far higher calibre with the rise and coming to power of historical fascism a hundred years ago:

> It we give the name form-of-life to this being that is only its own bare existence, and to this life that, being its own form, remains inseparable from it, we will witness the emergence of a field of research beyond the terrain defined by the intersection of politics and philosophy, medico-biological sciences and jurisprudence. First, however, it will be necessary to examine how it was possible for something like a bare life to be conceived within these disciplines, and how the historical development of these very disciplines has brought them to a limit beyond which they cannot venture without risking an unprecedented biopolitical catastrophe.[62]

That catastrophe, which may one day exceed both the *Naqba* and the *Shoah*, is upon us. To believe that the unknown numbers of so-called 'quarantine' camps built over the past two-and-a-half years were constructed in response to the specific threat of COVID-19 and in anticipation of future threats to public health is to ignore the history of the uses of camps. More importantly, it is to fail to recognise the legal state of exception to which they give a permanent spatial arrangement and the paradigm of government this has increasingly come to constitute across the globe. Already present in the former neoliberal democracies of the West, whether in immigration centres for refugees or torture facilities for prisoners abducted through the extra-legal process of extraordinary rendition, the coronavirus 'crisis' has justified and initiated the expansion of this spatial arrangement. As we have experienced, it was under a state of emergency that the populations of the West were governed for the two years of the 'pandemic' with little complaint and no organised forms of rebellion beyond protests and demonstrations, and the camps will make permanent this ostensibly temporary measure.

As Arendt insisted, the purpose of the camp is not to punish those who challenge the authority or break the laws of a dictatorial, despotic or tyrannical rule; the purpose of the camp is to serve the totalitarian system of which it is the goal. As the State of Israel has demonstrated for all the world to see and to which

---

62. Giorgio Agamben, *Homo Sacer*, p. 188.

the West has given its political approval and financial support, the aim of totalitarianism is to govern entire populations according to the biopolitical paradigm of the camp, in which some are criminals, some are political prisoners, some are guards and some are commandants, but in which the vast majority are human beings reduced to their bare life. In this society, there is no 'normal order' for the camp to remain outside, no 'rule of law' that has been temporarily suspended for its inmates; for the state of exception is now the permanent rule under which the population is governed, and the camp the new normal whose militarised border no longer serves to separate its extra-legal space from society, but which is coextensive with the obligations of the Global Biosecurity State. The aim of a totalitarian system is not to build so many camps that the whole population can be housed in them — something not even the People's Republic of China could achieve — but to turn the social space itself into a camp, and thereby subject the population to its paradoxical logic of being placed outside the law by the law, of being guilty in the absence of charge or sentence, of being citizens without citizenship, sick without sickness, humans deprived of human rights, housed while remaining homeless, stateless under the rule of the biosecurity state, of subsisting without being permitted to exist, the juridical person killed. If Auschwitz was the setting for the death of humanist man, Gaza is the post-historical time of our futureless present. Indeed, everything about the new forms of global governance emerging from this 'crisis' points to the conclusion that it is under the biopolitical paradigm of the camp that vast numbers of the global population will be forced to live in the Twenty-first Century.

9. The New Totalitarianism

'There is a great temptation to explain away the intrinsically incredible by means of liberal rationalisations. In each one of us there lurks such a liberal, wheedling us with the voice of common sense. The road to totalitarian domination leads us through many intermediate stages for which we can find numerous analogies and precedents. The extraordinarily bloody terror during the initial stage of totalitarian rule serves indeed the exclusive purpose of defeating the opponent and rendering all further opposition impossible; but total terror is launched only after this initial stage has been overcome and the regime no longer has anything to fear from the opposition.'

— Hannah Arendt, *The Origins of Totalitarianism*, 1951

It is a contradiction worthy of consideration that few in this country had any remaining belief in the integrity of one of the most corrupt Governments and, until he was forced to resign in July, untrustworthy Prime Ministers in modern British history; and yet the overwhelming majority of the population found a reason to believe and obey the 582 coronavirus-justified Statutory Instruments this Government made into law with little or no oversight by our elected representatives in a Parliament that has shown itself to be the worst in living memory. This spirit, or principle, or source of the law above those who made the thousands of regulations that suspended our rights and freedoms for two years has taken many and various forms, differentiated largely by class and party allegiance. For conservatives it's been pride in Britain and its 'world-beating Test and Trace system/race to develop a vaccine' (etc.); for middle-class liberals it's been a professional's trust in the 'apolitical' judgement of the technocrats in the Scientific Advisory Group for Emergencies; for the Left it's been an opportunity to point to other countries under nominally 'left-wing' governments imposing stricter restrictions as examples to which we should aspire; for the woke it's been a chance to sacrifice their individual freedoms in public for the 'common good'; and for the working class it's been the threat of arrest, fines and the courts. Indeed, the vast majority of UK citizens went beyond mere obedience to the letter of the laws that few of them had read, and subsumed their own will into the spirit that each, according to their own interests, identified behind them.

Today, however, the consequences of their more-than-obedience are becoming too unavoidable and terrible for all but the COVID-faithful to deny. Countries that were locked down for two years while trillions were injected into a collapsing financial system are now facing spiralling inflation and economic depression; the children kept masked and in a state of terror are showing the mental toll of bearing the brunt of their parent's compliance; the experimental 'vaccines' injected into billions is leaving a trail of permanently injured and dead; governments that temporarily suspended coronavirus-justified regulations in March are already threatening to reimpose them this autumn and winter; the number of billionaires in the world is increasing in direct proportion to the 250 millions that are being driven into extreme poverty; and the programmes and technologies of biosecurity are expanding the surveillance and control exerted by international technocracies over our lives without even the pretence of averting a threat to public health. Given which, how should we address those who obeyed the regulations and continue to be complicit in the crimes of the biosecurity state? Should we, even, try to communicate with those who contemptuously dismissed us as 'conspiracy theorists', and were willing to see us banned from participating in public life, including the means to make a living? If we should, by what categories of law and morality should they be judged and by whom? Most importantly of all, given the general moral collapse in the populations living in the Global Biosecurity State, how should we proceed to defend ourselves against the return of fascism not only in our politics, laws and culture, but in the servile obedience to authority and craven refusal to think of our fellow citizens? In the face of such willing collaboration with the new state apparatus of totalitarian domination, how do we continue to act, individually and with each other, morally and towards a future politics, in these dark times? Finally, who is this 'we' with whom I wish to speak — to them and with them — with the collective voice with which we must speak if we are to be heard?

1. The Right to Obey

The *Casa del Fascio* in Bolzano, Italy, was completed in 1942 in South Tyrol, which was annexed from the Austro-Hungarian Empire after the Great War. The former seat of the local Fascist Party, its facade is decorated with a 36-metre bas-relief by Hans Piffrader telling the story of *The Triumph of Fascism*. At the centre is a depiction of the Leader of Italian fascism, Benito Mussolini, on horseback giving the Roman salute; and between the horse's legs, somewhat awkwardly, is carved the fascist motto: '*Credere, obbedire, combattere* (Believe, obey, fight).' For years this was the object of protests by German-speaking Tyroleans, less for its celebration of fascism than because of Mussolini's suppression of the German language in the region's schools, newspapers and from official use. Although the building was owned by the state, who turned it into the State Financial Offices of the South Tyrol, it took until 2011, 68 years after the official fall of Italian fascism, for Silvio Berlusconi's Minister for Culture, Sandro Bondi, to agree not to remove the bas relief but to an intervention that placed it within its historical context. When this finally materialised in 2017, it took the form of neon letters placed over the bas-relief but not obscuring either it or the fascist motto, quoting Hannah Arendt. Despite over a century of Italianisation, South Tyrol is still a majority German-speaking population, and Arendt's original German is placed at the centre of the relief, translated on either side into, respectively, Italian and Ladin, the minority regional dialect. The German reads: '*Kein Mensch hat das Recht zu gehorchen* (No man has the right to obey)'.

The quote comes from an interview in 1964 in which Arendt, who the year before had published her book, *Eichmann in Jerusalem: A Report on the Banality of Evil*, commented on the SS-Obersturmbannführer's defence of his part in the transportation of Jews to the death camps with the claim that the guiding principle of his life was what the German philosopher of the Enlightenment, Immanuel Kant, argued was our duty to obey the law.[1] For Adolf Eichmann, obedience to the commands of the *Führer*, which in the Third Reich had the status of law, was the principle of his own will. In her book, Arendt had reported that Eichmann, despite

---

1. See Hannah Arendt, *Eichmann in Jerusalem: A Report on the Banality of Evil*, with an introduction by Amos Elon (London: Penguin Classics, 2006); and 'Hannah Arendt interviewed by Joachim Fest, 1964', Hannah Arendt Centre for Political Studies, Department of Human Sciences, University of Verona, 2016.

affecting a level of intelligence and culture he deemed appropriate for a member of the SS elite, had not finished either secondary school or his attempted training as an engineer, and constantly spoke in clichés, officialese and other inherited figures of speech in order to conceal what she heard as his inability to think for himself, or indeed from the standpoint of anybody else. Although Eichmann claimed to have read Kant's *Critique of Practical Reason* (1788), in quoting the central concept of his moral philosophy — the categorical imperative that must be obeyed in all circumstances — Eichmann, Arendt argued, had ignored the importance to Kant's moral philosophy of man's faculty of judgement, which is the antithesis of blind obedience. For Kant, the legislator is not the head of state, fascist or otherwise, but the moral self at the moment one begins to act. Not only those with juridical powers over others, therefore, but all people must be legislators; and the categorical imperative must function not as a moral justification for subjecting others to the laws of the state, but as a universal law applicable to all.

Arendt's response in this interview to Eichmann's defence was itself a paraphrase of a passage from Kant's *Religion within the Boundaries of Mere Reason* (1793), in which he commented on Acts, 5:29, in which the Apostles are put on trial:

> The saying: 'We should obey God rather than men,' signifies merely that, when men command anything which in itself is evil (directly opposed to the law of morality), we dare not, and should not, obey them.[2]

For Kant, the law of morality transcends man-made laws, and can only be established through judgement founded on practical reasoning. As an example of which, no one can rationally claim the freedom to kill others with impunity as a universal law, because in practice he himself would be subject to the same freedom of others to kill him. Arendt's paraphrase, however, adds something more to Kant's statement. She does not say that man has the 'right to disobey', which would, as it were, add disobedience of the law to the list of human rights. Such

2. Immanuel Kant, *Religion within the Boundaries of Mere Reason: And Other Writings*, edited by Allen Wood and George di Giovanni, with an introduction by Robert Merrihew Adams, Cambridge University Press, 2018.

an addition would undermine the rule of law with which human rights attempt to create a legal framework for justice. The right to disobey may sound like a declaration of freedom in the mouths of self-proclaimed 'rebels', but in practice it means the rule of the powerful and the violent. Instead, Arendt says that unthinking obedience to the law is not free from responsibility, and even from criminal prosecution for the consequences of our actions, on the grounds that we owed obedience to our professional, legal or political superiors.

I do not refer here to the enforcers of coronavirus-justified regulations, either the police or designated 'COVID marshals', who as functionaries of the state are above the laws they claim to enforce, and who throughout the 'pandemic' have restricted our rights and freedoms far beyond even their newly-made legal powers to do so. Nor do I refer to those responsible for making and justifying those laws, whether Secretaries of State and Cabinet Ministers or the senior members of the Scientific Advisory Group for Emergencies, the National Health Service and the UK Health Security Agency, all of whom, in different measure, are responsible for decisions with such far reaching and catastrophic consequences that no court in the UK could judge them, but which possibly amount, in the absence of a declared war, to crimes against humanity. My concern here, rather, is with those millions of citizens who, acting on their own conscience, willingly complied with, and thereby enabled the otherwise impracticable imposition of, the UK biosecurity state over two long years of cowardice and compliance. Medical professionals who continue to inject the population with experimental 'vaccines' that are still in clinical trials whose damning data is only now being released, and which were only officially approved for temporary authorisation under changes to existing legislation justified by a politically declared state of emergency, will no doubt claim that they were and are following orders and the judgement of their superiors in the MHRA, the NHS and the pharmaceutical industry; but their failure to exercise their judgement, as professionals but above all as moral individuals, will not relieve them from responsibility for the thousands of deaths and injuries to unknown millions that followed the injections they administered.[3]

---

3. On the parallel obedience of the medical profession to the ideology of National Socialism, see Omar S. Haque, Julian De Freitas, Ivana Viani, Bradley Niederschulte and Harold J. Bursztajn, 'Why did so many German doctors join the Nazi Party early?', *International Journal of Law and Psychiatry*, volume 35, issues 5-6 (September-December, 2012), pp. 473-479.

The same failure applies to care-home workers who kept their charges, the vast majority of whom had dementia, isolated in their rooms for months on end, leading to the appalling mortality rate in care homes during lockdown.[4] And to educational staff who kept children in their care masked, terrified, guilt-ridden, socially distanced from each other or even banned from school altogether at an age when months feel like years.[5] And, more generally, it applies to the millions of individuals who refused to serve, or to admit, or to continue to employ, or to speak to, or who denounced to the authorities anyone who didn't obey the regulations of biosecurity, whether that was wearing a face mask, or standing at a designated distance from others, or not entering or walking or sitting in proscribed places, or getting tested, or complying with contact tracing, or being injected as many times as they were ordered. And, perhaps most of all, it applies to those who, in person, or online, or in newspapers, or on radio, or on televised talk shows, or on news programmes, or in Parliament, demanded the full force of the rapidly expanding reach of the law and its ever increasing powers of punishment against the non-compliant, not only with censorship and fines and incarceration but with bans from public life that included the right to travel, to education, to employment, to healthcare and medical treatment, and, eventually, the right to remain at liberty.[6] These, too, will claim they were obeying the orders of their superiors in their

---

4. See Elisabeth Mahase, 'Covid-19: Neglect was one of biggest killers in care homes during pandemic, report finds', *BMJ* (22 December, 2021).

5. See Dr. Zenobia Storah, 'Psychology Report in respect of Civil Proceedings' (9 April, 2021); 'Laura Donnelly, 'Lockdown's hidden toll: million schoolchildren a year will need mental health help', *The Telegraph* (8 May, 2021); Jeremy Wilson, 'Exclusive: "Horrific" impact of third lockdown on schoolchildren's physical and mental health revealed', *The Telegraph* (10 May, 2021); and Lucy Kellaway, 'The anxious generation — what's bothering Britain's schoolchildren?', *Financial Times* (5 August, 2022).

6. See, for example, Dr. Michael Fitzpatrick, 'Anti-vaxxers' gospel of fear: Reckless, dangerous and irresponsible', *Daily Mail* (10 November, 2020); Dr. Alberto Giubilini and Dr. Vageesh Jain, 'Should COVID-19 vaccines been mandatory? Two experts discuss', *The Conversation* (25 November, 2020); Richard Littlejohn, 'No jab, no job — it's a no-brainer', *Daily Mail* (18 February, 2021); Nick Cohen, 'It is only a matter of time before we turn on the unvaccinated', *The Guardian* (27 February, 2021); Sean O'Grady, 'This is what we do about anti-vaxxers: No job. No entry. No NHS access', *The Independent* (18 May, 2021); Sarah Vine, 'We can't let selfish idiots who don't want free Covid vaccines that scientists worked around the clock to develop hold us hostage', *Daily Mail* (18 May, 2021); Andrew Neil, 'It's time to punish Britain's five million vaccine refuseniks', *Daily Mail* (9 December, 2021).

respective industries, their leaders in local, civic and central government, or what some celebrity, or poster campaign or nice-looking man on the television told them. But in moral matters there are no superiors, neither government nor state, law or duty. However much the circumstances may extenuate them in the eyes of the law, each of us is answerable for his or her actions, and none can escape the responsibility for their own moral judgement. This is what the neon words on the *Casa del Fascio* mean.

Within three years of them being turned on, however, Giuseppe Conte, the Prime Minister of Italy since 2018 — and himself a jurist, former professor of law and member of the Italian Bureau of Administrative Justice — placed Italy under lockdown. The greatest suppression of constitutional rights in the history of the Italian Republic since it was founded in 1945 following the fall of the Fascist Government was implemented through prime-ministerial decrees issued under a politically-declared state of emergency. The first government in the West to do so, this juridical and medical model was soon followed by almost every Western government when it became apparent that their populations had been sufficiently terrified by the corporate media to obey without thinking. It quickly became apparent that, rather than recalling Arendt's insistence that no man has the right to obey commands that go against the moral law, almost everyone was happy to believe the lies of their leaders, to obey the removal of our constitutional rights, and to join in the imaginary fight against a threat that never existed outside the stories about the 'War on COVID' told every day and to fantastical lengths by our governments, the media, the health industry, information technology companies and the organisations of global governance they form. In February 2021, in the face of criticism over the already catastrophic economic effects of a year in lockdown, Conte resigned and the President unilaterally appointed Mario Draghi as the new Prime Minister with the task of forming a technocratic government. The former Governor of the Bank of Italy and President of the European Central Bank, Draghi immediately reimposed the temporarily lifted lockdown, and in October of that year Italy became the first country in the world to require the EU COVID certificate of 'vaccination' — popularly known as the 'Green Pass' — as a condition of employment for the entire national workforce. This was soon extended to participation in all recreational activities, and the following year injection was made compulsory for those over 50 years of age, with a fine of

€1,500 for non-compliance. Fascism, and not Kant's categorical imperative that every man be the legislator of his actions, is the order under which we have lived in the West ever since.

2. The Moral Collapse

In December 2021, with the threat of vaccine passports and the re-imposition of lockdown looming, the division in the UK between the 'vaccinated' and those who had refused outright or were deemed by the Government to be insufficiently 'vaccinated' was at its highest. For two long years, the obedient had sat at home as the elderly, reduced to the legal status of bare life, were abandoned by the state to die alone in care homes, had put the health and lives of their own children at risk for the sake of a summer holiday when ordered to do so, then willingly injected themselves with experimental 'vaccines', and yet still they were in chains. And now they wanted revenge — not on the Government they had obeyed but on us, the non-compliant. Three months later, with the revoking of the cultic practices of the biosecurity state precisely two years after they were first initiated by The Coronavirus Act in March 2020 — whose two years' expiry date had been written into Section 89 with remarkable foresight — the COVID-faithful were having to confront the extent of their gullibility, their political naivety, their susceptibility to manipulation by the corporate media, their ignorance of elementary biology; and like all religious fanatics awakened to rude reality, it wasn't a pretty sight. Belatedly demanding evidence of the medical justification for which they had substituted religious conviction for two long years, they were now forced to confront the truth of the lies on which their beliefs were founded: that their publicly displayed 'virtues' were nothing more than craven obedience to the cynical abuse of power; that the so-called 'medical measures' they had slavishly obeyed were nothing more than the demonstration of the extent of their subservience to authority; that the legal enforcement of thousands of 'coronavirus regulations' and the exaggerated punishments for breaking them were the whims of politicians laughing up their sleeves at them at drunken parties in Downing Street; that they had sold two years of their children's lives, watched their parents die from another room, and injected poison into their own veins and that of their family to enable one of the greatest transfers of wealth from the poor to the rich in history; that everything they had denounced so confidently and with such contempt as 'conspiracy theories' was being implemented with an equally contemptuous lack of deception, and was now threatening to crash through the windows of their frightened middle-class world.

So how are those who have behaved like willing slaves for two years reacting now, as they begin to find out just how duped they were? The answer, of course, is as the middle-classes always behave: with new moral declarations of allegiance to what they must know in their hearts if not in their made-up minds was the biggest lie in modern history; with new declarations of support for the brutality of police forces enforcing the same restrictions in countries further down the road to fascism; with arrogant declarations that what really matters is the apparently completely unrelated primary legislation that is making permanently into UK law what coronavirus-justified Statutory Instruments imposed on a temporary basis; with chants of 'my body my choice' at rallies protesting the US Supreme Court's overturning of Roe vs. Wade and the right to abortion by liberals also demanding that those attending are 'vaccinated'; with the distraction of the threat of war with Russia and their renewed chance to mount, once again, the battlements of Leftist irrelevance and start protesting about sovereign states and national autonomy and the abuse of human rights in foreign countries. Without shame or the slightest hint of self-awareness, they obediently repeat the declarations about rights and freedom and democracy from the heads of Western governments who, at the beginning of the year, had unleashed the paramilitary weapons of their police forces against their own people.[7]

Like that preceding the triumph of fascism, this intellectual cowardice, of which the coronavirus 'crisis' has been the triumphant demonstration, has been many years in preparation. 2022 is not only the hundredth anniversary of fascism forming its first government in Italy but also, not coincidentally, of the *Annus Mirabilis* of modernism, at least in the English-speaking world, with the publication of James Joyce's *Ulysses*, T. S. Eliot's *The Waste Land* and Ludwig Wittgenstein's *Tractatus Logico-Philosophicus* — to which I would add the beginning proper of Ezra Pound's *Cantos*. Besides its authors being Irish, American and Austrian, this is, of course, an artificially frozen moment in the history of modernism in literature,

---

7. See Prime Minister of Canada, 'Prime Minister announces additional support for Ukraine and shared priorities at G7 Summit in Germany' (28 June, 2022).

art and music that had been initiated in Europe more than a decade before, and in philosophy, painting and poetry fifty years before that, and which, by the time it ended — let's say for argument in the 1970s — could make some claim to being matched only by the European Renaissance in imagination, brilliance and achievement. Yet all this appears to have been forgotten today, willingly erased from our memory and practices. It's a genuine question from a former art historian: does art even exist anymore? It's death-knell has been sounding for over a century, yet when the time came to lower its body into the ground and the tombstone laid reverently but firmly over its last resting place, it has instead been tossed onto the bonfire of capitalism like so much litter. As for the great emancipatory philosophies and movements of the Twentieth Century — communism, anarchism, existentialism, poststructuralism, feminism, post-colonialism, black power, gay liberation — they have all been discarded for the radical conservatism of identity politics and its fascist offspring, woke. We live in a theatre in which Beckett was never staged, in which Kafka's writings were never saved from the flames, in which Foucault never excavated the discourses of biopower, in which Agamben is slandered and censored by the new burners of books. The greater our advance into the technologies and programmes of the new totalitarianism, the more rapidly our ability to understand and resist them has been discarded, until all we have left is the puritanism and show trials of political correctness, in which snap moral judgements have supplanted discursive thought.

In the formation of this totalitarian kitsch, the middle classes, liberals, academics, artists, writers, and the shambles of the Left, have all been complicit. In the previous chapters I have attempted to analyse the historical, ideological, juridical, economic, psychological, cultural, political and biopolitical formation of this new force of social homogeneity and conformity in the West, which has emerged as the model of citizenship in the Global Biosecurity State. In this chapter, however, my interest is in judgement of their culpability in this formation. Over the past two-and-a-half years, the political parties, radical organisations, trades unions, socialist, communist and anarchist groups, left-wing journals and liberal newspapers, and what passes for an intelligentsia in this most anti-intellectual of countries, have either remained silent or declared their servile allegiance to the greatest transfer of money from the public to the private sector on record, the greatest increase in the power of the political establishment since the neoliberal revolution four decades ago, and the severest restrictions on our human rights and freedoms in modern history. Not only do they present not the least resistance to the hegemony of state kitsch and woke law as the new orthodoxies of the Global Biosecurity State, but they are now the enemies of its enemies, employing the language of critique developed over a century of philosophical and political theory and practice not to question and challenge power but to entrench its authority further in the apparatus of the state and denounce those who dare to oppose it. It is on their complicity with power, their intellectual and moral cowardice, their bad faith and collaboration, that the biosecurity state has been constructed.

And now, as it creeks into action on the world stage, they have emerged from their hiding places to raise their hands in obedient salute to their new masters. As I argued in chapter 5, war is the *raison d'être*, the justification for and inevitable outcome of fascism, and the COVID-faithful in social media's auditorium, who had almost fallen silent in doubt and fear as the curtain was drawn back on the scenes of state violence and totalitarian control in Canada, Austria, Italy, Belgium, France, Lithuania, Australia, New Zealand and other theatres of fascism, haven't hesitated to raise their clarion calls for Act Two in the Ukraine. The fact that it's a proxy war, waged by a puppet government installed by a US-engineered coup, at the head of a state that until recently was universally denounced as neo-Nazi, led by a former dance show contestant and professional comedian whose most famous role was playing the President of Ukraine in a soap opera, who has recently banned opposing political parties and media outlets and blacklisted journalists and academics critical of his leadership, yet is now celebrated across the Western World as a champion of democracy and compared in the UK to Winston Churchill, is only the icing on the three-tiered cake of their extraordinary political naivety, their readiness to believe anything the media tells them, their complete denial of reality.

The world we live in — I take London to be representative of the fate of the West, as few places have been more colonised by capital, more subjected to the technologies of biopower — is not the real world. It is, to reference Jean Renoir's 1937 film about class allegiances during the Great War, a *Grande Illusion*. But we are forced to live in this illusion, to labour in its factories of unproduction, to earn its grudging exchanges, to shop in its palaces of alienation, to interact with each other under its intrusive gaze, for one simple though not exhaustive reason: because everything else — the real world and all it contained — has been stolen from us, including the land and all it once yielded, our common being with other forms of life, our community with each other, for which it has substituted the unceasing ravages of capital. The sphere of ideology in which we wander as if in a nightmare is there to protect us from perceiving to what depths of servitude, stupidity and inertia the human being has been reduced. What is real — to adopt Jacques Lacan's tri-partite classification of psychoanalytic phenomena — is what is most traumatic, threatening to pierce the cataracts of lies and self-deception that cover our transfixed eyes, the bad faith in which we live out our attempts to accommodate ourselves to the four walls of our windowless cell.[8]

The mandatory blue masks that fill our garbage heaps and litter our oceans are only the latest and most blinding form of these cataracts. One day soon, if we continue on our current trajectory, the entire human face will be erased and only our bodies will remain, micro-chipped and monitored by the Internet of Bodies, our biometric data uploaded to a centrally-controlled Health Code modelled on that currently used in the People's Republic of China, our movements and access to sustenance, care and housing, perhaps our very continuation as a living organism, contingent upon obedience to a global system of surveillance, monitoring, control, reward and punishment.[9] The citizen of the nation state, with its imperfect freedoms and rights, will be reduced to the bare life of the digitally-augmented organism. As Hannah Arendt argued in *The Origins of Totalitarianism*, one of the goals and definitions of totalitarian domination is to make human beings, with our spontaneity, our initiative and our powers of judgement, 'superfluous' to the running of the state. This, above all that I have written about the biosecurity state, is the dream of fascism, which began a century ago with a discourse of degenerate races, diseased bodies and useless mouths, and proceeded to attempt to subsume the human being within the mass mechanised machine of the military. 'Total War', the watchword declared by Joseph Goebbels in 1943 as the Red Army began its long defeat of the Third Reich, was the fascist

---

8. See Dylan Evans, *An Introductory Dictionary of Lacanian Psychoanalysis* (Routledge, 1996), pp. 159-161.

9. See Maria Gardner, 'The Internet of Bodies Will Change Everything, for Better or Worse', *RAND Corporation* (29 October, 2020).

ideal long before it was imposed as a military policy, the realisation of its dream of total domination, in which every constituent member, every biological body and its every action, was subsumed within the totalitarian state.[10]

Perhaps the strongest argument, however, for the return of fascism as the ideological superstructure of the Global Biosecurity State is the abject cowardice shown by 95 per cent of the populations of Western nations over the past two-and-a-half years by people who, living for longer and in greater physical security and material comfort than any generation in history, have reacted to an imaginary threat to public health with a cravenness that can never be wiped from living memory as surely as it will be erased from the historical records, and which marks a significant downward step in our decline as a civilisation and perhaps as a species. As a child of parents who lived through the Second World War, I've always wondered what it was like to have come through the mass compliance in mechanised slaughter. I know now that the overwhelming emotion was not one of relief that they had survived, or pride in those who helped 'defeat fascism' as they were told by their governments, or even horror at the unprecedented violence and ruin it had unleashed, but rather shame that, as a civilisation, the West had ever allowed such an obscenity to happen. I can imagine this shame because I see it all around me now. I see it in the belated re-emergence of the masked-up Left to protest against Government legislation removing our right to protest, because that's all it's capable of doing any longer in the wake of its collaboration with the biosecurity state. I see it in the triumphant return of Extinction Rebellion and its subsidiaries to our streets, declaring yet another 'health crisis', yet another 'emergency', insisting that we should all be 'terrified', demanding 'zero-carbon' and that we 'Follow the Science!' — as if the last two years has not revealed what such absolutist and religious rhetoric is serving. I see it in the pathetic conviction with which the COVID-faithful cling to their masks, plastic dividers, social distancing and the fourth, fifth and next dose of whatever 'vaccine' they're told to take against whatever new virus or pox the media conjures into existence. And I see it in the nostalgic longing with which the apostles of 'zero-COVID', led by the religious zealots in lab coats, point at the latest figures on hospital admissions in

---

10. See Joseph Goebbels, 'People, Rise Up, and Storm, Break Loose!', 18 February, 1943; collected in *Landmark Speeches of National Socialism*, edited and with translations by Randall Bytwerk (Texas A&M University Press, 2008), pp. 112-139.

the hope that another lockdown will be imposed — to which the governments of the West appear willing to concede. Above all, I see this shame in the sudden and far too eager readiness of the Western World to resume its utterly bankrupt defence of human rights in the Ukraine. Indeed, I feel this shame myself every time I see another person wearing a face mask — the shame that a fellow human being in whom I recognise myself can so easily be haltered, tamed and ridden.

Or perhaps it is no more complex than observing that, having developed such total power over the populations of the West, why wouldn't the international technocracies of global governance turn fascist, as they have with alarming rapidity and almost contemptuous ease? Last August I watched Ettore Scola's 1977 film *Una giornata particolare*, this 'special day' being 4 May, 1938, when Hitler visited Mussolini in Rome. It was an all-too-familiar study of the unrelenting propaganda of the state and the willing collaboration of the masses that propaganda had formed out of the working and middle classes, when being an 'anti-fascist' meant being an enemy of the state and being a fascist meant participating in public displays of blind conviction and moral righteousness. Seen from within the fascist state, it shows the dependence of the unity of homogeneous society on fear of its real or imagined subversive elements, the poles of attraction to the Leader and disgust with the ostracised that bound the Italian people together, the role of state spectacles in creating and maintaining these polarities, and the consensus of violence enacted against anyone who didn't belong, let alone dared to resist.

All these are returning — have returned today — on a cultural palette wiped clean of memory and knowledge, in the wake of a general moral collapse in which behaviour contrary to the previous norms of liberal democracies and violating our former rights and freedoms has become the new civil norm. The culture, philosophy, thought, art, literature of the West over the past century appear to have been forgotten in a vast act of willed amnesia, and in its place have been erected the statues of an ersatz culture founded no longer on covert but now on blatant and even celebrated acts of censorship, on equally blatantly manufactured and manipulated fear, on exacerbated and directed hatred against enemies within and without, on the suppression of disagreement in thought, speech and writing, on enforced acceptance of state orthodoxies hiding behind the plurality of opinion, on the authority of an increasingly militarised state power, on the punishment of apostasy without crime (what the Online Safety Bill calls 'legal but harmful'), on pride in publicly-declared stupidity, on ignorance of even the immediate past, on the adolescent certainties of woke ideology, the state kitsch of totalitarianism.

Orwell's vision of the future in *Nineteen Eighty-Four* was of 'a boot stamping on a human face — for ever'.[11] If the new totalitarianism has an equivalent image, it is of a medical mask in which a plastic window shows the wearer's smile, and which requires that smile never to fade. But then, what part of Orwell's dystopian image of the future doesn't describe our present? The police helicopters spying on us not only in the street but even in our own homes. The home workouts to instructions from a screen we never turn off. The children denouncing their parents for Thought Crime. The control of desire by pornography. The control of thought by Newspeak. The 24-hour surveillance under which we live. The indoctrination into doublethink. The energy shortages. The fake food we're told is better than the real thing. The selection of wars and allies for the spectacle of war. The squandering of wealth on armaments for a permanent state of war with enemies both real and imagined. The deliberate immiseration of the workers. The erasure of memory and the rewriting of history.

In 'Personal Responsibility under Dictatorship' — the public address she delivered in 1964 in response to the furore touched off by her book on Eichmann — Arendt recalled that what had 'morally disturbed' her during the first years of the Third Reich was not the brutal behaviour of the stormtroopers or the violence of the speeches made by National Socialist politicians and officials, but rather the 'overnight change of opinion that befell a great majority of public figures in all walks of life and all ramifications of culture' and the 'incredible ease with which life-long friendships were broken and discarded'.[12] Similarly, over the past two-and-half years it has not been the political behaviour of my enemies that has so disturbed me — for what else should we expect of those in positions of power except its abuse? — but rather the moral behaviour of those I had reason to believe were my friends or comrades, or in whom I could recognise some shared

---

11. George Orwell, *Nineteen Eighty-Four*; Everyman's Library, with an introduction by Julian Symonds (Alfred A. Knopf, 1992), p. 280.

12. Hannah Arendt, 'Personal Responsibility Under Dictatorship', collected in *Responsibility and Judgement*, edited and with an introduction by Jerome Kohn (New York: Schocken Books, 2003), p. 24.

moral principles beyond our differences of political opinion or understandings of the world. All that has been sacrificed to the new 'common good' of biosecurity. And just as happened in post-war Europe, after the shame of collaboration have come the denials of complicity, the justifications for compliance, the blanket amnesia and the attempts to rewrite recent history in their favour.[13] It took Germany a generation even to begin the process of coming to terms with its fascist past, and all it has produced is the hegemony of neoliberalism in a Europe it continues to dominate economically and politically, a historically revisionist culture devoted to equating socialism with fascism, and a 'Holocaust' industry that justifies, among other things, the apartheid State of Israel and the imperialism of the West.[14] And for all the forced celebrations this March even among those who opposed lockdown and refused to obey biosecurity regulations, our World War is not over. Indeed, to quote the great class-warrior himself, this is not the end. It is not even the beginning of the end. But it is, perhaps, the end of the beginning. But the beginning of what? If the initial stage of totalitarian rule, as Hannah Arendt wrote in the epigraph to this chapter, serves to render all further opposition impossible, now that impossibility appears to have been achieved and the international technocracies that rule our lives have nothing to fear from an opposition that never materialised beyond the largest protests in British history buried by the media and ignored by both Parliament and Government, how do we respond to the next wave of terror the Global Biosecurity State is about to release upon us?

The recent sight of public figures who for two years stood up and voiced their resistance to the biosecurity state from a broadly libertarian standpoint — as distinct from the millions who were protesting against the managed destruction of their jobs and businesses — now tugging their forelocks in deference to the Queen at the obscene spectacle of the Platinum Jubilee, or participating in the spectacle of the Wimbledon tennis championships from which Russian and Belarusian

---

13. See, among numerous recent examples, Jim Pickard, 'Liz Truss labels Boris Johnson's handling of Covid crisis "draconian"', *The Financial Times* (25 August, 2022); and Aubrey Allegretti, Nicola Davis and Caroline Davies, 'Sunak accused of "rewriting history" by saying No 10 ignored lockdown harms', *The Guardian* (25 August, 2022).

14. See Simon Elmer, 'Memorials of Forgetting: Art and Architecture in Berlin', *Architects for Social Housing* (21 July, 2016); and 'Dresden Diary: Architecture, History and Politics', *Architects for Social Housing* (6 July, 2018).

players were banned, or declaring to anyone who will listen that local communities in London resisting immigration snatch squads intent on sending refugees to Rwanda threatens law and order in the UK, or complaining that striking rail workers are 'holding the country to hostage', or repeating Theresa May's specious argument that — notwithstanding the fact that, over the past two-and-a-half years, the Bank of England pumped £895 billion in quantitative easing into the crashing financial sector while the Government spent £410 billion on lockdown — there's no 'magic money tree' with which to pay immiserated workers, or, most recently, joining the national queue to pledge their allegiance as loyal subjects to the King and all his descendants, indicates how much of their resistance came not from political conviction but from its infringement on their personal liberties.[15] Now those liberties have temporarily been restored, many of those who formed that resistance appear happy to go back to being the passive consumers of war, sport, monarchy, patriotism, police violence and the media's hatred of the working class. Like Friedrich Hayek, their definition of freedom is the personal freedom to buy and sell, to make money and spend it — the freedom of the entrepreneur and consumer. Their resistance, in other words, neither proposes an alternative to the periodic crises of finance capitalism that are paid for by the global working class nor forms an opposition to its new forms of global governance. What they oppose is having their dream of a free market exposed for what it is: the bad faith with which the middle classes have excused forty years of neoliberalism so long as the benefits 'trickle down' to them while the gap between rich and poor grows ever wider.

As both Eco and Hayek — and before them Orwell and Trotsky — observed, historical fascism drew its converts from the impoverished middle-classes, whose fear and hatred of the working class made them ready to accept any political system that promised to save them from the same fate. Without an understanding that the Global Biosecurity State is the logical consequence of the financial and political monopolies created by forty years of neoliberalism and a global financial system built on credit, what chance is there that middle-class libertarians facing the greatest drop in their standard of living in generations will continue to bite the hand that feeds them? Is it the case, as Orwell predicted, that unless we create a

---

15. See Atlantic Council, 'Global QE Tracker'; and Philip Brien and Matthew Keep, 'Public Spending during the COVID-19 pandemic', *House of Commons Library* (29 March, 2022).

socialist party with a genuinely revolutionary programme, this newly impoverished middle class will, to the contrary, form the cadre of the new fascism? History tells us they will. Indeed, they have already shown themselves only too willing to be the bureaucrats of the new totalitarianism.

And yet, in the name of a future politics whose foundation we cannot yet see, it is the fools who believed the Government, media and medical industry, the cowards who didn't but obeyed everything they said anyway, and even the collaborators who hoped to benefit from both, that we must continue to try to bring over to our side — the side of freedom, which will only be won in non-compliance, civil disobedience and mass resistance to the Global Biosecurity State.[16] We cannot repeat the catastrophic accusation of 'social fascism' with which the Communist International from 1928 dismissed every other party opposed to fascism, and in particular the Social Democrats, right up to and even past the election of Hitler to power in Germany in 1933, and which was only dropped as a policy when the Third Reich ruthlessly set about annihilating the Communist Party of Germany. Only in 1935, at the Seventh World Congress of the Comintern, was the ultra-left position of the Third Period finally abandoned and, in its place, Georgi Dimitrov announced the policy of bringing together opposition from across the political divides in an 'Anti-fascist People's Front'.[17] Within a year this policy brought Popular Front governments to office, however briefly and ineffectually, in France and Spain. In the UK, the Labour Party, fulfilling its historical role of suppressing any threat to capitalism from the working class, declined to form a Popular Front alliance with communists, liberals and even rebellious conservatives against the appeasement of Hitler by successive National Governments; and in the US the Socialist Party of America similarly declined the overtures of the communists. That these Popular Front governments ultimately collapsed in the face of fascist invasion and the betrayal of Republican Spain by Léon Blum's French Government is only another in the long history of the failures of the Left. But if, today, fascism has once again taken political power in the West, it has done so not only with the help of the Left's customary betrayals of workers in favour of its parliamentary aspirations, but this time with its willing and total

---

16. For examples, see the pages titled 'Non-Compliance with the UK Biosecurity State', part 3 of 'The UK "Vaccination" Programme. Part 3: Resistance', *Virtue and Terror*, pp. 127-134.

17. See Georgi Dimitrov, *The United Front: The Struggle Against Fascism and War* (London: Lawrence & Wishart, 1939), pp. 27-28.

collaboration. What in the 1930s was a tragedy that opened the catastrophe of the Second World War is being replayed today on a stage no less catastrophic for being implemented on the greatest farce in modern history. If a Popular Front government is ever to seize power in the future, it will have to start as a People's Front formed outside the control of existing parliamentary parties, whose aspirations extend no further than finding a seat at the new table being laid by the international technocracies of the Global Biosecurity State.

It is becoming increasingly difficult — I am struggling to find reasons — not to call the political, juridical and cultural forces produced by this revolution in Western capitalism 'fascist', and to describe the Global Biosecurity State these forces are imposing on the West as 'totalitarian'. As I argued in the previous chapters, the collaboration of governments and parliamentary oppositions across Europe and the West has demonstrated for those of us still interested that Left and Right no longer exist as political positions in the Global Biosecurity State, and any opposition to its hegemony based upon this division only serves to entrench it further in our political system. If you're on the side of the masked and armed police assaulting and arresting protesters demanding the return of their human rights and civil liberties, you're on the side of the fascists enforcing the Global Biosecurity State. If you're on the side of the people opposing them, you're on the side of freedom. The choice is as clear as it is unavoidable, and it's for each of us to make alone and then form ourselves into a People's Front against fascism. But what chance is there of such a thing happening? There is a world of difference between what needs to be done to bring down the new form of global governance by which we are now ruled and the realities of resistance after forty years of neoliberalism; and calls for a revolution that exists only in the dreams and programmes of revolutionaries serve only to divide opposition and justify the lack of resistance to the most decisive and long-prepared revolution in modern history to a new form of totalitarianism.

3. A Novel Form of Government

Not every fascist state has been totalitarian — for Arendt, neither Franco's Spain nor Mussolini's Italy (despite Mussolini's numerous claims to the term) ever qualified as such; and not every totalitarianism has been fascist — with Stalin's

Soviet Union and Xi Jinping's China being the primary examples; yet the evidence of the present is that the Global Biosecurity State will soon be both, if it is not already. For the first year-and-a-half of the coronavirus 'crisis', in the more than two dozen articles I wrote on the implementation and expansion of the UK biosecurity state and why and how we should resist it, I repeatedly warned that, with the removal of our rights, freedoms and politics and their replacement with the regulations and programmes of biosecurity, we were in danger of enabling the revolution of Western capitalism into a totalitarian society. Over the past year, however, when I have been able to reflect on where the previous two years have brought us, I have revised my opinion. It appears clear to me now that, in the UK and across most if not all of the West, we have been living in a proto-totalitarian society for some time, at least since '9/11' and the colonisation of neoliberal democracies by the US model of the National Security State.[18] What libertarians opposed to lockdown, Digital Identity and 'vaccine' mandates refuse to see is that the model for the Global Biosecurity State is not only the Social Credit system of the People's Republic of China but also, and primarily, the United States of America, whose financial services sector is its prime instigator and financier in the West.

When our every online search is used to build up a profile of our consumer interests, sexual predilections and political affiliations; when the record of our every consumer transaction is available to the highest bidder for undisclosed uses; when our faces are recorded at the checkout of every supermarket and linked to our bank accounts on the spurious basis of prohibiting theft; when every photograph of ourselves and our friends we have posted online is being used to build up a database for facial recognition technology covering the entire population; when those of us foolish enough to carry a Smart Phone have to comply with its scan of our own face in order to use its other facilities; when our presence in every street, alley, shop, office, civic building, train station, airport, sporting venue, housing estate and every other public space is recorded by a CCTV camera; when our ability to leave and enter the country is contingent upon being herded like cattle, interrogated like criminals and subjected to retinal scans

---

18. In the two decades between the attack on the World Trade Centre in September 2001 and the declaration of the 'pandemic' in March 2020, no less than 12 terrorism Acts, amendments and measures were made into UK law. See Simon Elmer, 'Legislation for the UK Surveillance State', section 3 of 'The New Normal (Part 1. Programmes and Regulations)', COVID-19, pp. 198-202.

and now DNA swabs; when we live under the threat of assault with impunity from one of the largest and most well-armed and equipped police forces in the world — I find it difficult to describe the society in which we have lived for the past twenty years as anything but the preparation of our laws, technologies and behaviours for the Great Reset, and therefore as pre-totalitarian. As Larry Fink, the CEO of BlackRock, candidly remarked in 2011:

> Markets don't like uncertainty. Markets like totalitarian governments, where you have an understanding of what's out there. Obviously, the whole dimension is changing now with the democratisation of countries. And democracies are very messy, as we know in the United States. In Northern Africa and the Middle East we're going to have an uncertain environment for many years, until we have an understanding of where this is all going to take us.[19]

Ten years later, he's got what the financial sector wanted. Now that our right to protest against any Government policy or legislation is dependent upon the good will of an increasingly politicised and ideological police force; now that the state has denied us not only the financial means but even the legal right to challenge the decisions of the Government and other public bodies in the law courts; now that the corporate media has become the unified propaganda arm of the state tasked with censoring anything the Government judges to be 'fake news', including the consequences of its own legislation; now that our citizenship can be removed on the judgement of a Government Minister without scrutiny by our elected representatives in Parliament or judgement by the judiciary; now that corporate-funded 'fact checkers' dismiss as 'conspiracy theory' any criticism of both the corporations funding them and the governments they fund; now that our opinions on anything from politics, 'vaccines' and war to corporate transparency and the new cultural and legal orthodoxies of woke are subjected to scrutiny and erasure by social media platforms soon to be empowered by legislation to censor anything the Government considers 'lawful but harmful'; now that our human rights are being replaced by the obligations of citizenship to the UK biosecurity state; now that our civil liberties are contingent upon compliance with the

---

19. See Erik Schatzker, 'BlackRock's Fink "Worried" About Stocks Amid Unrest', *Bloomberg* (3 March, 2011).

unaccountable decisions of organisations of global governance run by international corporations and the unelected technocrats of nation states; now that Digital Identity carrying our biometric data is being made a condition of access to everything from travel, healthcare and education to voting, welfare and work; now that our currency is on the verge of being limited, programmed and linked to our carbon footprint and medical 'status'; now that medical interventions on the cusp of being made mandatory will carry the technology to register compliance with whatever mandates the international health technocracy imposes; now that the opinions and publications of writers, academics and other researchers must comply with the official policies of the UK biosecurity state or face *ad hominem* attacks by the British Broadcasting Corporation; now that all workers in contact with the public, including teachers, are compelled to undergo indoctrination into woke orthodoxy through programmes like 'unconscious bias' and 'equality, diversity and inclusion' training; now that parental consent is no longer required before the state makes experimental mRNA 'vaccines', puberty blockers and irreversible medical procedures available to their children; now that journalists reporting from the Ukraine who do not parrot the Government's narrative have their bank accounts frozen and their assets seized; now that police are using live facial recognition technology to stop and search members of the public without cause; now the cameras recording us at supermarket checkouts are using the same technology to add to the data banks; now that we can be arrested by the police for posting a comment online that in their estimation has the potential to cause someone else 'anxiety' or 'offence' or carrying a banner that might cause a 'disturbance of the peace'; now that we are being herded into a system of Social Credit by which obedience to Government-dictated norms of behaviour and not merely the law will become a condition of citizenship in the biosecurity state; now that the biopolitical paradigm of the camp is being expanded into a permanent spatial arrangement of the state of emergency that will embrace the whole of society — it has become impossible not to describe the society in which we live now as totalitarian.

But what is totalitarianism? What I have described here is different from the criteria by which the political scientists, Carl Joachim Friedrich and Zbigniew Brzezinski, defined it in their 1956 book, *Totalitarian Dictatorship and Autocracy*. These included the following:

1.   Single political party, typically but not always led by a dictator;

2.   Elaborate ideology, to which every member of society is supposed to adhere;

3.   System of terror, using secret police and exploiting modern science to control the population;

4.   Government monopoly of all means of mass communication;

5.   Government monopoly on the ownership and use of all weapons;

6.   Centrally controlled economy through bureaucratic co-ordination of corporate entities.[20]

Formulated ten years into the Cold War, these criteria have been used by Western critics ever since to denounce authoritarian socialist governments in order, as I discussed in chapter 7, to distract our attention from the West's own collusion with authoritarian capitalist governments; but although many of them (particularly criteria 2-5) are not unrecognisable in the new form of governance emerging from the Global Biosecurity State, they are outdated as a description of the totalitarianisms of the Twenty-first Century, in which global technocracies and corporate monopolies of markets and governments in thrall to finance capitalism — and not authoritarian socialism — present the greatest threat to our freedoms in the West. What need is there for a single political party when the difference between parliamentary parties equally committed to crisis capitalism is in personnel and rhetoric and not policies or principles? What need is there for a centrally controlled economy when, as I discussed in chapter 7, our economy is run by international organisations of global governance? As for the rest, woke, as I discussed in chapter 6, is the newly emergent and soon to be dominant ideology of the Global Biosecurity State; the system of terror used to control the population, as we have witnessed and obeyed for two-and-a-half years, is biosecurity; and the monopoly on the use of weapons is not governmental exactly but, like our economy itself, administered by national governments on behalf of international arms dealers. As for our corporate-owned media, the ideological hegemony it has displayed in creating, manipulating and maintaining the manufactured 'crisis' in public health has never been witnessed before in the West, even during the professional wars we wage on sovereign states. Updated from the Cold War to

---

20. See Carl Joachim Friedrich and Zbigniew Brzezinski, *Totalitarian Dictatorship and Autocracy*, second edition (Harvard University Press, 1965), p. 22.

the Civil War national governments are waging against their own populations today, the Global Biosecurity State meets each of these definitions of totalitarianism. However, definitions require more than updating if we are to comprehend the new totalitarianism.

A far better definition of the particularity of totalitarianism as distinct from dictatorship, tyranny and despotism is provided by Arendt in *The Origins of Totalitarianism*, which although published five years before Friedrich and Brzezinski's book, more accurately describes our present. Although, in its third volume, Arendt identified the by now familiar criteria of replacing class differences with the politically indifferent masses, the emotional and irrational alliance formed between these masses and a charismatic Leader, the role of propaganda in forming and maintaining this alliance in the face of reality, the resulting subordination of the individual to the state, and the role of the police in enforcing and maintaining that subordination, in the second edition of her book, which was published in 1958, Arendt added a new concluding chapter titled 'Ideology and Terror: A Novel Form of Government'.[21] In this text, which was originally published separately in *The Review of Politics* in 1953, and in which she reflected on her larger study, Arendt laid out what was new and particular to totalitarianism as distinct from other forms of authoritarian government. And as one would expect of a political theorist with her perceptiveness and courage, Arendt's reflections on the novelty of totalitarianism as a system of government have far more to tell us about the new totalitarianism being imposed upon us today. Her text is so rich that it is difficult to summarise without losing much of its explanatory power, but I will try to confine my commentary to the elements that most illuminate our present and possible future. Arendt divides the novelty of this form of government into four essential aspects:

1. Obedience to the higher authority of a single idea
2. Rule by terror
3. Deductive logic of ideological thinking
4. Production of isolation and loneliness

---

21. See Hannah Arendt, 'Ideology and Terror: A Novel Form of Government', *The Review of Politics*, vol. 15, no. 3 (July 1953); reprinted in *The Origins of Totalitarianism*, second revised edition (Penguin Modern Classics, 2017), pp. 604-629.

1. Higher Authority

Arendt was neither a socialist nor a communist, and didn't flinch from comparing the totalitarianism of the Third Reich under Hitler to the Soviet Union under Stalin, for which she was widely criticised by the Left. However, far from wielding power in the interests of one man, which is was happens under a dictatorship like that of Mussolini, Franco or Pinochet, totalitarian regimes, despite being ruled by a Leader, posit a higher form of authority. Formulated irrespective of previously held conventions of right and wrong, it's from this authority, and not from the Leader, that the laws made by man derive their ultimate legitimacy. For National Socialism, this higher authority was the laws of Nature, under which those born with a form of disability or who were designated as members of a degenerate 'race' were killed; while, for Soviet Communism, it was the laws of History and those classes that stood in the way of the 'dictatorship of the proletariat'. Legally, this resulted in a state within the state by which the laws made by the executive, ratified by the legislature and administered by the courts to justify the crimes of the totalitarian state were constantly broken and made redundant by the declarations and actions of their Leaders.[22] In Nazi Germany, Hitler's words had the status of law the moment he spoke them; while in the Soviet Union, the constitution adopted in 1936, which guaranteed various rights, freedoms and democratic processes, was almost immediately made redundant by Stalin's purges of the party, army and ethnic minorities over the following two years. In both regimes, however, the Leader was the embodiment of this higher authority, whose laws it was the function of the population to realise, if necessary by their death. In the Third Reich, therefore, it was the laws of Nature and not man that justified the extermination of Jews, Poles, Slavs, gypsies, homosexuals and other 'undesirable' social elements; while in the Soviet Union it was the laws of History that justified the enforced famines, the purges and the gulag.

To these two abstractions, which took the place of religion in these officially atheist regimes, it was predictable that the laws of an equally abstract Science, which today has attained the same religious status across the West, would justify the totalitarianism of the Global Biosecurity State. As I discussed in chapter 5 on

---

22. On the functioning of 'The Dual State' in Germany under the Third Reich, see 'Repression and Resistance' in Richard J. Evans, *The Third Reich in Power* (Allen Lane, 2005), pp. 42-66.

the psychological structure of fascism, the COVID-faithful are as obedient to this apotheosised Science as communists and National Socialists were, respectively, to History and Nature. And as in the Third Reich, this obedience extends far beyond the letter of the law. Indeed, so rapidly and without justification or scrutiny were the 582 coronavirus-justified Statutory Instruments made into law at a rate of 6 per week in the UK that not even jurists were able to say at any one moment what was proscribed by the thousands of regulations by which a UK citizen could be fined or arrested. It was, therefore, as I stated at the start of this chapter, to the ideology of biosecurity, a new and legally undefined term in the West, that individuals attributed the source, the principle and the spirit of the man-made laws which few had read and fewer still understood. Indeed, the police forces tasked with enforcing this daily legislation openly stated that they did so not on the contents of the laws they are paid to officiate, which they complained were too numerous and changeable to follow accurately, but on what they decided were their spirit, and irrespective of the law.[23] In response to criticisms made by Jonathan Sumption, the former Justice of the Supreme Court, that the police were acting beyond their legal powers in enforcing lockdown restrictions on our freedom of movement, the Chief Constable of the Greater Manchester Police replied that, during a crisis, the police are free to do what they think is fit.[24] Sumption accurately described this as the definition of a police state.[25] In effect, the declarations made at the Government press-conferences that were held every day by a Minister flanked by scientists from SAGE and televised to the nation before their contents were even presented to Parliament had the force of law. But the unquestionable higher authority on which this legislation was made by Government Ministers whom few trusted but all obeyed was Science, which justified everything, including and above all the most unscientific justifications for the biosecurity state. This, unmistakably, is how the law operates within a totalitarian regime.

---

23. See Chris Matthews, 'Devon and Cornwall police clarify travel to exercise guidance', *Cornwall News* (2 April, 2020).

24. See Jonathan Sumption, 'Government by decree: COVID-19 and the Constitution', Cambridge Freshfields Annual Law Lecture, 27 October, 2020 (University of Cambridge, 2020).

25. See Jonathan Sumption, 'Former Supreme Court Justice: "This is what a police state is like", *The Spectator* (30 March, 2020).

2. Rule by Terror

What obedience to this higher authority means in practice is rule by terror, which is designed to translate the laws of Nature, History and now Science into reality. As I discussed in chapter 8 on the function of the camp as the new paradigm of governance, the purpose of terror is neither to suppress opposition to the government nor to punish those who disobey its laws, but rather to render human beings superfluous to the rule of the state in which the higher authority finds its realisation in the world. Terror only becomes total when it rules independent of all opposition, unhindered by human actions. Before its court and under its judgement, guilt and innocence become meaningless pleas. Neither the leadership nor the administrators of terror are guilty, since both execute a sentence in accordance with a higher tribunal. Indeed, even those upon whom judgement is executed are not guilty, since their sentence is dependent not on their agency, which a properly totalitarian regime has eradicated, but on their disposition within the laws of Nature, of History, or of Science. As the execution of this law, therefore, terror has as its goal not the welfare of the individual, which it eradicates for the sake of the species, but rather the fabrication of a new kind of human.

How often have we heard those forced to acknowledge the growing number of disabling and permanent injuries and deaths caused by the experimental COVID-19 'vaccines' dismiss the figures and documentation of victims unable to stand or walk, quivering uncontrollably, limbs amputated because of blood clots, previously healthy athletes collapsed from a heart attack or children dying in their sleep, with the argument that their suffering is worth it for the protection this experimental biotechnology has supposedly given to millions of others — the latest number conjured by Imperial College London is 20 million lives saved worldwide?[26] Under the judgement of this higher authority, the 1.5 million injuries and more than 2,200 deaths reported to the UK Medicine and Healthcare products Regulatory Agency, the 1.35 million injuries and nearly 30,000 deaths reported to the US Vaccine Adverse Events Reporting System, and the 4.4 million injuries and 45,300 deaths reported to the EU EudraVigilance, are either denied

---

26. See Emily Head and Dr. Sabine L. van Elsland, 'Vaccinations may have prevented almost 20 million COVID-19 deaths worldwide', *Imperial College London* (24 June, 2022).

outright as merely coincidental ('correlation without causality' being the mantra of the COVID-faithful) or dismissed as the collateral damage of a greater cause — this being biosecurity.[27] Under this judgement, therefore, neither the scientists who developed, the companies who produced, the doctors who authorised and the politicians who mandated these experimental 'vaccines' nor the medical professionals who administered them are responsible for their already catastrophic and as yet unknown consequences. Even the tens of thousands who have been killed in the West alone and the unknown millions who have been injured are not to blame. They were, are and will forever be those who fell to the judgement of Science. Arendt captured some of the cold indifference and passionate zealotry of the COVID-faithful when she writes: 'From the totalitarian point of view, the fact that men are born and die can only be regarded as an annoying interference with higher forces'.

In contrast, it is those of us who fail to comply with these higher forces — the so-called 'anti-Science anti-Vaxxers' — for whom the laws of man have been made, and the more who die from the judgement of Science, the harsher will be the laws made by our governments. It is not for us, however — the unbelievers in their dogma — that the totalitarian regime has been made, but for the COVID-faithful themselves. If, indeed, there is a purpose, and not merely opportunism and criminal negligence on a global and historical scale that deserves the description 'unprecedented', we cannot say yet what the purpose is of what numerous reports fear is the permanent damage to the immune systems and even disruption to DNA repair in the billions who willingly or under threats to their livelihoods have been injected with this experimental biotechnology.[28] But we can

---

27. See Medicines and Healthcare products Regulatory Agency, 'Coronavirus vaccine - summary of Yellow Card reporting'; Open VAERS, 'VAERS COVID Vaccine Adverse Event Reports'; and EudraVigilance, 'European database of suspected adverse drug reaction reports'. These figures have been analysed and compared to deaths from previous vaccines reported to the same organisations in 'At least 77K Dead and 7.3 Million Injured due to COVID Vaccination across USA, Europe, UK and Australia', The Exposé (11 June, 2022). As an example of how corporate Fact Checkers dismiss the evidence of these figures as 'misinformation' by ignoring such comparative analyses, see Reuters, 'Fact Check-VAERS data does not suggest COVID-19 vaccines killed 150,000 people, as analysis claims' (4 October, 2021).

28. For a clear and well-documented summary of these dangers, see Remnant, MD, 'First Principles: The Problem with Gene-based Injections — Part 1' (26 February, 2022); and 'Trojan

say that, like the totalitarianisms of the Twentieth Century, the Global Biosecurity State is intent on fashioning a new humankind in the Twenty-first Century, if not medically then psychologically, socially, culturally, legally and politically, the institutions of which all now operate in the service of the higher authority of Science according to the ideology of biosecurity. There was no shortage of transhumanists promoting their latest product at this year's annual meeting of the World Economic Forum, but pride of place should go to its Founder and Executive Chairman, Klaus Schwab, who at the Chicago Council on Global Affairs held in May 2019, a year before the 'pandemic' was declared, announced that: 'At the end, what the Fourth Industrial Revolution will lead to is a fusion of our physical, our digital and our biological identities'.[29]

3. Ideological Thinking

How this higher authority is constituted as a Nature that justifies genocide, or a History that justifies slave labour, or a Science that justifies lockdown is, of course, the work of ideology. For Arendt, ideology is not merely the political, legal and cultural superstructure of a given society, as it is within Marxist theory, but the third defining characteristic of totalitarian government, and one that solves a problem arising from the total domination of a population. Just as the laws of a constitutional government have a purely negative function, setting limits to actions rather than inspiring and guiding them, so terror is not sufficient to determine the behaviour of those who live in a totalitarian state. But since the goal of totalitarianism is to eliminate our capacity for action as it does our capacity for judgement, it substitutes, for a principle of action, our preparation to play the role of executioner or victim of the judgement of Nature, History or Science. This preparation is the function of ideology. What Nature was to National Socialism and History was to Soviet Communism, Science is to the Global Biosecurity State. The former is the higher authority of a single idea on which the rule of terror is justified, the latter the ideology through which that rule is implemented.

Horse: The Problem with Gene-based Injections — Part 2' (5 March, 2022); both published in *Perspectives in Medicine*.

29. See Klaus Schwab, 'World Economic Forum Founder Klaus Schwab on the Fourth Industrial Revolution', *The Chicago Council on Global Affairs* (13 May, 2019).

It is a characteristic of ideologies within a totalitarian state that they claim to explain everything by deduction from a single idea. In this respect, organised religions were the prototypes for totalitarian ideologies, and God the idea to which every higher authority aspires. But today, when Science has replaced God as the highest authority of Western secular societies, ideologies always claim to be scientific in their methods, whether they're formulating a discourse of race or class or — as in our own time — disease. That Science is the religion of the Global Biosecurity State is merely the apotheosis of the unquestionable character of the single idea from which all totalitarian ideologies derive their authority, and which allows them to explain not only the present but also the past and the future. Orwell expressed this in *Nineteen Eighty-Four* with the invented Party slogan: 'Who controls the past controls the future. Who controls the present controls the past.'[30] Ideology is the logic of the idea as it unfolds in history; and in that unfolding the idea is transformed into a first premise from which everything — and indeed anything — can be deduced. This unfolding is the process of logical deduction that totalitarianism substitutes for our human capacity for thinking. All ideologies have this character to a greater or lesser extent — with capitalism, for example, deducing the entire history of humanity from man's supposedly inherent competitiveness and desire for supremacy over others — but only in totalitarian regimes is the function of logical deduction without thinking fully revealed. 'War is peace / Freedom is slavery / Ignorance is strength.'[31] The lines inscribed on Orwell's Ministry of Truth are not the lies of a one-party state free to contradict itself in its own slogans; they are the logical deductions of ideological thinking in a totalitarian system that has returned today with slogans every bit as unthinking in the perfection of their logic. Obedience is freedom / Censorship is truth / Thinking is a crime.

According to Arendt, there are three elements peculiar to all ideological thinking that are specifically totalitarian. First, in their claim to total explanation, ideologies are always oriented towards history. Even when proceeding from the premise of Nature, as did the ideology of National Socialism, the struggle between competing races served to explain the movement of history, which it thereby reduced to an expression of Nature.

---

30. George Orwell, *Nineteen Eighty-Four*, p. 37.

31. George Orwell, *Nineteen Eighty-Four*, p. 6.

Second, ideological thinking is independent of all experience, from which it can and must never learn, deduced as it is from the higher authority of the idea concealed behind perceptible reality, which only the ideology allows its adherents to perceive. Today, the evidence of our own bodies is denied for the higher authority of Science, which through the fraudulent use of the RT-PCR test has fabricated the Truth of 'asymptomatic transmission', which has effectively turned COVID-19 into a disease without symptoms.[32] And as we are seeing with the almost total colonisation not only of our work practices but also of our leisure and pedagogical practices by the orthodoxies of woke, ideological indoctrination is the primary purpose of institutions within a totalitarian regime. As I discussed in chapter 6, the propaganda of totalitarian movements works to dissociate thought from experience and reality, for which it substitutes a hidden meaning which reveals itself only to the indoctrinated. And like woke, whose ideologues see and denounce an 'ism' in everyone not compliant with their ideology, as soon as a totalitarian movement comes to power it changes reality to fit its ideological claims. Perhaps the most telling example of this ideological thinking is the declaration, which all politicians, civic leaders and public figures must now repeat if they are to hold office or retain their position, that a biological male is in every respect a female if he declares himself to be a woman.

And third, since ideological thinking does not have the power to transform reality — to turn a man into a woman, a positive test into a disease, a locked-down country into a disease-free space, a face mask into a barrier to viral transmission, or gene therapy into a vaccine — its advocates and adherents must bring about the emancipation of thought from reality through methods of deductive demonstration. To this end, ideological argumentation deduces from

---

32. On 20 November, 2020, a Chinese study reported that, out of 9,899,828 residents and 92.9 per cent of the population of Wuhan tested between 14 May and 1 June a month after lockdown restrictions were lifted on 9 April, no new symptomatic cases and just 300 asymptomatic cases were identified. From the latter, no positive tests for SARS-CoV-2 were identified among 1,174 close contacts of asymptomatic cases. Further testing of 52,312 samples between 13 June and 2 July found no positive results; and two months after the screening of nearly 10 million residents, by 9 August there were still no newly confirmed cases of COVID-19 in the city most severely affected by COVID-19 in China. Statistically speaking, as a vector of infection, the asymptomatic transmission of SARS-CoV-2 doesn't exist. See Shiyi Cao, et al., 'Post-lockdown SARS-CoV-2 nucleic acid screening in nearly ten million residents of Wuhan', *Nature Communications* (20 November, 2020).

its first premise free from interference by experience or evidence or reality. Thus, the overwhelming evidence of the ineffectiveness and harms of face masks, lockdown and experimental 'vaccines' has done nothing to halt the demands by the COVID-faithful for their re-imposition this winter.[33] On the contrary, the greater the evidence for their dangers, the louder the ideologues of biosecurity call for their enforcement as part of their attempt to transform reality in accordance with their ideology, to turn a man into a woman simply because — indeed, precisely because — they have said so. If the sudden hegemony of trans-ideology over our politics, laws and culture has an explanation, it is in the power of the new totalitarianism to transform woke ideology into a weapon with which each citizen of the Global Biosecurity State can bring him, her, them, em, xem, per, ver, hir, aer or faer self into line with the rule of terror.[34]

What distinguishes the ideologies of totalitarianism from the previous ideologies of dictatorial, tyrannical or despotic regimes is that the 'idea' of the ideology is not its most important aspect. The most important aspect is the logical process deduced from the idea. Indeed, in the process of its realisation, the original basis on which the individual ideology made its appeal to the masses — whether that was saving the German nation from a Jewish conspiracy, emancipating Russian workers from the Tsarist autocracy, or saving the entire world from a deadly viral pandemic — is devoured by that process. Just as Germany under Hitler was reduced to ruins and Soviet workers had fewer freedoms under Stalin than they had under the Tsars, so global lockdown has killed more people and caused far more damage than COVID-19 could ever have done outside the fantastical predictions of its ideologues. But it is in the nature of ideological politics, Arendt argues, that the original content of the ideology that realises the idea in the world is devoured by the logic with which the idea is carried out.

In preparing the population to be either executioners or victims of the idea — and sometimes to be both in succession — the principle of action in a totalitarian ideology is not the ideology itself — whether racism or dialectical materialism or biosecurity — but its inherent logicality. According to this deductive logic, which

---

33. See Immanuel Marcus, 'Germany: New Corona Law Passes Bundestag', *The Berlin Spectator* (9 September, 2022).

34. See Lesbian, Gay, Bisexual, Transgender, Queer Plus (LGBTQ+) Resource Center, 'Gender Pronouns' (University of Wisconsin, 2022).

requires of its adherents nothing more than that they suspend their capacity to think, if A is true then B must also be true (in logical notation: A→B); and if B is true then so too is C; and if C is then so is D, all the way down the alphabet to whatever conclusion is desired for total domination. We don't have to look at the absurdities of the Moscow Show Trials of the 1930s or the Jewish conspiracy of Bolshevik bankers with which the German public was terrorised for examples of the coercive force of such logical deduction and where it can lead. It is by what Arendt calls 'the tyranny of logicality' that we have surrendered our inner freedom to think just as we have surrendered our freedom of movement. And to counter the possibility of anyone thinking, which is the opposite of the compulsory process of deduction, the self-coercive force of logicality is increased as the grip of totalitarianism tightens.

Today, having convinced the populations of the West to comply with an experimental programme of mass injection for a disease that presents no more of a threat to our health and medical infrastructure than seasonal influenza, the sudden increase in heart attacks in the young and healthy has been blamed on everything from solar storms, gardening, napping too much, warm weather and a poor diet to cold weather, skipping breakfast, drinking less alcohol than the NHS recommends, cannabis-use in the young, the stress of watching football, car fumes caused by breaking suddenly, shower habits, sleeping in the wrong position, rising energy bills, depression, an unnamed 'stealth disease' and, of course, COVID-19.[35] And by the same deductive logic, the climate 'crisis' is now

---

35. See Alice Klein, 'Solar storms may cause up to 5500 heart-related deaths in a given year', *New Scientist* (17 June, 2022); Terri-Ann Williams, 'Urgent warning to gardeners as soil "increases risk of killer heart disease"', *The Sun* (1 July, 2022); Christopher Sharp, 'Heart Disease: Day napping may increase risk of symptoms', *The Express* (13 August, 2022); Andrew Gregory, 'Hotter nights increase risk of death from heart disease for men in early 60s', *The Guardian* (28 March, 2022); Helen Puttick, 'Rise in heart attacks attributed to pandemic stress and poor diet', *The Times* (16 October, 2021); Helen Millar, 'What is the link between cold weather and heart attacks?', *Medical News Today* (29 June, 2022); Benjamin Lynch, 'Why skipping breakfast can increase your risk of having a heart attack', *The Mirror* (15 December, 2021); Victoria Allen, 'Drinking less than NHS alcohol guidelines could increase risk of heart attacks', *Daily Mail* (28 January, 2022); Karen Schmidt, 'Cannabis use disorder may be linked to growing number of heart attacks in younger adults', *American Heart Foundation* (8 November, 2021); Ollie Lewis, 'Football fans are "at risk of a heart attack" due to intense levels of physical stress while watching their team play, Oxford researchers claim', *Daily Mail* (24 January, 2022); Shaun Wooler, 'Car fumes from exhaust and heavy breaking raise risk of heart attacks, study suggests', *Daily Mail* (24 August, 2022); Simran

the cause of everything from a hotter than average summer in the UK to house fires and the rise in the cost of living. At the same time, the growing number of scientific reports on the causal connections between mRNA injections and myocarditis and pericarditis in the young and healthy, and the unavoidable but still denied connection between the trillions of dollars of money printed since September 2019 and our spiralling inflation, are dismissed as conspiracy theories by the ideologically indoctrinated.[36]

The hegemony of ideological thinking has the effect not only of concealing the actions and absolving of responsibility the actual agents of the observed 'crisis' — the individuals, companies and governments responsible for pollution, inflation, the rising cost of living and excess deaths — but also of making each citizen personally responsible for saving the planet, reducing inflation, saving energy and combatting the virus by their individual actions. This, inevitably, entails the personal and willing 'sacrifice' not only of our standard of living but also of our individual freedoms: not only our freedom of movement, assembly, association, privacy and expression but also, and primarily, the sacrifice of our freedom of thought.[37] Indeed, this self-coercing force of deduction is the necessary complement to the compulsion of total terror, the success of which can be

---

Arora, 'Heart attacks in healthy people: A popular shower habit could take the blame', *Times Now* (21 July, 2022); Zachary Mack, 'Sleeping in this position could be hurting your heart, studies say', *Best Life* (1 March, 2022); Neil Shaw, 'Energy bill price rise may cause heart attacks and strokes, says TV GP', *Wales Online* (3 February, 2022); A. Pawlowski, 'Depression worsened during pandemic, boosting heart disease risk, experts warn', *Today* (17 November, 2021); Vanessa Chalmers, 'Urgent warning as 300,000 Brits living with stealth disease that could kill within 5 years', *The Sun* (26 January, 2022); Saima May Sidik, 'Heart-disease risk soars after COVID — even with a mild case', *Nature* (10 February, 2022).

36. For a review of the scientific literature, see Samantha Lane, Alison Yeomans and Saad Shakir, 'Reports of myocarditis and pericarditis following mRNA COVID-19 vaccination: a systematic review of spontaneously reported data from the UK, Europe and the USA and of the scientific literature', *National Library of Medicine* (5 July, 2022).

37. Recent examples of this call to sacrifice include, in June, the German Foreign Minister and member of the Green Party, Annalena Baerbock, saying she would keep imposing sanctions on Russia 'no matter what German voters think'; the UK Prime Minister, Boris Johnson, on a visit to Kiev in August, announcing Britons would endure higher energy bills at home as part of Ukraine's 'sacrifice'; and the French President, Emmanuel Macron, the same month, declaring the French people would be facing 'sacrifices' for the sake of 'liberty'.

measured by the extent to which people have lost contact not only with each other but also with the reality of the world around them. Arendt writes:

> The ideal subject of totalitarian rule is not the convinced Nazi or the convinced Communist, but people for whom the distinction between fact and fiction (i.e., the reality of experience) and the distinction between true and false (i.e., the standards of thought) no longer exist.[38]

As I argued in the previous section on the moral collapse in the West during the two years of the politically declared 'pandemic', the Global Biosecurity State has succeeded in producing just such a subject as its ideal citizen, whose ideological deductions from a first premise are not confined to the regulations and programmes of biosecurity. In a recent protest by Doctors for Extinction Rebellion, held on 17 July two days after the UK Health Security Agency had declared a 'heat emergency', medical professionals broke the windows of the office of JP Morgan Chase, the international financial services and investment bank in London's Canary Wharf.[39] Their stated justification for doing so followed the following chain of deductions, which began with the by-now familiar premise that:

1. Global warming is increasing because of man-made climate change;
2. The primary cause of climate change is fossil fuels;
3. JP Morgan is the world's biggest financier of fossil fuels;
4. The two days in which the UK was predicted to have temperatures of 40 degrees Celsius are proof of this climate crisis;
5. Climate crisis is a health crisis that threatens life on earth;
6. Medical professionals sign a code of conduct that includes the obligation to: 'Act without delay if they believe that there is a risk to patient safety or public protection';
7. Patients under their care, including those suffering from dementia and mental stress, will die as a consequence of this two-day 'heatwave';

---

38. Hanna Arendt, *The Origins of Totalitarianism*, p. 622.
39. See UK Health Security Agency, 'Heat-health advice issued for all regions of England' (15 July, 2022); and Chris Newman, 'Doctors for XR crack glass at JP Morgan as UK declares heatwave "national emergency"', *Doctors for Extinction Rebellion* (17 July, 2022).

8. Therefore, it is the obligation of medical professionals to do all they can to stop the causes of this 'health crisis'.

The question of whether the earth is warming up because of human actions or because of a natural cycle of climate change is outside the parameters of this book; although I have written before about the attribution of climate change to the abstract figure of 'man' rather than to capitalism.[40] And one might question why medical professionals who obediently, repeatedly and without question or protest continue to inject experimental 'vaccines' into millions of UK citizens while ignoring the overwhelming evidence of their threat and damage to health and life are now so concerned about their code of conduct when they have ignored their Hippocratic oath to 'first do no harm' with far more immediate and devastating consequences than their predictions about the effects of two days of hot weather. One might also wonder about their willingness, in the wake of two years of lockdown restrictions, to so readily use the by now familiar language of 'health' and 'emergency' to advertise their protest, and ask whose agenda their protest is furthering. Nor do they appear to be interested in drawing attention to the investment of JP Morgan and other international financial institutions in the Agenda 2030 development programmes, to which just about every government of the member-states of the United Nations has signed up without consultation with their parliaments or populations; or to the influence such institutions have on the organisations of global governance they form, and which increasingly dictate the policies of our democratically-elected national governments.[41] And why should they, when it's precisely these programmes Extinction Rebellion has been formed to promote? Indeed, the ease with which protests on privately-owned land under some of the most extensive surveillance and strictest laws in the world gain unimpeded access to the property of some of the most powerful and protected corporations in the world raises the question of how and why Extinction Rebellion is able to circumvent not only the private security arrangements of these

---

40. See Simon Elmer, 'Extinction Rebellion: Socialist Revolution', *Architects for Social Housing* (24 April, 2019); and 'Capitalising on Crisis: Extinction Rebellion and the Green New Deal for Capitalism', *Architects for Social Housing* (10 October, 2019); and Antonino Zichichi, Renato Angelo Ricci and Aurelio Misiti, 'Petition on Anthropogenic Global Warming' (17 June, 2019).

41. See United Nations, 'Transforming our world: the 2030 Agenda for Sustainable Development', *Department of Economic and Social Affairs*.

companies but also the attentions of the Metropolitan Police Service, Transport for London and the UK's own security services. As someone familiar with the surveillance, attention and actions the police give to protests in this city, my only explanation is that, since Extinction Rebellion is furthering the agenda of crisis capitalism, the global technocracies pushing this agenda have told the London Mayor, the Metropolitan Police Service and every other institution of civic order in the UK and other Western nations to back off.[42] Totalitarian governments have always been adept at mobilising the masses into the spectacle of 'The People', whether in organised marches or in spontaneous protests, in order to further their control over the isolated and lonely individuals who, through their willing participation, imagine and are encouraged to believe that they constitute just such a political body, such a force for change towards a single great 'idea'.

My point in quoting the arguments of these protests by Extinction Rebellion here, however, is less to take issue with the factual content of their claims than to show how ideology functions to create, from a first premise derived from a widely accepted idea, an unbreakable chain of logical deductions that require no thinking from those who repeat and follow them to their seemingly logical and unavoidable conclusion, and which demand and justify extreme actions. A similar chain of deductions started from a similarly unexamined but widely accepted first premise:

1. Germany is in decline because of foreign influences on the Aryan people;
2. The primary cause of national decline is the international banking system;
3. Jews are the most powerful bankers in Germany;
4. Hyperinflation in the 1920s and the Great Depression in the 1930s are both proof of the national decline;
5. Financial crisis is a political crisis that threatens all of Germany;
6. Politicians swear allegiance to the German nation and must act without delay if they believe there is a threat to the safety of the state and people;
7. People under their governance, including Germans of Aryan blood living in poverty, will die as a consequence of the financial crisis;
8. Therefore, it is the obligation of politicians to do all they can to stop the causes of this financial crisis.

---

42. See Simon Elmer, *Inequality Capital: A Power Walk by Architects for Social Housing* (April 2019).

There were other and completely incompatible chains of deduction, including the influence of Russian Bolshevism, that the ideology of National Socialism drew from the decline of Germany, just as the environmental crisis is being used to further the rise of totalitarian programmes justified by the coronavirus crisis. But we all know where this ideological thinking led the German politicians who wanted to save the German people from the Jewish conspiracy of Bolshevik bankers. Of course, it should be clear from the previous chapters that I am in no way defending the actions of JP Morgan Chase and the other institutions responsible for the financial crisis of September 2019 that required the lockdown of the Western World in March 2020, both of which are the primary causes of the current inflation. And there is a world of difference between the windows of Jewish-owned businesses and synagogues smashed across the Third Reich on *Kristallnacht* in November 1938 and the windows of the international banks offering their investment and laundering services in the financial capital of the world on the promise from the UK Government that they will be bailed out by the UK public when their speculations melt into air. But there is a parallel between the deductive logic from a first premise that leads an Extinction Rebellion doctor to smash the windows of a bank and a National Socialist stormtrooper to smash the windows of a Jewish-owned business.

The collaboration of the medical profession in the manufactured health 'crisis' has shown that, behind their masks and coloured smocks, doctors and nurses are skilled technicians and nothing more, and with very few and honorable exceptions do not have the time, the education, the disposition or the intellectual capacity to make judgements about the efficacy, necessity or consequences of restrictions and programmes that have laid the foundations for the Global Biosecurity State. The absurd elevation of the profession in the eyes of the general public to the final arbiters of our politics, laws, rights and freedoms has undoubtedly gone to the heads of many of its members, not least the teary-eyed acolytes sitting hand-in-hand outside JP Morgan, and Extinction Rebellion has been quick to utilise this newly-accorded status in the service of their own agenda to promote the crisis capitalism I discussed in chapter 4. In this respect, although the ideology of environmental crisis preceded that of biosecurity, the latter replicated the former's logical deductions to arrive at conclusions with even greater consequences for the politics, laws and cultures of the neoliberal democracies of the West. No-one will be unfamiliar with this chain of deductions, every one of which has been proven to be either factually false or logically inconsequent — none of which, of course, has done anything to alter the apparently irrefutable argument they form in the minds of the indoctrinated:

1. Coronavirus is a new pathogen constituting an unprecedented threat that, if not stopped, will kill 40 million people globally in the first year alone;[43]
2. The virus is transmitted from person to person via surfaces, aerosols and droplets;
3. Asymptomatic transmission is the primary driver of infection, so everyone is a potential threat to the lives of others;
4. The huge numbers of infections and deaths recorded with a positive PCR test are proof of the virulence and fatality rate of the virus;
5. The public health crisis is a pandemic that threatens the world;
6. Citizens have an obligation to sacrifice their freedoms and rights for the greater good until the health crisis is over;
7. People will die if we don't all obey the regulations and programmes of biosecurity, including social distancing, mandatory masking, contact tracing, swab testing and lockdown restrictions;
8. Only mass vaccination of the entire population of the planet will allow governments to remove these restrictions and build back better to the new normal.

Just as this chain of deductions without thinking led us, in just two years, to the Global Biosecurity State, so too the environmental crisis, whose deductive logic, so far, has been almost universally adopted by the governments, civic institutions and private corporations of the West, will continue far beyond its current conclusions. Even as I write, global warming is being used to form a chain of deductions that, in their furtherance of totalitarian domination, parallel those of the Global Biosecurity State when it made injection with experimental gene therapy a condition of citizenship. In the Netherlands, which is the second-largest exporter of agricultural goods in the world after the USA, farmers are being forced

---

43. See Neil Ferguson, et al., 'Report 12 — The global impact of COVID-19 and strategies for mitigation and suppression', *Imperial College London* (12 June, 2020).

to kill a third of their livestock to meet their Government's 'zero-carbon' commitments.[44] And with the Government refusing to intervene on rocketing energy prices in the UK, it has been predicted that two-thirds of UK citizens, 45 million people, will be driven into fuel poverty by 2023.[45] While the President of the European Commission has proposed a mandatory target for reduced electricity use during peak hours in order, as she expressed it with a by-now familiar justification, 'to flatten the curve'.[46] Indeed, it is in the imminent programmes of Digital Identity, Central Bank Digital Currency, Universal Basic Income, Social Credit, Environmental, Social and Governance Criteria, Sustainable Development Goals, Pandemic Prevention, Preparedness and Response, and all the other programmes of Agenda 2030 that the deductions from these respective crises will meet in a new and properly totalitarian world order in which the entire natural world (estimated by the New York Stock Exchange at $4 quadrillion) will be monetised and converted into financial capital.[47] The more the two ideologies converge, the more they divest themselves, as Arendt said, of the ideas they claim to realise, whether that's saving us from a deadly virus or saving the planet from us, both of which are devoured by the logic of totalitarian domination. Every argument that starts with the terror of a crisis and then uses it to justify coercive action does so in order to circumvent critical thinking; and whether the Newspeak slogans are those of the UK Government displayed on the podiums from which they announced biosecurity regulations to the nation for two years ('Stay Home / Protect the NHS / Save Lives'), or those of Extinction Rebellion laid out on the pavements from which they continue to stage their promotions for Agenda 2030 ('Act Now / Stop Ecocide / Save Lives'), their aim is to form an unbreakable chain of deductions that obviates and indeed precludes our capacity for thinking.[48]

---

44. See Andy Bounds, 'Dutch farmers in uproar over plans to curb animal numbers to cut nitrogen emissions', *Financial Times* (3 August 2022).

45. See University of York, 'Two-thirds of UK households to be in fuel poverty by the new year, according to new report' (8 August, 2022).

46. See European Commission, 'Statement by President von der Leyen on energy' (7 September, 2022).

47. See Ellen Brown, 'Conservation or Land Grab? The Financialization of Nature', *The Web of Debt Blog* (5 November, 2021).

48. Extinction Rebellion signs, exactly mimicking those used by the UK Government, bearing these slogans were used in a Doctors for XR protest at the office of JP Morgan in Glasgow in

4. Isolation and Loneliness

Finally, the fourth characteristic of totalitarian government identified by Arendt are the subjective experiences produced by a form of governance whose essence is terror and whose principle of action is the logic of ideological thinking. The first of these is the isolation of individuals from and against each other, which often marks the beginning of terror and is always its result. Isolation transforms the class solidarity in which the worker found collective agency against the exploitation of capitalists into the masses in which fascism binds the population together under the false unities of nation, state and obedience to the Leader. Indeed, Arendt identified the transformation of classes into masses, which was the explicit goal of Italian fascism, with the consequent elimination of all collective solidarity, as the necessary condition of total domination; for terror can only rule absolutely over individuals who are isolated and therefore powerless to act together, and is, therefore, pre-totalitarian.

The individual produced by the masses of modernity was the 'man of the crowd', alone among the thousands of people on the street in a city of several millions; or the worker in the factory, repeating over and over his single contribution to the process of mechanical production, as alienated from his own labour as he was from his fellow workers, with whom he found solidarity in the consciousness of his class and the organisations by which that consciousness threatened to become a political force. It was precisely this that fascism sought to destroy. But totalitarianism went a step further, with loyalty to workers' unions supplanted by obedience to the so-called workers' party — something we see today with the unquestioning support UK unions give to the Labour Party, no matter how neoliberal its policies, how little it supports industrial action, how deferential it is to the UK monarchy. Today, though, the masses no longer exist on the street — which outside the spectacles of democracy have been all but banned to spontaneous manifestations of collectivity by the privatisation and policing of public space — but in the equally privatised and policed space of the online world. To date — though doubtless even more efficient technologies of

---

November, 2021. See Extinction Rebellion, 'Doctors stage die-in at JP Morgan Glasgow in ongoing campaign, demanding they end new fossil fuel investment' (5 November, 2021).

isolation await us — there is no better demonstration than social media of how the World Wide Web produces the isolated and politically impotent individual.

However, while isolation in the political sphere has always been a fundamental characteristic of all forms of tyranny, totalitarianism also produces, within the sphere of social interactions, loneliness. These two experiences, Arendt explains, are not the same:

> While isolation concerns only the political realm of life, loneliness concerns human life as a whole. Totalitarian government, like all tyrannies, certainly could not exist without destroying the public realm of life, that is, without destroying, by isolating men, their political capacities. But totalitarian domination as a form of government is new in that it is not content with this isolation and destroys private life as well.[49]

It's hardly necessary to say how accurately this passage describes the increasingly explicit goals of the Global Biosecurity State. If the creation of the masses as isolated individuals has been the product of the online world to which the international technocracies are restricting as much of our social and political interactions as possible, from business, commerce and entertainment to education, health and what remains of public debate, loneliness has been the deliberately produced result of biosecurity 'measures' that have justified the atomisation of each citizen from each other, exacerbating our fear of and distance from the world. Indeed, the digital and virtual replacement of the phenomenal and actual world of our five senses and lived experience is the stated goal of the technological companies that have modelled the Global Biosecurity State on the online world.

Our resulting loneliness, which has increased significantly since lockdown was imposed in March 2020, is a product of the experience of feeling one's self superfluous to the world, and with it of losing our capacity for thought and experience: our sense of both ourselves and the world in which we previously lived with others. In this respect, loneliness, which has been the experience of the modern masses since the First Industrial Revolution, when workers' actions were taken from them as alienated labour, and was sharpened in the Twentieth Century under the abstract and incomprehensible rule of finance capitalism, prepared man

---

49. Hannah Arendt, *The Origins of Totalitarianism*, p. 624.

for totalitarian domination by purging him of his capacity for thinking. As Arendt writes:

> The only capacity of the human mind which needs neither the self nor the other nor the world in order to function safely, and which is as independent of experience as it is of thinking, is the ability of logical reasoning whose premise is self-evident.[50]

In what appears to be a reference to Orwell's *Nineteen Eighty-Four*, which had been published only four years before, Arendt argues that, deprived of that common sense with which we share the world with other human beings, the isolated and lonely individual falls back on the truism that 'two and two equals four', which appears like the last place in which to stand in a drowning world where nobody is reliable and nothing can be relied upon. But this, she says, is an empty truth, or rather no truth at all, since it reveals nothing. Only the deductive logic of ideological thinking leads its adherents to the conclusion that — in an echo of Orwell — 'sometimes they are five'.[51]

From this experience of political isolation and social loneliness derives the extremism characteristic of totalitarian movements, whose ideological thinking — despite its claims to radicalism — always leads its adherents to the worst possible conclusions. Whether that's the civilisation-threatening virus proclaimed by the COVID-faithful or the imminent environmental catastrophe proclaimed by the acolytes of Extinction Rebellion, totalitarian thinking continues to rely on catastrophe as the principle of action. As numerous news platforms reporting on grass fires in Southern Europe during the two days of hot temperatures in July unanimously declared, this was a 'heat apocalypse'; and any attempt to point to the temporary area of low-pressure off the coast of Portugal drawing hot air from North Africa, or the contribution of residential development in forested areas to the artificial build-up of brushwood and other potential sources of fuel, was denounced as 'climate change denialism'.[52]

---

50. Hannah Arendt, *The Origins of Totalitarianism*, p. 627.

51. George Orwell, *Nineteen Eighty-Four*, p. 263.

52. See 'Europe's Heat Apocalypse', *The Guardian Weekly* (22 July, 2022).

This is where totalitarian government steps in. In a broadcast televised in March 2020, during which she denied her Government's intention to impose lockdown restrictions, the Prime Minister of New Zealand, Jacinda Ardern, who has since become one of the most zealous implementers of the Global Biosecurity State, warned the individual members of a national population she would subsequently isolate from each other and cut off from the rest of the world for longer than almost any other nation in the West, about listening to rumours and disinformation.[53] In a statement that would not sound out of place in the mouth of O'Brien in *Nineteen Eighty-Four*, Ardern in 2020 instructed the citizens whose rights and freedoms she was about to remove for the better part of two years not to listen to any source of information other than her Government:

> Dismiss anything else. We will continue to be your single source of truth. Take everything else you see with a grain of salt. Remember that, unless you hear it from us, it is not the truth. We will continue to provide everything you need to know.[54]

But, we might ask with Winston Smith in our online Room 101, how can we help seeing what is in front of our eyes? Two and two are four. Sometimes, is the response we've learned to accept from our governments. Sometimes, if the pharmaceutical companies say otherwise, they are five. Sometimes, if the Fact Checkers tell us, they are three. And sometimes, when the Global Biosecurity State says so, they are all of them at once. We are slow learners, but we're learning how to think ideologically. Follow the Science. Asymptomatic transmission is the primary driver of viral infection. My vaccine only works when you take yours. Your human rights end where mine begin. No-one is safe until everyone is safe. We will own nothing and be happy.

Arendt's final comments in her text, whose historical and political context was the Cold War and her fears for the future, are both a warning of the return of

---

53. For the severity and length of New Zealand's lockdown, see Hannah Ritchie, Edouard Mathieu, Lucas Rodés-Guirao, Cameron Appel, Charlie Giattino, Esteban Ortiz-Ospina, Joe Hasell, Bobbie Macdonald, Saloni Dattani and Max Roser, 'Policy Responses to the Coronavirus Pandemic', *Our World In Data* (Jan 2020-August 2022).

54. See Derek Cheng, 'Coronavirus: Jacinda Ardern dismisses nationwide lockdown speculation on social media', *New Zealand Herald*, 19 March, 2020.

totalitarianism as a 'potentiality' and an 'ever-present danger', and the hope — if that is what it still is — that totalitarian domination 'bears the germs of its own destruction.'[55] The danger for us, seventy years later, is not that the new totalitarianism of the Global Biosecurity State will establish a permanent world — for no world, not even a totalitarian one, lasts forever — but that it threatens to ravage a world 'in which everywhere seems to have come to an end', she writes, before the chance of a new beginning rising from this end and contained within it has a chance to germinate. This beginning, which Arendt says is identical with the freedom of man and born again with each of us, is what totalitarian domination seeks to eradicate by making humans superfluous to the form of its governance. As the ascendance of the camp as the biopolitical paradigm of the Global Biosecurity State demonstrates, this superfluity of humanity is at the heart of the post-human technologies and programmes of the Fourth Industrial Revolution.

---

55. Hannah Arendt, *The Origins of Totalitarianism*, p. 628.

10. Humanity in Dark Times

'We need to conceptualise an alternative political configuration that could escape the eternal oscillation — one that we have been witnessing for decades — between a democracy that degenerates into despotism and a totalitarianism that is shaped in an apparently democratic form. For a careful observer it is difficult to decide whether we live today, in Europe, in a democracy that uses increasingly despotic forms of control, or in a totalitarian state disguised as a democracy. It is beyond both that a new, future politics will have to appear.'

— Giorgio Agamben, 'Polemos Epidemios', *Babylonia*, May 2020

1. The Politics of Friendship

In 1959, eight years after the publication of her book on *The Origins of Totalitarianism*, Hannah Arendt gave a talk on the German Jewish Enlightenment writer, philosopher, dramatist and art critic, Gotthold Lessing, titled 'On Humanity in Dark Times'. Delivered in Hamburg, Germany, upon her acceptance of the Lessing Prize, it was Arendt's chance to reflect further on how a new beginning can germinate within a totalitarian world, and she does so around a discussion on the politics of friendship. This talk went on to become the introductory text to a collection of Arendt's profiles of twentieth-century intellectuals, some of whom were her friends, including Rosa Luxemburg, Karl Jaspers, Walter Benjamin and Bertolt Brecht, which was published in 1968 under the title *Men in Dark Times*.[1] By 'dark times' Arendt meant those periods in history in which the world becomes so obscured in darkness that people cease to ask any more of politics than that it guarantee their individual freedom and survival, a demand that precisely describes our own time, when the conditions of both have been made very clear to the compliant. Arendt's reference is to Brecht's famous poem, *To Those Born After*, written in 1939 on the brink of the Second World War, which begins: 'Truly, I live in dark times!'; and her book is an examination of how each of these more

---

1. Hannah Arendt, 'On Humanity in Dark Times', *Men in Dark Times* (San Diego: Harcourt Brace & Company, 1968), pp. 3-31.

or less public figures lived through them, and what light their work and life casts on the darkness.[2] Discussing the only figure in the collection not from her own century, the talk on Lessing introduces the importance Arendt attributed to friendship, which she elevates in this text to a political relationship both to others and to the world in which we live with others. The basis of her argument, which I want to draw on in this final chapter, is the distinction Arendt makes between the politics of fraternity and that of friendship.

To the *liberté* and *égalité* that had always been categories of the political demands of the oppressed, the exploited and the persecuted, the French Revolution of 1789 added *fraternité*. Insofar as this concept drew on eighteenth-century theories of a fundamental human nature underlying and transcending the multiplicity of nations, peoples, races and religions into which the human race has been divided by different ideologies, fraternity was understood as the fulfilment of humanity. This human nature, however, was manifested not through reason but in compassion, which was made an inseparable motive of the subsequent history of European revolutions. Indeed, insofar as it is an aspect of human nature that responds to the sight of suffering in others, compassion would seem to be an ideal basis on which to establish a society in which all of humankind might really become 'brothers'. A barrier to the formation of this society, though, was that humanity manifests itself in such brotherhood most frequently in 'dark times', and it does so primarily for persecuted peoples and enslaved groups. Humanity in the form of fraternity, therefore, is the great privilege of what Arendt calls 'pariah peoples', accompanied as it is by their radical 'loss of the world'.[3]

On the one hand, this loss creates an intimacy, intensity and warmth of human relationships of which human beings are otherwise scarcely capable. Those of us who participated in them experienced this in the marches against lockdowns and 'vaccine' mandates, which, without security of any kind and in the face of provocation and violence from the police, put millions of people on the street over the Spring and Summer of 2021 without a single incidence of violence of which I am aware or have heard about, which must be unique in the history of

---

2. Bertolt Brecht, 'To Those Born After', *The Collected Poems of Bertolt Brecht*, translated and edited by Tom Kuhn and David Constantine (New York: Liveright Publishing, 2019), pp. 734-736.

3. Hannah Arendt, *Men in Dark Times*, p. 13.

demonstrations in the UK.[4] On the other hand, as the privilege of pariah peoples, fraternity becomes a substitute for the world from which they are barred by their persecution and oppression. In the bond of fraternity, therefore, the element that is common to all humans and binds them together is no longer the world in which they live but the abstraction of 'human nature', whose qualities vary according to the requirements of the persecuted group. Most importantly of all, since fraternity is manifested in dark times, this human nature cannot be identified in a world common to all people at all times. Indeed, when those dark times have passed, however temporarily, and the world is once again open to previously pariah peoples, their fraternity, writes Arendt, 'dissolves into nothingness like phantoms'. This applies as much to the working class that nationalism, racism and religion have kept fighting among themselves for centuries as it does to Jews who survived the *Shoah* only to create the apartheid State of Israel founded on the same racial identity fabricated by the Third Reich. In words that should be embroidered on the flag of every protester against the renewed imposition of mask and 'vaccine' mandates, Arendt writes:

> The humanity of the insulted and injured has never yet survived the hour of liberation by so much as a minute. This does not mean that it is insignificant, for in fact it makes insult and injury endurable; but it does mean that in political terms it is absolutely irrelevant.[5]

Arendt is famous for saying and writing what nobody wants to hear or read, least of all those who turn to her for an easy truth; and it is partly for this reason that I have been drawing on her writings now, when our lives are being lived according to convenient lies and self-deceptions that have not attained such hegemony in public life in Europe since the rise of fascism a century ago. Indeed, the attacks on her after the publication of her book on Eichmann have been repeated in the attacks on the equally intransigent Agamben, their shared crime being that both abjure popular explanations of totalitarian programmes (then as now, that they have been imposed for the 'common good') for analysis of how

---

4. See Simon Elmer, 'March for Freedom: London, 29 May, 2021' (30 May, 2021), collected in *Virtue and Terror*, pp. 23-31.

5. Hannah Arendt, *Men in Dark Times*, p. 16.

they are created within the legal framework of democratic states.[6] And, unfortunate as it is to witness, Arendt's words here have been proven to be as true today as they were during the years immediately after the Second World War, when the Allied coalition that won the military struggle against fascism split into both old and new factions whose political divisions continue to this day, not least in the State of Israel and the widely-accepted equation of fascism with socialism.

Today, the fraternity among the 'unvaccinated' who faced unemployment and loss of freedom for their disobedience, the brief compassion of middle-class libertarians in the public eye for the overwhelmingly working-class protesters against lockdown, and the beginnings of solidarity between the non-compliant irrespective of their former allegiances to parliamentary parties or the redundant division between Left and Right — or indeed their depoliticisation as masses — have all dissolved with the removal of coronavirus-justified restrictions this March. Despite the fact that these restrictions have, by the admission of the UK Government, only been suspended and may be reimposed this winter as they already are in Germany; that the 'vaccination' programme has not only continued but been extended in this country to children as young as five and an appalling 6 months old in the US; that, far from being dropped, 'vaccine' passports are waiting to be implemented outside of any immediate threat of a 'pandemic'; that the programmes of biosecurity are being extended to encompass Central Bank Digital Currency, Social Credit and Universal Basic Income; and that a wave of new legislation and treaties are being made into law that will permanently remove the human rights and freedoms that were temporarily suspended over the previous two years — despite all this, the popular opposition to, non-compliance with and protest against the UK biosecurity state have all but vanished. Meanwhile, its former public spokespersons have returned to sniping at the Government on social media, with little or no attempt to form what is left of the former resistance of millions into a force capable of resisting what is in store for us in the future. As Arendt warned in *The Origins of Totalitarianism*, it is only when the first stage of terror has achieved its aim of rendering further opposition impossible that the regulations and programmes of totalitarian domination are

---

6. For a discussion of these attacks on Agamben by journalists, psychoanalysts, political theorists, philosophers, students and translators of his work, see Simon Elmer, 'Giorgio Agamben and the Biopolitics of COVID-19' (25 April, 2020), collected in *COVID-19*, pp. 53-65.

unleashed in full, and in the West we are totally unprepared to meet them with anything but more protests, bewilderment, submissive acceptance and willing collaboration.

This is where Arendt's discussion of friendship offers a political alternative to this already failed fraternity. For the Ancient Greeks, she writes, friendship among citizens (*philia*) was one of the fundamental requirements for the well-being of the city state (*polis*) on which Western democracy is based. This concept of friendship, however, is different from that held by the individual in modern or even our postmodern times. For us, friendship is experienced as the intimacy in which we escape our alienation from the world through exposure of the details of our private life in face-to-face encounters and, increasingly today, online. Friendship, therefore, is the opposite of our public lives within the social and political realm. But for the Greeks, citizens were only united in a *polis* — only constituted this public realm — in the constant interchange of talk. The essence of friendship, therefore, consisted in discourse, which was not the intimacy in which individuals talk about themselves, but that in which the world common to all is made manifest.

This is an important point for Arendt. For her, the world is only made human because it has become an object of discourse. However much they may affect us otherwise, the things of the world only become human when we discuss them with our fellow human beings. And, crucially, in the course of speaking, Arendt says, 'we learn to be human'.[7] The Greeks called this quality of humanness, which is only achieved in the discourse of friendship, '*philanthrōpia* (love of man)', since it manifests itself in a readiness to share the world with others. Misanthropy, in contrast, means an inability to find someone with whom to share the experience of the world. This concept subsequently underwent numerous changes to become Roman '*humanitas* (humanity)', the most important of which corresponded to the political constitution of Roman citizenship, which could be acquired by peoples of widely different ethnic origins, and who were thereby able to come together with other Romans and enter into discourse with them about the world. Humanity, therefore, was exemplified in friendship, which was not intimate and personal but, to the contrary, made political demands upon friends and retained, in their shared discourse, reference to the world they inhabit. For

---

7. Hannah Arendt, *Men in Dark Times*, p. 125.

Arendt, it is this that distinguishes the politics of friendship from the abstraction of human nature on which fraternity is founded.

It is, I think, a measure of the political potential of this concept of friendship that, for the two years during which we lived under restrictions on our freedoms justified by a politically declared 'pandemic', friendship was under unrelenting attack by the state. The space of friendship has been explicitly targeted by biosecurity 'measures' that continue to instruct us to maintain social distancing, are trying to erase our faces behind a permanently-worn mask, encourage us to see others as a threat to our health and lives, instructed people to remain in their homes for months on end, have normalised working from home for the always-obedient middle-classes, still promotes online interaction over personal relations, and more generally and progressively is removing our access to the world in which we live and whose revolutionary transformation into the Global Biosecurity State we have been banned from discussing. This attack, which continues to this day, has resulted in the widespread breakdown of relationships between the compliant and the non-compliant that, in my experience and that of everyone I know or who have talked to about this topic, has extended from friends, comrades and colleagues to families — dividing husbands from wives, parents from children, brothers from sisters. Once again, Arendt identified the loneliness in which totalitarianism isolates the individual as one of the definitions and conditions of this novel form of governance, each of us isolated from each other, no longer able to call on each other for support, fearing in each other a threat or source of denunciation. Perhaps most importantly, the concerted assault on friendship by the biosecurity state has served this political form most explicitly in the enforced ban on discussing the Brave New World into which we've been forced without debate in our Parliament, in our media, and largely in the absence of discussion among ourselves.

In my experience, as in that of many thousands and no doubt millions of others in the UK, those with whom in any other circumstances and on any other topic I would expect to be able to enter into such a discussion, debate and disagreement, have flatly refused to do so: either declaring themselves uninterested or 'too busy' to question what they've been told by sources they would previously not have trusted; or denouncing me, as they have millions of others, as a 'conspiracy theorist' who should be censored, or arrested, or worse.

Indeed, the discourse between citizens about the world that the Ancient Greeks identified as the foundation to the well-being of the state has not only been repressed but is now criminalised on the justification of that 'common good' by which bare life has been accorded an absolute value over the now subsidiary values of citizenship, friendship, freedom of speech and democracy. Indeed, perhaps the most distinctive character of the consensus on which the UK biosecurity state has been built in a little over two-and-a-half years is the willingness of the vast majority of the population, and of almost all our so-called intellectuals, not merely to submit to censorship but to abandon critical thinking. Those 'dangerous thoughts' that Arendt identified as the condition of all thinking have not merely been abandoned by the most intellectually craven generation in modern history but actively suppressed with their willing collaboration.[8] And as she argued, without that constant discussion by which the things of the world become humanised, our world has become less and less human, more and more inhumane, in direct correlation with our compliance with the post-human agenda of the Global Biosecurity State. It is not surprising, therefore, that the regulations of biosecurity have targeted precisely this political dimension of friendship, since it is on the erasure of the political — of that constant debate on which the democratic *polis* is founded, if more in principle than in practice — that the trans-human programmes and technologies of the Global Biosecurity State are being implemented.

At the start of the previous chapter, in which I discussed the moral collapse in the West over the past two-and-a-half years, I asked who is the 'we' to whom and with whom I wished to speak if we are to find that collective voice with which we must speak if we are to make ourselves heard above the imposed and policed silence in which we have been politically isolated from each other. The simple answer is: it is the we of friendship. If we are to formulate what Agamben, in my epigraph, called a 'future politics' founded neither on a democracy that is employing increasingly despotic forms of control nor on a totalitarian state disguised as a democracy, we must start by reclaiming the political dimension of friendship described by Arendt as a preferable foundation to such a politics than the abstraction of fraternity.

---

8. See Hannah Arendt, *The Life of the Mind*, edited by Mary McCarthy (Houghton Mifflin Harcourt, 1981), p. 176.

My attention to Arendt's talk was drawn by another talk, delivered by Agamben at a conference organised by Venetian students on 11 November, 2021, against the Italian Government's illegal imposition of the 'vaccine' Green Pass.[9] Agamben agrees with Arendt that friendship is the possible foundation for policy in the dark times that describe the Global Biosecurity State today as much as they did Europe under fascism: so long as we remember that friendship is what he calls 'a threshold that both unites the individual with, and divides him from, the community'; that rediscovering the politics of friendship means 'nothing less than trying to create a society, or a community within society, everywhere'; that faced with 'the growing depoliticisation of individuals', friendship means 'rediscovering in friendship the radical principle of a renewed politicisation'; and, finally, that on this rediscovery 'will depend the very possibility of living in a human way'. So what is this community in which individuals are both united with and divided from each other, that we must establish as the basis of a future society, that is founded on a radically politicised concept of friendship, and on which a human way of living will depend in what future is left to us?

Agamben argues that, before we live in a nation or a state, we live in a language, which is the condition of all other transformations of society. Ours is the language of modernity, which began with the First Industrial Revolution in England and the political revolutions in France and the USA, which implemented, among other things, the division of powers between the executive, the legislature and the judiciary that totalitarianism renders redundant. These economic and political revolutions were preceded, however, by the scientific revolutions of the European Enlightenment, which gave birth to a language of science that has progressively sought to eliminate any ethical, poetic or philosophical experience of the world in order to transform language into a tool for the mere exchange of information. Agamben calls this 'the illusion of reason', which allows us to account for and govern both the natural world and the lives of human beings. If science, whose revolutions have increased in number as they have expanded its domination over our politics and ethics, has nevertheless failed to increase either our freedom or our happiness, it is because science presupposes not the speaking being of poetry and philosophy but instead a mute biological body, the

9. See Giorgio Agamben, 'Speech at the conference of Venetian students against the Green Pass on November 11, 2021 at Ca' Sagredo', translated by Lena Bloch (3 January, 2022).

bare life that is the object of our increasingly totalitarian form of governance. As a sign displayed in the counter-demonstration against the Freedom Convoy against 'vaccine' mandates in Manitoba in February proudly announced, as though it were a declaration of objective truth: 'Science doesn't care about your beliefs'. In actuality, what the past two-and-a-half years have demonstrated is that this apotheosised Science has supplanted our beliefs, to the extent that it is now the dominant religion in the West. Today, under the Global Biosecurity State, whose mantra is to 'Follow the Science!', our relationship to language has been so transformed that — as Arendt said of the ideal subject of totalitarian rule — we are no longer capable of distinguishing a truth from a falsehood, fact from fiction, a cause of death from the criteria created to manufacture a 'pandemic', medical measures from the programmes of biosecurity, a vaccine from still experimental and evidently dangerous and increasingly fatal biotechnology.

This extends even, and perhaps above all, to those to whom we have looked to make precisely this distinction: doctors, scientists, jurists, who have instead accepted and embraced a language that has renounced and even banished questions about what is true and what is false. In this respect, they have come to resemble Adolf Eichmann as Arendt described him: unable to speak in anything but officialese, capable only of obedience to their superiors, incapable of thinking outside their particular fields of technical expertise, whether that's the biotechnology that is transforming the conditions of citizenship, or the artificial intelligence by which our compliance is monitored, or the emergency powers by which their imposition is enforced. It is for this reason that doctors, scientists and lawyers are the last people we should be listening to for the truth about this manufactured crisis, since they are, as the technocrats of the biosecurity state, at the forefront of the revolution in language through which thinking has become prohibited, not only in practice and principle but now in law. The result of their servile collaboration with power is that those we previously regarded as intellectuals with the ethical duties that entails are no longer capable, as they have shown themselves to be throughout this revolution, of doing anything but obeying orders.

How, then, do we reconcile Arendt's concept of friendship as the basis of a future politics with this still unrecognised and — given the bad faith in which the COVID-faithful continue to act — likely to remain unacknowledged betrayal? Not by forgetting, certainly, and, speaking for myself, not forgiving what, given the cowardice and consequences of their betrayal, is unforgiveable. Yet we cannot, as I have said, abandon these fools, these cowards and these collaborators to their stupidity, their cowardice and their complicity. That way lies disaster. On the contrary, we must continue to try to speak to those who refuse to speak to us, listen to those who long ago shut their ears to anything but the lies and threats of their superiors, try to educate and persuade those who were and still are willing to ban us from their society for our lack of belief in their dogma. Because if we don't, fascism will more surely triumph than it will, perhaps, do so anyway even if we do. And if only because, as Agamben wrote in the most poetic of the texts he has published since this 'crisis' began, 'When the House Burns', it is with these fools, these cowards and these collaborators that we must exchange a final look as the flames of the world we once inhabited rise about us, consuming us with it.[10] What we can imagine ourselves saying to them then we must say to them now, if only so that they may have the chance to add their voices to those silenced by the roar of a collapsing world.

2. Resistance

I want to end these considerations with an example of resistance drawn from Arendt's report on the trial of Eichmann in which she recounts the various means by which the so-called 'Final Solution to the Jewish question' was implemented across Europe. This was accomplished with the collaboration of most fascist governments, including those of France, Norway, Hungary, Slovakia, Romania, Croatia and Serbia, and of the populations under German occupation, including those of Poland, Austria, Greece, Belgium and the Netherlands. The one exception, she says, was Denmark. Arendt, as I said, was not given to offering simple answers to difficult questions or dispensing unwarranted praise, so we should listen when she writes that:

---

10. See Giorgio Agamben, 'Quando la casa brucia', *Quoblibet* (5 October, 2020); translated, with an introduction and notes, by Simon Elmer and Carlo Rimassa as 'When the House Burns: Giorgio Agamben on the Coronavirus Crisis' (15 October, 2020), collected in *Brave New World*, pp. 177-183; and by Kevin Attell in *When the House Burns Down* (Seagull Books, 2022), pp. 1-16.

One is tempted to recommend the story as required reading in political science for all students who wish to learn something about the enormous power potential inherent in non-violent action and in resistance to an opponent possessing vastly superior means of violence.[11]

While Sweden, which maintained a policy of neutrality, proved to be immune to anti-Semitism, and Italy and Bulgaria, although their governments placed both native and foreign-born Jews into concentration camps, contrived to sabotage German plans for their deportation to the death camps in the East, only Denmark dared to contest the policy. Having also declared itself neutral in September 1939, Denmark was nevertheless occupied by German forces in April 1940, after which the Danish Government and King functioned as a *de facto* protectorate over the country, with political independence in domestic matters. However, when ordered to introduce the Yellow Star for those designated under the laws of the Third Reich as Jewish, officials in the Danish Government threatened to resign. There was even a rumour that the King would be the first to wear it. As a consequence, the occupying German forces weren't even able to establish the distinction, which was key to the process of deportation across the rest of Europe, between Danes of Jewish origin and Jewish refugees from Germany who had been declared stateless by the Third Reich. Indeed, the Danish Government argued that, since the stateless refugees were no longer German citizens, the occupying forces could no longer claim them without its assent. Most surprising of all, although the Danish Government had denied naturalisation and even the right to work to these refugees before the war, they now took them under their protection. Faced with these decisions, the German occupying forces could carry out none of the moves preparatory to deportation, which was postponed until Autumn 1943.

With the German offensive in the Soviet Union having been defeated at Stalingrad in February 1943, the Afrika Korps having surrendered in Tunisia in May, the Battle of Kursk handing the initiative on the Eastern Front to the Red Army in August, and the Allied invasion of Italy finally launched in September, Danish workers decided the time was ripe to launch their own offensive on the home front. Industrial strikes and civil disobedience followed, with dock workers refusing to repair German naval ships in Danish shipyards. When the German army

---

11. Hannah Arendt, *Eichmann in Jerusalem*, p. 171.

tried to seize Danish vessels in port, the Danish navy scuttled 32 of its own ships. In response, the German military commander declared a state of emergency, banned assemblies in public, outlawed strikes, introduced curfews, censored the press and radio, and imposed martial law. In protest, the Danish Cabinet resigned (although the King never officially accepted their resignation), Parliament ceased to convene, and the running of the separate Ministries was effectively handed over to the Permanent Secretaries.

Just as the UK 'vaccination' programme was implemented under a politically declared 'emergency period' that allowed the temporary authorisation and promotion of unlicensed 'vaccines', it was under cover of this state of emergency that the German plan for the deportation of Denmark's Jews was relaunched. However, in the intervening years, the German officials had changed their attitudes, no doubt under the awareness that the war was already lost and a reckoning was coming. The military commander refused to put his soldiers at the disposal of the Reich Plenipotentiary, and even the SS units occasionally objected to their murderous duties. This was to have decisive consequences for the German plans. In 1943, the festival of Rosh Hashanah, the Jewish New Year, ended on Friday, 1 October, and with their customary sense of humour the Germans had designated Friday evening for the round-up of all the Jews in Denmark, sending police units brought in from Germany to undertake a door-to-door search of homes in Copenhagen. At the last moment, however, the Reich Plenipotentiary informed the police units that they were not permitted to break into private homes, since the Danish police might interfere, and a running battle between opposed police forces was bad for civic order. In the event, only those Jews who voluntarily opened their doors to the German police were deported, some 477 out of a population of more than 7,800 native and foreign-born Jews. Sent to the concentration camp at Theresienstadt in the Protectorate of Bohemia and Moravia (former Czechoslovakia), even these were treated better than their fellow inmates because of the constant enquiries after their status made by Danish officials and citizens, and only 48 died, most of whom were elderly, by the time the camp was liberated in May 1945.

Even more damaging to the success of the deportations, a German shipping agent, probably tipped off by the Reich Plenipotentiary, revealed the German plans to the Danish Government, which in turn informed the heads of the Jewish community in Denmark. In contrast to Jewish leaders in other countries — most notoriously and catastrophically in Hungary — these communicated the news in the synagogues during the New Year services, allowing the Jews to go into hiding. This was made easier by their long integration into Danish society, which viewed the attack on Danish Jews as an attack on Denmark, and therefore as a political rather than a humanitarian issue. They might have remained there, however, for the remainder of the war, were it not for the solidarity shown by the Swedish Government, which in August had cancelled its 1940 agreement to permit German troops to pass through the country, and now offered to receive all the Jews in Denmark, both Danish and German. With the help of the extensive Danish fishing fleet, 5,919 Jews were ferried to Sweden, where they all received permission to work. Extraordinarily, the relatively low shipping costs were largely paid by wealthy Danish citizens at a time when only wealthy Jews could afford the small fortunes required to bribe corrupt officials across Europe for exit visas, and poor Jews, consequently, had no chance of escape.

For Arendt, the most interesting aspect of this story, politically and psychologically, is what happened to the German occupying forces in Denmark. In the face of open and principled resistance from a people, and not just a government, that refused to carry out the dictates of a totalitarian regime, the formerly iron resolve of the German authorities melted away. Indeed, some of the authorities even began to show the beginnings of courage. The vaunted 'toughness' of the Aryan master race was shown to be a myth of self-deception, concealing what Arendt called 'a ruthless desire for conformity at any price'. At the subsequent Nuremberg Trials, not a single one of the defendants tried to defend the ideology of National Socialism, with every one either claiming they had always been opposed to it or, like Eichmann, blaming the abuse of their loyalty on their superiors, while denouncing each other in an attempt to save their own lives.

It is incumbent on us, perhaps, to compare this story of courage, resistance and solidarity with how we in the UK have behaved under different but comparable circumstances, at a time when the new totalitarianism is still very much in the process of being implemented. Part of the self-deception and lies that continue in the wake of the temporary lifting of lockdown restrictions in the UK is the denial of just how appallingly the British people have behaved towards each other over the past two-and-a-half years, and only by acknowledging and confronting that behaviour can we begin to start behaving like the citizens of a democracy, reclaim our rights and freedoms from the criminals to whom we've so cravenly conceded them, and begin to create that future politics we so desperately need if the new totalitarianism is not to so ravage the world that its overthrow will lie beyond any future we can see or predict. Unsurprisingly, the comparison with the behaviour and actions of the Danes under occupation by the Third Reich does us no favours.

It goes without saying that our hereditary Head of State, unlike the Danish King, collaborated fully and obediently with the UK Government in promoting every regulation of the biosecurity state, from lockdown restrictions to the 'vaccination' programme, while at the same time playing host to parties of unmasked, unsocially-distanced heads of state from the G7 countries while the rest of the country was under threat of fines, arrest and imprisonment for doing the same. That Her Majesty's Government was itself doing the same and more at drunken parties the night before the burial of her husband, during whose funeral service she continued to play her part in the charade of masking, social distancing and bans on indoor socialising, was, in my opinion, insufficient retribution for her collaboration with this criminal Government. The first question her heir and successor, King Charles III, has to answer is whether he will continue to be an obedient spokesman for the Great Reset, Agenda 2030 and the World Economic Forum, an organisation whose openly-declared aim is the creation of a global government of unelected leaders that will replace democratic nation states like the UK as the model of governance in the West.

Also needless to say, not a single Member of Parliament, let alone the Cabinet, resigned in protest against the Government's removal of the rights and freedoms of the electorate they were voted to represent. Indeed, on the few occasions when coronavirus-justified legislation was presented for their brief scrutiny and obedient approval before it was made into law, the level of debate, if one can call it that, presented a spectacle of servile collaboration, intellectual cowardice and professional incompetence fully the equal of any puppet Parliament under occupation during the Second World War. No Member of what I have consistently called the worst Parliament in British history should ever be permitted to hold any public office again. All are complicit in enabling if not actually implementing the UK biosecurity state, and are collectively responsible for the ongoing damage and harm it is doing to the UK and its people.

But the collaboration didn't stop there. While the Danes refused to separate native-born Jews from Jewish refugees from Germany, the British people recognised, embraced and policed the arbitrary distinctions by which the Government divided us from each other, whether that was between those who were and were not exempt from the various restrictions, or between those designated 'vaccinated' and 'unvaccinated'. Those who declared themselves exempt from masking, or who paid for fake proof of injection, merely gave the appearance of legality to what were illegally imposed regulations; while those who declared that wearing a mask or getting 'vaccinated' was a personal decision they had chosen to make, in doing so turned their back on the consequences of their actions for those who took a principled stand against what mass compliance was enabling.

In comparison to the Danish workers who refused to comply with the German occupation and even dared to sabotage the German war effort, no such stance or action was made by our unfailingly servile unions, who instead responded to the state of emergency by abandoning those workers who refused mandates on wearing masks at work to 'vaccination' as a condition of employment, and joined the political Left in and out of Parliament in refusing to join and instead denouncing the overwhelmingly working-class opposition in marches and demonstrations as right-wing conspiracy theorists. The recent strikes by the Rail, Maritime and Transport Union only demonstrate what could have happened if the unions had had the courage to do more than demand higher wages for their workers, and had instead defended all workers against the greatest transfer of wealth and power from the poor to the rich in modern UK history.

As for the military, while even the occupying German forces refused to participate in the Final Solution in Denmark, necessitating the arrival of German police units to do their dirty work, the British military, rapidly formed into the 'COVID Support Force', was visibly present on our streets.[12] Ostensibly employed to aid with the building of temporary Nightingale Hospitals that were never used or to carry out medically fraudulent tests that justified further lockdowns, the presence of the military was a threat to suppress any civil unrest during the state of emergency. Since Caesar crossed the Rubicon with his legions and entered Italy in defiance of Roman law, the presence of the military on home soil has been

---

12. In March 2020, 20,000 British military personnel were placed on standby in anticipation of civil unrest in response to the Government-imposed lockdown of the UK. A further 3,000 were added in April. See Ministry of Defence, 'Military stands up COVID Support Force' (19 March, 2020).

a sign that a society is living under a dictatorship, and the fact that ours was constitutional does nothing to change that truth. Indeed, the Government threatened to use the army against protesters if the demonstrations against lockdown and 'vaccine' mandates continued.[13]

In the event, the army wasn't required. Arendt argues that one of the characteristics of totalitarian governments is that the police forces have greater power than the armed forces, and since lockdown was imposed the already great powers of the UK police forces have increased exponentially, to the point where they now constitute a politicised police force whose primary function is to enforce adherence not merely to the regulations of the biosecurity state but also to its totalitarian ideology. Again, while the Danish police force presented a barrier to the German police conducting door-to-door searches for Jews, UK police forces the length and breadth of the country, whether empowered to do so by new regulations as in Wales or without that legal power in England, did not hesitate to break into private homes to enforce lockdown restrictions. And now, in the wake of those restrictions being lifted, the same invasion of privacy beyond even their newly created legal powers is being conducted by police for such newly-created crimes as posting comments on social media that have caused someone, somewhere, offence or anxiety.[14] For this our police have rightly been compared to the fictional 'Thought Police' of Orwell's Nineteen Eighty-Four, and the ideology they're enforcing is composed of the orthodoxies of woke. Those who have dismissed fears about the uses to which the raft of new legislation will be put have already been corrected by how ready and willing our ideological police force is to punish the newly designated crimes to the letter of the new laws and beyond.

And while the heads of the Jewish community in Denmark risked their own lives to give the members of that community a chance to escape the imminent pogrom, the equivalent heads of communities in the UK, not only of the Jewish community but of the Muslim, Christian, Asian and Black communities, have instead provided a crucial conduit between the imposition of biosecurity regulations and programmes and communities which, from long experience, have learned to distrust central, municipal and local governments. Indeed, SAGE's sub-

---

13. See John Simpson, 'Coronavirus raves and protests may need army, advisers warn', *The Times* (1 August, 2020).

14. See Harry Miller, 'The Police crackdown on social media has gone too far', *The Spectator* (1 August, 2022).

group on Social and Behavioural Impacts (SPI-B) explicitly targeted community leaders as the key to compliance in these religious, ethnic and racial communities.[15] It's to their credit that the Black community, particularly in London, has in general refused the criminal 'vaccination' programme, and constitutes one of the highest demographics of non-compliance. This is something the middle classes arrogantly attribute to that community's ignorance and lack of education, but which is clearly attributable to its far greater experience and knowledge of the corruption and lies of officialdom.

With the honourable exception of a handful of public figures who have dared to put their heads above the parapet of conformity and compliance (and who were very quickly targeted by the corporate propaganda arm of the biosecurity state for doing so), none of the UK's immensely wealthy and potentially influential individuals have raised a finger to help, let alone offered to assist financially, those most affected by the restrictions of the biosecurity state. These are, as always, the working class and the poor, who rightly understand this politically-declared 'pandemic' as a global form of class war — something the middle classes are only now, perhaps, beginning to recognise as the cost of living soars. Otherwise, what Arendt described as 'a ruthless desire for conformity at any price' continues to rule the public life of the UK biosecurity state as it did that of Germany under the Third Reich.

And while Danish civic institutions and individuals alike held on to as much of the pastoral care they could over the Jews deported to Theresienstadt, to the marked diminishment of their fatality rate, in the UK, in contrast, individuals and institutions alike have abandoned those in their care to the bare life they become as soon as they pass the doors of our hospitals and care homes: incubated, injected with powerful sedatives, denied resuscitation and refused visits from anyone outside the legal state of exception to which these medical facilities give spatial permanence. And, worst of all, those who, either personally or professionally, should have done everything they could to protect the vulnerable from these dehumanising and in most cases fatal conditions, were happy to

---

15. See Scientific Advisory Group for Emergencies, 'SPI-B Summary: Key behavioural issues relevant to test, trace, track and isolate' (6 May, 2020); and 'SPI-B: Consensus Statement on Local Interventions' (27 July, 2020).

participate in their disappearance into the biosecurity archipelago, which continues to this day.

Finally, and once again to its credit, just as Sweden was largely immune to the ideology of anti-Semitism and the authority of Race the occupying German forces tried to force upon it in the 1940s, so its Government and people have been more immune to the ideology of biosecurity and the authority of an apotheosised Science than any other country in Europe, having refused to deny work to the 'unvaccinated' as did the UK Government.[16]

The only comparison in which we can recognise ourselves with parity is the backtracking, rewriting of history and denials of having joined in the imperious demands for masking, lockdown, mandatory 'vaccines' and COVID passports by public figures both in and out of office who, like the occupying German authorities in Denmark, suspect the war might be lost and that, one day, the Nuremberg trials so many opposed to their criminal behaviour have called for will be convened. This shows how ignorant they are of the revolution in capitalism they have served, and of which they have been the more or less unwitting tools. Unfortunately, the war has only just begun, and whatever trials may one day bring these collaborators to justice lie on the other side of the long defeat of the Global Biosecurity State.

As I know well and have on occasion been guilty of myself, in attempting to warn about our descent into totalitarianism, it is easy to fall into mimicking its ideologues' predictions of catastrophe. Both must be resisted by a practice of thinking and action that, while not averting its eyes from this descent, retains its hold on the world of experience from which our moral collapse increasingly separates us. While it is more than evident that the Danish people, in civil society and their social interactions, continued to think, continued to debate and continued to humanise the totalitarian world the occupation forces of Germany tried to force upon them, we have just as evidently stopped thinking, stopped debating and given up even trying to humanise the Global Biosecurity State whose

---

16. See the data on Sweden in Hannah Ritchie, et al, 'Policy Responses to the Coronavirus Pandemic', *Our World In Data* (January 2020-August 2022). For a comparison between the restrictions imposed by Sweden and the rest of Europe and the effects they had over the first 4 months of the 'pandemic', see the pages titled 'Comparative Government Responses' and 'Alternatives to Lockdown' in Simon Elmer, 'Lockdown: Collateral Damage in the War on COVID-19'; collected in *COVID-19*, pp. 138-145.

governance, laws and ideology we have embraced with the same cowardice as those who, willingly or under threat, collaborated with the implementation of the Final Solution. Indeed, over the past two-and-a-half years of active collusion and passive compliance, the people and civic institutions of the UK have failed, at every turn, to act as the people and civic institutions of Denmark acted under occupation by the Third Reich, and have instead experienced something like that 'moral collapse' that Arendt said gripped the German people during the twelve years of the latter's political existence. And like the German people then, we are not alone in that collapse, which like fascism in the 1930s has spread across Europe in the 2020s. Unfortunately, the Government of Denmark has, if anything, distinguished itself this time by the brutality of the enforcement of this ideology, rather than its resistance to it. But as we look forward to the reinstatement of many of the restrictions and obligations of the Global Biosecurity State and the implementation of many more with which we are currently being threatened, it is not too late to learn from the historical example of Danish resistance, as Arendt wrote, 'to an opponent possessing vastly superior means of violence'. It is, at its most simple, a question of our courage, of refusing the right to obey, of reclaiming the space of friendship, of sowing the seeds of a future politics in the ground of the present — however dark the time grows.

Conclusion

'So you wait, and you wait. But the one great shocking occasion, when tens or hundreds or thousands will join with you, never comes. That's the difficulty. If the last and worst act of the whole regime had come immediately after the first and smallest, thousands, yes, millions would have been sufficiently shocked. But of course, this isn't the way it happens. In between come all the hundreds of little steps, some of them imperceptible, each of them preparing you not to be shocked by the next. And one day, too late, your principles, if you were ever sensible of them, all rush in upon you. The burden of self-deception has grown too heavy, and some minor incident collapses it all at once, and you see that everything, everything, has changed and changed completely under your nose. The world you live in — your nation, your people — is not the world you were born in at all. The forms are all there, all untouched, all reassuring, the houses, the shops, the jobs, the mealtimes, the visits, the concerts, the cinema, the holidays. But the spirit, which you never noticed because you made the lifelong mistake of identifying it with the forms, is changed. Now you live in a world of hate and fear, and the people who hate and fear do not even know it themselves; when everyone is transformed, no one is transformed.'

— Milton Mayer, *They Thought They Were Free: The Germans, 1933-45*, 1955

What, then, are the grounds for arguing for the return of fascism in the West today, and what are the benefits and pitfalls of doing so? Historical fascism came out of the heart of Europe during one of the worst crises in the history of Western capitalism, and soon spread across the continent, not only in conquered nations like France, which didn't take much to adopt its political, juridical and cultural practices, but before that in much of Central, Southern and Eastern Europe. The later attempt to equate fascism with socialism is, as I have argued, part of the neoliberal project to dissociate pre-war fascism from the West's post-war history of overthrowing, by military invasion or political coup, any country that elected a socialist party into government, and installing, in its stead, brutal military dictatorships in South America, Africa, the Middle East and South-east Asia. This was not merely a result of the Cold War and the fight against international communism. It was and is easier for the West to extract the resources and wealth of countries ruled by dictatorships they themselves have installed, rather than governments, no matter how flawed or corrupt they may be, that identify as socialist. Whether those dictatorships should be described as 'fascist' is not the question this book is trying to address. My question is whether it describes the current revolution in Western societies to authoritarian forms of governance and totalitarian methods of control that haven't been seen in Western Europe since historical fascism, and in Eastern Europe since the dissolution of the Warsaw Pact.

As I have argued, this emergent form of governance is not a form of communism, including that form currently governing the People's Republic of China, even though the latter has provided the model for many of its restrictions and programmes. China, like the Soviet Union before it, is a one-party state ruled by an authoritarian form of government employing a totalitarian system of surveillance and control, but it is not fascist. If fascism has any meaning as a term, it describes how an authoritarian system of governance, which in the case of Nazi Germany produced a totalitarian system of control but in other forms of fascism did not, can be implemented within a capitalist economy on the ruins of a failed democracy. If fascism is not capitalist it has no specificity distinct from other forms of dictatorship in non-Western countries. Indeed, I would argue that fascism is particular to Western dictatorships, which, once again, have not been seen in Europe since the 1970s in Spain, Portugal and Greece — although the wars and crimes against humanity that followed the breakup of the Socialist Federal Republic of Yugoslavia in the 1990s demonstrated once again the presence of the axe blade of fascism in capitalism, and how violently the latter's bundle of politics, law and culture unravels when the bonds binding them together are severed. It's for this reason that I believe it is legitimate to use the term 'fascism' to describe the wielding of this axe blade today and the shredding of the social contract that contained its violence — or, more accurately, directed it against other states rather than the populations of its own.

The question of terminology, however, is only partially one of legitimacy, which has played a minor part in my decision to call the Global Biosecurity State 'fascist'. By far the more important question is what job a concept does in being formulated. What does calling the emergent superstructure of Western states 'fascist' tell us about this revolution in capitalism? Does it work to illuminate or obscure its emergent governmental, juridical and cultural forms? Capitalism, as we have seen, has been only too eager to consign fascism to the past, just as it has socialism, even while the transformation of capitalism itself increases at ever greater speed, to the point where it no longer resembles what it was a mere fifty years ago before the neoliberal revolution, let alone in the time of historical fascism. And the more it fails to resemble itself, the more fanatically its ideologues defend it with terms like 'free market', 'private enterprise' and 'competition' that have been redundant as a description of how capitalism operates for hundreds of years. The eternal present of capitalism, which is always in the process of revolution into the imaginary future promised to the consumer, is predicated on the erasure of the past, from which nothing can or should ever be learned. The insistence with which the ideologues of neoliberalism define fascism as the inevitable conclusion to ill-advised and thankfully dispelled beliefs in socialist equality can only serve to deny fascism's continuing and now resurgent presence in Western capitalism. The past, however, and nowhere more so than in the economic, political and cultural circumstances that gave rise to historical fascism a hundred years ago, is our best lesson, I believe, in understanding what is happening in the West now and where it is leading us. If that is the case — and this book has been my attempt to argue for the relevance of this past to our present understanding of the future — then the term 'fascism' will succeed in doing its conceptual work.

As for the pitfalls of using this term, they are many and considerable. Even before reading what I have written, commentators with little understanding of either the past or the present have dismissed my use of the term. As I have said, this is as much a product of the history of fascism we have been taught as it is of the refusal to face the brutal reality of contemporary capitalism. The insistence with which even its critics fall back on calling the Global Biosecurity State 'communist' in order to describe what has happened to the West since March 2020 is a testimony to how little we understand either fascism or socialism. This is to be expected of a neoliberal system of 'co-ordination' that has long since penetrated not only our economics and politics but also our media, culture and education industries. Indeed, it is only on the basis of such coordination that the aberration of woke ideology could have attained its current hegemony.

Finally, the reluctance to use this term to describe the world we live in today, which with a wave of a hand and a snort of derision is 'quite clearly' not fascist, is another expression of our refusal to face a reality to which, at every moment, we are offered a virtual alternative. Although we continue to do so in proportion to the increasing complexity of the world and the cloud of ideology through which we view it, we should not base our political opinions on aesthetics or find solace in the state spectacles to which we are increasingly subjected. For the vast majority of us, our image of fascism is a product of Hollywood cinema and BBC documentaries, to which the equivalent depictions of our neoliberal democracies today bear no resemblance. But this is precisely the purpose and function of the 'Holocaust' industry to which the Third Reich and the history of fascism has been almost entirely reduced in the UK — enshrined as the incomparable and therefore ahistorical crimes of the past from which we cannot and must not learn, rather than the lessons of the economic, political and cultural history of twenty-first-century capitalism. This, apparently, is of considerable comfort to those who insist on the certainty with which they dismiss any comparisons between the UK biosecurity state and historical fascism; but it offers neither hope nor instruction to those of us who are trying to understand and oppose how those who control our present are rewriting the past to produce the future they want.

I started this book not with a decided answer to this question in my own mind, but in order to formulate its terms and to discover, through the process of writing, what the answer is. Notwithstanding the evident ease with which my thesis is dismissed by those who have themselves stopped thinking and are intent on stopping it in others, my answer now, after ten chapters examining the Global Biosecurity State in its historical, ideological, juridical, economic, psychological, cultural, political, biopolitical, governmental and moral aspects, is a qualified 'yes'. Qualified, because a single book cannot hope to change the ideological contexts in which the meaning of this word today has been safely and deliberately consigned to the past. But then, part of the task of this study has been to challenge precisely those contexts, by exposing how the term itself is a contested point in the history of Europe since the Great War, and a key strategy in the geopolitics of Western capitalism since the Second World War. Understanding the complexity of the present, therefore, means changing our understanding of the past to one in which fascism is the bloody axe at the heart of the political economy of capitalism. It is an axe which, as I write, is cutting its way through the bonds of moral law, democratic politics and cultural freedom to wield its blade over the citizens of the Global Biosecurity State.

Appendix: Laws for the Protection of People and State

'It would be more honest and, above all, more useful to investigate carefully the juridical procedures and deployments of power by which human beings could be so completely deprived of their rights and prerogatives that no act committed against them could appear any longer as a crime.'

— Giorgio Agamben, *Homo Sacer* (1995)

In May 2020, when I first drew comparisons between the state of emergency under which Germans lived through the 12 years of the Third Reich and the politically-declared 'emergency period' under which coronavirus-justified regulations were being imposed on UK citizens without parliamentary scrutiny or approval, a member of the already forming cult of the COVID-faithful responded that my doing so was 'beneath contempt'.[1] Then in September 2020, when I compared the biopolitical paradigm of the laws that had removed the human rights and civil liberties of German citizens with the laws doing the same in the UK, I was told of the dangers of doing so by the journalist, Peter Hitchens, who warned me that 'the vultures circling high in the sky and waiting to feast on your flesh will see it and dive down on you'.[2] He was right, as in response the Architects Registration Board accused me of 'anti-Semitism' and initiated a 6-month investigation that threatened Architects for Social Housing with public censure, a fine or even removing our right to practice as architects.[3]

By the end of 2021, however, with England under its second national lockdown, this comparison had become commonplace, although not without drawing down the wrath and demands for censorship and punishment from Zionists and other keepers of the sanctity of the 'Holocaust'. In December 2021, the Conservative MP, Marcus Fysh, compared the so-called 'Plan B' restrictions

---

1. See Simon Elmer, 'Manufacturing Consensus' (1 May, 2020), collected in *COVID-19*, pp. 66-93.

2. See Simon Elmer, 'The New Normal: What is the UK Biosecurity State? (Part 2. Normalising Fear)' (28 August, 2020), collected in *COVID-19*, pp. 224-270.

3. See Simon Elmer and Francis Hoar, 'In our Defence: Freedom of Speech in the UK Biosecurity State' (16 June, 2021), collected in *Virtue and Terror*, pp. 141-215.

in the UK, and in particular the Government's threat of imposing 'vaccine' passports, to the restrictions on civil liberties in Nazi Germany.[4] And in January 2022, the journalist, Naomi Wolf, published a three-part article in which she compared the willingness of US 'liberals' to comply with and enforce practices of discrimination since March 2020 with the complicity of Germans with National Socialist rule in the early years of the Third Reich.[5] Indeed, few of the predictions that were contemptuously dismissed as the dangerous rantings of 'conspiracy theorists' in 2020 and 2021 have failed to come true in 2022, where they are now equally hysterically proclaimed as necessary to the protection of the people and the safety of the state by the same congregation of the COVID-faithful. This cult has grown to become the *de facto* Church of England, having received the ecclesiastical endorsement of its dogma and rituals last Christmas by the Archbishops of Canterbury and Westminster, the former of whom declared that 'vaccination' was not a question of human rights but a moral issue, and suggested that refusing to comply was a sin.[6] What was once denounced as impossible, ridiculous or obscene is now demanded by the same apologists, the same opportunists, the same ideologues of biopower. Caught between public displays of virtue and obedience to the rule of terror, our collective memory of the past has been voluntarily erased for little more than the promise of rewarded compliance.

However, for those of us who believe that our previously inalienable rights and freedoms should not be tossed aside at the first sign of a 'crisis', it is important not to be cowered, bullied and threatened into forgetting why it was thought necessary to inscribe those rights in European and International law after the Second World War. As I have argued, we have for some time now been living in the West in a pre-totalitarian society, which has prepared us for a Global Biosecurity State that no longer even requires the justification of this manufactured health 'crisis' to remove, with all the violence of the state, the last vestiges of our democracy. The Acts of Parliament and International Treaties that are being made into law or signed by the Government this year, together with the programmes and technologies of the Global Biosecurity State being implemented

---

4. Rob Merrick, 'Covid Plan B restrictions like "Nazi Germany" and Soviet "gulag", say rebel Tory MPs', *The Independent* (13 December, 2021).

5. See Naomi Woolf, 'On the Subtlety of Monsters', *Outspoken* (28 January, 2022).

6. See Ellen Teague, 'Get vaccinated, say Archbishops Nichols and Welby', *The Tablet* (21 December, 2021).

largely without the knowledge and certainly without the vote of the UK public, are the ample evidence of this. However, Hannah Arendt argued that the Third Reich did not become properly totalitarian until September 1939, when the Second World War provided it with the necessary cover to commit its crimes against humanity. Comparing the removal of the human rights and civil liberties of Jews and other 'undesirables' in the Third Reich from 1933 with those of the 'unvaccinated' in the UK biosecurity state since 2020 allows us to see what equivalent date and law we have reached today, and perhaps what the future holds for us unless we overthrow the governments imposing these laws for the protection of people and state.[7]

- On 28 February 1933, the Decree for the Protection of People and State (commonly known as the Reichstag Fire Decree) suspended most of the human rights of German citizens, including the rights of public assembly and of freedom of association, privacy of postal, telegraphic and telephonic communication, freedom of expression and of the press, as well as *habeas corpus*.

- On 21 March 1933, the Malicious Practices Act made it illegal to speak against, question or criticise the Third Reich or its leaders, including making anti-Nazi jokes or 'spreading rumours' punishable by fines or imprisonment. This led to a vast number of denunciations of fellow Germans to the Secret State Police.

- On 23 March 1933, the Law to Remedy the Distress of People and State (commonly known as the Enabling Act) gave the German Cabinet plenary powers to pass laws by decree, without parliamentary approval, and to override fundamental aspects of the Weimar Constitution. Given a 4-year lifespan unless renewed by the Reichstag, this Act was extended twice, in 1937 and 1941, and Germany was still legally under its emergency powers at the end of the Second World War.

- On 7 April 1933, as part of the National Socialist programme of 'co-ordination [*Gleichschaltung*]', the Law for the Restoration of the Professional Civil Service dismissed political opponents of the Third Reich (communists, social

---

7. See William F. Meinecke and Alexandra Zapruder, 'Law, Justice and the Holocaust', *United States Holocaust Memorial Museum*, July 2014.

democrats and trades unionists), as well as Jews and designated 'non-Aryans', from their positions, including as teachers, professors, judges and other civil servants.

- On 11 April 1933, the First Ordinance on the Implementation of the Civil Service law extended the terms of this ban on political opponents and non-Aryans to doctors, nurses, lawyers, notaries, tax consultants and musicians, all of whom were dismissed from their positions.

- On 14 July 1933, the Law on the Revocation of Naturalisations and the Deprivation of German Citizenship revoked the citizenship of naturalised Jews and those the Government deemed to be 'undesirables'. This included communists and anyone granted citizenship under the previous Weimar Government between 9 November, 1918 and 30 January, 1933. The law also applied to those German citizens residing abroad whose loyalty to the Third Reich had been placed in question by their conduct. If they refused to return to the Reich, their citizenship could be forfeited, rendering them stateless, and their property confiscated by the Government.

- On 14 July 1933, the Law for the Seizure of Assets of Enemies of the People and State allowed the Government to confiscate the assets of communists and other designated enemies of the Third Reich.

- On 14 July 1933, the Law against the Founding of New Parties banned or dissolved all other political parties.

- On 14 July 1933, the Law for the Prevention of Offspring with Hereditary Diseases allowed the Government to forcibly sterilise people with physical or mental disabilities.

- On 4 October 1933, the Law on Editors banned Jews from working in journalism, and newspapers were banned from publishing any information that could 'weaken the strength of the Reich abroad or at home'.

- On 24 November 1933, the Law Against Dangerous Habitual Criminals empowered the Secret State Police to take persons suspected of pursuing activities hostile to the state into 'protective custody [Schutzhaft]' without warrant, specific charge, right of appeal, access to a lawyer or judicial review. Incarcerated for an indefinite period of time in a prison or concentration camp, this extra-legal practice was sometimes defended as being necessary for the protection of the individual. The Supreme Court failed to challenge or protest this loss of judicial authority.

- On 18 May 1934, the Flight Tax imposed in 1931 to dissuade wealthy Germans from leaving the country during the Great Depression was amended so that Jews who left Germany had to pay a tax of 25 per cent of their assets. This included those imprisoned in concentration camps outside the borders of the Third Reich.

- On 3 July 1934, the Law on the Unification of Health Care took what had been under the jurisprudence of individual German states into centralised federal legislation and administration, under which doctors administered treatment according to the principles of National Socialism, which superseded their Hippocratic oath to 'first do no harm'.

- On 19 August 1934, in a national referendum, 90 per cent of the German electorate approved the merger of the offices of Chancellor and President, making Adolf Hitler both head of government and head of state. This merged office was designated as the Leader [Führer], whose word now became law.

- On 20 August 1934, the Oath of Loyalty sworn by all state officials was changed from loyalty to the German constitution to loyalty to the Führer.

- On 15 September 1935, the Law for the Protection of German Blood and German Honour banned Jews and other non-Aryans from marital and sexual relations with 'citizens of German or related blood'.

- On 15 September 1935, the Reich Citizenship Law deprived German Jews of their citizenship, and with it their civil and political rights, including the right to vote or hold political office, and instead made them 'subjects of the state [Staatsangehörige]'. This was defined as 'a person who enjoys the protection of the state and in consequence has specific obligations towards it.'

- On 18 October 1935, the Law for the Protection of the Hereditary Health of the German People required all prospective marriage partners to obtain from the public health authorities a certificate of fitness to marry. These were refused to anyone with a contagious disease.

- On 14 November 1935, the first supplemental decree to the Reich Citizenship Law defined 'Jews' not as members of a religious or cultural community but as a race defined by hereditary. This is a definition retained today by both the International Holocaust Remembrance Alliance and the State of Israel.

- On 26 November 1935, the Ministry for the Interior extended the Reich citizenship Law to Roma, Sinti and Afro-Germans.

- On 3 December 1935, anti-Jewish signs near the site of the Winter Olympics, which were held in Garmisch-Partenkirchen from 6-16 February 1936, were removed to avoid international criticism.

- Throughout 1936, to protect the Third Reich from criticism by foreign countries during the Summer Olympics that were held in Berlin from 1-16 August, the making of new legislation for the protection of people and state, and in particular against Jews, was paused.

- On 17 June 1936, the Main Office of the Security Police united the Criminal Police (*Kripo*) with the Secret State Police (*Gestapo*).

- On 15 October 1936, the Ministry for Education banned Jewish teachers from public schools.

- On 9 December 1936, the Supreme Court expanded the definition of 'sexual relations' in the Nuremberg Laws of September 1935 to include all 'natural and unnatural' sexual relations between members of the opposite sex in which 'sexual needs' were in any way gratified, even if it did not involve bodily contact.

- On 14 December 1937, the Decree for Preventative Police Action Against Crime gave the Criminal Police unlimited powers of surveillance and the power of 'preventative arrest [*Vorbeugungshaft*]' to confine in concentration camps anyone on the mere suspicion of criminal activity, or for engaging in anti-social or criminal behaviour, without requiring evidence of a specific criminal act. 'Anti-social' was defined as anyone whose attitude did not fit with that of the 'national community [*Volksmeinschaft*]', including gypsies, prostitutes, pimps, tramps, vagrants, beggars, hooligans and the long-termed unemployed, whose identities were obtained from labour exchanges. Those arrested had no right of appeal or access to a lawyer, and arrests were not liable to judicial review.

- On 26 April 1938, the Order for the Disclosure of Jewish Assets required Jews possessing more than 5,000 Deutschmarks in assets to register their property. This policy was subsequently introduced by fascist governments in France, Hungary, Romania, Bulgaria, Croatia and Slovakia.

- On 31 May 1938, the Law for the Confiscation of Products of Degenerate Art allowed for the confiscation without compensation of thousands of works of art from museums and private collections.
- On 11 July 1938, the Ministry of the Interior banned Jews from attending health spas in order to remove the risk of infection from association with a people defined by National Socialist medicine as vectors of disease both physical and moral.
- On 23 July 1938, Jews were ordered to apply for Identification Cards which had to be shown to police or officials on demand. These were marked with a red letter 'J'.
- On 17 August 1938, the Executive order on the Law on the Alteration of Family and Personal Names ordered Jews without Government-approved forenames to add the name 'Israel' (for males) or 'Sara' (for females) to their own.
- On 3 October 1938, the Decree for the Confiscation of Jewish Property regulated the transfer of assets from Jews to non-Jews, forcing the former into penury and homelessness.
- On 12 September 1938, Jews were banned from attending cinemas, concerts and the opera. Like the ban on health spars and sexual relations, this was a biosecurity 'measure' that reduced the former citizenship of German Jews to the bare life of 'subjects of the state'.
- On 12 November 1938, the Decree for the Exclusion of Jews from German Economic Life banned Jews from owning businesses, selling goods or services or having a trade, forcing them into bankruptcy, unemployment and poverty.
- On 15 November 1938, the Ministry of Education banned Jewish children from attending public schools. This biosecurity 'measure' was justified as a means to protect Aryan children from the risk of infection not only by the bodies but also by the beliefs of Jews, which culturally were dismissed as 'Bolshevik' and religiously as 'anti-Christian'.
- On 21 November 1938, the Atonement Tax for Jews of German Nationality forced Jews with assets of 5,000 Deutschmarks or more to pay 20 per cent in four instalments between 15 December, 1938 and 15 August, 1939. A fifth payment was added in October 1939, bringing the total tax to 25 per cent.

- On 28 November 1938, the Ministry of the Interior restricted freedom of movement and travel for Jews, who were only permitted to leave the Third Reich with 8 per cent of the monetary value in Reichsmarks of their assets.

- On 3 December 1938, the Decree on the Utilisation of Jewish Property made 'Aryanisation' of all Jewish businesses compulsory, imposed a deadline for the sale or liquidation of all businesses, stocks and securities, and blocked all Jewish-owned bank accounts.

- On 14 December 1938, the Executive Order on the Law on the Organisation of National Work cancelled all state contracts with Jewish-owned businesses.

- On 21 December 1938, the Law on Midwives banned all Jews from the profession.

- On 21 February 1939, the Decree concerning the Surrender of Precious Metals and Stones in Jewish Ownership required Jews to turn in gold, silver, diamonds and other valuables to the state without compensation.

- On 18 August 1939, the Reich Committee for the Scientific Registering of Hereditary and Congenital Illnesses initiated the Aktion T4 involuntary euthanasia programme. By the end of the Second World War, between 275,000 and 300,000 people designated as 'life unworthy of living [Lebensunwertes Lebens]' had been killed in hospitals in the Third Reich or under its control. By the end of 1941, this programme had 'emptied' over 93,500 hospital beds for those wounded in the war.

- On 5 September 1939, the Decree against Public Enemies made any crime against person, property, community or public security that was committed under cover of the conditions of war (such as blackouts or air-raids) punishable by death.

- On 27 September 1939, the Reich Security Head Office (RSHA) united the Criminal Police (Kripo) and the Secret State Police (Gestapo) with the SS Intelligence Service (SD), effectively placing all police services in the Third Reich under the central control of the SS (Schutzstaffel).

- On 15 January 1940, the Decree on the Treatment of Enemy Property blocked the existing ownership of all property owned either directly or indirectly by designated enemies of the Third Reich.

- On 1 September 1941, Police Regulations on the Labelling of Jews prohibited Jews in the Third Reich who had reached the age of 6 from 'showing themselves in public without a Jewish star.' It was additionally forbidden for Jews 'to leave the area of their community without having a written permit from the local police'. The punishment for intentionally or negligently contravening these Regulations was a fine of up to 150 Reichsmarks or imprisonment for up to 6 weeks.

- On 1 October 1942, the Letters to All Judges, issued by the newly-appointed Minister of Justice, imposed official guidelines to be used by judges in interpreting the laws of the Third Reich and sentencing those who broke them to death.

- On 25 November 1941, the Eleventh Decree to the Reich Citizenship Law stripped Jews of their remaining rights as subjects of the state, stipulating that Jews living outside Germany were no longer citizens, and that the property and pensions of German Jews who had lost their nationality, including those deported, was to be confiscated by the Reich.

- On 24 April 1942, Jews throughout Greater Germany were prohibited from using public transport. Further prohibitions issued during the course of the Second World War included against using public telephones and ticket dispensing machines, congregating in railway stations, visiting restaurants, entering parks or forests, walking on lawns, obtaining newspapers or periodicals, keeping pets, smoking tobacco, and certain foods were banned, including meat, seafood, milk, white bread, fruit and sweets.

Between the Nuremberg Laws in September 1935 and the outbreak of World War Two in September 1939, more than 120 laws, decrees and regulations imposing over 400 legal restrictions were enacted by the Third Reich on the justification of protecting the health of the German People and the security of the German State. These constituted an epidemiological discourse no less legitimate under German law for being entirely manufactured by National Socialist doctors and scientists: of protection from disease and remedy when infected, and of identifying the infected and imprisoning (and finally exterminating) the diseased.

The 'Holocaust' to which the Third Reich is reduced by those who want to erase its history was preceded by 8 years of laws that so completely deprived

Jews of their rights that, by the time it was implemented in 1941, as Agamben wrote, no act committed against them could appear any longer as a crime. Those who denounce comparisons between the erasure of human rights in today's Europe and Nazi Germany are not only finding consolation in the fact that life in the Global Biosecurity State is not yet as bad as it was in the Third Reich, but are closing their eyes to how totalitarian states are constructed in the laws of democratic societies.

Between January 2020 and March 2022, under a politically-declared 'emergency period', 582 coronavirus-justified Statutory Instruments were made into law in the UK.[8] 537 of these were only laid before Parliament after they were made. 167 were laid by the Department of Health and Social Care, 151 of which were made under the unlawful exercise of powers conferred by the Public Health (Control of Disease) Act 1984.[9]

- On 10 February 2020, the Health Protection (Coronavirus) Regulations 2020 empowered the state to detain, isolate and take a biological sample from someone on the grounds that they 'may be' infected with SARS-CoV-2, in the enforcement of which a police officer may 'use reasonable force'.
- On 5 March 2020, under the first Amendment to the Health Protection (Coronavirus) Regulations 2020, COVID-19 and SARS-CoV-2 were added to the list of, respectively, 'Notifiable Diseases' and 'Causative Agents' that medical practitioners have a duty to record on a death certificate.
- On 16 March 2020, the 'Guidance and standard operating procedure: COVID-19 virus testing in NHS laboratories', issued by the National Health Service, recommended a thermal cycle amplification threshold (Ct) of 45 for reverse-transcription-polymerase chain reaction (RT-PCR) tests for SARS-CoV-2, with anything below 40 to be regarded as a 'confirmed' positive.
- On 16 March 2020, 'Guidance on social distancing for everyone in the UK' instructed the population to avoid contact with someone displaying

---

8. See Hansard Society, 'Coronavirus Statutory Instruments Dashboard, 2020-2022' (9 April, 2020-17 June 2022); and Jennifer Brown and Esme Kirk-Wade, *Coronavirus: A history of 'Lockdown laws' in England,* House of Commons Library (22 December, 2021).

9. See Simon Elmer, 'Bonfire of the Freedoms: The Unlawful Exercise of Powers conferred by the Public Health (Control of Disease) Act 1984' (5 November, 2020), collected in *Brave New World*, pp. 9-24.

symptoms of infection; to use public transport only when essential; to work from home when possible; to avoid gatherings in public places, or with friends and family; and to contact medical services online rather than in person. Despite having no legislative backing, this guidance was enforced through criminal sanctions, including fines and arrest.

- On 17 March 2020, the National Health Service was radically reprioritised, resulting in up to 25,000 hospital patients being discharged into care homes without first being tested for SARS-CoV-2.

- On 19 March 2020, the Ministry of Defence announced the formation of the COVID Support Force comprised of 20,000 military personnel tasked with assisting with implementing the Government's response to the COVID-19 'crisis'. On 2 April, this force was increased by a further 3,000 reservists.

- On 23 March 2020, the Health Protection (Coronavirus, Business Closure) (England) Regulations 2020 required all shops selling non-essential goods to close, as well as libraries, playgrounds, outdoor gyms and places of worship.

- On 25 March 2020, the Coronavirus Act 2020 modified mental health and mental capacity legislation to extend the time a patient can be detained from 72 hours to 120 hours prior to sectioning; empowered a doctor who had not seen the deceased to certify the cause of death as COVID-19 without the body being referred to a coroner before cremation of the remains; removed the requirement for a jury to establish whether COVID-19 was the cause of a death, as is the case with other Notifiable Diseases; extended the time limit for the state's retention of the biometric data of UK citizens; empowered the state to close educational institutions; prohibited attendance at public gatherings or other premises; empowered a police officer to use whatever force is necessary to cover someone's face with a mask, remove them to a place of detention, take a biological sample without their permission and impose restrictions on their movements, actions and contacts for a further 14 days; authorised the awarding of billions of pounds of public money to private contractors as part of the response to the 'pandemic'; and postponed all elections until May 2021.

- On 26 March 2020, the Health Protection (Coronavirus, Restrictions) (England) Regulations 2020 imposed the first national lockdown on England, restricting the movements of the public to shopping for basic necessities, one form of exercise per day, receiving or delivering medical needs, and travel to essential work, with gatherings of more than two people in public prohibited, and compliance enforced by criminal sanctions.

- On 30 March 2020, the Cabinet Office announced that the Government's Rapid Response Unit was working with social media companies to remove any information about coronavirus published online that contradicted its own.

- On 31 March 2020, the Office for National Statistics announced that, for a death to be included in its records of COVID-19 deaths, the disease merely had to be 'mentioned' anywhere on the death certificate, without it being listed as the 'main cause of death', including as a 'contributing' factor; or when a doctor diagnosed a 'possible' case of COVID-19 based on 'relevant symptoms' but with no test for SARS-CoV-2 having been conducted; or when the deceased tested positive post-mortem.

- On 7 April 2020, under Section 22 of the Prosecution of Offences Act 1985, the Coronavirus crisis protocol for the effective handling of custody time limit cases in Magistrates Court and the Crown Court extended the time a defendant could be kept in custody before trial from 56 days to 182 days.

- On 10 April 2020, the Care Quality Commission introduced a 'new way' to understand whether COVID-19 was 'involved in the death' of someone in a care home. This merely required a statement from the care home provider that COVID-19 was 'suspected', and which 'may or may not' correspond to a medical diagnosis, a positive test result for SARs-CoV-2, or even be reflected in the death certificate.

- On 20 April 2020, the World Health Organization issued guidelines to medical practitioners instructing them that, if COVID-19 is the 'suspected', 'probable' or 'assumed' cause of death, it must always be recorded as the underlying cause of death on death certificates, and instructed medical professions to 'always apply these instructions, whether they can be considered medically accurate or not'.

- On 21 April 2020, the House of Commons approved a motion facilitating 'hybrid proceedings' that allowed a maximum of 50 MPs into the Chamber of 650 seats, with 120 MPs able to participate online, proceedings reduced from 8 to 2 hours, and all questions published in advance.

- On 21 April 2020, the Investigatory Powers (Communications Data) (Relevant Public Authorities and Designated Senior Officers) Regulations 2020 extended the power to obtain communications data under the Investigatory Powers Act 2016 to five additional public bodies.

- On 28 April 2020, Public Health England announced that every death in the UK to occur in a care home or otherwise outside a hospital in which a positive test for SARS-CoV-2 has been made pre- or post-mortem would be added both retrospectively and in the future to the official number of COVID-19 deaths.

- On 28 April 2020, the National Health Service announced that it would include on its publication of COVID-19 deaths all deaths for which there has been no positive test for SARS-CoV-2 but for which COVID-19 has been entered on the death certificate as the 'underlying cause of death'.

- On 28 April 2020, the Office for National Statistics and the Care Quality Commission issued a joint transparency statement clarifying that their recording of a death as being the result of COVID-19 'may or may not correspond to a medical diagnosis or test result, or be reflected in the death certification'.

- On 28 April 2020, the Chief Executive of NHSX, the unit that sets national policy and best practice for the NHS on digital technology, announced that, in collaboration with companies specialising in Artificial Intelligence technology, they were exploring the creation of 'immunity passports'. These would require a facial recognition check that matches a Government-approved form of identification linked to biometric data, to confirm a citizen's health 'status' via a Quick Response (QR) code whenever they enter any space using the biosecurity system.

- On 30 April 2020, the National Police Chiefs Council announced that, in the month since the Health Protection Regulations had come into force, it had received reports from public informants of more than 194,300 coronavirus-related incidents in England and Wales (over 5,700 reports per day), and that 9,176 fixed-penalty notices had been issued.

- On 10 May 2020, the Prime Minister announced the launch of the Joint Biosecurity Centre, a privately-run monitoring system designed to require businesses to collect a wide range of data, including biometric samples, on their employees, customers and visitors, based on which it would set the COVID-19 Alert Level as part of an 'extended infrastructure to address biosecurity threats to the UK'.

- On 11 May 2020, the Government presented to Parliament 'Our plan to rebuild: The UK Government's COVID-19 recovery strategy', which included the NHS Test and Trace programme administered through the NHS COVID-19 smartphone app, economic support estimated at £100 billion for the Government's response to COVID-19 and £330 billion (equivalent to 15 per cent of GDP) in the form of guarantees and loans for businesses, 'robust enforcement measures' as the UK moves into the 'next phase', and a 'rapid re-engineering of government's structures and institutions'.

- On 1 June 2020, under the third Amendment to the Health Protection (Coronavirus, Restrictions) (England) (Amendment) (No. 3) Regulations 2020, public protests were banned in the UK.

- On 5 June 2020, following lobbying by the governments of the G7 countries, the World Health Organization revised its 'Advice on the use of masks in the context of COVID-19' to recommend their use, with their reasons for doing so including 'reminding people to be compliant with other measures' and 'encouraging public acceptance of protection measures in general'.

- On 15 June 2020, the Health Protection (Coronavirus, Wearing of Face Coverings on Public Transport) (England) Regulations 2020 made face coverings mandatory on public transport.

- On 29 June 2020, 412,000 people in the City of Leicester were placed under lockdown restrictions on movement, association and closures of premises.

- On 2 July 2020, the Department of Health and Social Care published guidance instructing the owners of public houses, bars, restaurants, cafes, hotels, museums, cinemas, hairdressers, town halls, civic centres, libraries and places of worship to refuse entry to, service in, or employment by their establishments to visitors, customers or staff who refuse to supply their personal details, including their name and contact number or e-mail address, as well as the time of their visit, purchase or shift; and to share this information with the NHS Test and Trace programme.

- On 18 July 2020, the Health Protection (Coronavirus, Restrictions) (England) (No. 3) Regulations 2020 empowered local authorities to give directions imposing prohibitions, requirements or restrictions to close or restrict entry to premises, events or public outdoor places.

- On 23 July 2020, the Health Protection (Coronavirus, Wearing of Face Coverings in a Relevant Place) (England) Regulations 2020 made face coverings mandatory in shops, shopping centres, banks, post offices and transport hubs.

- On 27 July 2020, the National Police Chiefs Council announced that, in the two months between 27 March and 25 May, 17,039 fixed-penalty notices bad been issued in England and Wales.

- On 31 July 2020, The Health Protection (Coronavirus, Restrictions) (Blackburn with Darwen and Bradford) Regulations 2020 placed 528,000 people under lockdown restrictions on movement, association and closures of premises.

- On 31 July 2020, the Government announced an 'independent panel' to examine reform of judicial review, the means by which citizens can challenge whether the decision of the Government or any other public body is within the laws enacted by Parliament.

- On 4 August 2020, the Health Protection (Coronavirus, Restrictions on Gatherings) (North of England) Regulations 2020 placed 6.6 million people under lockdown restrictions on movement, association and closures.

- On 8 August 2020, the Health Protections (Coronavirus, Wearing of Face Coverings in a Relevant Place) (Amendment) Regulations 2020 extended the mandatory wearing of face coverings to places of worship, community centres, crematoria and chapels, hotels and hostels, concert and exhibition halls, cinemas, museums, galleries, indoor tourist sites, bingo halls and public libraries.

- On 8 August 2020, the Health Protection (Coronavirus, Restrictions on Gatherings) (North of England) (Amendment) Regulations 2020 placed 141,000 people in Preston City Council under lockdown restrictions on their movements and associations, as well as closures of their businesses and public premises, because of a reported increase in 'cases' to 61 people testing positive for SARS-CoV-2.

- On 25 August 2020, the Government issued Guidance that children in secondary schools in England must wear face coverings in communal areas.

- On 27 August 2020, the Health Protections (Coronavirus) (Restrictions on Holding of Gatherings and Amendment) (England) Regulations 2020 raised the fine for organising unlawful gatherings of more than 30 people to £10,000.

- On 27 August 2020, the Health Protection (Wearing of Face Coverings in a Relevant Place and on Public Transport) (England) (Amendment) Regulations 2020 raised the fine for not wearing a face covering where mandated to a maximum of £6,400.

- On 24 September 2020, the Health Protection (Coronavirus, Wearing of Face Coverings in a Relevant Place and on Public Transport) (England) (Amendment) (No. 3) Regulations 2020 made the wearing of a face covering mandatory for staff or other workers in certain retail, hospitality and leisure settings, and for anyone entering a pub or restaurant, with fixed penalty notices for non-compliance raised to a maximum of £6,400.

- On 28 September 2020, the Health Protection (Coronavirus, Restrictions) (Self-Isolation) (England) Regulations 2020 raised the fixed penalty notice for breaking quarantine to a maximum of £10,000.

- On 30 September 2020, the Coronavirus Act 2020 was renewed for the first time by a vote of 330 in favour to 24 against in the House of Commons.

- On 14 October 2020, the Health Protection (Coronavirus, Local COVID-19 Alert Level) (Medium) (England) Regulations 2020, the Health Protection (Coronavirus, Local COVID-19 Alert Level) (High) (England) Regulations 2020, and the Health Protection (Coronavirus, Local COVID-19 Alert Level) (Very High) (England) Regulations 2020 empowered the Secretary of State to divide England according to three tiers of regulations (later increased to four), with the maximum fixed penalty notice for non-compliance set at £6,400 for individuals and £10,000 for businesses.

- On 16 October 2020, the Human Medicines (Coronavirus and Influenza) (Amendment) Regulations 2020 modified The Human Medicines Regulations 2012 to allow temporary authorisation of unlicensed COVID-19 vaccines, and extended complete immunity from civil liability to the scientists, pharmaceutical companies and medical professionals responsible for their manufacture, distribution and administering to the public.

- On 5 November 2020, the Health Protection (Coronavirus, Restrictions) (England) (No. 4) Regulations 2020 imposed a second national lockdown on

England. Approved by a vote of 516 MPs to 38 after a 3-hour debate in the House of Commons the previous day, this was the first time since the beginning of the 'crisis' that coronavirus-justified Regulations had been presented to Parliament before being made into law.

- On 26 November 2020, the Government allocated £4 billion to build sufficient prisons to incarcerate 18,000 new inmates (a 23 percent increase in the prison population of the UK), plus an additional £275 million to recruit 20,000 more police officers (a 13 per cent increase).

- On 2 December 2020, the Medicines and Health products Regulatory Agency granted temporary authorisation to the Pfizer/BioNTech messenger RNA 'vaccine' for COVID-19 just seven months after the start of clinical trials that are due to be completed in February 2023.

- On 3 December 2020, the Vaccine Damage Payments (Specified Disease) Order 2020 added COVID-19 to the list of diseases against which payments made to individuals severely disabled as a result of 'vaccination' are limited to a one-off Vaccine Damage Payment of £120,000.

- On 30 December 2020, the Medicines and Health products Regulatory Agency granted temporary authorisation to the AstraZeneca/Oxford viral vector 'vaccine' for COVID-19, the trials for which are due to be completed in February 2023.

- On 6 January 2021, the Health Protection (Coronavirus, Restrictions) (No. 3) and (All Tiers) (England) (Amendment) Regulations 2021 imposed a third national lockdown on England.

- On 8 January 2021, the Medicines and Health products Regulatory Agency granted temporary authorisation to Moderna/NIH messenger RNA 'vaccine' for COVID-19, the trials for which are due for completion in December 2022.

- On 15 February 2021, The Health Protection (Coronavirus, International Travel) (England) (Amendment) (No. 7) Regulations 2021 imposed fixed-penalty notices of up to £10,000 for failing to take an RT-PCR test or to remain in quarantine upon entry from 'red list' countries from which travel to England and Wales was banned, with a prison term of up to 10 years for incorrectly identifying the country from which they had returned.

- On 8 March 2021, the 'Roadmap out of lockdown', published by the Government, laid out four-steps for lifting restrictions on social contact,

271

education, travel, businesses, activities and events over the next three months, on condition of mass compliance of the UK population with the COVID-19 'vaccination' programme, with the fourth step being delayed four weeks until sufficient numbers had been injected at least once.

- On 25 March 2021, the Coronavirus Act 2020 was renewed for the second time by a vote of 484 MPs in favour to 76 against in the House of Commons.

- On 29 March 2021, the Health Protection (Coronavirus, Restrictions) (Steps) (England) Regulations 2021 raised fixed penalty notices for breaking lockdown restrictions to a maximum of £5,000 for attempting to leave the UK without a reasonable excuse, £6,400 for gatherings of more than 15 people, and £10,000 for gatherings of more than 30 people.

- On 1 April 2021, Public Health England was merged with the NHS Test and Trace programme and the Joint Biosecurity Centre to form the UK Health Security Agency.

- On 7 May 2021, the UK Health Security Agency made the NHS COVID Pass available to use as a condition of travel, entry or service by both private businesses and public institutions.

- On 28 June 2021, the National Police Chiefs' Council reported that, in the 15 months between 27 March 2020 and 20 June 2021, they issued 366 Fixed Penalty Notices for large gatherings incurring a £10,000 fine.

- On 13 August 2021, the UK Health Security Agency and the National Health Service announced that children under the age of 16 would not require parental consent to be injected with the Pfizer/BioNTech 'vaccine' if they are 'Gillick competent'.

- On 13 September 2021, the Chief Medical Officers of England, Scotland, Wales and Northern Ireland authorised the injection of 3.15 million 12-15-year-old UK children with one dose of the Pfizer/BioNTech mRNA 'vaccine'.

- On 27 September 2021, the Government published 'Proposal for mandatory COVID certification in a Plan B scenario', a policy paper mandating not only face coverings but also what it called 'COVID-status certification' requiring that access to aspects of public life in the UK would be contingent upon proof not of immunity from SARS-CoV-2 produced by antibodies or even a negative test but of being 'fully vaccinated', which it defined as a 'course of doses' of undefined number and content.

- On 19 October 2021, the Coronavirus Act 2020 was renewed for the third time without a vote in the House of Commons.
- On 9 November 2021, the Secretary of State for Health and Social Care announced to Parliament that National Health Service staff who refused to be injected with a COVID-19 'vaccine' would be sacked from their job.
- On 11 November 2021, the Health and Social Care Act 2008 (Regulated Activities) (Amendment) (Coronavirus) Regulations 2021 made a 'complete course' of COVID-19 'vaccines' mandatory for all care home workers and those entering care homes to work.
- On 3 February 2022, the Medicines and Health products Regulatory Agency granted temporary authorization to the Novavax protein adjuvant 'vaccine' for COVID-19, the trials for which are due for completion in July 2023.
- On 1 April 2022, the Department for Health and Social Care awarded the contract to develop the NHS COVID Pass to the Danish IT firm, Netcompany Ltd. The scope of works for the project stated: 'This enables a quick response if/when the Government invokes a mandate. If a citizen is fully vaccinated, medically exempt or has been in a clinical trial, they will be eligible for an "all venues" (mandatory) pass. If a citizen only has natural immunity or negative test results, they will only be eligible for a "limited venues" (voluntary) pass.'
- On 28 April 2022, the Health and Care Act 2022, as part of the NHS Long Term Plan, furthered the privatisation and outsourcing of the National Health Service, granted the Secretary of State authority over the NHS, and made 42 integrated care systems statutory bodies with power over NHS commissioning and spending in England.
- On 28 April 2022, the Police, Crime, Sentencing and Courts Act 2022 empowered the police to impose conditions on public demonstrations and protests, including where they are held, and that they do not cause 'unease', 'annoyance' or 'disruption', failure to comply with which was made a criminal offence punishable by up to 10 years in prison; granted police access to private education and health records; as well as the power to stop and search citizens without cause; and criminalised trespass on private-owned land.
- On 28 April 2022, the Nationality and Borders Act empowered the Home Secretary, without prior notification, to revoke the British citizenship of anyone who is not born in the UK, who is of dual nationality, who is judged

to be a threat to national security, or whose behaviour is deemed to be 'unacceptable'; and criminalised asylum seekers who arrive in the UK via unsanctioned routes.

- On 28 April 2022, the Judicial Review and Courts Act 2022 empowered the law courts to suspend and limit challenges to the legality of, and redress for, the decisions and actions of the UK Government and other public bodies.

- As of 28 September 2022, the Medicines and Healthcare products Regulatory Agency had received 464,0171 reports of 1,517,640 injuries following injection with a COVID-19 'vaccine', including 2,272 deaths within 7 days of injection, with an unknown number having died outside this time limit.

Bibliography

Academy of Medical Sciences. *Preparing for a challenging winter 2020/21* (14 July, 2020).

Action Aid Global, et al. Open letter – Corporate capture of global governance: The World Economic Forum–UN partnership agreement is a dangerous threat to UN System', *International Network for Economic, Social and Cultural Rights* (20 June, 2021).

Agamben, Giorgio. *Homo Sacer: Sovereign Power and Bare Life*. Meridian: Crossing Aesthetics, series edited by Werner Hamacher and David E. Wellbery. Translated by Daniel Heller-Roazen. Stanford University Press, 1998.

_____. *State of Exception*. Homo Sacer II, 1. Translated by Kevin Attell. University of Chicago Press, 2005.

_____. *Stasis: Civil War as a Political Paradigm*. Homer Sacer II, 2. Translated by Nicholas Heron. Stanford University Press, 2015.

_____. *Remnants of Auschwitz: The Witness and the Archive*. Homer Sacer III. Translated by Daniel Heller-Roazen. Zone Books, 2002.

_____. 'Capitalism as Religion', in *Creation and Anarchy: The Work of Art and the Religion of Capitalism*. Meridian: Crossing Aesthetics, series edited by Werner Hamacher and David E. Wellbery. Translated by Adam Kotsko. Stanford University Press, 2019, pp. 66-78.

_____. 'The Invention of an epidemic', *Il manifesto* (26 February, 2020); collected in *Where Are We Now? The Epidemic as Politics*. Second updated edition. Translated by Valeria Dani. Eris, 2021, pp. 11-13.

_____. 'A Question', *Quodlibet* (13 April); collected in *Where Are We Now?*, pp. 34-37.

_____. 'Bare Life: Interview with Ivar Ekman for Swedish Public Radio (19 April 2020); collected in *Where Are We Now?*, pp. 38-41.

_____. 'New Reflections', *Neue Zürcher Zeitung* (27 April); collected in *Where Are We Now?*, pp. 34-37.

_____. 'Medicine as Religion', *Quodlibet* (2 May, 2020); collected in *Where Are We Now?*, pp. 49-54.

_____. 'Biosecurity and Politics', *Quodlibet* (11 May, 2020); collected in *Where Are We Now?*, pp. 55-58.

_____. 'Polemos Epidemios: Interview with Dimitra Pouliopoulou, *Babylonia* (20 May 2020); collected in *Where Are We Now?*, pp. 59-71.

_____. 'What is Fear?', *Quodlibet* (13 July, 2020); collected in *Where Are We Now?*, pp. 88-95.

_____. 'Quando la casa brucia', *Quoblibet* (5 October, 2020); translated, with an introduction and notes, by Simon Elmer and Carlo Rimassa as 'When the House Burns: Giorgio Agamben on the Coronavirus Crisis', *Architects for Social Housing* (15 October, 2020); and by Kevin Attell in *When the House Burns Down* (Seagull Books, 2022), pp. 1-16.

_____. 'Bare Life and the Vaccine', *Quodlibet* (16 April, 2021); collected in *Where Are We Now?*, pp. 96-98.

_____. 'Speech at the conference of Venetian students against the Green Pass on November 11, 2021 at Ca' Sagredo', *Quodlibet* (11 November, 2021); translated by Lena Bloch (3 January, 2022).

Ahronheim, Anna. 'Israel completes upgraded barrier with the Gaza Strip', *The Jerusalem Post* (7 December, 2021).

Albert, Angeline. 'CQC uncovers "serious concerns" of human rights breaches linked to blanket do not resuscitate orders', *Care Home* (18 March, 2021).

Allegretti, Aubrey, Nicola Davis and Caroline Davies, 'Sunak accused of "rewriting history" by saying No 10 ignored lockdown harms', *The Guardian* (25 August, 2022).

Allen, Victoria. 'Drinking less than NHS alcohol guidelines could increase risk of heart attacks', *Daily Mail* (28 January, 2022).

Alzheimer's Society, 'Facts for the media about dementia' (19 July, 2022).

Amaro, Silvia. 'Greece imposes monthly fines of 100 euros on the over-60s who refuse a Covid vaccine', *CNBC* (1 December, 2021).

Americans for Tax Fairness. 'After 2 years of COVID, U.S. billionaires are $1.7 trillion, or 57%, richer' (11 March, 2022).

Amnesty International. *Israel's Apartheid against Palestinians: Cruel System of Domination and Crimes against Humanity*, 2022.

Anon. 'UK and Israel sign military agreement', *5 Pillars UK* (7 December, 2020).

_____. 'The Queen and Royal Family host G7 leaders for joint dinner at Eden Project', *ITV News* (11 June, 2021).

_____. 'Energy crisis: Why gas prices have soared and left UK facing prospect of food shortages', *Sky News* (22 September, 2021).

_____. 'How recent vaccine mandate laws in Lithuania and throughout Europe have upended my family's life', *The Rio Times* (1 October, 2021).

_____. 'Covid green pass: How are people in Italy reacting to the new law for workplaces?', *The Local* (15 October, 2021).

_____. 'What changes about life in Italy in February 2022?', *The Local* (1 February, 2022).

_____. 'Chelsea boss Thomas Tuchel says fans should not have sung Abramovich's name during minute's applause', *ITV News* (7 March, 2022).

_____. 'Partygate: A timeline of the lockdown gatherings', *BBC* (19 May, 2022).

_____. 'Al Jazeera to refer journalist Shireen Abu Akleh's killing to ICC', *Al Jazeera* (26 May, 2022).

_____. 'At least 77K Dead and 7.3 Million Injured due to COVID Vaccination across USA, Europe, UK and Australia', *The Exposé* (11 June, 2022).

_____. 'Europe's Heat Apocalypse', *The Guardian Weekly* (22 July, 2022).

_____. United Kingdom inflation rate', *RI* (17 August, 2022).

_____. 'COVID: German cabinet signs off on rules for autumn and winter', *DW* (24 August, 2022).

Arendt, Hannah. *The Origins of Totalitarianism*. Schocken Books, 1951. Second revised edition. Penguin Modern Classics, 2017.

_____. 'Ideology and Terror: A Novel Form of Government', *The Review of Politics*, vol. 15, no. 3 (July 1953); reprinted in *The Origins of Totalitarianism*. Second revised edition. Penguin Classics, 2017, pp. 604-629.

_____. 'On Humanity in Dark Times' (1959); collected in *Men in Dark Times*. San Diego: Harcourt Brace & Company, 1968, pp. 3-31.

_____. *Eichmann in Jerusalem: The Banality of Evil*. Viking Press, 1963. Revised and enlarged edition, with an Introduction by Amos Elon. Penguin Classics, 2006.

_____. 'Hannah Arendt interviewed by Joachim Fest, 1964'. Hannah Arendt Centre for Political Studies. University of Verona, Department of Human Sciences, 2016.

_____. 'Personal Responsibility Under Dictatorship' (1964), collected in *Responsibility and Judgement*. Edited and with an introduction by Jerome Kohn. Schocken Books, 2003.

_____. *The Life of the Mind*. Edited by Mary McCarthy. Houghton Mifflin Harcourt, 1981.

Arora, Simran. 'Heart attacks in healthy people: A popular shower habit could take the blame', *Times Now* (21 July, 2022).

Atlantic Council. 'Global QE Tracker'.

Auken, Ida. 'Welcome to 2030: I own nothing, have no privacy and life has never been better', *Forbes* (10 November, 2016).

Auschwitz-Birkenau: Former German Nazi Concentration and Extermination Camp. 'The Organizational Structure'.

Austin, Lloyd J. 'The Department of Defense Releases the President's Fiscal Year 2023 Defense Budget' (28 March, 2022).

BAE Systems. 'BAE Systems brings its military aircraft expertise to the development, manufacture, integration and sustainment of the F-35'.

Bank of England. 'Central Bank Digital Currency: An update on the Bank of England's work — speech by Tom Mutton' (17 June, 2021).

_____. *Monetary Policy Report*, August 2022.

Bank of International Settlements. *Annual Economic Report*, June 2019.

Barber, Sarah, Jennifer Brown and Daniel Ferguson. 'Coronavirus: lockdown laws', *House of Commons Library* (14 July, 2022).

Barrett, Emily, and Jesse Hamilton. 'Why the US Repo Market Blew Up and How to Fix It', *Bloomberg UK* (6 January, 2020).

Bartsch, Elga, Jean Boivin, Stanley Fischer and Philipp Hildebrand. 'Dealing with the next downturn: From unconventional monetary policy to unprecedented policy coordination', *BlackRock Investment Institute* (August 2019).

Bataille, Georges. 'The Psychological Structure of Fascism' (1933-34), collected in *Visions of Excess: Selected Writings, 1927-29*. Edited, translated and with an introduction by Allan Stoekl. Theory and History of Literature, Vol. 14. University of Minnesota Press, 1984, pp. 137-160.

Benjamin, Walter. 'The Work of Art in the Age of Mechanical Reproduction' (1936), collected in *Illuminations*. Edited and with an introduction by Hannah Arendt. Translated by Harry Zohn. Fontana Press, 1992, pp. 211-244.

_____. 'Theses on the Philosophy of History' (1940), collected in *Illuminations*, pp. 245-255.

Berman, Lazar. '"We do not agree": UK rejects Amnesty report accusing Israel of apartheid', *The Times of Israel* (4 February, 2022).

Board of Governors of the Federal Reserve System. 'Federal Reserve Actions to Support the Flow of Credit to Households and Businesses' (15 March, 2020).

Boffey, Daniel. 'EU must consider mandatory Covid jabs, says Von der Leyen', *The Guardian* (1 December, 2021).

Borger, Pieter, et al. 'Corman-Drosten Review Report. External peer review of the RT-PCR test to detect SARS-CoV-2 reveals 10 major scientific flaws at the molecular and methodological level: consequences for false positive results' (27 November, 2020).

Bounds, Andy. 'Dutch farmers in uproar over plans to curb animal numbers to cut nitrogen emissions', *Financial Times* (3 August 2022).

Brady, Dr. Michael. 'How to have sex while managing the risk of COVID-19', *The Terrence Higgins Trust* (7 August, 2020).

Brecht, Bertolt. 'To Those Born After', *The Collected Poems of Bertolt Brecht*. Translated and edited by Tom Kuhn and David Constantine. Liveright Publishing, 2019, pp. 734-736.

Breton, André. 'Open Letter to Paul Eluard', collected in *Free Rein (La Clé des champs)*. Translated by Michel Parmentier and Jacqueline d'Ambrose. French Modernist Library, series edited by Mary Ann Caws, Richard Howard and Patricia Terry. University of Nebraska Press, 1995, pp. 229-231.

Bridge Initiative Team. 'Factsheet: Torture at Guantánamo Bay Detention Centre', Georgetown University (19 July, 2020).

Brien, Philip and Matthew Keep. 'Public Spending during the COVID-19 pandemic', *House of Commons Library* (29 March, 2022).

British Security Agency. 'Automated Facial Recognition: ethical and legal use' (25 October, 2021).

Brock, Thomas. 'Environmental, Social, and Governance (ESG) Criteria', *Investopedia* (28 May, 2022).

Brown, Ellen. 'Another Bank Bailout Under Cover of a Virus', *The Web of Debt Blog* (18 May, 2020).

_____. 'Conservation or Land Grab? The Financialization of Nature', *The Web of Debt Blog* (5 November, 2021).

Brown, Jennifer. 'Coronavirus: enforcing restrictions', *House of Commons Library* (27 July, 2021).

Brown, Jennifer and Esme Kirk-Wade. *Coronavirus: A history of 'Lockdown laws' in England*. House of Commons Library. 22 December, 2021.

Brown, Natalie. '"Scare campaign": Underlying health issues involved in 92 per cent of Aussie Covid deaths', *News* (16 February, 2022).

Butler, James. 'Follow the Science', *London Review of Books* (16 April, 2020).

Bytwerk, Randall, ed. *Landmark Speeches of National Socialism*. Texas A&M University Press, 2008.

Cabinet Office. 'Implementing the Sustainable Development Goals' (15 July, 2022).

_____. 'Roadmap out of lockdown' (22 February, 2021).

Canales, Katie. 'China's "social credit" system ranks citizens and punishes them with throttled internet speeds and flight bans if the Communist Party deems them untrustworthy', *Business Insider* (24 December, 2021).

Campaign Against Arms Trade. 'Israel: Frequently asked questions' (13 May, 2021).

Cao, Shiyi, et al. 'Post-lockdown SARS-CoV-2 nucleic acid screening in nearly ten million residents of Wuhan', *Nature Communications* (20 November, 2020).

Cecco, Leyland. 'Justin Trudeau takes a knee but is silent on reforms to policing', *The Guardian*, 6 June, 2020.

Centre for Evidence-based Medicine at Oxford University. 'Viral cultures for COVID-19 infectivity assessment. Systematic review' (4 August).

Center for Health Security. 'The Event 201 Scenario: A Global Pandemic Exercise' (18 October, 2019).

Chalmers, Vanessa. 'Urgent warning as 300,000 Brits living with stealth disease that could kill within 5 years', *The Sun* (26 January, 2022).

Cheng, Derek. 'Coronavirus: Jacinda Ardern dismisses nationwide lockdown speculation on social media', *New Zealand Herald*, 19 March, 2020.

China Copyright and Media. 'Planning Outline for the Construction of a Social Credit System (2014-2020)' (14 June, 2014).

Cohen, Nick. 'It is only a matter of time before we turn on the unvaccinated', *The Guardian* (27 February, 2021).

Collins, Paul. 'IPCC climate report 2022 summary: The key findings', *Climate Consulting by Selectra*, 2022.

Connolly, Kate. 'German government drops plan for Covid vaccine mandate', *The Guardian* (8 April, 2022).

Corman, Victor M., et al. 'Diagnostic detection of 2019-nCoV by real-time RT-PCR', *Eurosurveillance*, 22 January, 2020.

Cotton, Johnny. 'Belgian police fire water cannon, tear gas during COVID curbs protest', *Reuters* (23 January, 2021).

Council of Europe. 'European Social Charter', collected texts (7th edition) (updated: 1 January, 2015), p. 14.

_____. 'Covid-19 vaccines: ethical, legal and practical considerations', Council of Europe Resolution 2361 (27 January, 2021).

Crego, Maria Diaz, Costica Dumbrava, David de Groot, Silvia Kotanidis, and Maria-Margarita Mentzelopoulou. 'Legal issues surrounding compulsory Covid-19 vaccination', *European Parliamentary Research Service* (14 March, 2022).

Dalio, Ray. *Principles for Dealing with the Changing World Order: Why Nations Succeed and Fail*. Simon and Schuster, 2021.

Davis, Nicola. 'Do Covid vaccine mandates work?', *The Guardian* (3 December, 2021).

Davis, Nicola, Ashley Kirk and Pamela Duncan. 'Covid lockdown shows signs of working in England, expert says', *The Guardian* (19 November, 2020).

Department for Digital, Culture, Media and Sport. 'The Fourth Industrial Revolution' (16 October, 2017).

_____. 'Code of practice for wireless network development in England' (7 March, 2022).

_____. 'UK digital identity and attributes trust framework' (14 June, 2022).

Department for International Trade. 'Open general export licence (exports in support of joint strike fighter: F-35 Lightning II)' (6 January, 2014).

Department of Transport. 'Reported road casualties Great Britain, annual report: 2019' (30 September, 2020).

DeSilver, Drew. 'For most U.S. workers, real wages have barely budged for decades', *Pew Research Centre* (7 August, 2018).

Dimitrov, Georgi. *The United Front: The Struggle Against Fascism and War*. London: Lawrence & Wishart, 1939.

Dimitropoulou, Alexandra. 'Economy Rankings: Largest countries by GDP, 2022', *CEO World Magazine* (31 March, 2022).

Donnelly, Drew. 'China Social Credit System Explained — What is it and How Does it Work?', *NH Global Partners* (22 July, 2022).

Donnelly, Laura. 'Lockdown's hidden toll: million schoolchildren a year will need mental health help', *The Telegraph* (8 May, 2021).

Durden, Tyler. '"The Fed Was Suddenly Facing Multiple LTCMs": BIS Offers A Stunning Explanation Of What Really Happened On Repocalypse Day', *ZeroHedge* (9 December, 2019).

Dutt, R. Palme. 'The Question of Fascism and Capitalist Decay', *The Communist International*, Vol. XII, No. 14 (July 20, 1935).

Eco, Umberto. 'Ur-fascism', *The New York Review of Books* (22 June, 1995); collected in *How to Spot a Fascist*. Translated by Ricard Dixon and Alastair McEwan. Harvill Secker, 2020.

Elmer, Simon. 'Memorials of Forgetting: Art and Architecture in Berlin', *Architects for Social Housing* (21 July, 2016).

_____. 'Dresden Diary: Architecture, History and Politics', *Architects for Social Housing* (6 July, 2018).

_____. 'Supply and Demand in Centre Point Residences', *Architects for Social Housing* (6 November, 2018).

_____. *Inequality Capital: A Power Walk by Architects for Social Housing* (April 2019).

_____. 'Extinction Rebellion: Socialist Revolution', *Architects for Social Housing* (24 April, 2019).

_____. 'Whatever Happened to the Middle Class? Bad Faith and the Culture Industry', *Architects for Social Housing* (10 May, 2019).

_____. 'Capitalising on Crisis: Extinction Rebellion and the Green New Deal for Capitalism', *Architects for Social Housing* (10 October, 2019).

_____. 'The Labour Party Manifesto on Housing', *Architects for Social Housing* (21 November, 2019).

_____. 'COVID-19 and Capitalism', *Architects for Social Housing* (18 March, 2020).

_____. 'Sociology of a Disease: Age, Class and Mortality in the Coronavirus Pandemic', *Architects for Social Housing* (24 March, 2020).

_____. 'Language is a Virus: SARS-CoV-2 and the Science of Political Control', *Architects for Social Housing* (3 April, 2020).

_____. 'Coronazombies! Infection and Denial in the United Kingdom', *Architects for Social Housing* (9 April, 2020).

_____. 'Giorgio Agamben and the Biopolitics of COVID-19', *Architects for Social Housing* (25 April, 2020).

_____. 'Manufacturing Consensus: The Registering of COVID-19 Deaths in the UK', *Architects for Social Housing* (1 May, 2020).

_____. 'The State of Emergency as Paradigm of Government: Coronavirus Legislation, Implementation and Enforcement', *Architects for Social Housing* (12 May, 2020).

_____. 'Lockdown: Collateral Damage in the War on COVID-19', *Architects for Social Housing* (2 June, 2020).

_____. 'The Science and Law of Refusing to Wear Masks: Texts and Arguments in Support of Civil Disobedience', *Architects for Social Housing* (11 June, 2020).

_____. 'The New Normal: What is the Biosecurity State? (Part 1: Programmes and Regulations)', *Architects for Social Housing* (31 July, 2020).

_____. 'The New Normal: What is the UK Biosecurity State? (Part 2. Normalising Fear)', *Architects for Social Housing* (28 August, 2020).

_____. *COVID-19: Implementing the UK Biosecurity State*. Architects for Social Housing, 2020.

_____. 'Bonfire of the Freedoms: The Unlawful Exercise of Powers conferred by the Public Health (Control of Disease) Act 1984', *Architects for Social Housing* (5 November, 2020).

_____. 'The Betrayal of the Clerks: UK Intellectuals in the Service of the Biosecurity State', *Architects for Social Housing* (12 November, 2020).

_____. 'Bread and Circuses: Who's Behind the Oxford Vaccine for COVID-19?', *Architects for Social Housing* (25 November, 2020).

_____. 'Bowling for Pfizer: Who's Behind the BioNTech Vaccine for COVID-19?', *Architects for Social Housing* (9 December, 2020)

_____. 'Five Stories Under Lockdown', *Architects for Social Housing* (1 December, 2020).

_____. 'Our Default State: Compulsory Vaccination for COVID-19 and Human Rights Law', *Architects for Social Housing* (8 January, 2021).

_____. 'Lies, Damned Lies and Statistics: Manufacturing the Crisis', *Architects for Social Housing* (27 January, 2021).

_____. *'Cui bono*? The COVID-19 "conspiracy"', *Architects for Social Housing* (19 February, 2021).

_____. *Brave New World: Expanding the UK Biosecurity State through the Winter of 2020-2021*. Architects for Social Housing, 2021.

_____. 'Behind the Mask, the Conspiracy!', *Architects for Social Housing* (17 May, 2021).

_____. 'March for Freedom: London, 29 May, 2021', *Architects for Social Housing* (30 May, 2021).

_____. 'The Impact of Lockdown on UK Housing', *The People's Inquirer* (14 June, 2021).

_____. 'The UK "Vaccination" Programme: Part 1. Adverse Drug Reactions and Deaths', *Architects for Social Housing* (15 September, 2021).

_____. 'The UK "Vaccination" Programme. Part 2: Virtue and Terror', *Architects for Social Housing.* (22 September, 2021).

_____. 'The UK "Vaccination" Programme. Part 3: Resistance', *Architects for Social Housing* (1 October, 2021).

_____. *Virtue and Terror: Resisting the UK Biosecurity State.* Architects for Social Housing, 2021.

_____. 'Open Letter to Left Lockdown Sceptics', *Left Lockdown Sceptics* (17 October, 2021).

Elmer, Simon and Francis Hoar. 'In our Defence: Freedom of Speech in the UK Biosecurity State', *Architects for Social Housing* (16 June, 2021).

Engelbrecht, Torsten, and Konstantin Demeter. 'COVID-19 PCR Tests are Scientifically Meaningless', *Bulgarian Pathology Association* (1 July, 2020).

EudraVigilance. 'European database of suspected adverse drug reaction reports'. European Commission. 'Identifying conspiracy theories'.

_____. 'Statement by President von der Leyen on energy' (7 September, 2022).

European Council. 'An international treaty on pandemic prevention and preparedness' (25 March, 2022).

Evans, Dylan. *An Introductory Dictionary of Lacanian Psychoanalysis*. Routledge, 1996.

Evans, Richard J. *The Coming of the Third Reich*. Allen Lane, 2003.

_____. *The Third Reich in Power*. Allan Lane, 2005.

Extinction Rebellion. 'Doctors stage die-in at JP Morgan Glasgow in ongoing campaign, demanding they end new fossil fuel investment' (5 November, 2021).

Faustino, Didier, and Kostas Grigoriadis. 'The Logic of Guantanamo', *The Funambulist* (19 December, 2016).

Federal Deposit Insurance Corporation. 'Basic FDIC Insurance Coverage Permanently Increased to $250,000 Per Depositor' (21 July, 2019).

Federal Reserve. 'The Primary & Secondary Lending Programs'.

Feldner, Heiko and Fabio Vighi, *Critical Theory and the Crisis of Contemporary Capitalism*. Critical Theory and Contemporary Society, series edited by Darrow Schecter. Bloomsbury Publishing, 2015.

Ferguson, Neil, et al. 'Report 9. Impact of non-pharmaceutical interventions (NPIs) to reduce COVID-19 mortality and healthcare demand', *Imperial College London* (16 March, 2020).

_____. 'Report 12. The global impact of COVID-19 and strategies for mitigation and suppression', *Imperial College London* (12 June, 2020).

Fiore, Fiorella De, and Oreste Tristani. '(Un)conventional Policy and the Effective Lower Bound', *BIS Working Papers*, No. 804 (August 2019).

Fitzpatrick, Dr. Michael. 'Anti-vaxxers' gospel of fear: Reckless, dangerous and irresponsible', *Daily Mail* (10 November, 2020).

Forsberg, Dr. Lisa, Dr. Isra Black, Dr. Thomas Douglas and Dr. Jonathan Pugh. 'Compulsory vaccination for COVID-19 and human rights law', UK Parliament Joint Committee on Human Rights (22 July, 2020).

Foucault, Michel. *The Will to Knowledge*. Volume 1 of *The History of Sexuality*. Translated by Robert Hurley. Penguin Books, 1998.

Friedrich, Carl Joachim, and Zbigniew Brzezinski. *Totalitarian Dictatorship and Autocracy*. Second edition. Harvard University Press, 1965.

Furedi, Jacob, Jane Caplan, Roger Griffin, Kevin Passmore and Bruno Waterfield. 'What is . . . Fascism?', *Battle of Ideas*, 29 October 2017.

Gardiner, Laura, and Hannah Slaughter. 'The effects of the coronavirus on workers', *Resolution Foundation* (16 May, 2020).

Gardner, Maria. 'The Internet of Bodies Will Change Everything, for Better or Worse', *RAND Corporation* (29 October, 2020).

Gehrke, Laurenz. 'Germany to tighten coronavirus restrictions', *Politico* (1 December, 2021).

Gibson Dunn Lawyers. 'BlackRock, Vanguard, State Street Update Corporate Governance and ESG Policies and Priorities for 2022' (25 January, 2022).

Giubilini, Alberto, and Vageesh Jain. 'Should COVID-19 vaccines been mandatory? Two experts discuss', *The Conversation* (25 November, 2020).

Golbert, Max. 'Russian News Channel RT Has UK License Revoked By Regulator Ofcom', *Deadline* (18 March, 2022).

Gorton, Gary B. 'Questions and Answers about the Financial Crisis', *National Bureau of Economic Research, Working Paper 15787* (February 2010).

Gove, Michael. '"Homes for Ukraine" scheme launches', Department for Levelling Up, Housing and Communities (14 March, 2022).

Government Digital Service. 'How to score attributes' (2 August 2021).

Government of Canada. 'Mandatory COVID-19 vaccination requirements for federally regulated transportation employees and travellers' (6 October, 2021).

Greeley, Brendan. Central Bankers rethink everything at Jackson Hole', *Financial Times* (25 August, 2019).

Greenberg, Clement. 'Avant-Garde and Kitsch' (1939), collected in *Art and Culture: Critical Essays*. Beacon Press, 1961, pp. 3-21.

Gregory, Andrew. 'Black Lives Matter: Keir Starmer takes knee in solidarity with "all those opposing anti-black racism"', *The Independent* (9 June, 2020).

_____. 'Covid passports could increase vaccine uptake, study suggests', *The Guardian* (13 December, 2021).

_____. 'Hotter nights increase risk of death from heart disease for men in early 60s', *The Guardian* (28 March, 2022).

Grimley, Naomi, Jack Cornish and Nassos Stylianou. 'Covid: World's true pandemic death toll nearly 15 million, says WHO', *BBC* (5 May, 2022).

Gross, Judah Ari. 'IDF says it launched major offensive on dozens of rocket launch tubes in Gaza', *The Times of Israel* (11 May, 2021).

Gupta, Dr. Sunetra, Dr. Martin Kulldorff and Dr. Jay Bhattacharya. 'The Great Barrington Declaration' (4 October, 2020).

Hansard Society. 'Coronavirus Statutory Instruments Dashboard, 2020-2022' (9 April, 2020-17 June 2022).

Harriss, Lydia and Philippa Kearney, 'Smart Cities', *Research Briefing, UK Parliament* (22 September, 2021).

Haque, Omar S., Julian De Freitas, Ivana Viani, Bradley Niederschulte and Harold J. Bursztajn. 'Why did so many German doctors join the Nazi Party early?', *International Journal of Law and Psychiatry*, volume 35, issues 5-6 (September-December, 2012), pp. 473-479.

Harari, Yuval Noah. *21 Lessons for the 21st Century.* Jonathan Cape, 2018.

Hart, Robert. 'Nobody Is Safe Until Everyone Is Safe': World Leaders Call for Global Pandemic Preparedness Treaty', *Forbes* (30 March, 2021).

Harvey, David. *Seventeen Contradictions and the End of Capitalism* (Profile Books, 2014).

Hayek, Friedrich. *The Road to Serfdom: Texts and Documents*. The Collected Works of F. A. Hayek, volume II. The Definitive edition. Edited by Bruce Caldwell. University of Chicago Press, 2007.

Head, Emily, and Dr. Sabine L. van Elsland. 'Vaccinations may have prevented almost 20 million COVID-19 deaths worldwide', *Imperial College London* (24 June, 2022).

Hersey, Frank. 'UN explores digital identity sector to inform legal identity progress', *Biometric* (15 November, 2021).

_____. 'France announces user-controlled mobile digital identity app for use with national ID', *Biometric* (28 April, 2022).

Hickel, Jason. 'The World's Sustainable Development Goals aren't Sustainable', *Foreign Policy* (30 September, 2020).

Hickman, Becky. 'The biggest cause of accidental injuries at home are falls — how can we prevent them?', *RSA* (12 October , 2021).

HM Government. 'Our Plan to Rebuild: The UK Government's COVID-19 Recovery Strategy' (May 2020).

Home Office. 'Islamist terrorist group Hamas banned in the UK' (26 November, 2021).

_____. 'Nationality and Borders Bill: Deprivation of citizenship factsheet' (March 2022).

Hudson, Frank and Aaron Kulakiewiscz. 'Potential Merits of a universal basic income', *House of Commons Public Library* (13 June, 2022).

Human Rights Watch. 'Saudi Arabia: Migrants Held in Inhuman, Degrading Conditions' (15 December, 2020).

_____. 'Gaza: Apparent War Crimes During May Fighting' (27 July, 2021).

Hussein, Mohammed, and Mohammed Haddad. 'Infographic: US military presence around the world', *Al Jazeera* (10 September, 2021).

Huxley, Aldous. *Brave New World*. With an introduction by John Sutherland. Everyman's Library, 2013.

Infectious Disease Society of America. 'Predicting infectious Severe Acute Respiratory Disease Syndrome Coronavirus 2 from Diagnostic Samples' (22 May, 2020).

_____. 'Correlation Between 3790 Quantitative Polymerase Chain Reaction-Positive Samples and Positive Cell Cultures, Including 1941 Severe Acute Respiratory Syndrome Coronavirus 2 Isolates' (28 September, 2020).

Inman, Phillip. 'Is a global recession coming? Here are seven warning signs', *The Guardian* (25 August, 2019).

Institute of International Finance. 'IIF Quarterly Global Debt Monitor 2019' (5 August, 2019).

Institute for the Study of Global Antisemitism and Policy. 'ISGAP Fellows Reject Antisemitic Tropes in Amnesty Report' (23 April, 2022).

International Holocaust Remembrance Alliance. 'What is antisemitism? Non-legally binding working definition of antisemitism'.

_____. 'Information on endorsement and adoption of the IHRA working definition of antisemitism'.

International Monetary Fund. 'Financial Intermediation and Technology: What's Old and what's New?' (7 August, 2020).

John P. A. Ioannidis, et al. 'Age-stratified infection fatality rate of COVID-19 in the non-elderly informed from pre-vaccination national seroprevalence studies', *medRxiv* (13 October, 2022).

Jamal, Urooba. 'Facebook is reversing its ban on posts praising Ukraine's far-right Azov Battalion, report says', *Insider* (25 February, 2022).

Javid, Sajid. 'Health Secretary statement on Vaccines as a Condition of Deployment', Department of Health and Social Care (9 November, 2021).

Jolly, Jasper and Mark Sweney. 'Big oil's quarterly profits hit £50bn as UK braces for even higher energy bills', *The Guardian* (2 August, 2022).

Jones, Dr. Rosamond, et al. 'First Do No Harm', *Us For Them* (7 November, 2020).

Kant, Immanuel. *Religion within the Boundaries of Mere Reason: And Other Writings.* Edited by Allen Wood and George di Giovanni, with an introduction by Robert Merrihew Adams. Cambridge University Press, 2018.

Kabra, Archana. '20 Richest Companies in the World by Market Cap 2022', *The Teal Mango* (25 June 2022).

Kellaway, Lucy. 'The anxious generation — what's bothering Britain's schoolchildren?', *Financial Times* (5 August, 2022).

Klein, Alice. 'Solar storms may cause up to 5500 heart-related deaths in a given year', *New Scientist* (17 June, 2022).

Klein, Naomi. *The Shock Doctrine: The Rise of Disaster Capitalism.* Knopf Canada, 2007.
_____. 'The Great Reset Conspiracy Smoothie', *The Intercept* (8 December, 2020).

Knapton, Sarah. 'High Covid death rates skewed by people who died from other causes, admits Sajid Javid', *The Telegraph* (19 January, 2022).

Knipp-Selke, Andrew and Heike Riedmann. 'Die Spaltung der Gesellschaft ist längst in den Schulen angekommen', *Die Welt* (1 December, 2021).

Kundera, Milan. *The Book of Laughter and Forgetting.* Translated by Michael Henry Heim. Penguin Books, 1983.

Lackey, Brett. 'New Zealand Parliament grounds set on fire as Kiwis lose it', *Daily Mail* (3 March, 2022).

Lane, Samantha, Alison Yeomans and Saad Shakir. 'Reports of myocarditis and pericarditis following mRNA COVID-19 vaccination: a systematic review of spontaneously reported data from the UK, Europe and the USA and of the scientific literature', *National Library of Medicine* (5 July, 2022).

LaPointe, Jacqueline. 'CMS Updates Healthcare Worker Vaccine Mandate Guidance', *RevCycle Intelligence* (18 January, 2022).

Lazaroff, Tovah. 'UN: There is no 'safe place' in Gaza, 72,000 people displaced', *The Jerusalem Post* (19 May, 2021).

Lee, Amanda. 'What is China's social credit system and why is it controversial?', *South China Morning Post* (9 August, 2020).

Lenin, Vladimir. *Imperialism, the Highest Stage of Capitalism*. Selected Works, volume 1. Moscow: Progress Publishers, 1963.

Leonard, Tom. 'Inside Guantanamo Bay: Horrifying pictures show the restraint chairs, feeding tubes and operating theatre used on inmates in terror prison', *Daily Mail* (27 June, 2013).

Lesbian, Gay, Bisexual, Transgender, Queer Plus (LGBTQ+) Resource Center. 'Gender Pronouns' (University of Wisconsin, 2022).

Levesque, Catherine. '"Stand with Swastikas": Emergencies Act debate turns ugly as opposition grows', *National Post* (16 February, 2021).

Lewis, Ollie. 'Football fans are "at risk of a heart attack" due to intense levels of physical stress while watching their team play, Oxford researchers claim', *Daily Mail* (24 January, 2022).

Liboreiro, Jorge and Shona Murray. 'Ukraine war: What is SWIFT and why is expelling Russia a "last resort"?', *my.europe* (26 February, 2022).

Ling, Justin. 'Ottawa protests: "strong ties" between some occupiers and far-right extremists, minister says', *The Guardian* (16 February, 2022).

Littlejohn, Richard. 'No jab, no job — it's a no-brainer', *Daily Mail* (18 February, 2021).

Livingston, Grace. 'Margaret Thatcher's Secret Dealings with the Argentine Military Junta that Invaded the Falklands', *Declassified UK* (29 January, 2020).

Lorizzo, Ellie. 'Royal Opera House cancels Bolshoi Ballet London tour', *The Independent* (25 February, 2022).

Lynskey, Dorian. 'Wall of love: The incredible story behind the national Covid memorial', *The Guardian* (18 July, 2021).

Löwenstein, Karl. 'Law in the Third Reich', *Yale Law Journal,* vol. 45 (1936), pp. 779-815.

Lynch, Benjamin. 'Why skipping breakfast can increase your risk of having a heart attack', *The Mirror* (15 December, 2021).

Mack, Zachary. 'Sleeping in this position could be hurting your heart, studies say', *Best Life* (1 March, 2022).

MacLean, Howard, and Karen Elphick. 'COVID-19 Legislative response — Human Biosecurity Emergency Declaration Explainer', Parliament of Australia (19 March, 2020).

Mahase, Elisabeth. 'Covid-19: Neglect was one of biggest killers in care homes during pandemic, report finds', *BMJ* (22 December, 2021).

Mahlburg, Kurt, 'In Canada it's truck versus tweets and the trucks are winning', *Mercatornet* (11 February, 2021).

Marcus, Immanuel. 'Germany: New Corona Law Passes Bundestag', *The Berlin Spectator* (9 September, 2022).

Marx, Karl. 'The Eighteenth Brumaire of Louis Bonaparte', collected in *Selected Writings*. Edited by David McLellan. Oxford University Press, 1977, pp. 300-325.

_____. 'Preface to *A Critique of Political Economy*', collected in *Selected Writings*, pp. 388- 392.

Massa, Annie, and Caleb Melby. 'In Fink We Trust: BlackRock is Now "Fourth Branch of Government"', *Bloomberg* (21 May, 2020).

Mayer, Milton. *They Thought They Were Free: The Germans, 1933-45*. With a new afterword by Richard J. Evans. University of Chicago Press, 2017.

Matthews, Chris. 'Devon and Cornwall police clarify travel to exercise guidance', *Cornwall News* (2 April, 2020).

Medicines and Healthcare products Regulatory Agency. 'Coronavirus vaccine — summary of Yellow Card reporting'.

Meek, James. 'Red Pill, Blue Pill', *The London Review of Books* (22 October, 2020).

Meinecke, William F. and Alexandra Zapruder. 'Law, Justice and the Holocaust'. *United States Holocaust Memorial Museum*, July 2014.

Merrick, Rob. 'Covid Plan B restrictions like "Nazi Germany" and Soviet "gulag", say rebel Tory MPs', *The Independent* (13 December, 2021).

Millar, Helen. 'What is the link between cold weather and heart attacks?', *Medical News Today* (29 June, 2022).

Miller, Harry. 'The Police crackdown on social media has gone too far', *The Spectator* (1 August, 2022).

Mills, Claire and John Curtis. 'Military assistance to Ukraine since the Russian invasion', *House of Commons Library* (15 August, 2022).

Ministry of Defence. 'Military stands up COVID Support Force' (19 March, 2020).

Ministry of Health NZ. 'COVID-19: Mandatory Vaccinations' (last updated 1 August 2022).

Ministry of Justice. 'Prisons, courts and victim services will benefit from spending review funding' (26 November, 2020).

_____. 'Human Rights Act Reform: A Modern Bill of Rights' (post-consultation paper for the consultation opened 14 December, 2021, closed 19 April, 2022).

Mishra, Manas. 'Health costs pushed or worsened poverty for over 500 million', *Reuters* (13 December, 2021).

Momtaz, Rym. 'Emmanuel Macron on coronavirus: "We're at War"', *Politico* (16 March, 2020).

Monbiot, George. 'It's shocking to see so many leftwingers lured to the far right by conspiracy theories', *The Guardian* (22 September, 2021).

Munson, Sarah, 'A history of care homes', *Care home* (7 August, 2020).

Mussolini, Benito, and Giovanni Gentile. *The Political and Social Doctrine of Fascism*. Translated by Jane Soames. Hogarth Press, 1933.

National Health Service England. 'Guidance and standard operating procedure: COVID-19 virus testing in NHS laboratories' (16 March 2020).

_____. 'Important and Urgent — Next Steps on NHS Response to COVID-19' (17 March 2020).

National Police Chief's Council. 'Update on Coronavirus FPNs issued by police – June 2021' (28 June, 2021).

National Records of Scotland. 'Deaths involving COVID-19 by pre-existing conditions, by age group, March 2020 to November 2021'.

Neil, Andrew. 'It's time to punish Britain's five million vaccine refuseniks', *Daily Mail* (9 December, 2021).

Newman, Chris. 'Doctors for XR crack glass at JP Morgan as UK declares heatwave "national emergency"', *Doctors for Extinction Rebellion* (17 July, 2022).

Nice, Alex, Raphael Hogarth, Joe Marshall, Catherine Haddon and Alice Lilly. 'Government emergency powers and coronavirus', *Institute for Government* (22 March, 2021).

Nicholson, Kate. 'Rishi Sunak Proves That The Conservative Power Stance Lives On', *Huffington Post* (13 July, 2022).

O'Dell, Liam. 'Jacinda Ardern admits New Zealand will become a two-tier society between vaccinated and unvaccinated', *The Independent* (24 October, 2021).

O'Grady, Sean. 'This is what we do about anti-vaxxers: No job. No entry. No NHS access', *The Independent* (18 May, 2021).

O'Neill, Aaron. 'Life expectancy (from birth) in the United Kingdom from 1765 to 2020', *Statista* (21 June, 2022).

Office for National Statistics. 'Leading causes of death, UK: 2001 to 2018' (27 March, 2020).

_____. 'Suicides in England and Wales: 2019 Registrations' (1 September, 2020).

_____. 'Deaths from influenza and pneumonia 2015-2020' (30 November, 2020).

_____. 'Deaths from COVID-19 with no other underlying causes' (16 December, 2021), FOI Ref: FOI/2021/3240.

_____. COVID-19 deaths and autopsies Feb 2020 to Dec 2021' (17 January, 2022), FOI Ref: FOI/2021/3368.

Olliaro, Piero, Els Torreele and Michel Valliant. 'COVID-19 vaccine efficacy and effectiveness — the elephant (not) in the room', *The Lancet* (20 April, 2021).

Oltermann, Philip. 'Austria plans compulsory Covid vaccination for all', *The Guardian* (19 November, 2021).

Open VAERS. 'VAERS COVID Vaccine Adverse Event Reports'.

Orlowski, Andrew. '"Mass formation psychosis" gets a warning from Google', *The Post* (5 January, 2022).

Ortelier, Orlando. 'The "Chicago Boys" in Chile: Economic Freedom's Awful Toll', *The Nation* (10 October, 2016).

Orwell, George. *The Road to Wigan Pier* (1937), collected in *Orwell's England*. Edited by Peter Davison, with an introduction by Ben Pimlott. Penguin Books, 2001. pp. 51-216.

_____. 'What is Fascism?' (1944), collected in *Orwell and Politics*. Edited by Peter Davison, with an introduction by Timothy Garton Ash. Penguin Books, 2001, pp. 321-325.

_____. '"The Intellectual Revolt": Pessimists' (1946), collected in *Orwell and Politics*, pp. 418- 419.

_____. *Nineteen Eighty-Four* (1949). With an introduction by Julian Symonds. Everyman's Library, 1992.

Osborne, Samuel. 'COVID-19: Australian riot police fire rubber bullets at anti-lockdown protesters in Melbourne', *Sky News* (22 September, 2021).

Pawlowski, A. 'Depression worsened during pandemic, boosting heart disease risk, experts warn', *Today* (17 November, 2021).

Paxton, Robert O. *The Anatomy of Fascism*. Penguin Books, 2005.

Perotti, Enrico. 'The Roots of Shadow Banking', *Centre for Economic Policy Research*, Policy Insight No. 69 (December 2013).

Peter G. Peterson Foundation. 'US Defense Spending Compared to Other Countries' (11 May, 2022).

Pfizer. 'Cumulative analysis of post-authorization adverse event reports of PF-07302048 (BNT162B2) received through 28-Feb-2021.

Pickard, Jim. 'Liz Truss labels Boris Johnson's handling of Covid crisis "draconian"', *The Financial Times* (25 August, 2022).

Piggott, James. '2022 Analysis of UK Government Strategic Suppliers', *Tussell* (19 May, 2022).

Prime Minister of Canada. 'Prime Minister announces additional support for Ukraine and shared priorities at G7 Summit in Germany' (28 June, 2022).

Preussen, Wilhelmine. 'Von der Leyen's warning message to Italy irks election candidates', *Politico* (19 October, 2022).

Public Health England. 'Understanding cycle threshold (Ct) in SARS-CoV-2 RT-PCR: A guide for health protection teams' (October 2020).

Puttick, Helen. 'Rise in heart attacks attributed to pandemic stress and poor diet', *The Times* (16 October, 2021).

Randerson, James. 'UK's Liz Truss: I support Brits who take up arms against Putin', *Politico* (27 February, 2022).

Rawlinson, Kevin. 'Neo-Nazi groups recruit Britons to fight in Ukraine', *The Guardian* (2 March, 2020).

Reilly, Jessica, Muyao Lyu and Megan Robertson. 'China's Social Credit System: Speculation vs. Reality', *The Diplomat* (30 March, 2021).

Reiss, Dr. Karina, and Dr. Sucharit Bhakdi. *Corona False Alarm? Facts and Figures*. Chelsea Green Publishing, 2020.

Remnant, MD. 'First Principles: The Problem with Gene-based Injections — Part 1', *Perspectives in Medicine* (26 February, 2022)

_____. 'Trojan Horse: The Problem with Gene-based Injections — Part 2', *Perspectives in Medicine* (5 March, 2022).

Richardson, Edward. 'Learning for Life: Funding a world-class adult education system', *CBI* (October 2020).

Richter, Wolf Richter. 'Fed Cut Back on Helicopter Money for Wall Street and the Wealthy', *Wolf Street* (23 April, 2020).

Ritchie, Hannah, Edouard Mathieu, Lucas Rodés-Guirao, Cameron Appel, Charlie Giattino, Esteban Ortiz-Ospina, Joe Hasell, Bobbie Macdonald, Saloni Dattani and Max Roser. 'Policy Responses to the Coronavirus Pandemic', *Our World In Data* (January 2020-August 2022).

Robespierre, Maximilien. 'On the Principles of Political Morality that should Guide the National Convention in the Domestic Administration of the Republic' (1794). Collected in *Virtue and Terror*. Texts selected and annotated by Jean Ducange, translated by John Howe, with an introduction by Slavoj Žizek. Verso, 2007, pp. 108-125.

Robinson, Martin. 'How "Pariah Russia" is steadily being cancelled by the West', *Daily Mail* (2 March, 2022).

Rosalind English. 'Compulsory vaccination — the next step for Covid 19?', *UK Human Rights Blog* (5 November, 2020).

Rugaber, Christopher. 'Federal Reserve to lend additional $1 trillion a day to large banks', *PBS* (20 March, 2020).

Rule of Law Education Centre, 'Victorian Pandemic Management Bill' (2 November, 2021).

Saadi, Altaf, Maria-Elena De Trinidad Young, Caitlin Patler, Jeremias Leonel Estrada and Homer Venters. 'Understanding US Immigration Detention', *National Library of Medicine* (22 June, 2020).

Sabbagh, Dan. 'Britain and Israel to sign trade and defence deal', *The Guardian* (28 November, 2021).

Schatzker, Erik. 'BlackRock's Fink "Worried" About Stocks Amid Unrest', *Bloomberg* (3 March, 2011).

Schmidt, Karen. 'Cannabis use disorder may be linked to growing number of heart attacks in younger adults', *American Heart Foundation* (8 November, 2021).

Schwab, Klaus. *The Fourth Industrial Revolution*. With an introduction by Marc R. Benioff. Portfolio Penguin, 2017.

_____. *Shaping the Future of the Fourth Industrial Revolution: A Guide to Building a Better World*. With a foreword by Satya Nadella. Portfolio Penguin, 2018.

_____. 'World Economic Forum Founder Klaus Schwab on the Fourth Industrial Revolution', *The Chicago Council on Global Affairs* (13 May, 2019).

Schwab, Klaus, and Thierry Malleret. *COVID-19: The Great Reset*. Forum Publishing, 2020.

Scientific Advisory Group for Emergencies. 'Options for increasing adherence to social distancing measures' (22 March, 2020).

_____. 'SPI-B Summary: Key behavioural issues relevant to test, trace, track and isolate' (6 May, 2020).

_____. 'SPI-B: Consensus Statement on Local Interventions' (27 July, 2020).

Scott, Malcolm, Paul Jackson and Jin Wu. 'A $9 Trillion Binge Turns Central Banks into the Market's Biggest Whales', *Bloomberg UK* (7 July, 2021).

Sharma, Ruchir. 'The billionaire boom: how the super-rich soaked up Covid cash', *Financial Times* (13 May, 2021).

Sharp, Christopher. 'Heart Disease: Day napping may increase risk of symptoms', *The Express* (13 August, 2022).

Shaw, Neil. 'Energy bill price rise may cause heart attacks and strokes, says TV GP', *Wales Online* (3 February, 2022).

Siddique, Haroon. 'New bill quietly gives powers to remove British citizenship without notice', *The Guardian* (17 November, 2021).

Sidik, Saima May. 'Heart-disease risk soars after COVID — even with a mild case', *Nature* (10 February, 2022).

Simpson, John. 'Coronavirus raves and protests may need army, advisers warn', *The Times* (1 August, 2020).

Sorensen, Reed J. D. et al. 'Variation in the COVID-19 infection–fatality ratio by age, time, and geography during the pre-vaccine era: a systematic analysis', *The Lancet* (24 February, 2022).

Sovereign Wealth Fund Institute. 'Top 100 Largest Central Bank Rankings by Total Assets'.

Stanley, Jason. 'The antisemitism animating Putin's claim to "denazify" Ukraine', *The Guardian* (26 February, 2022).

Stone, Jon. 'UK Government backs Israel's bombardment of Gaza', *The Independent* (20 May, 2021).

Sumption, Jonathan. *Trials of the State: Law and the Decline of Politics*. Profile Books, 2019.

_____. 'Former Supreme Court Justice: "This is what a police state is like", *The Spectator* (30 March, 2020).

_____. 'Government by decree: COVID-19 and the Constitution', Cambridge Freshfields Annual Law Lecture, 27 October, 2020. University of Cambridge, 2020.

_____. 'Where is Parliament?', *The Critic* (8 November, 2020).

Táíwò, Olúfẹ́mi O. 'How BlackRock, Vanguard, and UBS Are Screwing the World', *New Republic* (7 March, 2022).

Taylor, Ciaren, Andrew Jowett and Michael Hardie. 'An examination of Falling Real Wages', *Office for National Statistics* (January 2014).

Teague, Ellen. 'Get vaccinated, say Archbishops Nichols and Welby', *The Tablet* (21 December, 2021).

Thompson, Henry. 'Latest Updates on UK Government COVID-19 Contracts and Spending', *Tussell* (29 March, 2022).

Tidy, Joe. 'Pegasus: Spyware sold to governments "targets activists"', *BBC* (19 July, 2021).

Trilateral Commission. 'Task Force Report on Artificial Intelligence' (25 March, 2018).

Trotsky, Leon. *What Next? Vital Questions for the German Proletariat* (1932). Marxists Internet Archive.

Trump, Donald. 'Executive Order 13887 — Modernizing Influenza Vaccines in the United States To Promote National Security and Public Health' (19 September, 2019).

Truss, Liz. 'United Nations Human Rights Council, 1 March 2022: Foreign Secretary's statement', *Foreign, Commonwealth and Development Office* (1 March, 2022).

UK Government Chief Scientific Advisor. 'The Internet of Things: Making the most of the Second Digital Revolution' (December 2014).

UK Health Security Agency. 'COVID-19 vaccine surveillance report: Week 10' (10 March 2022).

_____. 'Heat-health advice issued for all regions of England' (15 July, 2022).

United Nations. 'Transforming our world: the 2030 Agenda for Sustainable Development', *Department of Economic and Social Affairs*.

United Nations Educational, Scientific and Cultural Organization. 'Universal Declaration on Bioethics and Human Rights' (19 October, 2005).

United Nations High Commissioner for Refugees, 'Figures at a Glance' (16 June, 2022).

University of York. 'Two-thirds of UK households to be in fuel poverty by the new year, according to new report' (8 August, 2022).

U.S. National Library of Medicine. 'Phase III Double-blind, Placebo-controlled Study of AZD1222 for the Prevention of COVID-19 in Adults' (1 April, 2020).

_____. 'Study to Describe the Safety, Tolerability, Immunogenicity, and Efficacy of RNA Vaccine Candidates Against COVID-19 in Healthy Individuals' (30 April, 2020).

_____. 'A Study to Evaluate Efficacy, Safety, and Immunogenicity of mRNA-1273 Vaccine in Adults Aged 18 Years and Older to Prevent COVID-19' (14 July, 2020).

Vengattil, Munsif, and Elizabeth Culliford. 'Facebook allows war posts urging violence against Russian invaders', *Reuters* (11 March, 2022).

Vighi, Fabio. 'Slavoj Žižek, Emergency Capitalism, and the Capitulation of the Left', *The Philosophical Salon* (24 May, 2021).

_____. 'A Self-fulfilling Prophecy: Systemic Collapse and Pandemic Simulation', *The Philosophical Salon* (16 August, 2021).

_____. 'The Central Bankers' Long Covid: An Incurable Condition', *The Philosophical Salon* (18 October, 2021).

_____. 'Red Pill or Blue Pill? Variants, Inflation and the Controlled Demolition of the Economy', *The Philosophical Salon* (3 January, 2022).

_____. 'From COVID-19 to Putin-22: Who needs friends with enemies like these?', *The Philosophical Salon* (14 March, 2022).

Vine, Sarah. 'We can't let selfish idiots who don't want free Covid vaccines that scientists worked around the clock to develop hold us hostage', *Daily Mail* (18 May, 2021).

Wallace, Tim. 'Bank of England tells Ministers to intervene on digital currency programming', *The Telegraph* (21 June, 2021).

Ward, Sarah. 'Mandatory ESG reporting is here, and Finance needs to get ready', *KPMG* (20 May, 2022).

Weaver, Matthew. Cardiff Philharmonic removes Tchaikovsky performance over Ukraine conflict', *The Guardian* (9 March, 2022).

West, Dave. 'NHS hospitals have four times more empty beds than normal', *HSJ* (13 April, 2020).

Weston, Katie, Chris Matthews and Peter Allen, 'French Freedom Convoy crackdown: Riot police teargas terrified diners at pavement cafes in Paris', *Daily Mail* (12 February, 2022).

Whipple, Tom. 'Professor Neil Ferguson: People don't agree with lockdown and try to undermine the scientists', *The Times* (25 December, 2020).

White, Ed, Andy Lin, Dan Clark, Sam Joiner and Caroline Nevitt. 'How China's lockdown policies are crippling the country's economy', *Financial Times* (1 June, 2022).

Whyte, Jessica Whyte. *Catastrophe and Redemption: The Political Thought of Giorgio Agamben.* State University of New York Press, 2013.

Wilkie, Christina, and Thomas Franck. 'Biden asks congress for $33 billion to support Ukraine through September', *CNBC* (28 April, 2022).

Williams, Terri-Ann. 'Urgent warning to gardeners as soil "increases risk of killer heart disease"', *The Sun* (1 July, 2022).

Wilson, Jeremy. 'Exclusive: "Horrific" impact of third lockdown on schoolchildren's physical and mental health revealed', *The Telegraph* (10 May, 2021).

Wimbledon. 'Statement Regarding Russian and Belarusian Individuals at The Championships 2022' (20 April, 2022).

Wong, Tess. 'Henan: Chinese Covid app restricts residents after banking protests', *BBC* (14 June, 2022).

Greg Woodfield, John R. Kennedy and Keith Griffith. 'Trudeau's trucker crackdown begins', *The Daily Mail* (18 February 2021).

_____. 'Ottawa police arrest 100 protesters and remove 21 trucks using emergency act powers', *Daily Mail* (19 February, 2022).

Woolf, Naomi. 'On the Subtlety of Monsters', *Outspoken* (28 January, 2022).

World Bank Group. 'Practitioners Guide' (October 2019).

World Economic Forum. 'The Forum of Young Global Leaders'.

_____. 'Identity in a Digital World: a new chapter in the social contract', Insight Report (September 2018).

_____. 'A brief history of globalization' (17 January, 2019).

_____. 'World Economic Forum launches COVID-19 Action Platform to fight coronavirus' (11 March, 2020).

_____. 'This is what a new model of governance could look like' (17 January, 2022).

_____. 'G20 Global Smart Cities Alliance' (February 2022).

World Health Organization. 'Global Vaccine Safety Summit' (2-3 December, 2019).

_____. 'WHO Director-General's opening remarks at the media briefing on COVID-19 - 11 March 2020' (11 March 2020).

_____. 'International guidelines for certification and classification (coding) of COVID-19 as cause of death' (20 April, 2020).

_____. 'Advice on the use of masks in the context of COVID-19' (5 June, 2020).

_____. 'Coronavirus disease (COVID-19): Herd immunity, lockdowns and COVID-19' (15 October, 2020).

_____. 'World Health Assembly agrees to launch process to develop historic global accord on pandemic prevention, preparedness and response' (1 December, 2021).

Wright, Nicholas. 'Coronavirus and the Future of Surveillance', *Foreign Affairs* (6 April, 2020).

Yardeni, Dr. Edward, and Mali Quintana. 'Central Banks: Monthly Balance Sheet' (April 2022).

Yeadon, Dr. Mike. 'What SAGE Has Got Wrong', *The Daily Sceptic* (16 October, 2020).

Yeadon, Dr. Mike, Dr. Paul Birkham and Barry Thomas. 'How Likely is a Second Wave?', *The Daily Sceptic* (7 September, 2020).

Young, Iona. 'Edinburgh Festival cuts ties with Russian conductor Valery Gergiev over Putin support', *Edinburgh Live* (28 February, 2022).

Yu, Verna. 'China puts 65m people into semi-lockdown ahead of party summit', *The Guardian* (5 September, 2022).

Zenobiah, Dr. Storah. 'Psychology Report in respect of Civil Proceedings' (9 April, 2021).

Zetkin, Clara. *Fighting Fascism: How to Struggle and How to Win*. Edited by Mike Taber and John Riddell. Haymarket Books, 2017.

Zichichi, Antonino, Renato Angelo Ricci and Aurelio Misiti. 'Petition on Anthropogenic Global Warming' (17 June, 2019).